THE LYTTELTON
HART-DAVIS
LETTERS
Volumes 5 and 6

Books by Rupert Hart-Davis

HUGH WALPOLE
a biography

THE ARMS OF TIME
a memoir

A BEGGAR IN PURPLE
a commonplace book

Edited

THE LETTERS OF OSCAR WILDE

SELECTED LETTERS OF OSCAR WILDE

MORE LETTERS OF OSCAR WILDE

THE LYTTELTON HART-DAVIS LETTERS

TWO MEN OF LETTERS
R. C. Hutchinson & Martyn Skinner

and works by
Max Beerbohm, George Moore,
William Plomer, Arthur Ransome, Siegfried Sassoon

THE LYTTELTON HART-DAVIS LETTERS

Correspondence of George Lyttelton
and Rupert Hart-Davis
Volumes Five and Six 1960–62

Edited and introduced by
RUPERT HART-DAVIS

Th' entente is all, and naught the letters' space.
CHAUCER

I rattle on exactly as I'd talk
With anybody in a ride or walk.
BYRON

JOHN MURRAY

First published in paperback 1987
by John Murray (Publishers) Ltd
50 Albemarle Street, London W1X 4BD

Printed and bound in Great Britain by
The Bath Press, Avon

British Library Cataloguing in Publication Data
Lyttelton, George
The Lyttelton Hart-Davis letters:
correspondence of George Lyttelton and Rupert Hart-Davis.
Vols. 5 and 6: 1960–62
1. English letters
I. Title II. Hart-Davis, Rupert
826'.914'08 PR1347
ISBN 0-7195-4381-9

This double volume is dedicated
by its editor to
REGGIE GRENFELL
and to the joyous memory
of his darling wife
JOYCE
also to
ROSALIE NUGENT
who with her beloved husband
TIM
was responsible for all this
correspondence

INTRODUCTION

This last double volume will need no introduction to the faithful, but new readers may demand a little guidance.

In 1926 I had been taught by George at Eton, where he was an outstanding teacher and housemaster. In my last year he started an English course, and it was then that I fell under the spell of his infectious enthusiasm for literature. After I left Eton our ways parted. George taught for a further twenty years before retiring to Suffolk. We met again in 1949 and thereafter saw and wrote to each other occasionally, but the origin of this correspondence was a dinner-party in 1955, during which George complained that no one wrote to him in Suffolk, and I accepted his challenge.

To avoid repetitive footnotes I should say that Comfort was my wife; Bridget, Duff, and Adam my children. Ruth Simon had been my beloved prop and stay since 1946.

As before, in the first letters I have retained the opening and signature, which are afterwards omitted, since they are almost always the same: any variation is printed. Similarly I have given our full home addresses in the early letters and then abbreviated them. From Monday to Friday I lived in a flat above my publishing office at 36 Soho Square. At the beginning of this volume George was almost seventy-seven and I was fifty-two.

RUPERT HART-DAVIS

Marske-in-Swaledale
August 1986

4 January 1960 *36 Soho Square*

My dear George

I can see that it's going to be another week before this correspondence resumes its normal level. Towards the end of last week I was submerged by what you and Shakespeare would call a whoreson cold, and was obliged to cancel my week-end plans and stay here streaming —but greatly cherished by Ruth. Today I am nearing normal again, and your letter has been forwarded from Bromsden.

So glad you approve of Adam, who, as you may have guessed, is the apple of his mother's eye—and indeed of his father's. I now find that you can't put a boy up for the M.C.C. till he's *seventeen*, so I shall hang on to the form and submit it for your signature in June. What a gay time you examiners have in Cambridge—movies every night indeed! I have finished *Coningsby* and enjoyed it all, though I'm sure *Sybil* is a better book. I long to know the name of the don who told you I was doing wonders for the London Library, but perhaps you never knew it.

Ruth and I are both sad to know that you won't be at the Lit. Soc. And who will protect me from the Knight of the Rueful Countenance?[1] Your visit to Bromsden was enormously popular with all ranks, and I rejoiced to see Pamela looking so well.

I expect you saw Raymond Mortimer on Hotson[2] in the *Sunday Times*. Priestley in *Reynolds News* (but who reads it?) was much more forthcoming and pronounced himself entirely converted. I shall eagerly await your opinion. As always, vested interests will be massing on the other side: if Hotson could be proved right, all their damned text-books would have to be rewritten. We ran into John Wain to-day,

[1] Cuthbert Headlam.

[2] *Shakespeare's Wooden O* by Leslie Hotson (1960), in which he sought to prove that the London theatres of Shakespeare's time were literally 'in the round'.

just married again and very cheerful—no sign of the Angry Young Man about him except that he wore no tie.

Now I must do some of the mass of work which Xmas and my cold have caused to pile up. You shall get a proper letter from Bromsden next week.

Ruth sends her love.

Yours ever
Rupert

6 January 1960 (77th birthday!) *The Timbralls Eton*

My dear Rupert

I did not know of the new M.C.C. rule about entry, but anyway my support of Adam remains, whatever vagaries the Committee may indulge in.

My three days at Cambridge were oddly busy, partly because what you regard as my masochistic instincts made me go to two films; one, *Great Expectations*, excellent, the other—My God! It was called *Expresso Bongo*,[1] all din and glitter and semi-nudity, and acrobatic dancing, and prestissimo dialogue, mostly to me inaudible, but, they told me, crackling with wit and satire—which made it particularly unfortunate that all the w. and s. I did hear was insipid beyond words. I felt 150 years old. My colleagues—intelligent young-middle-aged men—were as pleased with it as Mr Peter Magnus said his friends were when he signed himself 'Afternoon'.[2] Have you or has Ruth seen it? If either of you didn't think it dreadful rubbish, I shall give up trying to keep up.

The don who spoke of you and the London Library was *either* Duff of Trinity (son of T.D. Duff) or Denis Robertson (eminent economist) or Stanley Bennett (bibliographer, Chaucerian, fellow of Emmanuel), a genial friendly chap, commonly known in charitable Cambridge circles as 'Backstairs Bennett'—they all pull strings, but apparently he does it more successfully than most. All three are men who do not talk nonsense, and never talked less than when they praised R.H-D.

[1] The film of a musical play by Wolf Mankowitz (1958).

[2] In *Pickwick Papers*, chapter xxii.

I haven't yet got round to Leslie Hotson, as I have been tackling *The Owl of Minerva*[1] which is not a short book. What a grim and disillusioning series of experiences! Why, I wonder, though always interested, did I feel vaguely unsatisfied? Is it that his experiences are somehow not digested—or that the style, when at all elaborated, often misses the target? I don't know. I am in fact a hopeless critic. Amis would know, Leavis would know. The sop to my humiliation is my confident certainty that both, in their separate ways, would know wrong, as Dizzy said was the defect of great thinkers. I must try *Coningsby* again.

At Cambridge I always find Trollope best for bedtime reading, after reading third-rate manuscripts all day. And shall I be lynched if I say how awfully bad *The Warden* seems to me? All its issues go below its surface—the whole business of John Bold and Eleanor left in the air, and he does not succeed in persuading me, at least, that the Archdeacon is not essentially a man of four letters, which he appears to want to do. I forget whether you are a Trollope fan—or share perhaps Gosse's distaste for 'the listless amble' of Trollope's style? I wonder if anyone in England has *all* his novels. I have read scores, it seems, but am always coming across the names of many I haven't. No second-hand bookshop ever has any beyond the Barchester lot. Odd.

I am sorry to miss the Lit. Soc. (though perhaps it is no bad thing not to attend *all* the dinners). I met a lady at tea with Christopher Stone—do you know him?—who asked if Sir Cuthbert was still (a) very handsome, and (b) carping, as he was when she knew him thirty years ago. My answer was yes and no (to which adjectives do you think?).

We go back on Friday, and a day or two later shall be housing my youngest, Mary, and her family. You would like her. The Lord Cranworth—*aetat* eighty-two—thinks she is the most fascinating young woman he has ever seen, to the frank amusement of M. and her husband. How the Ancient of Days does like making fools of us.

Do you ever do things quite wrong, misquote etc, as I am always doing, e.g. in a crib supplied to examiners in the G.C.E. Because here is the perfect defence: 'What is obvious is not always known, what is known is not always present. Sudden fits of inadvertency will surprise

[1] The autobiography of Gustav Regler (1959).

vigilance; slight avocations will seduce attention, and casual eclipses of the mind will darken learning.' Isn't it perfect? Johnson of course. I do hope it isn't too familiar to you. But even if it is you won't mind turning it over your tongue in the new year. Best love to Ruth. See you both in Feb—and even the wolf-month doesn't last for ever. But don't forget it is apt to show its teeth round about the 20th. *Verb. sap.*

Yours ever
G.W.L.

9 January 1960 *Bromsden Farm*
Henley-on-Thames
Oxon

Your excellent letter, written on your birthday, makes me fear you never got my birthday card. When I asked the girl in the shop whether she had any special ones for 77th birthdays she seemed amazed, so I had to make do with an ordinary one embellished with an apt quotation. Perhaps it will catch up with you.

I'm happy to say my whoreson cold has departed, and I am almost fit for what at Cambridge should clearly be called Examiners' Licence. *Expresso Bongo* indeed! It'll be strip-tease next, mark my words. I certainly haven't seen *E.B.*, nor has Ruth: we call for sterner stuff. I am not a Trollope fan, but only perhaps through lack of leisure. I mean, I'm all *for* him but haven't read many. Certainly I'm not in any way *anti*, and the professional hardheadedness of his writing habits, which so scandalised the readers of his *excellent Autobiography*, endears him to me. The Ivory Tower is not necessary for the production of literature, as I'm sure you'll agree. Where exactly does that splendid bit of Johnson come from ('What is obvious is not always known' etc)? It's a splendid Editor's Defence and I should like to have it by me, with chapter and verse.

Yesterday I, as they say, 'took delivery' of a new car—a Morris station-waggon, like our old one but seven years more up-to-date. Heinemann's[1] have bought it for me, and we are all delighted with it. Never before have we enjoyed a car with a *heater* in it, and today, in

[1] My publishing firm had been taken over by William Heinemann Ltd.

glorious sunshine, we drove snugly through the cold, at the sedate speed which 'running-in' demands, to the Cotswolds to lunch with Comfort's darling old stepmother. On the way I snatched half an hour in the antiquarian department of Blackwell's and emerged with five good books. Next Wednesday I am to spend the night with Sparrow at All Souls and attend a Christ Church gaudy as the guest of J.I.M. Stewart (the Michael Innes of detective story fame): you shall hear of it all next week, and of Tuesday's Lit. Soc.

Yesterday morning I took Diana Cooper to the crypt of St Paul's for a private view of Duff's memorial tablet (carved by Reynolds Stone), which is to be unveiled later this year. All the cathedral's heating is in the crypt, which is always warm and to me full of beauty and romance—with Nelson and Wellington sleeping out eternity side by side in vast hideous sarcophagi—though Wellington's battle-flags are wonderfully romantic and threadbare. Upstairs in the Cathedral proper the huge hanging Epstein strikes me as a fine thing in the wrong place. The surroundings are altogether too classical for such savage individuality.

Arthur Ransome, whom I visited on Tuesday, has had to give up chess, which he has played all his life, because at seventy-five he says it gives him a blinding headache. He is proposing to give all his chess books to Adam, much to A's delight.

Did I ever mention my friend Christopher Devlin? He is a Jesuit priest, brother of Patrick Devlin the judge and William Devlin the actor, and a charming person. He helped me a lot with the Gerard Manley Hopkins papers which were left unfinished when Humphry House died, and soon afterwards he (C.D.) was sent out to South Africa as a missionary. At first he hated it but gradually became reconciled. I have sent him books and occasional letters. Just before Christmas I got a scrawled note to say he was being flown home for a serious operation. Poor creature, he had cancer of the rectum: can you imagine anything more agonising? He had the operation just after Christmas and is apparently going on all right. His sister-in-law (the judge's wife) rang up to say he could have visitors, so I'm going to see him on Monday: he's at Cheam in Surrey. He's about my age: isn't it awful! I suppose one ought to be grateful every moment that one is well and without pain, but one never thinks of such things until someone one knows is involved. I suppose Christopher will somehow reconcile this appalling event with God's infinite mercy, but it will take some doing.

To end on a lighter note, Duff has discovered a new restaurant in Leicester Square called 'Guinea and Piggy'. You pay a guinea each as you go in, and you can eat as much as you like of over a hundred dishes hot and cold. Duff and his girl ate two kinds of fish, roast chicken, Boeuf Stroganoff, casserole of pheasant and two sweets—ah, youth, youth! I fear they'd make money on me.

14 January 1960 *Finndale House*
Grundisburgh
Suffolk

Your admirable birthday card arrived all right, many thanks, but at least two days late—after I had written. Never have I known the Xmas post so haywire. It was a very good quotation—dreadfully true. My Johnson sentence for you was from the magnificent preface to his Dictionary. Was ever a defence so complete—and every noun and adjective and verb is exactly the right one. I remember a large majestic youth called Keele giving it at the Fourth of June speeches on J's bicentenary, and the sight of Augustine Birrell's rich enjoyment of it in the audience. Keele spoke it beautifully, and I can still hear the final sentence: 'I therefore dismiss it with frigid tranquillity, having nothing to fear or to hope from censure or from praise.' Keele was killed in the first war. He was a fine chap. The preface is bound to be in the Johnson book which you published.

Exciting about your new car. I hope it means Heinemann has seen the light and is no longer tiresome. We too find the heater a great boon at the moment. The great frosts and snows are ten days early, damn them. Tyres have no real grip, and I walk to the post-box like Agag. The answer to Shelley's optimistic question 'Can Spring etc.' is 'Yes, a devilish long way.'

You must be, at the moment of writing, dining with John Sparrow and Michael Innes. Alington always put his detective stories at the very top. I liked some (viz *Hamlet, Revenge!*) but found some *too* ingenious, and one, *Stop Press* was it, curiously dull. You will have good company. I have a feeling that at All Souls talk flows more freely than at the Trinity high table, where the ghost of A.E. Housman still seems to exercise its costive sway. Do you remember his frigid comment on Wilfrid Blunt's saying in his diary that he thought A.E.H. would much prefer to remain silent. 'He was quite right.'

I like your remark about Epstein in the Abbey—nail on the head. You remember Johnson on the point 'A cow is a very good animal in a field, but we turn her out of a garden.' Things, high and low, must be in the right environment.

'Guinea and Piggy' sounds delicious. I can remember a dozen friends of sixty years ago who would have bust the restaurant in a week—but that, no doubt, is why *all* of them are no longer alive. How long did Mr Woodhouse[1] live on his gruel—'thin but not too thin', and his not very strong belief that 'an egg, lightly boiled, is not unwholesome'? I feel inclined to echo Marlow's 'Ah youth, youth'[2] at my youngest daughter and son-in-law who are going off on grossly unsafe roads this evening six miles to see Danny Kaye. They find the Suffolk climate a bit grim after Malaya, though frankly admitting that you *can* get tired of feeling sticky every day.

The three children regard their grandfather as an old funny. 'Out of the mouth of babes and sucklings' etc but they are great fun. Not that I share *all* their tastes. I suspect you too have outgrown your enthusiasm for snowballing or even making a snow-man. I hate the stuff more every winter.

By the way, I hope that grand Alpine book you sent me is selling well—oh yes *The White Spider* by name.[3] It has had very good reviews. I re-read bits of it and the pictures still give me a delicious shudder. Sleeping on a four-inch ledge half way up a precipice with the thermometer at zero—riotous fun it must be! Mountaineers must resemble chess-champions, possessing something in their make-up which others not only don't have but cannot even understand.

Tell me of your visit to Devlin. What awful things Fate can and daily does do. A cousin, whose memorial service I attended last week,

[1] In Jane Austen's *Emma*.

[2] In Conrad's 'Youth'.

[3] An account of climbing the Eiger by Heinrich Harrer (1959).

had had several years of absolute immobility from arthritis, and for the last year had been stone-blind. 'Fatherlike he tends and spares us!'

I have a pain in the chest—probably some form of dyspepsia. My family cheerfully suggest angina pectoris. How scored off they would feel if they turned out right! Was it not Walter de la Mare who said what splendid names for heroine and villain Lady Angina Pectoris and Sir Rheumatoid Arthritis would be?

To-morrow I stay a night with one XYZ, who wants to find out what exactly Eton has that no other school has, with a view to articles in the *Evening Standard* or *Daily Express* (which hates Eton). But how can it be put into words?

16 January 1960 *Bromsden Farm*

Almost as soon as I'd written to you last week I realised that the Johnson quotation must come from the preface to the Dictionary, and found it there. What a splendid piece of writing it is: perhaps I shall persuade Adam to recite it at Speeches when he's in Sixth Form.

The new car has survived its baptism of snow, though yesterday Comfort had to employ spade and sacks on her way to school. Heinemann's paying for it is, I fear, more like hush-money than anything more encouraging—but we shall see. I'm sure you'd be wise to put in central heating: I'd do it here if I had the money. As it is I hug the library fire, whence I can watch the nuthatch bullying the tits on the bird-table.

Yes, *The White Spider* is selling well. This week I shall be sending you a brief memoir called *The Witch*,[1] which delighted me. The author was an émigrée Russian princess, and is now married to Edward Hulton, the newspaper tycoon.

Last week began with my visit to poor Christopher Devlin: it took me three hours, though I was with him for only twenty minutes. He is in a Catholic hospital at Cheam—an endlessly sprawling and flat section of what I believe is now called Subtopia. I took him some flowers and books, and I think he was pleased to see me, though he was clearly in pain: I shall try to go again next week.

[1] By Nika Hulton (1960).

On Wednesday I lunched with a beautiful and intelligent woman called Margaret Lane (when she writes) and Lady Huntingdon in private life. With her I went to my second meeting of the General Advisory Council of the B.B.C. (again quite amusing) and then caught a train to Oxford, where the arrangements for getting taxis at the station are barbaric and involved standing for ages in the snow with F.C. Francis, the Director of the British Museum, whom I ran into there. There were 101 diners in the festal lights of Christ Church hall, but I spoke only to my host, Michael Innes, a very shy Canon on my other side, and Masterman, the Provost of Worcester. I saw at once that, as regards the menu, it was all or nothing, so I went doggedly through the seven courses and six wines, all excellent (list enclosed), and was no whit the worse. M. Innes is a most civilised and amusing chap: he has written all those thrillers to educate his five children. I think the two best are *Lament for a Maker* and *The Journeying Boy*—but I daresay I've said so before. At about eleven I walked back through the snow to All Souls, where I found the Warden sound asleep by his study fire in the Lodging. He woke refreshed and kept me up till one, showing me all his latest book-acquisitions. The house is thoroughly comfortable, with a cherishing old manservant. I hadn't had a bath run for me since I left the army in 1945. Next morning Sparrow nobly drove me to catch the 9 a.m. train. I enjoyed it all.

Sparrow has promised to read all my Oscar proofs, and will probably review the book in *The Times Literary Supplement*, if his enthusiasm conquers his procrastination.

Meanwhile the plans for the London Library sale at Christie's go forward: I have a meeting about it on Monday, and *three* meetings on Monday and Tuesday about the Phoenix Trust. Adam is coming up for the night on Tuesday (the last of his holidays) and Ruth and I are taking him to *The Importance of Being Earnest* at the Old Vic. I feel that a few grains of general culture must be added to his strictly scientific diet.

Have you ever read anything so drearily turgid as Eden's memoirs? They're like chunks of the day-before-yesterday's newspapers written by a civil service clerk. I've always thought him a weak dull mediocrity (although he was at my tutor's) and here is proof positive. He deserves to have these tedious pages read back to him at dictation-speed by a Foreign Office Spokesman.

This is really the dead vast and middle of the winter—when, according to M.D. Hill[1], all the great frosts of the past century have begun. But all our six inches of a week ago are no more, save for a patch or two, and the usual sulky rawness, child of the East wind, has taken its place. The neighbourhood is stricken with fowl-pest and an obscure hepatic complaint is wiping out all the foxes. Not that I was ever a hunting-man. To sing 'John Peel' in my bath was as near as I ever got to being one. It was a kindly dispensation of Providence to see that I weighed thirteen stone when I was sixteen, so that my economical father would not run to what would practically have been a shire horse—certainly by the time I was eighteen and weighed fifteen stone I should have needed one whose neck was clothed with thunder, like the great Suffolk punch, Naunton Prince, over whose demise his late Majesty and I shed tears together.

I like your idea that Adam should speak the Johnson preface; it should certainly recur every fifty years. I suppose A. will be in Sixth Form about 1962. A great moment. I have told the library to get *The World of Paul Slickey*.[2] How you will jeer! I am having a row with them at the moment, as they are hesitant about getting *The Rainbow Bridge* by R.W. Livingstone.[3] They probably think it is a *San Luis Rey* whimsy whereas it is educational, and he is about the best writer on the subject. I have gently suggested that it would find more readers than *Biscay Harbourages and Anchorages*, *Hors d'oeuvres and Cold Table*, *A Concise Textbook of Midwifery*, *Asparagus*, *The History of Grocery*, and *Your Poodle*, all of which are recent acquisitions. The pretence that many human beings—especially officials—are sane must surely soon be abandoned.

Thank you for your Oxford menu. Very toothsome. Did I tell you about *my* lunch at the Ecu de France with XYZ, a nice journalist? All out of the Beaver's[4] pocket, I am glad to say. The peas and beans we ordered were shown to us beforehand in their pods. No deception,

[1] Eton master.

[2] A play by John Osborne (1959).

[3] Classical scholar (1880–1960). President of Corpus Christi College, Oxford 1933–1950. Knighted 1931.

[4] Lord Beaverbrook.

12/6 a helping (no, sorry, no such thing at the E. de F.—*a portion*). And after seeing the Beaver's face in this week's *Radio Times*, I wish I had asked for asparagus (15/-). I am sorry to see old C.H. Wilkinson of Worcester is dead.

All Michael Innes's whodunits are in the Ipswich library (with *Your Poodle*) and at the moment *not one* is on the shelves. Popularity!

I cannot agree with you about Eden's memoirs, for the simplest of reasons. I read half the first one and was too crushingly bored to read another line—for my line is Johnson's 'If I pick up a skein and find it packthread, I do not expect on going further to find it silk.' He must be the driest of sticks; I couldn't see a gleam of interest. Surely *The Times* will drop a packet over the stuff.

I had got to here yesterday, and this morning *The Witch* was on the breakfast-table, from the best and kindest of men, whose good deeds shine ever more brightly as the world grows naughtier—and sillier. Pamela instantly pounced upon it, saying she had nothing to read, so what will you. I am *pro tem.* up-to-date with my R.H-D. books, so got yesterday from the library Coleridge's Letters Vol IV, but they look a little daunting. You know of course Carlyle's perfect picture of C. in *John Sterling* 'Glorious islets too I have seen rise out of the haze (of C's talk)—islands of the blest and the intelligible'. Ten per cent genius and ninety per cent bore—an uncomfortable blend, but perhaps not a very uncommon one, e.g. daddy Wordsworth too—in his poetry as well as (I expect) his conversation.

I must go and hew wood.

23 January 1960 *Bromsden Farm*

Adam is due to leave Eton in July 1961, so he'll have to reach Sixth Form before then—perhaps this September. He went back cheerfully on Wednesday with an enormous stack of kit and rations. The night before, Ruth and I took him to dine in Soho (whitebait, steak, Beaujolais, cream cake) and on to the Old Vic, where we all three thoroughly enjoyed Oscar's masterpiece. The production wasn't frightfully good and Fay Compton couldn't get anywhere near Lady Bracknell, but the words and jokes are good enough to survive almost any acting (have you read the play lately?). Edith Evans was the Lady B of all time, and, as John Gielgud once said to me, any perfect performance spoils a part for a generation. E. Evans has similarly spoiled Millamant, and the Nurse in *Romeo*, but her Cleopatra was an agonising disaster.

Your lunch at the Ecu de France sounds pretty shameful: do you realise that all those restaurants would close down in a week if no one were allowed to eat on expense-accounts? Still, I'm glad you ate your way through a helping of beans at Lord Beaverbrook's expense.

Preparations for the London Library sale at Christie's are going forward, and since everything must be assembled *eight weeks* before the sale (which we hope will be at the end of April or beginning of May) I've got to try and collect it all by the end of February. My secretary (nice but stupid and oh so *slow*) is mercifully leaving on Feb 15, and I have hired a new one who promises much better, but she will not arrive in time to be much help with the sale.

Ruth and I were going down to Worthing on Monday to spend the day with the Eliots, but they can't bear it (Worthing—not the thought of us) any more and are returning to London on their way to Tangier. Like Jonah, T.S.E. suffers from breathlessness.

Last week we had a meeting of the Phoenix Trust, which, considering there was no progress to report, took an unconscionable time. I've told them that until the London Library's plight is dealt with, I can't give much time to the P.T.

I am going to include FitzGerald in my Reynard Library series. Except for *Omar* and a few oddments, the volume will consist entirely of letters—and jolly good ones too. There is no edition in Everyman or World's Classics. You will have to do your best to promote the sale in Suffolk. The editor is a nice woman called Joanna Richardson: I hope she won't make a mess of it.

I am deep in a 700-page-typescript history of the Franco-Prussian War (which I shall publish) and other manuscripts await my pleasure —or disgust. I have had specimen pages of Oscar, but as yet no date for first proofs: I rather long to get back to it and finish it off.

I see Diana's baby is safely christened, with Roger at the font: I trust he will take his duties seriously and in due course lead the boy to the Bishop. Every grinning press-photograph of your old chum

Cantuar confirms my dislike of the canting old sadist. He may be a good chairman, but that means nothing, as I know full well.

And now back to Moltke and the Siege of Paris—

28 January 1960 *Grundisburgh*

I read *The Importance* a few years ago, when with a spurt of imbecility, unusual even for them, the Oxford and Cambridge Board set it in the Higher Cert. And Harrow, if you please, had to have a special paper, and I had to set it, when there were quite simply no more questions to ask. I suggested that we should ask for a suggested comment by Oscar on his play being set for examination; they grinned but wouldn't have it; they (rightly) feared reflections on the Board. Of course Edith Evans made any other Lady B. impossible. And I often read how the other parts are spoilt by the performers' obvious consciousness that they are being funny. They often strike me as very stupid people in the way they force things. E.g. *Hassan*[1] was nearly ruined by some farcical over-playing. But, as you say, the language of the play is unspoilable. Don't our sillier young critics object to any attempt to use words with grace and point, or is that fatuous little fashion on the way out? I am dubious. The hosts of Philistia, constantly changing their uniforms, seem to me to grow pretty steadily. But then I am frequently charged with pessimism. Well, I don't know. It depends on how far you look. I am not one, as regards friends and family etc., but I suppose that fundamentally anyone who has no belief whatever in a future life may or must be called a pessimist. Do you know that magnificent paragraph of Arthur Balfour's about the almost contemptible brevity of the human race's sojourn on the earth, which some day, 'tideless and inert, will no longer tolerate the race which has for a moment disturbed its solitude'?[2] Nowhere that I know is the stark factuality of science so majestically garbed in language. Bertrand Russell has a similar passage somewhere, but, as that old devil Logan Pearsall Smith noted, it is vitiated by a slight self-con-

[1] By James Elroy Flecker. First published 1922, produced at His Majesty's Theatre 1923.

[2] From *The Foundations of Belief* (1895).

sciousness; he quotes it in *Trivia* and adds 'By jove, that's a stunt!' The old lynx-eye!

I have just heard from the library that *Paul Slickey* is waiting for me, so by next week I shall have given it the minute attention that 'so great a work of art' (Alan Brien etc) deserves. But I am afraid you never went to see it. Pamela has *The Witch*, but as you might guess is so full of household chores that she is asleep before reading at night and up too early to do so in the morning. Hotson is tough but rewarding—like mountaineering.

Odd people, journalists. XYZ wanted to know all about Eton, and expressed great admiration etc. A very pleasant and civilised man. I told him plenty, but as I was fifteen years out of date, referred him to Oliver Van Oss[1]. I wrote to V.O. and told XYZ all was well. XYZ saw him and a few minutes later his articles appeared (though he had told me he would show them to me before they did). And all through this he has not sent me a line of thanks, information, or the articles in proof or print. I suppose when a journalist has got what he wants from A. that is the end of A. as regards courtesies etc. Or am I oversensitive? Very likely. They don't much like the articles at Eton. Perhaps his professed love for E was bogus; perhaps he is all bogus. He was once on the *Daily Express*. 'Shameful' is the right word for the Ecu de France luncheon. Easily overpowering the savours of rich viands and vegetables, the stink of money pervaded the place. Jowls, dewlaps and paunches were much in evidence. If, as I believe, some lunch there every day, have I not, as Wordsworth wrote, reason to lament what man has made of man?

I remember liking one or two Gerhardi novels, one of which was certainly *The Polyglots*. Is G. dead? Probably you know him quite well. What a mysterious job is yours. How *do* you spot a best—or even a good-seller? That page in *The Times* has a positive genius for dealing with books that I, at least, feel no desire to read. Do you find that?

I will do all I can for your Reynard FitzGerald. Isn't it time his letters were properly edited, or am I out of date? I have only Aldis Wright's two vols, which aren't really edited at all. Nobody and nothing alluded to ever have an explanatory note. A.W. was an old humbug. I remember him at Trinity—one of those absurdly formid-

[1] Eton master, later Headmaster of Charterhouse.

able-looking old dons, grim, rigid, incurably 1850. 'Sound your alarum, sir' was his angry injunction to an undergraduate on a bicycle who nearly ran him down (or have I told you that?). F. was a crusty, humorous old homo, almost forgotten in Woodbridge. He died the year I was born, but I have spoken to a man at whom F. aimed a mild blow with his stick when he got in his way. This man was ninety-eight.

Must I read Coleridge's letters? I opened a vol recently in the library and read 'So beautiful a countenance [Byron's] I scarcely ever saw, his teeth so many stationary smiles, his eyes the open portals of the sun.' Of course I read on, but soon lost my way in the purple fog of his English. But perhaps I should have persevered?

Love to Ruth. See you both on Feb 9.

30 January 1960 *Bromsden Farm*

The only thing Adam left behind this half was his electric torch, which is two foot long, made of rubber, and contains *five* batteries: a very jolly thing to pack. He is now in First Hundred and starting English Extra Studies (nowadays lowlier specialists don't do any E.S.).

I thought your Mr XYZ's articles were some of the worst (or rather, most pointless) of all time. What was the *reason* for them? Or didn't he know?

On Thursday Ruth and I had drinks with the Eliots in their flat. He is terribly breathless, poor old boy, but very amusing and nice. We talked of Max Beerbohm, whom he loved and admired, and he read me Ezra Pound's lines on Max, remarking on E.P.'s vision of Max's Jewishness. The lines run:

> The sky-like limpid eyes,
> The circular infant's face,
> The stiffness from spats to collar
> Never relaxing into grace;
>
> The heavy memories of Horeb, Sinai and the forty years,
> Showed only when the daylight fell
> Level across the face
> Of Brennbaum 'The Impeccable'.

Whatever one may think of Ezra (and I don't think much), these lines are rather fine, don't you think? And they start new trains of thought. The Eliots have now flown to Morocco, where they stay till March.

You will be disappointed to hear that I *don't* know William Gerhardi, though he is undoubtedly alive, and I imagine pretty hard up. It's usually impossible to forecast what books are going to sell, unless the author already has a steady public. I always assume that anything I particularly like will not sell at all, but publish it nevertheless. If one abandons one's own opinion in an attempt to gauge the market, one is lost indeed. It's a mug's game.

I loved the Aldis Wright anecdote: it now looks as though my Reynard FitzGerald may not materialise, since the American who has been editing the Letters for twenty years, and seemed to have died on them three years ago, has now announced that his labours are almost completed.

The only way to tackle Coleridge's letters is one or two at a time, skipping: otherwise you'll assuredly get bogged down.

A very sprightly letter from Edmund Blunden in Hong Kong contains two brief epigrams, *viz*:

ON CERTAIN MEMOIRS

Does EDEN call to mind *Paradise Lost*?
One thing was not in Eden—well, a Frost.

K. LEAR continues

Let them anatomise Eden. My fierce daughter
Poured poison on me, this boss pours cold water.

When are you coming up to London next week? If I don't hear to the contrary I'll post on Sunday to Grundisburgh, and in any case we shall expect you at six at Soho Square on the Tuesday. I shall have had a London Library meeting in the afternoon. Dear old Masefield has offered a set of all his books in print (about twenty), with something specially written in each. Tomorrow morning I am driving round to John Piper and Osbert Lancaster to collect their contributions to the sale. It all takes a lot of time and work.

Last week Ruth and I went to *two* entertainments—the film of *Our Man in Havana*, which was enjoyable if not frightfully good, and the Eugene O'Neill play *A Moon for the Misbegotten* at the Arts Theatre, which is gripping and excellently acted.

I found I hadn't got the first volume of Froude's *Carlyle* here, so I've started the *Life of Sterling* instead, and am finding it most enjoyable.

Estimates on Oscar show that it will make 850 *large* pages, and if I can't somehow manage to print more than 3000 copies the price will have to be *five guineas*. (The setting up of the type will cost £1500, and the more copies one can spread this over, the cheaper each copy will be.) My chief hope is that the American publishers will agree to my printing their edition at the same time as mine. If they do, and I can print a total of 10,000 copies, I can publish at *three* guineas, which is a little better. See with what mundane considerations the purity of scholarship is beset!

We have some aconites in flower, and a few tiny snowdrops, but there is water, water everywhere. Take care you don't go under.

4 February 1960 (the day Carlyle died) *Grundisburgh*

I wonder who does English Extra Studies now. It is very important. Only Macnaghten of my colleagues knew that it was a more exacting job than nearly any other. He used delightfully to say 'Anyone can teach Latin and Greek', which of course isn't quite true, or why do so few manage to do it? But he did realise what a razor's edge one is on, rousing interest in Eng. Lit. And among *my* bouts of melancholy, which all old men have, one of the worst is 'how much better I could do that job now!' An old story of course. My successor was H.K. Prescot, a man I always found rather gloomy. He was apt to talk about Chekov (spelling?) and on one occasion took them through 'The Turn of the Screw', which to me verges on the outlandish as a set study for adolescents. Tell me how Adam gets on. I suspect that he will get more light on Eng. Lit. from his father than from anybody else.

Those are good lines of Ezra P's (a tremendous ass, by his comments on other and better men—and of course the war). *Was* M.B. a Jew? I miss the allusion to Brennbaum ('That's it!' cried Michael Finsbury, 'Very stupid!').[1]

[1] In *The Wrong Box* by R.L. Stevenson and Lloyd Osbourne.

I am sorry about your FitzGerald. I had already been preparing the Woodbridge library for its reception and dissemination. And those two admirable epigrams of E.B. He is wasted at Hong Kong.

You might be amused to hear the story of XYZ. He rang me up at Eton, saying he was about to write four articles on Eton, poured gallons of butter over me ('everyone tells me you are the one who' etc etc) and mentioned as great friends of his several O.E's whom I knew to be good chaps. So I had that disgraceful lunch with him and subsequently told him plenty about Eton—which he professed to admire immensely. He was excessively friendly, and really very pleasant. *BUT* in the next few days I wrote to him three or four times apropos of introducing him to Van Oss, and generally smoothing the way for him at Eton. He never sent one word of acknowledgement or thanks. Last Friday I lunched with Birley[1], who wanted to know all about the background of the articles, as the Governing Body might want to know. He was much amused at my not knowing that geniality is part of a journalist's stock-in-trade, and that they turn it off as soon as they have got from you all they want. (Incidentally, I had gently reminded XYZ that he had said I should see the articles before they appeared. I didn't—or afterwards either.) I have now got hold of the articles, and very poor stuff they seem. Several facts are wrong, and very many of the inferences etc drawn from those that are right. I lent XYZ a small book on Eton, and have sent a *not* very effusive postcard asking for its return. He hasn't yet sent it, and I am rather hoping he won't, as in the small hours a letter has been taking shape in my mind, of which the gist or nub is that its loss is a small price to pay for the revelation of what a Beaverbrook journalist regards as civilised behaviour, and ending by saying this is so far from the normal view that he may be surprised at my being able only in irony to call myself his sincerely. One or two more ponderings at 5.30 a.m. will do to polish it up. How I do loathe the Press!

There is a good deal of abusive stuff in the life of Middleton Murry which I am in the middle of.[2] Did you know him at all? If not I expect you have heard plenty about him from T.S.E.—one of the many who at any given moment one is not quite sure are or are not on speakers

[1] Robert Birley (1903–1982), then Headmaster of Eton. Knighted 1967.
[2] By F.A. Lea (1959).

with M.M. A very odd chap. I can't make much headway with all that introspection and metabiology, whatever that may ultimately be, but I rather like him. I don't much like K. Mansfield, and still less D.H. Lawrence (an old *bête noire*).

Last week I sat under your old hero the Archbishop of C. He was full of fun. He is resigning the Chairmanship of the G.B.A. and there is a movement on foot for the committee to give him a dinner (£3 a head). The cream of the joke is that I think it will fall just beyond the date on which my term on the committee comes to an end. But I must tread warily; they may suggest a retrospective levy. A portentous man called Sir Griffith Williams is the moving spirit, and, like Habakkuk, is *capable de tout*. He is one of those men who *look* far more important than anyone can possibly *be*—as Desmond MacCarthy said very young elephants do.

I go to London on *Tuesday* and then stay for two nights at 7 The Grove, Highgate Village, N.6.

6 February 1960 *Bromsden Farm*

Adam reports that his English Extra Studies are divided equally between Keats (please send me an edition, he adds) and some novel published last month. No such nonsense would have been permitted in G.W.L.'s day.

I imagine the Beerbohms may have had Jewish blood: 'Brennbaum' was simply a slender disguise for 'Beerbohm'. All the literary blokes mentioned in those particular poems of E.P.'s are given fictional names.

My FitzGerald volume is not yet finally kiboshed, so don't let the Woodbridge library lose interest. I did just know Middleton Murry (I was at Cape's when they published his autobiography and other books) but only slightly. An interesting but intolerable man, I should say, though I haven't yet read this new biography.

I am gradually collecting objects for the London Library sale. Leonard Woolf has sent copies of the first six Hogarth Press books, which he and Virginia set up and printed by hand: they should fetch a lot. And the splendid old G.M. Trevelyan says that he can never repay the London Library, without which his early books could not have been written. He is giving us drawings by Domenichino, Romney and Edward Lear, as well as the manuscript of his own autobiographical essay!! He apologised for not bringing them to London, as he is too blind, so I am to collect them at Cambridge on Monday afternoon. I shall go down after lunch, attend a dinner at Trinity Hall as Graham Storey's guest, spend the night (chastely, *bien entendu*) with Humphry House's widow, catch the 8.45 a.m. train to London, and prepare for the London Library meeting, the Lit. Soc. *and* your visit to Soho Square. I do hope you won't have too much difficulty getting there from Highgate. Thank goodness the Railway Strike isn't till the following week. Last Monday was a foretaste of things to come. When I got to Paddington at 9.45 a.m. there were three hundred people queueing for taxis, and more for buses, so there was nothing to do but walk. Unfortunately I had two heavy bags, and when I reached Soho Square an hour later I was, as the Americans say, 'fit to be tied.' Every street was solid with stationary vehicles, loud with curses, and heavy with the fumes of petrol.

I have just been sent the proofs of the first volume of an American (two-volume) biography of Mrs Besant. She's certainly ripe for a volume, but will she stand *two*? And is this chap (a university professor in Chicago) the man for the job? I must start on it tonight. This morning my eye fell on *The Egoist* (I have a battered first edition—three vols—which belonged to Augustine Birrell) and I took down the first vol, found the first chapter enchanting, and quickly put the book back on the shelf in case I should be so beguiled that my work would go by the board. If I ever have a free day I'll go a bit further: when did you last try it?

Today the *sun* came briefly out, and I did my first spell of garden-work for many months: rain is prophesied for tomorrow, so Mrs Besant may get a look in.

I have sent for that new life of Conrad, which sounds excellent. The author is a nice intelligent fellow, very industrious and thorough.[1] No proofs of Oscar yet: Ruth and I are both longing to get at them—and we're both looking eagerly forward to 6 p.m. on Tuesday.

[1] Jocelyn Baines (1924–1972).

11 February 1960 *Grundisburgh*

Again some of us lingered on after the rest of you had gone—Ivor, Roger, Tim, and Martin Charteris, because the divine good fortune emerged that Ivor Brown was on M.C.'s way home and that that home is only a few hundred yards from where I am, so a long and tedious journey was avoided. I was very well placed between Ivor B. and Tim. I didn't notice who your neighbours were: I hope they were good value. Did those empty chairs mean defaults at the last moment? Where was Peter F? Where, so to speak was Bohun?[1]

My sister took me off to a film yesterday—*Anatomy of a Murder*. Nice and long and mainly consisting of an American trial for murder. I enjoyed it, though my ears missed a good deal, and it was never really clear whether the young wife *had* been raped or not. All hinged on a pair of panties, a psychiatrist, and the fact that Mary was not the mistress of the murdered raper but his daughter. Perhaps the book will make all clear. There were several passages of which Queen Victoria would not have approved.

Life is full of mystery. This evening a photographer and young woman turned up out of the blue to take snaps of me talking about the family to the young woman. This is all for the *Queen* newspaper—unfamiliar to me—run by Francis Wyndham, a cousin of Pamela's and once in my house. A good lad with brains (something of a writer).

The railwaymen are obviously insane. We *may* escape something very like a general strike, but hadn't the boil better burst? How obvious it is that we can't go on in this atmosphere of perpetual strikes threatened or actual. But how is it to be tackled? The trouble is that democratic government demands (1) more brains (2) more unselfishness (3) more patience, and (4) more imagination than there is the smallest reason to suppose human nature will be able to produce for several hundred years. Aphorism by GWL.

Just finished another Trollope in the train, *Sir Harry Hotspur*—not very good, though of course readable as always. The characters are all black and white, and the young lady really does die of a broken heart, which they tell me does *not* happen—especially as the young man who broke it was a blackguard of vintage strength and cheated at cards.

[1] 'Where's Bohun?' (Bernard Shaw, *You Never Can Tell*, act iv).

Did you ever read the Tranby Croft baccarat case[1]—and if so tell me *why* Sir William cheated. His income was about £7–8000 a year. But my uncle who was in his regiment said he was suspected long before of cheating at cards by his brother-officers. Very rum. Who was the duchess who frankly cheated and they used to say 'Now, duchess, keep your hand up—no sly work below the table'? I like those old aristocrats, e.g. the one with kleptomania, whose valet's chief duty was to return in the morning the silver cruets and spoons which his master had brought from last night's dinner.

14 February 1960 *Bromsden Farm*

My Saturday writing plan broke down yesterday, for we were out all day, driving over to lunch with Patrick Devlin, the judge, and his wife at Pewsey, near Marlborough, where they have a beautiful centrally-heated Georgian house. My friend Christopher D., Patrick's brother, is there recovering from his ghastly operation, and I went up and saw him after lunch. Our new car has now had a radio installed—the first time we've ever had such—and on the way back we listened to the rugger international from Twickenham.

Duff reports that he is on the short list for a Commonwealth Fellowship (interview in March) and that three skeletons have been dug up in the excavation for a new building at Worcester College: victims of the Black Death, says Duff.

Did you realise that I was feeling exhausted and stupid on Tuesday? I hope it didn't show too much. My dinner neighbours were Tony Powell and Jo Grimond, whom I like very much. Peter had simply shirked, thinking the dinner was next week. I'm so glad you got a lift back to Highgate—what a stroke of luck! We must make sure that all future candidates are strategically placed round London to convey you home. Have you got your deaf-aid yet? It's no use going to the movies if you can't hear who has raped whom.

I might have known that Francis Wyndham was a cousin of Pamela's—everyone interesting is. His mother Violet, as I'm sure you

[1] For a full account of this famous case, see *Cheating at Cards* by John Welcome (1963).

know, was the only child of Oscar's friend Ada Leverson (née Beddington) whom Oscar called The Sphinx. I have got a lot of O's letters to her, and I need Violet's permission to print a letter from her father, Ernest Leverson, who was a rich diamond-merchant, as well as a number of Ada's contributions to *Punch* (some very amusing) which I unearthed.

The day after I saw you, old Jonathan Cape died suddenly, and his *Times* obituary, which I had promised to do eighteen months ago, had to be dashed off in a couple of hours. Did you see it on Thursday? It was exactly as I wrote it, except that the editor had inserted the sentence about *Earlham*, which in my haste I had forgotten. All the same, 'best-seller' is an exaggeration in reference to *E.* The first edition consisted of 750 copies, and I suspect that the rushed reprints were of 500 each.

I'm delighted the strike is off, even though I shall now have to attend Cape's funeral at Petersham, near Richmond, at noon on Monday. I am also supposed to be writing Diana Cooper's obituary for *The Times*, but I find the task unsympathetic to the point of impossibility when the subject is alive and flourishing.

I think Sir William cheated because he liked winning, so that his wealth had nothing to do with it. Mind you fire that last shot at the unspeakable XYZ—don't weaken!

Next Wednesday I have to take the chair at a Foyle's Literary Lunch (I've never been to one before) in honour of Priestley's massive new tome *Literature and Western Man*, of which I've read a good chunk: it's a remarkable achievement, though I can't quite understand why he took the trouble to write it, or who exactly is expected to read it.

The American publishers of Oscar's letters have proved most cooperative, and I shall now be able to price the book (850 large, closely-printed pages) at 63/- maximum, and possibly 45/-. Anyhow the printers have at last been given the go-ahead, and proofs should start coming in before the end of March. Then the fun begins!

E.M. Forster has offered to give the manuscript of *A Passage to India* for the London Library sale! He says it's messy and incomplete, but it should fetch a tidy sum. I fear I shan't get it without another journey to Cambridge, and I'm always so short of time. You've no idea how often I envy you your comparative leisure to do and read what you want.

18 February 1960 *Grundisburgh*

I didn't think you were in the least stupid last Tuesday, but that you were rather tired. And added the mental rider, 'and who wouldn't be?' Has any friend of yours *not* said at one time or another that you work at too many things? I trow not (though never quite certain what 'trow' means). How good you are at 'keeping your friendships in repair'; hardly a letter does not mention a visit to some ailing friend.

Old Cape must have been a good man. Your excellent obituary didn't mention, what some other did—that he had always had a particularly intelligent succession of readers, one of which was R.H-D. Does *Earlham* still sell? Very doubtful I imagine. To take trouble over *how* one says what one has to say on paper is still out of fashion. The man Naipaul who called *E.* 'estimable but rather dreary' still flourishes.

The first batch of your old letters will be shortly on their way home. I must see that they are in order. The fly in the amber of leisure to read all one wants to is that it belongs to a period of life when one gradually becomes more conscious of 'Time's hurrying footsteps' and Winston's 'surly advance of decrepitude'. The grim Scottish aurist says a permanently flat drum in my left ear is not temporary but eternal, i.e. old age. But some kind of hearing-aid will probably materialise in a week or two. They tell me the defect of it is that what one hears most clearly is one's breathing and the beating of one's heart. We shall see.

Alas, the man XYZ has returned the book I lent him with a tremendously smarmy letter, in which he pours far too many coals of fire on his own head and far too much oil and melted butter on mine. So the beautiful letter I was preparing for him is wasted. Housman would no doubt have kept it for the next harmless German who said something about the enclitic δή which H. disapproved of. These great scholars are very absurd with their pedantry and thin skins. They *sit* too much and get dyspepsia. Who was the scholar of Milton's day who was for some reason cut open after death, and his tummy was found to be half full of sand?

The Witch is delightful. I love the demure way she records the really incredible deeds and words of those irresistibly comic fairies—and the doctor, too old to know the sex of his patient, and the countess, buried, or rather not buried, in her hat. And I have enjoyed Nicolas Bentley's *A Choice of Ornaments*, though perhaps he does quote too often and too lengthily. Do you know him? I always liked whatever his father wrote—except of course his 10,000 leaders for whatever his paper was. He had an excellent style and any amount of humour and sense. Wouldn't you put *Trent's Last Case* very near the top of all 'whodunits'? I like the final scene at Simpson's, when Trent begs Mr Cupples to speak lower when asking for a glass of milk, on the grounds that the head waiter has a weak heart.

I am sure you are right about Sir William's motive—the same really as Iago's and T.J. Wise's. And perhaps the murderer(?) Wallace who in the end got away with what J. Agate called the perfect murder.[1] Bernard Darwin tells me there is no doubt that W. did it, but I don't know that there is any fresh evidence.

Tell me all about the Foyle lunch. I am always rather pro-Priestley, but I know nothing much about him. He may have jawed us a bit too much in the war, but he does, *me judice*, talk a great deal of sense.

20 February 1960 *Bromsden Farm*

I rather enjoy the false glow of non-stop activity which your letters cast on me: without them I might be overwhelmed by my own idleness, procrastination and lack of method, but I have only to remind myself 'George thinks I never stop working' to feel reassured once more.

Jonathan Cape's funeral on Monday was icy, and the clergyman so thin-voiced, old and doddery that I feared he might have to be shovelled into the same grave. The church at Petersham is a lovely old building with high pews, and a gallery round three sides of it. I travelled down by tube and taxi, but got a speedy lift back from a chartered accountant (Cape's and mine). He said that for years he had tried to persuade Jonathan to give some of his fortune to his five children, and so avoid at least part of the crippling death-duties, but the old boy always refused. Power to such as he is simply money, and if

[1] See volume iv of these letters, p. 150.

you part with any of your money you must lose some of your power. I understand this attitude without sympathising with it. I have never had any money (nor shall ever have) and my love of power is minimal: the Treasury will be lucky if they ever get anything out of me. Jonathan was in fact, despite my obituary notice, one of the tightest-fisted old bastards I've ever encountered, though his partner Wren Howard is even tighter. Still, one doesn't engrave a man's faults on his tombstone, does one?

The thought of my first batch of letters winging their way home is a sobering one, but perhaps one day I shall bless them and you—but the latter I do continually.

I'm longing to bawl into your hearing-aid, and only wish it was an ear-trumpet. My paternal great-grandmother used one, and she lived to be ninety-five.

I like your attribution of pedants' dyspepsia to their sitting too much, and hasten to quote (not, I fear, for the first time):

> 'Don't come flying out of your chair like that, Mr Venus!'
> 'I ask your pardon, Mr Wegg. I am so soured.'
> 'Yes, but hang it,' says Wegg argumentatively, 'a well-governed mind can be soured sitting!'

I only wish I had Dickens at my finger-tips, as Bernard Darwin has. Perhaps one day . . . ?

So glad you liked *The Witch*: the author was beginning to be rather a nuisance, sending her chauffeur round to every bookshop in London (including antiquarian ones) to ask if they had copies of the book, but mercifully she has now set off round the world by air, and by the time she gets back her detective ardour may have cooled. Nick Bentley is indeed a friend, and a most delightful fellow. Last year he too had a nasty go of jaundice, and his first drink (after, I think, the prescribed period of abstinence) produced such a severe relapse that he was in bed again for weeks. His father I saw but never knew: *Trent's Last Case* and the Clerihew should put his immortality beyond question.

The Foyle lunch was hard work. I took an old friend as my guest, a most amusing widow called Josephine Bott (see my *Hugh Walpole*, *passim*), and when we arrived Miss Foyle (dolled up to the tens and immensely refined) asked if I would receive the guests. I said I was her servant, so Jo and I stood solemnly inside the door and warmly shook hands with dozens of people as an enormous man in red called out their names with a roar. Tiny little old women with purple dresses and white fur hats and a surprising number of men. Jo almost got the giggles and tried to abandon me, but I made her stay, pointing out that we were in a strong position, since none of the guests had the faintest idea who *we* were, whereas we knew at least all their names. Several hundred people sat down to what proved a surprisingly palatable lunch (sole, chicken, ice-cream and peaches, white wine). I was between the two Priestleys, which was fun. After lunch I made a brief introductory speech, then Richard Church spoke well but dully about Priestley, and J.B.P. replied in his happiest and least combative vein. He said: 'When I arrived, the Chairman asked me why I always arrive at a function in my honour with a face of thunder (as I indeed had), and I'll tell you. Most of the time I'm glum because I'm not being praised, and on the rare occasions when I *am* praised I'm ashamed because I haven't done better.' Which I thought rather charming. The whole thing took more than two hours.

25 February 1960 *Grundisburgh*

Back of my hand to you six times! Your picture of yourself as a *dolce far niente* devotee, muddling through a slackish day, is on the same level of truth as Himmler's obituary reference to the unspeakable Heydrich as 'this good and radiant man'. Ask Ruth if it is an accurate self-portrait—or indeed anyone who knows you.

I see there was a side to old Cape which you touched on very lightly in *The Times*, but, as in epitaphs, a man is not on oath in an obituary. There are/is a number of people mentioned in your letters to me who will cut a very different figure after your letters—selected!—have been published. If the Lit. Soc. is on March's second Tuesday, that happily cuts out the Johnson Club dinner on the same day. How nice it is to make a choice between A. and B. when there is no rivalry. I hope Harold Nicolson will be at the Lit. Soc. dinner, as I want to tackle him about a remark he is reported to have made on Thomas

Carlyle—in today's *Times*, *viz* that he was 'a horrid old thing' whom he was delighted to think that nobody now read. If not misreported, it is below the level we expect from H.N. even as an *obiter dictum*—and as to the last statement, has not R.H-D just been reading the horrid old thing? So you must join in tackling him.

My hearing-aid is not yet to hand, in fact I still await a summons to the clinic. It is a rather sinister fact that several people who have the thing quite rarely use it. Like another friend whose first action when taking his seat at table, is to remove his dentures, which he says are just tolerable except when eating!

I notice in today's literary page in *The Times* that there is a sudden revival of interest in Southey, of all dreary dogs. Are you aware of this? It seems to be his political writings rather than his poetry. Or are people murmuring the tale of old Kaspar as they trudge to their work? I have always thought his couplet the most pathetic thing in the *Oxford Book* (except of course, for a different reason 'Meet we no angels, Pansie?')

> Yet leaving here a name I trust
> That will not perish in the dust.

—and hitherto, surely no hope has seemed less likely of fulfilment? Or am I addressing one whose heart always misses a beat when he thinks of how the water comes down at Lodore—easily the least impressive waterfall I have ever seen?

The ear-trumpet, yes. An aunt of mine had one, and one bawled into it placed in front of one at meals, not looking at her—rather like talking into the mike I imagine. Now and then it went out of order and screamed piercingly on one high note like a railway engine. She couldn't hear that and when it happened during a play or concert, she was not popular—in fact more than once had to leave the building.

At last, after really a very kind winter, we have one of those days which has, more than once in the past, been the prelude to thirty-six hours' rain. They say it is the same all over England. The sort of day which makes some take to drink. Do you know, by the way, the three reasons given by an American for declining an invitation to 'liquor up'—(1) that it was the anniversary of his brother's death, who had died of D.T. (2) that he was a teetotaller (3) that he had liquored up only ten minutes earlier? Not bad, I think, considering it dates from Victorian times.

Odd you should mention Dickens, because I have been recently re-reading all the *Martin Chuzzlewit* bits in which Mr Pecksniff and Mrs Gamp come (and *of course* the whole story of M.C. and Mark Tapley in America). Gosh! the man's mind was simply a *ceaseless* bubbling-up of fun and fantasy and the right words for embodying every notion, big and little. And how magnificently bad his character-drawing is! All his folk are black or white, e.g. Jonas Chuzzlewit and Tom Pinch—no iota of good in one or bad in tother—and both therefore very tedious. And Macaulay called *Martin Chuzzlewit* frivolous and dull, and refused to review it because he had dined with Dickens—a lovely Victorian blend of stupidity and gentlemanliness!

Your vignette of the Foyle lunch is lovely, and what a good remark of Priestley's. I haven't seen his new book yet, but the Ipswich librarian knows that there is such a book.

I am rather sorry that the new record for the high jump has been made by a man called John Thomas. We don't want any D.H. Lawrence in the athletic world.

27 February 1960 *Bromsden Farm*

I'm sorry to start this week by quoting your least favourite author, but Comfort has been reading *Pride and Prejudice*, and she says I am exactly like Mr Bennet: 'In his library he had been always sure of leisure and tranquillity; and though prepared, as he told Elizabeth, to meet with folly and conceit in every other room in the house, he was used to be free from them there.' I see what she means, and try hard to be charitable, but this room, which I made out of an old dairy so as to get away from the children, is now so much the warmest and cosiest room in the house that they tend to congregate here. Duff came over from Oxford for lunch, and Bridget is here for the week-end.

This morning I drove over to visit the Poet Laureate[1] at Burcote Brook, between Dorchester and Abingdon. One bumps up a dismal

[1] John Masefield (1878–1967).

drive to a low-slung desolate-looking house standing in the midst of much unkempt grass, with the swollen Thames flowing sullenly past. The old poet couldn't have been more charming: says he's getting shortsighted, but otherwise quite all there. We didn't mention his wife's death (I had sent him a letter of sympathy) and for all I know it may have been a great relief to him. He had ready for me three cartons, all packed and labelled by him, containing no fewer than *128* of his own books and pamphlets, in each of which he had written something—a quotation or other remark, sometimes about the London Library—and signed his name. It was all most touching. As I was leaving he said 'Is there anything else I can do to help?' I said: 'Certainly not: you've done quite enough—unless you can find us a tame millionaire'. 'Alas,' he said simply, 'my millionaire's dead.'

Talking of millionaires, did I tell you that I have managed to extract £500 from Mr Roy Thomson, the owner of the *Sunday Times* and many other papers? We have now passed the £10,000 mark—half way there!

On Wednesday I travelled again to Cambridge and visited E.M. Forster at King's. I found the dear old man surrounded with sheets of the manuscript of *A Passage to India*, which he was vainly trying to put in order for me. I told him I'd do all that for him, swept it up and took it back to London. After two evenings of sorting (when I should have been doing a hundred other things) I've got it into pretty good order, despite his appalling handwriting, and it should fetch a pretty penny. After all this sweat and toil we've received only some fifty lots, and we need 120. Somehow I must try to assemble the other seventy by the end of March, so that the cataloguer can get to work. T.S.E. has been laboriously copying out *The Waste Land* in Morocco, and yesterday I got a postcard from him, beginning:

> Oh Chairman, my Chairman,
> The fearful task is done!

I expect you saw the leader in today's *Times* rebuking Harold N. for his remarks about Carlyle: I'm sure it was written by Sir William Haley himself.

I long for further news of your hearing-aid. Perhaps you'll hear, not only your own heart beating and clothes rustling, but the bats squeaking in your belfry, the chip creaking on your shoulder, and the bees buzzing in your bonnet. Every man his own concert-party!

I can't help having a soft spot for old Southey, though I was quite unaware of any general feeling in that direction. Landor thought the world of him: a much greater poet than Wordsworth, said the old silly. But isn't the *Life of Nelson* rather good? I have the feeling that if one had the time and patience one might succeed in compiling a readable *short* anthology from S's works. A good biography of him was published in 1945 by Jack Simmons (or perhaps Simmonds: the title-page says one, the binding the other): it's worth reading.

I've always loved *Martin Chuzzlewit* (what a splendid name), but I remember thinking that Dickens's view of some of the characters had undergone considerable change as the book slowly appeared in its monthly parts. I can't remember now, but don't the Pecksniff daughters (particularly the one who marries Jonas) turn from monsters into almost sympathetic figures of tragedy? Or am I quite mistaken? One of the first things I shall do when I retire to N.W. Yorkshire is to re-read the whole of Dickens: there's something to look forward to!

2 March 1960 *Grundisburgh*

Pride and Prejudice is the Jane Austen I like best. As to the others my resentment (as of course you know) is composed partly of annoyance at myself for not seeing what so many great and good men are apparently unanimous in praising, and partly impatience with the amount of *Schwärmerei* there is about her by Walkley and David Cecil and all those voluble women. I believe to like *P. and P.* best is to join the groundlings who put *Pickwick* top of Dickens (where did I read lately of a piece of research which revealed the striking frequency of the occasions on which Mr Pickwick drank too much?).

What marvellous work you are doing for the London Library—Masefield, Forster, T.S.E. etc. I (knowing nothing at all about it) still feel that eventually an American tycoon will cough up a really fat sum. Or do they remember too well what Carlyle said about them? There was much to forgive in what Dickens wrote. I was amused and pleased by the *Times* leader putting H.N. firmly and justly in his place about T.C.—one of what I suppose to be the rare occasions on which H.N. spoke foolishly. But of course the thrawn old dyspeptic, like Milton, does arouse a really fierce antipathy in some. You, thank Heaven, are not one of them. And please read the very last paragraph in his *Reminiscences*, just after he had finished with Wordsworth, and tell me how can one *not* love the man who wrote that?[1]

Now, your letters. How you will laugh at me (and possibly, perhaps, be faintly pleased). I started arranging the bundle, re-read the first one or two, and without a pause settled down to re-reading *every single one*. I have nearly finished (each one took about five minutes); they range from October '55 to March '58. They are superb! What fun posterity will have, and how easily I foresee an able editor observing kindly that (if you reprint any), though G.W.L.'s are not in the same class, they at least did quite a good job in the midwife line. You will see some odd cabalistic signs in places—in one the name 'Gubby' makes a mysterious entry. Many questions and problems arise, and I must be sparing of them. In one place tears seem to have fallen, springing perhaps from acute sympathy with your railway accident in December '55. What is the story of 'Two Zoologists and a Flea' which you proposed to tell me and then didn't? Have you beaten Adam at chess since January '56? Wellington at the ceremony apropos of Borodino? Duff Cooper's 27 hats, Oscar's protest about his cress sandwich, Winston on his gaping flybuttons—the fun and fertility are inexhaustible, and if you please, in strong contrast with mine, you repeat yourself exactly once. If you think I am exaggerating, hand any three or four to Ruth and ask her candid opinion. She may find, as they did in Dr Jekyll's bible (was it?), some 'annotations of startling indecency (blasphemy)' made of course by Mr Hyde: some extremely funny flashes from the smoking-room, but she will take the same view

[1] In a few years, I forget in how many and when, these Wordsworth appearances in London ceased; we heard, not of ill-health perhaps, but of increasing love of rest; at length of the long sleep's coming; and never saw Wordsworth more. One felt his death as the extinction of a public light, but not otherwise. The public itself found not much to say of him, and staggered on to meaner but more pressing objects. Why should I continue these melancholy jottings in which I have no interest; in which the one figure that could interest me is almost wanting! I will cease.

of them as Landor did of the naughtinesses in Catullus's poems, and if she doesn't laugh at e.g. Mencken's story of his revenge on his traducer—but the hypothesis is absurd.

I *shall* bring this batch to you on Tuesday at 6, taking all the precautions that James Bond, when on the trail, took whenever he entered his room or got into a train. How absurdly readable Ian Fleming is. I couldn't resist *Dr No* in a Penguin. By page 40 (as far as I have got in bed) J.B. has already foiled four attempts to kill him. Dr No is as incompetent as Professor Moriarty.

My hearing-aid is still delayed. I don't think they trouble to be very quick with N.H. patients. My dour Scotch specialist clearly looks upon them as Himmler did on the Jews.

You put old Southey higher than I do (so far, by your letters, about the only thing we strongly disagree about is custard, which I love). I haven't read his *Nelson* for years. I remember admiring the end of it. I suppose Landor could be just as dogmatic and wrong in his judgments as Ruskin.

I see Oliver Van Oss has written what seems to me an excellent review of old Priestley's book in the *National Review*. It has the breadth and humanity of Priestley himself, and how nice to find a modern reviewer uttering full-throated praise. Do tell me what you think of it. And also, why J.B.P. gives a short parenthesis and no more to Milton; how can *he* be deaf to the organ-voice? Another question. The excellent N. Bentley has a lovely remark about M. Arnold's 'chilblained mittened musing', which is shrewd and telling about a good many of his poems, but what about Sohrab, Thyrsis, and Scholar Gypsy? Do tax him with this little catechism. We all have blind spots, and he *may* share this anti-Arnold spirit with Edith Sitwell and Lytton Strachey. M.A. *was* too pontifical of course and invited a sharp deflating punch in the stomach.

5 March 1960 *Bromsden Farm*

Truly you're better than any tonic. I got home last night utterly exhausted after a trying week and not a trifle despondent. There waiting for me was your splendidly long letter in which you tell of *re-reading* and *enjoying* all my old letters. Isn't that enough to raise anyone's spirits? As Yeats wrote:

> We have no gift to set a statesman right;
> He has had enough of meddling who can please
> A young girl in the indolence of her youth,
> Or an old man upon a winter's night.[1]

A momentary pleasure, when they arrive next day, is all one can hope for one's letters—and here are you, a man of the utmost taste, discernment, and, I'd have sworn, honesty, affirming that my old ones have amused you years after they were written. Can you wonder that today I wear my rue with a difference? One day I will pay you back by re-reading all *your* letters and overwhelming you with praise. Alas, I have forgotten every remnant of the story of the two zoologists and the flea (why on earth didn't I pass it on?). Now it must join Ould Grouse in the gunroom.[2]

I forgot to tell you that I asked J.B.P. about his unhappy trip to Australia, where he clearly put the natives' backs up, as he inevitably does wherever he goes. 'What did you say to upset them?' I asked. 'Nothing at all,' says he—and then, after a pause, 'I did say that their big cities reminded me of Wolverhampton after a long dry spell—but nothing else.'

On Thursday Christie's sent out a 'press release' about the London Library sale, and I was rung up by every newspaper in London. After lunch the B.B.C. telephoned to ask if I would be interviewed on television. I felt I must agree, but stipulated that I must be conveyed to Alexandra Palace and back in a B.B.C. car. This they arranged. I was on view for two minutes, twenty-one seconds, and the whole thing took exactly *three hours*! Have you ever been to A.P.? It was North London's answer to the Crystal Palace, and it stands like a monstrous folly on quite a high hill. One drives up a long circular drive, like the rings round a sand-castle on the beach. After dark the endless vista of coloured lights all round is very beautiful. Inside, the building is

[1] 'On Being Asked for a War Poem.'

[2] The anecdote mentioned, but never told, in Goldsmith's *She Stoops to Conquer*.

purely functional—studios and control-rooms and so on. I rehearsed my interview four times, trying desperately without watch or clock to keep within the allotted fragment of time. They were all very charming and helpful.

Next morning a widow sent the library a cheque for £2000, but no amount of flattering unction can persuade me that this had any connexion with my TV appearance. Be that as it may, we have now indubitably received £12,500 of the £20,000 we need, and the balance looks more possible daily. Also I have persuaded one of the independent TV companies to subscribe £250 *a year*!

I have, as you ordered, read the last passage of Carlyle's *Reminiscences*—with delight. I started my TV interview: 'The London Library was founded in 1841 by the *great writer* Thomas Carlyle . . . .' I knew you would approve.

Many of Landor's pronouncements were not literary judgments at all, but rather expressions of personal loyalty. He loved Southey as a man and didn't care for W.W. Therefore S. was the better poet. Incidentally, Southey's last recorded words were: 'Landor, ay, Landor.'

Your memory is not the only one that's going: I can't remember whether I told you about Ruth's son, Timothy. He is thirty and got married a few months ago, just bought his first house. Now he has to undergo the most serious heart-operation imaginable—they have done it only for a year or less, and it involves stopping the heart while they do the job. Apparently many recover completely, but others don't. To make bad intolerable they can't find room for him at Guy's for another fortnight, and in the interim the young couple are staying with Ruth, and you can imagine the underground tension. The boy is wonderfully cheerful and brave, and so, outwardly, is Ruth, but when she gets away to Soho Square she naturally relaxes and I do my best to comfort her. I don't know if she'll manage to be there at 6 on Tuesday, but if she does I thought you'd better be in the picture.

Did you know that the German for ice-hockey is Eishockey? I just found out, and it amused me, partly perhaps because Ei is the German for egg. Little things please little minds. A letter from America the other day referred to me accidentally as a 'publusher'—a lovely word. I am on the last chapter of Diana Cooper's last volume: it has been a fearful job, but there are some charming things in the book. I shall expect you on Tuesday, bringing *my* sheaves.

10 March 1960 *Grundisburgh (Summer-house)*

Once again a perfect London visit with the highlight 6–7 p.m. on the Lit. Soc. evening, which is itself, in my experience, of excellent quality. Am I curmudgeonly in saying that Gerry Wellington is *almost* first-class company? But anyway we had a good crack. Poor old Cuthbert shrinks visibly; he must weigh under eight stone and will just twinkle away one of these days. As my surgeon (a great man) once bluntly put it 'Yer know, Lyttelton, excluding accidents, there are, when yer come to it, only two ways of dying; you either dry up or swell up, and the first is more comfortable. You'll do the second.' A nice brutal man. But to go back to 6–7. How brave of the lovely Ruth to turn up and show no sign of strain. Honestly I cannot remember so striking a blend of charm and sympathy and sharp intelligence (how I should hate to say something really stupid to her—and I suspect I have). Which brings me to the blunt question (awfully non-U I expect) how is it possible *not* to be in love with her? So there—and I shan't be surprised if the answer to this is in the third person closing the correspondence. Still it has been a good one.

There are other problems an editor will some day have to tackle besides the two zoologists, *viz* was 15 January 1956 the last time you beat Adam at chess? What were you to tell me about the dentist at Didsbury (a ridiculous name)? And won't more light be wanted about the man who had a dipsomaniac daughter who was electrocuted by an electric iron at Beersheba, whose husband was manager of the Sodom waterworks?

In one letter you said your *Hugh Walpole* might be coming out in a Penguin. What has happened about that? I feel it should have precedence over *Lady Chatterley*.

That was a good party of Roger's—ultimately a benefaction of Lord Beaverbrook's. Rose Baring is a charmer, and Pamela's sisters are—well, Pamela's sisters. I nearly missed the 4.30 at Liverpool Street.

What business have all the No 9 buses to be full up at 3.30? Grotesque. What fun—if it is on, which it won't be—one would have in the next world contemplating London traffic in 1980. It was some ass of a saint who said that one of the chief pleasures of the saved *through all eternity* would be watching the torments of the damned. But *all* the time?

How they do go on about the *St Joan* Epilogue. My opinion (not that anyone ever asked it) is that it is quite in order but that the *expression* of it should be more dignified. They shouldn't all appear equally *little* men. What do you think?

I had nothing to read in bed last night, so picked up (why?) *Vile Bodies*[1] oh dear! I should have preferred the Koran, though it would have kept me awake longer.

I do hope there will soon be good news about Ruth's boy. My love to her.

12 March 1960 *Bromsden Farm*

Two little things I forgot to tell you last week: (1) when I looked out of my bedroom window here at 7.30 on Monday morning, just as it was getting light, I was enchanted to see five wild deer, grey and ghostly, in the field. By the time I had had my bath they had vanished into the wood, and now I only *just* believe in their existence. (2) Coming down exhausted in the train on Friday evening I was irritated from Paddington to Henley by two schoolgirls, who talked and giggled loudly without a break. I could have slapped them both with pleasure, and then one of them said, quite seriously, 'I've given up being beastly to Daddy for Lent,' and my wrath subsided.

What, if anything, makes you cry? I asked Harold Nicolson this question at the Lit. Soc. dinner, and he said: 'Three things only—patriotism, injustice righted, and misunderstanding explained. Tragedy never.' I agree whole-heartedly about patriotism: I can't see the Queen on a newsreel without a lump in my throat; but am less sure about the other two.

Poor old Cuthbert made an effort to sit next to me, but I had already buttressed myself with Roger and Martin Charteris—and then, when

[1] Evelyn Waugh's second novel (1930).

I saw Cuthbert silent, and his neighbour Tony Powell wilting with boredom, I felt a few tiny pangs of compunction.

I shall have to show Ruth some sentences in your letter, if only to sustain her during the last week of waiting for the boy's operation, now fixed for Monday 21st.

I think that 15 January '56 was almost certainly the last time I beat Adam at chess—and jolly nearly the last time I played with him, for he quickly got much too good for me. The dentist at Didsbury rings a bell almost as faint as that rung by the zoologists. My *Walpole* never appeared as a Penguin because the Penguin people ratted, after suggesting the idea to me. I was most disappointed, and so were Hugh's brother and sister, to whom I had told the good news.

I thoroughly enjoyed the luncheon-party and was charmed by both Pamela's sisters, please tell her. What is the other one's name?

I agree exactly with what you say about the Epilogue to *St Joan*, but it's many years since I saw it acted.

This morning I drove over to Oxford and fetched Duff home for his last vac. The traffic in the city was *épouvantable*. The new paper, the *Farming Express*, on which Bridget is working, will burst on an astonished world next Thursday, and she claims to be rushed silly in her office. The demise of *Time and Tide* is not unexpected, and it had sunk to a miserable rag since Lady Rhondda's death, when the subsidy was cut off. Still, I reviewed thrillers for it for fifteen years, and now there will be no more. I hadn't time for them anyhow.

The reason I've sent you no books lately is that I haven't published any: my absence last summer (when no new books were taken) is now making itself felt. However, we start again at the end of April, so look out!

Sunday morning.

Refreshed, and also slightly stupefied, by nine and a half hours of sleep, I return to the charge. The sky is grey, the bird-table thronged, the library fire most comforting. Surely you can't be in your summer-house today?

I have a few proofs to look over, but no manuscripts to read. In a fortnight the Oscar proofs will begin to arrive, and directly Fleming has finished his book about Younghusband, I shall have to go over it with a blue pencil. In fact I foresee a ceaseless stream of publishing work until June takes me back to Kisdon. And then, who knows?, *How Green etc* may tempt me! Now I am about to embark on that new life of Conrad by Jocelyn Baines: I can't remember whether you've read it. So far there hasn't been a good life of C.—oh yes, I have had a letter from Professor Theophilus Boll of the University of Pennsylvania. Clearly a fictional name—don't you think? but which novelist? Not quite outrageous enough for Wodehouse perhaps. You will know at once.

A nuthatch has just driven off the tits and is wrestling with some bacon-rind. It is raining steadily.

Next week looks like being a little less busy than last, and I am planning to try and take Thursday off, so as to take Ruth to Brighton for the day. We always love such excursions, and I think diversion is what she needs just now. You shall hear all about it.

17 March 1960 *Grundisburgh*

We are not at home at present as a new Aga and a new boiler are being installed, so we are with Pamela's sister at Wickham Market, hoping to be back by Sunday. But you know how it always is: 'Some of the pipes cannot be used again, being so silted up that it is a mystery how you got *any* hot water etc'. It is no crisis except in so far as old age can be called a crisis. P. goes over (seven miles) every day, having discovered how much better and quicker work is done if the owner is present and doesn't mind fussing, nagging, girding, protesting. I never can dismiss that horrid conviction that practically all work—not only of this sort—is done more speedily and competently by Germans. Don't *you* rage over the new pound notes where the important number is on the side under the counter's thumb? It is not inconvenient, it is imbecile. Incidentally isn't it a pity that the effigy of our pretty little Queen on it should bear no resemblance to her at all? No wonder old Carlyle more than once expressed exasperation at men's 'cursed ways of going on'.

Your deer! That sight was what Geoffrey Madan in his enchanting *Livres sans nom* called 'Sights of the Kingfisher', i.e. bits of dazzling luck. And I like your schoolgirl's Lenten resolve. I told two noisy schoolgirls on the top of a bus recently that they shouldn't make so much din in a public place, and to my astonishment they never uttered another sound. I suppose they thought I really *was* the great Panjandrum with the little round button at top.[1]

I cry repeatedly (like Winston) certainly at some aspects of patriotism, some ridiculously obvious sob-stuff in e.g. a cinema, but mainly at *words*, used as they are in e.g. 2 *Samuel* ch. 18, *Matthew* 26, the end of *Earlham*, of 'Sohrab and Rustum', of *Lear* (which old Samuel couldn't bear to re-read, though he was editing it!) and of course the 'Thus with the year' at the beginning of *Paradise Lost*, Book Three. As Cocteau (I think) said 'It isn't the pathetic that moves us, but the miracle of a word in the right place', which has a lot of truth in it. I agree with you that there is something very moving about the sight of our little Queen.

Oh yes, and I think I must tell *you*. My Aunt Lucy (Lady Frederick Cavendish)'s husband was murdered in Phoenix Park, Dublin, in 1881 and it broke her heart. She was very religious and quite enchanting, so full of humour and understanding; we children all loved her. Well, the murderers were rounded up and several put to death. The ringleader, Casey, nicknamed 'Skin-the-goat,' was to be hanged on a certain day, and the evening before Aunt Lucy sent his wife the little gold crucifix she always wore, as a sign of forgiveness—and other things. Of course *she* never told anyone, but Mrs. C. probably did. Anyway *old* George Trevelyan tells it in his Life of Macaulay, and says it is the most beautiful human action he ever heard of. That makes me cry whenever (very rarely) I have told it. It *could* be misunderstood, but Aunt L. was the most entirely genuine person that ever lived.

How right you are about Pamela's sisters—Sibell and Lettice both, like P. (and Madeline with whom we now are) magnificent people, *special* targets of fate. S. has lost two husbands and an only son, Lettice a husband and two sons—one in the war, the other, two years ago, run over by an underground train, of all fantastic ends; he thought he could nip across the line.

[1] From a rigmarole composed by Samuel Foote (1720–1777).

Time and Tide is the Chessman[1] of the periodical world. I see it has again been reprieved. Revivals *do* happen; I once again peruse *John o' London* in the Ipswich library, though how long I can stand the underbred swaggering cocksureness of Colin Wilson is doubtful. I read that he avers that Casanova was not immoral. Words are turning their coats. 'Dirty' will soon be a word of praise—just as 'brutal' was in 1937 Germany.

Theophilus Boll is straight from Peacock—like Dr Virgil Wigwam who writes about Scriptistics, whatever they may be. I always love the names which on the screen precede an American film. Even in the G.C.E. we get increasingly odd ones, e.g. two years ago Bee, Bones, Baffin, Bulger, and Blim. None such from Eton. There are still the ancient hierarchies of Campbell, Foljambe, Serocold, Howard and Hart-Davis.

I haven't read Conrad yet, but have just got the new book on Kipling and—in bed—an unread Raymond Chandler. As usual practically whenever Marlowe calls on a man the man is there all right—but dead. Why do I read him? God knows.

By the way will you send me my paper on reading without the schoolmaster, which I once wrote for Van Thal. The series it was meant to figure in perished a few months before it was due. What the devil was the paper called? I want to read it to the Leys School in a few weeks. Perhaps you have put it, as my father would have said, behind the fire.

I do hope all will go well with poor dear Ruth's lad on the 21st. I think of it constantly. Please give her my love. I don't pray much but aren't hundred-horse-power hopes prayers?

19 March 1960 *Bromsden Farm*

Your letter was faithfully waiting for me on Friday evening (yesterday). I do hope you're safely home by now, with all pipes flowing. I very much like and approve Cocteau's phrase (if it is his) about the

[1] Caryl Chessman, having at Los Angeles in 1948 been sentenced to death for multiple crimes, spent twelve years in the death-cell at St Quentin and was finally executed on 2 May 1960.

miracle of a word in the right place. My friend Humphry House couldn't read aloud 'whose dwelling is the light of setting suns' and the lines around it, without tears. On the other hand my Uncle Duff habitually cried when he was reading, and in the theatre, at almost any emotional passage, and in a way I rather envy that extra enjoyment of his. Your Aunt Lucy's action is certainly most moving—a beautiful and lovely story. Thank you for telling me. And now I shall go to bed and write more in the morning.

Sunday morning

The sun is shining, and Comfort is planting vegetables all over the place. A brick path demands my attention, the wild daffodils are out, and a few tame ones. Duff shot a deer last week (on Peter's orders) and I can't help being sorry, remembering that 'kingfisher sight' in the early morning. I'm against killing anything.

What is Lettice's surname?—her charming manner gave no hint of her tragic history. The agony of Ruth and her family has been protracted by the postponement of the operation to next Thursday, so concentrate your thoughts then. The boy is now in Guy's, being prepared for the ordeal. They keep telling him, or at any rate his young wife, the most grisly details, and mercifully they don't seem to upset her. For instance, while the heart is stopped and the operation in progress, the blood is pumped through the body by a machine, which, they cheerfully announced, has to be primed (like a pump) with three pints of someone else's blood. The whole thing makes me feel sick, but all I can do is to distract and comfort Ruth as much as possible.

What can I tell you of last week? It began in an underground 'dive' and finished in Henry's holy shade. Leonard Russell, the literary editor of the *Sunday Times*, asked me to lunch on Monday at a place called The Paint Box in a back-street near the B.B.C., which he had seen advertised. I arrived first and found it to be a pitch-dark basement with faint lights round the edges and a hidden gramophone playing incessantly. Two solitary men and a couple were sitting at widely spaced tables, groping for their food in the gloom. A strong smell of bad cooking pervaded everything. I sat down at a tiny bar to wait. Presently some curtains on one side were pulled back to reveal a tiny stage, on which a stark-naked Eurasian girl was reclining on the floor, with her back against a chair. She had a fine figure, but was clearly not allowed to move an inch for fear of breaking the law. None of the half-dozen people in the room paid the faintest attention to her, but I thought it only civil to face in her direction until my host arrived. He was extremely embarrassed and kept his back firmly towards the girl, who must, I fear, have been frozen. We played for safety with cold ham and an omelette. After about half an hour the curtains were drawn again, and soon the girl appeared in the restaurant, rather scruffily dressed and far less prepossessing. Later she carried on a piercingly loud telephone conversation in what I took to be Malayan, a few yards from our table. Apparently London and our other cities are full of such places, where tired business men can eat nasty food with a frozen nude in front of them. Perhaps even in Ipswich . . . ?

The best London Library news is that James Strachey (to whom I wrote soliciting) is going to give us the manuscript of Lytton's *Queen Victoria* for the sale! Willie Maugham is sending the manuscript of a long short-story, and Nancy Mitford a whole novel.

Our day in Brighton was the greatest fun and change. We walked by the sea, had an excellent lunch, briefly inspected *four* secondhand bookshops, and went to the movie *Anatomy of a Murder*, which we both enjoyed. I can't remember if you liked it?

Yesterday Adam was confirmed along with a hundred others, including Oscar's grandson. We had to sit on the knifeboard, under which run extremely hot pipes. The Bishop of Oxford spoke for much too long, and the boys grew restive. I suppose no-one can stop a bishop when the bit's between his teeth, but he ought to sense the right moment to stop. Afterwards we had a poorish lunch at London Airport and went to an amusing movie in Slough, called *Two-Way Stretch*. This is Adam's first half in the top Science division and he has come out second in the half's order, which seems pretty good. Bridget has started to mow the lawn and is calling for assistance.

23 March 1960 *Grundisburgh*
(Summer-house)

Yes, it *was* Cocteau, though I don't know which work it comes from, being, let me tell you, wholly unacquainted with his writings. I am in fact a contemptible French scholar. I imagine your Uncle Duff was a very good one. I particularly like to hear of his crying over a book and in the theatre. When he had once got over my being a beak, I feel we should have got on very well—and frequently we should have mingled our tears.

Yes, deer must be shot I suppose, but not in my presence, thank you. One can think of a cow, pig, or sheep lying down but who ever pictured a deer other than moving with incomparable grace at whatever speed you like? (interval for instruction: a cheetah is the fastest of all—about 70 m.p.h.: in two seconds from stationary its speed is 45 m.p.h. A botfly goes 400 yards in one second, i.e. 818 m.p.h. End of interval for instruction).

Lettice was married to Geoffrey Colman (Oxford XI about 1913–14). A grand chap; head eventually of the great mustard firm, and one of those who really would have helped industrial relations. He was badly wounded in 1916, and died in about 1930, endocarditis I think they called it, the result of the wound. Never was there a sisterhood of greater courage than the Adeanes.

I shall certainly think of Ruth to-morrow. The tactlessness of doctors is very odd—and almost universal. I suppose if you are trained to regard the heart as a pump or a muscle, you just can't think of it as the 'fountain of sweet tears', or dancing with daffodils. *Do* our thoughts and hopes have the faintest effect on the Ancient of Days? Who knows? I find it hard to feel the confidence that many say they do, that all will be perfectly clear to us the moment we arrive in the next world. And I rather like old Allan Monkhouse's remark that he was not going to be easily convinced by what he called The First Cause's explanation of his main puzzles in his lifetime. Ruth will know that, with all the host of friends, every wish and hope I have is hers on Thursday.

Your story, by the way, of the man who had lost his memory has had a good press in Suffolk.[1] My doctor I thought would pass out, he

[1] See volume iv of these letters, p. 163.

laughed so much. I may tell you I am quite shameless in retailing them to fit audiences. You know the lovely Audrey Van Oss? She recently had a spell in hospital—often depressed, not getting well very quick. I told her in a letter of Winston's reply apropos of his fly-buttons,[1] and three days later she was back home. Of course the cure is an old one, and I need not remind you of Dr Battie whose impersonation of Punch made an ill boy laugh so much that his quinsy burst and the boy recovered—and Henry VII hired a man for six shillings and eightpence 'to eat coals before him.' It was, as far as I remember, about the only thing he ever did laugh at.

Your 'dive' adventure is grand. Every facet of it is a-gleam with character and fun. Fancy you *not* having time to write. Monstrous unfairness. I love your climax, viz the hypothesis that even in Ipswich there may be a place or places where tired business men eat nasty food with a frozen nude. I must do some research; there should be something bizarre in the alluringly-named Silent Street.

I much enjoyed *Anatomy of a Murder*, also *Battle of the Sexes* which was quite funny. But all the last week we have been at Madeline Wigan's (P's sister) while our stoves were being put in, and had our bellyful of TV non-stop from 5.00 to 10.30. Altogether about four things worth seeing, chiefly of course the Calcutta Cup match and a boxing match. Otherwise one is almost killed by the amount of *jaw*, as there is apparently hardly any music. By Tuesday I felt I never again wanted to hear what anybody thought about anything. No, I shall never have one. I shall go to a neighbour's to watch the Boat Race. Oxford is to win, they say, probably because they put the oars in the water with their feet, as the rowing-manual at Spottiswoode's said was essential. Tuppy always maintained 'with' meant in company with and not by means of. It *always* annoyed wetbobs when he mentioned it.

On Tuesday C.M. Wells's[2] dinner, his ninetieth birthday. He hasn't changed in the last twenty years. His forty-to-fifty-year-old pupils have—bald, fat, dewlapped, limping etc. G.O. Allen was there. He had just seen Statham who told him that Hall, 6 ft 5, was *much* the fastest bowler he or anyone else had ever seen; not even Cowdrey really enjoyed facing him. C.M.W. of course repeated W.G.'s saying

[1] See volume ii of these letters, p. 35.

[2] Former Eton master.

about fast bowling, *viz* that the faster it was the better he liked it. I gathered that G.O.A. regarded himself as of much the same pace as Larwood etc. But D.R. Jardine told me L. was a good deal quicker. John Christie[1] is the spit of Mr Pickwick, in good form. Only one eye and subject to angina pectoris, but quite contemptuous about both.

Our old stove would have lasted another ten weeks at most, our Aga another three or four, so we haven't acted too soon. Pamela purrs audibly whenever she enters the kitchen.

Adam's scholastic career is most impressive. I imagine you chatting with him on a summer evening about specific gravity. Who teaches him? In the Nineties all the science-beaks were absurd, though Porter had a touch of genius, and was a fine showman. He told K. Fisher who was brought in to re-organise Eton science (which P. thought was unnecessary) that all the science-teaching at Eton except his own was mere wind, and got the Johnsonian retort: 'But even so, my dear Porter, is it not better that we should have organised wind instead of casual flatulence?' K. Fisher was a good man.

P.S. I don't think you reached the sentence in my letter in which I expressed a mild wish to get from you the typescript of my paper called I think 'Letter to a Schoolboy'. It was all about how to read without having any truck with a beak.

26 March 1960 *Bromsden Farm*

I love finding your letter waiting for me, and any Friday evening at seven you can imagine me, newly changed into my comfortable old clothes, relaxed in my armchair by the library fire with a glass of hot whisky and the latest budget from Finndale House.

Last week was a nightmare of anxiety and strain. Ruth's daughter flew home from Italy to stand by, and that meant another person to cope with. Poor Ruth could settle to nothing, so I took her and the daughter to the cinema two nights running to distract them. (One of the films, *I'm All Right Jack*, was excellent, and I suddenly realised that I, a confirmed non-cinemagoer, had been to four within a week—one at Brighton, one at Slough, two in London.) On Thursday the

[1] Eccentric millionaire (1882–1962). For some years an Eton master. Founded the Glyndebourne Music Festival on his own estate 1934.

operation began at 9 a.m., and we were told to expect news about noon. In fact it wasn't till almost *two* that we heard all so far was well, and you can imagine the stress of the morning. They found his heart even worse than they had expected and say they can't guarantee how fit he will ever be. On the other hand, they say he couldn't have lasted more than a few months without the operation. I have just (11 p.m.) spoken to Ruth. She saw the boy today for the first time, and they say all is going splendidly, though his condition must be considered critical for another forty-eight hours.

In between all this I attended Jonathan Cape's memorial service at St Martin's, and took the chair for my old friend William Plomer when he read some of his poems to a collection of old dames in Foyle's bookshop. On Thursday I attended a dinner-party twenty strong, given at the Ivy by the head of the U.S. publishing firm Harper's. I had the ill-luck to sit next to Mrs Woodham (*Florence Nightingale*) Smith, who is voiceless and inaudible at nine inches' distance. Altogether the week was endlessly wearing—and next Tuesday the Oscar proofs start rolling in. Oh for Kisdon Lodge! I backed Eagle Lodge in the National, but it's still running.

Sunday morning

A cold grey day with a bitter north-east wind. I lit the library fire and it went straight out. Duff is kindly coping with it. Did I tell you that he failed to get a Commonwealth Fellowship? He was very disappointed, but on the whole I'm not sorry. By the time he came back from America he would have been twenty-six, without prospects and thoroughly used to being subsidised. Now he will have to get a job after he comes down from Oxford in June.

Yesterday I drove over and had tea with Lytton Strachey's brother James, a charming old boy with a white beard, blind in one eye, who lives with his psychoanalyst wife in a fine centrally-heated, book-infested house in a wood above Marlow. He has now translated eighteen of Freud's twenty-three books into English and still seems quite cheerful. He gave me the complete manuscript of *Queen Victoria*, beautifully legible, together with corrected typescript, corrected page-proofs, and a number of notebooks in which L.S. planned the book and took notes for it—what a haul! I found it difficult to thank him adequately. What will it fetch? I posted your 'Letter to a Schoolboy' to you on Friday. So sorry I forgot to mention it last week. Altogether I feel rather bad about your batch of essays, having seized them enthusiastically and then gone dead on them. The trouble is that there isn't quite enough, it seems to me, to make a book, and I don't suppose you feel like writing any more. Please let me have this one back when you've delivered it, so that they are all kept together.

I have started to re-read Dover Wilson's *What Happens in 'Hamlet'* and can't put it down. I expect you know the book?

30 March 1960 *Grundisburgh*

What a dreadful time poor Ruth has been having. I hope the acute anxiety is now past. It is a tremendous burden for a young man to shoulder just at the dawning of all his hopes and prospects. Can we agree with John Keats who in a letter wrote that when a great misfortune came to a man he felt inclined to congratulate him on being so challenged to show the resources of his spirit? I can't find the passage in what must be much the worst edited book in the world, *viz* K.'s letters edited by Colvin. In the first three pages there are six unexplained allusions and names. It is as bad as Aldis Wright's two vols of FitzGerald's letters. What did those old men *think* their job was? K. is of course fundamentally right in regarding man as capable of *any* degree of heroism and fortitude. Most of us, happily, are spared the uttermost tests.

You omitted to say what the menu at the Ivy dinner was. I lunched there four times and dined once, and the provender was superb. Is it still? I have some notion that the famous chef has gone.

Are you writing a detailed account of your money-raising activities for the L.L.? Because it really is a grand story. Strachey's *Q.V.*! Just imagine if you have two opulent Yankee fans in opposition! The price could rival those fantastic sums paid for pictures, many of which *can't* be worth all that. I suppose Agnew's will make a packet on that Gainsborough, was it?[1] My old pupil[2] must have done some fine reconstruct-

[1] *Mr and Mrs Robert Andrews*, bought by Agnew's for 130,000 guineas at Sotheby's on 23 March 1960. Now in the National Gallery.

[2] Geoffrey Agnew. Knighted 1973.

ing of the firm's fortunes; it was in very hot water fifteen years ago.

Many thanks for the 'Letter to a Schoolboy' which you shall have back in due season. I shall use quite a lot of it for the Leys School in May. The line I have in mind is not anti-science (though I shall have a little swipe or two at Hogben and co) but rather to show how *clarity* of style is essential to both literature *and* science—and how they can and must almost entirely acquire that on their own, with very little help from the beak. Do you think that is at all a promising line? Of course I am not anti-science (it is important that Adam should not think that) but only arrogant ignorant scientists—e.g. Hogben.

There is a good deal of fun in the papers just now. Are you well up in Francis Bacon's painting? His 'Sleeping Figure' in to-day's *Daily Telegraph* has strong emetic value (hailed of course as of immense power and originality). And I like the brothers Cheeryble on p. 19 who are suing the Attorney-General and a brace of policemen for £10,000, for charging them (successfully) with swindling. America of course does well with a 'special tariff' for black men at an eating-house which charges them 17/9 for a cup of coffee and then summons them for making a disturbance. But I feel no great liking for the boy of ten who can't quite remember whether he did or did not stab to death a girl of nine.

Pamela is now rejoicing over a new sink, which looks to me very like a quite competent old one, but in which she sees a score of superiorities. Women!

2 April 1960 *Bromsden Farm*

The Oscar proofs have begun to pour in, and I am already overwhelmed with sheets and sheets of paper, all requiring checking and titivation. I shall not badger you at this tiresome stage, but perhaps when the proofs are paged and manageable (in some months' time) you might be amused to read them and look for howlers?

I'm happy to say that Ruth's son appears to be mending most satisfactorily: her acute anxiety is over, but she is suffering a little from reaction after strain. I shall try to advance our Yorkshire holiday—to May if possible.

Colvin was not only the idlest of editors, but also the most unscrupulous. We shan't know exactly how much he cut, expurgated and bowdlerised Stevenson's letters until they're edited afresh from the originals, but I know of one letter which R.L.S. (in the midst of a haemorrhage) signed 'Yours in buckets of blood, R.L.S.' Colvin printed 'Yours, R.L.S.', with no sign of omission.

I'm sorry to say that the Ivy dinner wasn't up to much gastronomically—smoked salmon, *huge* segments of tough duck liberally soused in orange, and a goodish pudding. I fancy the chef must have fled, as you suggest.

The London Library sale is now fixed for the *evening* of June 22—which should give Christie's plenty of time to circulate the catalogue in the States. No astonishing acquisitions last week, except the manuscript of Rosamond Lehmann's last novel *The Echoing Grove.* Also Macmillan's coughed up 100 guineas, to bring our cash receipts above £15,600.

I think your suggested address to the Leys School is admirable, and am only sorry I shan't be there to hear it. Francis Bacon's pictures are too revolting for words—stockbrokers with two heads and no trousers, elemental horrors crawling up walls—give me *Dracula* any day!

Last week I dined out three nights running—nothing worth recording, but all very exhausting. Adam came home covered with glory, *viz* (1) Trials Prize, which seems to me to make him the top Science specialist in the school at sixteen, though he modestly says that several of his rivals were away on scholarships; (2) a prize for his *sixth* Distinction in Trials; (3) a prize for his third sent-up-for-good. Withal he remains his old self, very affectionate and simple and undemanding.

Duff has now cut all the grass, and in its ring of daffodils the garden looks very trim and springlike. P. Fleming has dumped on me twenty-three out of the twenty-four chapters of his Younghusband book, which we are now thinking of calling *Bayonets to Lhasa*—a better title, I think, than his original one, *Tibet 1904.* I shall have to read these chapters comma by comma, correcting and making notes or suggestions, and naturally I long only to pore over the Oscar proofs.

I'm delighted to see that Donald Somervell has expressed his intention of attending the Lit. Soc. on the 12th: he must indeed be much better. Will you be there? I do hope so.

You didn't answer my question about Dover Wilson, whose book I am still enjoying, alongside Bloggs Baldwin's new book, *The Mac-*

donald Sisters,[1] which has a lot of amusing new material in it.

I have refused an offer of £25 to drive to Teddington next Sunday and appear on Commercial Television with Ian Fleming, discussing his new book of short stories (which I haven't read). The money is tempting, but Sunday is precious for work and rest.

Today I drove over to Pewsey and lunched with the Devlins. My friend Christopher (the judge's brother) seems to be making a good if slow recovery after his frightful operation, and I am encouraging him to occupy his mind with a monograph on Christopher Smart[2], for which I have sent him cargoes of books from the London Library. He is a charming person, of the utmost naturalness and courage, and he's the only priest I've ever known (he's a Jesuit) who is *completely* unparsonic.

My publishing activities, having lain dormant since January, will start up again on April 28: nothing very exciting, I fear, or very saleable—except for a frightful book about the Wolverhampton Wanderers football club. The ghost-author is always unobtainable and the book is almost a year late—luckily perhaps, since W.W. are now in the Cup Final, and may win the League as well. Our first edition of 5000 copies looks like being exhausted before publication, which is more than can be said of most of my precious literary books. It only goes to show! Now Younghusband calls.

6 April 1960 *Grundisburgh*

What a relief about Ruth's boy! You and Kisdon will remove her strain, which must have been like a dead weight on every minute of her day. Give her, please, a message of deep affection from me. You needn't perhaps add the egotistical note that I rejoice delightedly to find that, at seventy-seven, the heart's blood is not dried up.

I shall love to be associated with your Oscar in any office. The most menial if you like. The best judges are agreed that few tie up parcels better than I do. I will help in any way I can.

Those old editors were curiously shameless. Macaulay who hated

[1] By A.W. Baldwin, younger son of the Prime Minister, whose mother was one of the sisters.

[2] Poet (1722–1771).

Croker (as apparently most people did) more than cold boiled veal, had no difficulty in showing up the monstrous liberties C. took with his edition of Boswell, and Froude—though I have forgotten the details—was pretty loose with the Carlyle material. I have been browsing once again in the Life, with the same feelings as of old. C's conviction (the same as Dean Inge's) was that democracy was a more than dubious form of government. Those who say that C's prophecies of disaster have been disproved, don't know or have forgotten that the *ultimate* crash that he foresaw might not happen for a century or two. *All* his lamentations a hundred years ago—love of money, lowering of standards, political humbug, impotence of religion etc—would surely be intensified to-day, if indeed the English language could carry any more than he put into it. If Gladstone on Ireland, and Dizzy on the Franchise, nearly killed him with exasperation, what would Barbara Castle have done? His imperviousness to feminine charm always amuses me—the obviously personable young lady from U.S.A. who called on him and was tersely designated as 'a diseased rosebud', Margaret Fuller 'a strange, lilting, lean old maid, not nearly such a bore as I expected'. And his horror at the portraits of himself is also rewarding: 'the portrait of an idiot who has taken glauber salts and lost his eyesight;' 'a delirious-looking mountebank, full of violence, awkwardness, atrocity and stupidity,' and of course the early one which he said was 'like a flayed horse'.

With Bradman as captain that black team would have won the rubber—or M.A. Noble. Both of them, they tell me, immensely superior to any English captain. Jardine just as intelligent, but cordially disliked by *both* sides—as I keep in reserve for any more than usually smug Wykehamist. (It is simple historical fact that the only tour in Australia led by a Wykehamist nearly disrupted the Empire.)

How proud you must be, and ought to be, of Adam. If it would give him the smallest pleasure, convey to him my congratulations. I forget whether he knows my grandson Lawrence. He too is an interesting boy, but lacks A's cutting edge. At the moment he is on the way to Greece with a party. I hope he will see the Acropolis by moonlight, *and* with the southern sun on the rich marble of the Parthenon—quite unique and unforgettable. The light seems to be coming out of the marble. It is worth remembering (or is it?) that Bernard Shaw wrote to Ellen Terry that he was glad to get away from Athens 'with its stupid classic Acropolis and smashed pillars'. One of his pronouncements that make one's toes itch.

I have just got into Priestley's book. Very enjoyable. I skip a certain amount when he is among foreign playwrights, but reluctantly, because he has a wonderful gift of phrase. He must be grand company. I wish he would write more regularly in the weekly press; his comments on the prevailing asininities are always refreshing.

I note that in the publisher's advertisements of *Breakdown* by Bratby, it is clear that we have now reached the point at which 'vulgar, tasteless, a beast of a book, repellent, garbage-can' are regarded if not as actually laudatory, at least likely to attract readers. And there are still those who approve of the general taste of readers in 1960!

I have been reading in bed about the absurd life of Selfridge. Nothing in the book has given me as much pleasure as the figure of Arnold Bennett in one of the illustrations. Every single item of his dress is wrong and the total effect is an overwhelming picture of the provincial snob. He never quite shed his upbringing did he? In one of his reminiscent volumes there is a snap of him and Dorothy in deck-chairs on the sands somewhere. A.B. is still wearing ordinary black *boots*. None the less he always strikes me as a good chap.

What *excellent* news about D. Somervell. He must have recovered marvellously. I wish I could be at the Lit. Soc. on Tuesday, but my sister is to be here for two days, and I must shirk. *What Happens in 'Hamlet'* I remember thinking *superb*, but I must read it again *at once*. Thank you for reminding me.

9 April 1960 *Bromsden Farm*

It's angelic of you to say you'll help with the Oscar proofs. I think I'll keep you for the page-proofs later in the year: they'll be much more convenient to read—just like an unbound book—and I hope less scrappy than these galley-proofs which are now pouring in daily. Eight expert well-wishers in various parts of the world are reading sets, and it looks as though their comments and queries may be longer than all Oscar's works put together. Endless minor points need attention, but there is no time. Mercifully the London Library sale is now complete except for a few stragglers, and the cataloguers are at work. Elisabeth Beerbohm's sister has given us two Max drawings for it.

Having finished *Sterling*, which I much enjoyed, I have embarked on T.C.'s *Reminiscences*. I found I hadn't got the first two volumes of Froude's biography, so that is postponed.

Adam's reports were the best I've ever seen, but he is in no way changed or spoiled by his success.

I thought you'd enjoy the Priestley book: I skipped too, here and there, but found much to admire.

I have just finished the manuscript of Peter's book about the Younghusband expedition—at present called *Bayonets to Lhasa*. It's a fascinating story very well told, but I can't see it selling as well as *The Siege at Peking*: it lacks comedy, and the Dowager Empress, and a proper climax, but you'll like it, I'm sure. It should be out in October or November.

I was sorry to read of Crace's death:[1] I was never up to him, but he was a friend of yours. Now I shall put the clocks on and resume this turgid scrapbook in the morning.

Sunday morning

A gale is blowing, and once again it looks like the library fire for me. I'm happy to say that Ruth's son is getting on splendidly: from tomorrow he is to be allowed non-family visitors, so Ruth won't have to battle her way to Guy's every day.

Last week I saw Diana Cooper, fresh from the De Gaulle banquet at Buckingham Palace. She reported Winston as totally *non compos*, and scarcely able to walk. I fear the old hero has lived too long.

Once again I dined out three nights running—too much food and drink, too much time wasted: 'So much to do, so little done.'[2]

I expect you saw that Peter Davies threw himself under a train. The poor fellow had for years been dying of some incurable disease, but this does seem to me a particularly inconsiderate form of suicide: just think of the driver of the train, and the people who have to pick up the remains! Sleeping-pills are surely the most civilised means, and

[1] J.F. Crace, Eton master.

[2] Tennyson, *In Memoriam*. Said to have been the last words of Cecil Rhodes.

going to sleep is itself pleasurable, but I suppose they don't work instantaneously and might leave time for a change of heart. Hemlock itself wasn't all that quick, was it?

We still haven't decided exactly when to go to Kisdon, but it may well be in May, which would mean my missing that Lit. Soc.—we'll see. The Oscar proofs are going to take so long anyhow that we can almost disregard them in our plans: they'll go with us for sure. Last week I got copies of the last nine letters which had hitherto evaded me, and now I know of none that I haven't got, though many more probably lurk here and there—especially in America. You must forgive my harping on Oscar: he is much on my mind just now.

Did I tell you that I have stupidly agreed to open the Antiquarian Book Fair on April 27? What on earth am I to say? This is only the third year they've held it, and the two previous openers were Lord Birkett and Miss Phyllis Calvert. Clearly they've tried Brains and Beauty, and are now reduced to the Beast. Somehow I must try and learn to say NO politely—a thing I've always found it hard to do.

13 April 1960 *Grundisburgh*

How good that Ruth's boy really is getting on well. I suppose it is still too early to say whether he will in due course be able to do a full day's work with head or hand. What a rum thing the whole of man's existence is—how, why, whence, whither—not one of the four questions ever answered. You will find many reflections of that sort in Carlyle's reminiscences. The *fundamental* difference between him and Macaulay is that C. never lost his sense of mystery, and M. never had one. I expect you may find C's lamentations for Jane a bit too much. In any recollections connected with her he writes as if she had died the moment before, and as if she simply was unique—body, soul, and mind. The old man had extraordinary tenderness, and yet you can see, from what she quotes in her letters of what he said, that this usually had a grumpy sound. I suppose the Scots are like that—his family especially. 'Pithy, bitter-speakin' bodies' some neighbour said about the whole clan.

I shall be greatly honoured by having the very smallest bit to do with the Oscar letters. Will the chorus of indolent reviewers see the immense trouble you have taken with it? Some will, no doubt, and the rest don't matter. You will have every right to be wholly indifferent to what they say—like T.C., content with the knowledge that you have done every blessed thing that you could.

Jan Crace was a great friend of mine, and I spent many hours last week writing a thing about him for *The Times*. They must have got it on Monday, but so far nothing has appeared. I have heard more than once that the present obituary editor is rather a cross-grained chap, and he has probably reacted rather violently from the too ample notices of Eton beaks in the past, but they ought not to ignore men of marked distinction in some line the public know nothing about (as I shall tell the bloke on Sunday, when demanding my manuscript back for the *Eton College Chronicle*). If you are director of a company, you are sure of at least six-eight inches, and giving intelligent boys a love and knowledge of the classics is better work in the world than passing a dividend. They will of course plead lack of space. Luckily Pamela insisted on copying it out and sending it to Jan's widow, who seems thoroughly happy about it and not to care twopence if *The Times* prints it or not. Very like J.F.C. himself!

I got recently a tiny volume of poems by Susan Glyn who is apparently about sixteen years old. They seemed to me very distinguished and wholly unintelligible (the bucket with a hole in it blaming the inefficiency of the pumps filling it!). She says she knows you (and of course gets a thrill out of it) but so far, she says, hasn't dared to tell you that she has written poetry. I have reassured her about your ability to survive such a shock, and I rather think left her with the impression that you are a prince among patrons. I wonder how you met her. Do you know her father, who for some obscure reason has changed his name from Geoffrey Davson to Anthony Glyn. I don't think his mother at all approves and I don't wonder.

I am *much* enjoying Priestley. Surely his pages on Wordsworth, Coleridge, Scott, Byron, Shelley, Keats could not be better—and what a lot he says in really very little space.

Where did I read recently a complaint about T.S. Eliot's dulness in conversation? Not that he is alone among great men. Housman could be deadly—partly from disdain, partly because, just like Kipling, he didn't *want* to give his opinions about this and that, except on rare occasions in congenial company, and with just the right amount of the right food and drink inside him. Too often, as Max Beerbohm said, he should have had a poached egg in his room. But he was very greedy, so paid much attention to the fare and none to his fellow-guests.

A poor day—dark, windy, wettish, and the cherry-trees and almond are looking somehow snubbed; all they ask is a little sun. But the brevity of the life of spring blossom saddens me every April and May—less than a week for many things. We should be having the nightingale here in a day or two, but somehow he is not the bird he was, or perhaps my ears are at fault. I have had my aid fitted, but I doubt if I shall wear it much. There is too much fiddling with adjustment and parking of batteries etc. They tell me I shall get used to hearing my own voice (my daughters rudely say that surely I must be *that* by now). I think I may find it useful when sitting on a committee, and so avoid (which old Monty Rendall[1] *didn't*) announcing as the next item on the agenda the matter they had just finished discussing. On Tuesday I go to a Christie play just to test the thing. If I could resume playgoing that *would* be a great gain. *Nous verrons.*

I didn't know Peter Davies, though I did all the others—a lively and attractive lot. I agree with you. Sleeping-tablets or a jump out of a window, but not in front of a train at Sloane Square. But suicides are incalculable—wasn't it Brutus's wife who died by swallowing red-hot charcoal? 'Many the ways, the little home is one'.[2] I suppose a doctor can do it without pain or delay.

Good luck to Duff and his Greats. Remind him at the right moment if necessary that all the greatest men got seconds. There is a lot of luck about it. You *can't* bore me about Oscar, so there.

Easter Saturday, 16 April 1960 — *Bromsden Farm*

Undeterred by celebrations of the Crucifixion, our postman de-

[1] 1862–1950. Headmaster of Winchester 1911–1926. In retirement he restored and transformed Butley Priory, near Woodbridge in Suffolk, and was chairman of many committees.

[2] T.L. Beddoes, *Death's Jest Book*, act 1, scene 1.

livered your letter faithfully yesterday morning, so my holiday began most agreeably. I haven't got to Jane Carlyle yet, but was much touched by the tribute to T.C.'s father, and am now deep in the account of Edward Irving—it's all splendid stuff.

So far less than a quarter of the Oscar galley-proofs have arrived, but already my inner ring of helpers are flooding me with pertinent comments and queries. On Monday I am to dine at All Souls and receive Sparrow's animadversions to date. Most of the chorus of indolent reviewers will fail to appreciate the notes, but to hell with them. If *you* are pleased and satisfied I shall not have laboured in vain.

So glad you're enjoying Priestley. Why don't you write him a fan-letter?

By the way, I have just re-read *The Bridge of San Luis Rey* by Thornton Wilder, which I hadn't looked at since I bought and much enjoyed it when it first appeared—in 1927, when I was twenty. To my astonishment I now think it *first-rate*—a shaped and finished work of art—contrived, admittedly, but none the worse for that. Do read it again and see whether you agree. It seems to me to have improved and mellowed in thirty-three years, and I don't see why it shouldn't be read and enjoyed as long as books are read. I shall nervously await your reaction to this *ex cathedra* pronouncement.

You must give the deaf-aid a proper hearing, to coin a phrase, before you miss any of Cuthbert's witticisms.

The other day I was trying to find words to explain my dislike of Henry James's old-age revisions of his early work—and today I find that Max (I might have guessed) put it perfectly:

> One . . . wasn't glad that for the definitive edition of his works he did a lot of re-writing—a process akin to patching pale gray silk with snippets of very dark thick brown velvet. It was a strange sad aberration: and a wanton offence against the laws of art.

That was written in 1949, when Max was seventy-seven. Age couldn't wither him, any more than it can an old East Anglian friend of mine. Now to bed with T. Carlyle and Edward Irving.

Sunday noon.

On the Resurrection morning I slept till 10.30, and over my breakfast (one slice of bread and marmalade, one mug of tea) I read the second volume of a book called *La Jeunesse d'André Gide*, from which I was happy to learn that the French translation of *Wuthering Heights* is called *Les Hauts de Hurlevent.* Gide hasn't met Oscar yet, so I must push on.

Ian Fleming's new book, *For Your Eyes Only*, consists of five superbly readable long short stories, one of which might have been written by W.S. Maugham.

Bridget has gone riding, Adam (after attending Holy Communion in the village church) is pursuing pigeons with his gun, Comfort is scrubbing the kitchen floor, Duff is with his sweetheart in Wales. There is much rough work to do in the garden—clipping and path-laying and stone-carting: the sun is shining through the window, and I must away. I like to think of you sunning in your summer-house, perhaps thinking up a joke or a quotation for next week's letter. How many words, I wonder, have we now exchanged? A quarter of a million each? My *Hugh Walpole* is 180,000, but most of them are other people's words. Sorry about this ink—fountain is the right name for my pen. A lovely nib but an incontinent belly.

20 April 1960 *Grundisburgh*

Would Priestley care one twopenny damn for a letter of appreciation, however genuine, from an elderly nonentity in Suffolk? I wish his book had been out when I was lecturing on Eng. Lit. I should have used it lavishly. Is it too 'advanced' for the School Library? Adam in due course would get a lot out of it, unless, as old Warre[1] said of M.D. Hill, he is 'delivered, body and soul, to science.'

I have just been reading R.W. Livingstone's *Rainbow Bridge*, all about education—very wise and urbane about science and 'vocational' studies etc. It was all the more surprising to find him describing Carlyle as 'that illustrious master of cant and self-deception'. 'Self-deception' of course you can saddle anyone with, whose opinions you don't share, but '*cant*'? If L. is thinking of its dictionary meaning of 'false or affected assumption of lofty morality' he is surely about as wrong as one can be about a man who, in his large output, mainly

[1] The Rev. Edmond Warre (1837–1920). Headmaster of Eton 1884–1905.

attacked various forms of cant. It strikes a crude and violent note which is quite uncharacteristic. (Like the tale I found recently of T.S.E. showing a fierce thing he had written to Ezra P. who said: 'No, that's not your style at all. You let *me* throw the bricks through the front window. You go in at the back door and take the swag'.)

My hearing-aid. Well, yes I do hear better with it, but it is, somehow, not all that gain. One hears so much else, plus a sort of old gramophone background noise. But I missed very little at the theatre last night, where we all went to see *The Unexpected Guest* by Agatha Christie. Very good fun. She is really devilish clever in making one suspect *everyone* in the affair, except the right one in the last minute. I think I shall keep the aid for such occasions—and especially committee-meetings, where everyone mumbles, and one sits at a long table. I shall *not* bring it to the Lit. Soc. and Sir Cuthbert's acidities shall waste their sweetness on the desert air. I am delighted to hear that Donald Somervell was there—because you don't attend the Lit. Soc. unless mind and body are functioning pretty well.

I am browsing in Johnson's Lives, *not* of the poets but of others, and constantly turning up nuggets, e.g. the reason for Blake (Admiral) not getting a fellowship at Merton, because of 'his want of stature, it being the custom of Sir Henry Savile, then warden of that college, to pay much regard to the outward appearance of those who solicited preferment in that society'. In fact Sir H.S. was a —? I will send you more as I find them. Meanwhile let me remind you that when he and Boswell supped with a farmer at Armadale, the fare put on the table was minced collops, fricassee of fowl, ham and tongue, haddocks, herrings, frothed milk, bread pudding, and syllabubs made with port wine. Those were the days.

I shall certainly read *San Luis Rey* again. I remember greatly liking it, and it is high time for a *re*-reading—on the whole life's greatest pleasure. I do like to think of you in the T.C. reminiscences—savouring (as so few seem to) the old man's tenderness and perception and never-ceasing consciousness of the eternities on which man's life so obscurely rests. His 'eternities' are now *jokes*—like Milton's God the Father. Priestley, the wise man, points out very pertinently that we haven't *emerged* from C's pessimistic forecasts; we are in the middle of them. The mills of God!

Les Hauts de Hurlevent is delicious. Do even the cleverest Frenchmen understand English fully? It may not of course have been a very clever Frenchman who translated 'The English always love the under-dog' into 'Les Anglais aiment toujours le ventre du chien'.
P.S. Love to Ruth (treble the normal because of not seeing her. But how is 'treble' possible?).
P.S.2. There is nothing in life I enjoy more than this correspondence.
P.S.3. So there!

23 April 1960 *Bromsden Farm*

I think you should write to Livingstone and take him up on Carlyle's 'cant'. Almost the only thing I have learned in thirty years of literary life is that *all* authors, whatever they pretend, *love* getting appreciative letters from readers. Authorship is a lonely business, and after the nine days' wonder of reviews etc, the ripples are apt to subside, and as far as the author knows no one is reading or enjoying his book. The most acceptable letters, therefore, are the ones that come after the initial splash has subsided. *Verb. sap.*
Where did you come across that splendid tale of T.S.E. and Ezra Pound?
So glad the hearing-aid is some use. We shall definitely be back before the Lit. Soc. dinner in June. Ruth's son is leaving hospital next week. I visited him in Guy's last week, and was amazed at how well he looked: modern surgery is astonishing.
I'm loving T.C.'s *Reminiscences*—still on Edward Irving.
Last Monday (Bank Holiday) I heard my first cuckoo (and another one today). The wild cherries just failed to wear their white for Eastertide, but are full out now. On Monday evening, after a lot of gardening, I drove over to Oxford; the road was filled with vehicles bumper-to-bumper in both directions; I hit the main road behind two 'coaches' and was unable to pass them for sixteen miles. Dinner at All Souls was uphill work. Besides the Warden there were only three other Fellows there—a rather dried-up Professor of Comparative Religions, a young philosopher with long hair, and the black Fellow (from Ghana perhaps) who never spoke. When the daylight died and the only light came from the seven-branched candlesticks on the

table, you couldn't see him at all against the dark panelling of the Common Room until he opened his mouth and his very white teeth flashed out. Sparrow told me afterwards that the servants had complained of this fact. I gathered that they all regret having elected the poor fellow—falling over backwards to avoid any hint of segregation—and I daresay he feels pretty miserable too.

On Tuesday I lunched (chez Herbert Agar) with Sir Fordham Flower, brewer and chairman of the Stratford Theatre, and Alfred Francis, chairman of the Old Vic. As a result I think both these great concerns will contribute mildly to the Phoenix Trust. Flower was interesting about the results of advertising his beer on commercial TV, describing how the demand rose hugely *next morning*! whereas they reckon that ordinary advertising (press, posters and what they call 'point of sale') takes at least *three years* to produce any visible result. No wonder the TV companies are so rich.

On Wednesday I lunched in state with the Governors of the B.B.C., which was more fun than I had expected, since I sat between Hugh Greene, Graham's brother, an old friend, now Director General, and Thelma Cazalet, another old friend. Afterwards a meeting of the General Advisory Council, at which I spoke not a word. There was much discussion of B.B.C. interviews on sound and television, and it was generally agreed that, whereas private people being interviewed should be treated with care and consideration, public men were, as it were, fair game and could be more roughly handled.

On Wednesday evening I gave dinner again at the Garrick to my north-country poetess Phoebe Hesketh. Altogether it was a short but exhausting week. Two hundred Oscar galleys have now come in—just over a third of the whole—and the amount of detailed finicky work they need is appalling. I see no hope of their going back to the printer to be made up into pages before July or August.

This morning Comfort got a letter to say someone had left her £100 and I got a very grand one from Windsor Castle signed by Michael Adeane and saying that the Queen, God bless her, will present a book to the London Library sale. This was Harold Nicolson's doing, and the publicity value should be considerable.

Adam is ending his holidays with a dance every night, and will go back to Eton on Wednesday a wreck. On the same day I have to open the Antiquarian Book Fair at 11 a.m.—what next? I can't wait for the sheep and the curlews. I shall try and get the sitting-room in the flat redecorated while we're away—which will entail moving all those books. Many of them haven't been dusted for ten years—heigh ho!

27 April 1960 *Grundisburgh*

I think I shall see Livingstone when I go to Oxford in May or June. His Carlyle remark is such an oddly crude and shallow one for a good man to make. But you know practically all the modern remarks one comes across on T.C. (Harold N.'s for instance) are based, if not on sheer ignorance of him and his best work, on a view of him which is limited to his *Latter-Day Pamphlets* pro-Germanism, Might is Right, and the greatly overdrawn picture by Froude of his inconsiderateness to Jane. It must not, too, be forgotten that the old man never meant his *Reminiscences* to be published at all, with their morbid self-accusations, exaltation of Jane, and consequent denigration of almost everybody else. There is a sort of conspiracy to ignore his rectitude, courage, independence, insight and depth of feeling. Stimulated by your interest (which I find nowhere else) I have just re-read his magnificent essays on Johnson and Burns and am deep in 'The Diamond Necklace'. He will come back some day when the present silly queasiness about writing of any richness has gone. I think that T.S.E. and Ezra tale came in a review of some Yank who has just been explaining T.S.E.—the man whose book is reviewed in last week's *Spectator*—a review of which I understand hardly a single sentence.

Your daily doings once again fascinate and appal me. How do you get *any* work done? My letters must be very small beer after the talk you must come in for almost daily. But All Souls, like Trinity, was clearly disappointing (but for Sparrow). So many dons are dried-up or contemptuous or—like Housman—both. The exceptions—e.g. Jim Butler[1]—are good value, or old George Trevelyan, still foaming with rage over some injustice several centuries old.

[1] James Ramsay Montague Butler (1889–1975). Regius Professor of Modern History at Cambridge 1947–1954. Chief historian of the official war-history of 1939–1945. Knighted 1958.

You must be nearing the £20,000 mark for the L.L. Are you wearing black about your person for old Chapman?[2] I thought him a stiff old thing on first meeting him, but he thawed considerably in a few minutes. He gave us—I forget if you were there—a very slatternly talk at the Johnson Club, quite obviously implying that if any of his audience thought he was going to take any more trouble about it than a few random thoughts between snoozes, on the way from Oxford to London, could throw up, they were much mistaken. But I suppose he did plenty of good work in his prime.

Adam will find the half very restful after the holidays. It always amused me that Long Leave—meant as a mid-term *rest*—always sent the boys back exhausted with late hours and divers skylarking. And the clever beaks always arranged their football match v. the School on the Tuesday—and always won it, though often beaten in the first match. How does A. face a game of *cricket* to-morrow? Here to-day is simply a goodish day in mid-February. The cuckoo showed up (as always) on Shakespeare's birthday, but since then has got no further than 'cuck'. These hard dry Aprils are very tedious—and frequent. I should like to go and fell a tree, but my anile leech forbids it with the same tactless insistence with which he cuts off ham and bacon—my two favourite comestibles. I steadily gravitate to the condition of Sir Cuthbert.

30 April 1960 *Bromsden Farm*

I have spent most of this lovely sunny day kneeling in the garden, picking stones out of the new November-sown lawn. Excellent therapy, no doubt, but I am now suffering from some sort of double housemaid's knee and move with groans. Whether or not Carlyle intended his *Reminiscences* to be published, I am enjoying them almost more than anything of his—certainly more as a whole, for in most of his works one has to wade a good deal to get to the plums, if you will forgive a peculiar metaphor. This book is *all* enjoyable, the writing much more unbuttoned and less strained than elsewhere. I particularly like the description of a Warwickshire serving woman: 'correct as an eight-

[2] R.W. Chapman, editor of Jane Austen and Dr Johnson (1881–1960).

day clock, and making hardly as much noise', and when T.C. rode over to Hagley and thereafter 'Lord Lyttelton's mansion I have ever since in my eye as a noble-looking place', I raised a special cheer. I trust you to put Livingstone severely in his place.

The London Library fund has now reached £16,300, so we need only £4000 from the sale, which in fact I hope will produce more and so provide us with a much-desired surplus.

The Oscar proofs are now approaching the half-way mark, and the galleys themselves are becoming a burden. The trouble with a book of this length and complexity is that one needs an index at the type-script stage, and another for the galley-proofs, for unless one can remember exactly where each letter and each note come (which one can't) one wastes hours in searching. When we get to page-proofs (which you shall see) I shall have to compile *the* index, which will take many weeks.[1]

I was sorry to read of old Chapman's death: rude and curmudgeonly though he often was, he was a 'character' and he did the state of letters some service.

I have sent for Roger's new book,[2] and shall bear it happily off to Kisdon on Tuesday week—blessed day! We've been looking forward to it actively since last August, and now are like prep-school boys counting the days.

Last Wednesday I opened the third Antiquarian Book Fair at the brutal hour of 11.30 a.m. A few stray thoughts and an hour's feverish cramming produced a short speech which went down well, but I knew my audience (mostly antiquarian booksellers) and one day I shall leave it too late and dry up. Yehudi Menuhin was surprisingly in the audience, and I was introduced to him afterwards—very young and small and intelligent he looked.

On Thursday evening Ruth and I went with an American friend to *A Passage to India*, which we thoroughly enjoyed. The Indian lady-dramatist has made an excellent job of it, and the leading part is brilliantly played by a Pakistani actor. Afterwards we had a first-class supper with John Gielgud at Prunier's (*oeufs en gelée*, steak, an excellent claret, and a melting-in-the-mouth piece of cake).

[1] It took six months.

[2] *Hanover to Windsor* by Roger Fulford (1960).

John G. regaled us with a variety of good stage anecdotes, told with punch and finish. Vague and dreamy about most things, he is exact and always amusing about the theatre, having been, as he says, stage-struck all his life.

On Tuesday I dined with the James Lavers in the Boltons. Vyvyan Holland (Oscar's son) and his wife were there, and I was able to enlist Mrs V.H.'s support in my campaign to prevent V.H. from expurgating anything in the Letters. He owns the copyright and must be appeased.

Did I tell you that Bertie Van Thal is making a one-volume anthology from Agate's works (all of which are now out of print)? I shall probably publish it early next year, but I daresay it won't sell. Jock Dent has written an introduction. Bertie is miserable in his present job with Weidenfeld, and I've told him I'll take him on as an editor-cum-reader on July 1. I'm fond of him, and he's full of ideas for books.

I've still got those Max Beerbohm letters to edit, and I shall take them to Kisdon, just in case I have time there or feel inclined—though generally we find that looking after the cottage, fetching water from the spring etc, takes up most of our time, and when it's fine we just lie or sit in the sun. Write here this week: I'll be here next week-end. Now for more Oscar.

4 May 1960 *Grundisburgh*

How right you are about 'unbuttoned' Carlyle. That is why his letters are in the main so good (so much better than the overpraised Jane's, in which there is a spate of stuff about tweenies etc and her ailments). Some day you must browse in *Frederick* which has some of the fine 'grisly humour' praised by Meredith. What about his comparison of the activities of various dryasdusts who nose out a good deal of scandal with 'those dogs that after closely scrutinising the parts of shame of another dog, eventually depart with satisfied air, as though from a problem solved'. Not quoted alas, only remembered, and life even in Suffolk is not long enough to search all 7 volumes. I remember the allusion to 'Lord Lyttelton's mansion'—which, alas, after a life of exactly two hundred years is almost sure to be sold—if anyone will buy it. I don't quite remember how much my grandfather did about starting the London Library, but no doubt you will. He was a fine old chap—a good deal of an oddity. Have you come across Carlyle's perfect snapshot of Sir William Harcourt, 'a lawyering, parliamenteering, loud man', which my uncle Alfred particularly loved?

You were the big noise in the literary pages of the *Sunday Times* this week. I hope your chatty Leonard Russell may have been helpful with his allusions to the work you are doing. It will be grand when the sale is over, and the world knows how you have saved the L.L. 'Sir Rupert' is, *me judice*, an absolute certainty. Just as it should be.

I read in *Punch* an excellent review of *A Passage to India* by Eric Keown—known to you of course. He always seems to me pretty good. But how devastatingly unfunny—and often quite unintelligible—are the pictures nowadays, and I was much disheartened by the face of Cyril Connolly, all chin and conceit, and virosity. Dreadful! The two leaders in last week's *T.L.S.* were on an architect I had never so much as heard of, and *Pilgrim's Progress* which I have on the whole read enough about. The Pryce-Jones tradition continues; and he goes on with that insipid chatter on Thursdays.

The admirable Richard Martineau has written a first-rate obit of poor Audrey Van Oss, who was ill, off and on, for twelve years and fought throughout with unfailing courage. She won a county golf-championship *after* the doctors had told her she could never play again. She was forty-seven. Lovely to look at and (she was a great friend of ours) we can get some comfort from 'Adonais'—that is all there is for a death in the prime of life. I forget whether you knew her.

I hope there will be no expurgating by Vyvyan Holland. I trust you to make rings round him. That is interesting about Bertie Van Thal. I had thought he was with Barker. He was very friendly at one time—he and wife actually stayed a week-end here, but then he dropped me for, no doubt, excellent reasons. Was there no more sale for any Agates? The poor old thing was convinced of the immortality of the *Egos*. And they are surely much better than Arnold Bennett's *Journals*. Though A.B. met on the whole bigger people, he mostly made very little of them. But perhaps A.B. too is out of print? I will eat my hat if J.A.'s criticisms of Shakespeare plays are not jolly good.

You say nothing about taking *How Green* to Kisdon! You will never read it. I have some books like that, e.g. I know I should like Creevey, but I simply cannot start on him. Something Freudian I suppose.

I listened to and judged on Monday the Ipswich declamation prize. Not very good. Boys rarely seem to realise that you must get not only the meaning but the whole mood and tone and colour of a passage—feel it, in fact, before you can repeat it remotely well. They declaim 'Kubla Khan' as if it was Kennedy's gender-rules. But anyhow *not one* in the Cassius passage pronounced 'controversy' like the damned B.B.C.—with the stress on the second syllable. Don't you hate that?

7 May 1960 *Bromsden Farm*

Eves of departure are usually hurried and confusing. At *4 a.m.* on Tuesday we shall leave Soho Square in Ruth's tiny car, breakfast at 8 at Bawtry, near Doncaster, lunch on the moors high above Wensleydale, and reach our cottage in the benevolent farmer's tractor at about 2.30 p.m. Before then a thousand loose ends must be tied or hidden away, countless details seen to. My pockets are stuffed with *aide-mémoires*, and all the time the Oscar galleys are piling up.

The weather today was perfection—lilac and apple-blossom out, wallflowers giving out their lovely smell. I drove over to Pewsey and lunched with the Devlins. The judge is charming, and I think might be a good Lit. Soc. member. Adam reports clean-bowling an opponent with his first ball of the season: perhaps the umpire hadn't called 'Play'.

I have finished the first volume of T.C.'s *Reminiscences* and am keeping the second for Swaledale. (By the way, T.C. refers to the Yorkshire moors as 'those mute wildernesses and their rough habitudes and populations'.) I particularly enjoyed, and sympathised with, the plight of poor John Murray (Byron's one)—do you remember?

> Stupider man than the great Murray, in look, in speech, in conduct, in regard to this poor *Sartor* question, I imagined I had seldom or never seen! Afterwards it became apparent to me that partly he was sinking into the heaviness of old age, and partly, still more important, that in regard to this particular *Sartor* question his position was an impossible one; position of a poor old man endeavouring to answer yes *and* no!

My ageing publisher's heart goes out to the poor old fellow: I know that feeling so well.

After watching the royal wedding[1] yesterday (I hired a television set for the day, so that all the staff could see it—and we all loved it) I think £25,000 was a very modest outlay for such general enjoyment and beneficial outlet for emotions. Reflect also that a great deal of the money goes in wages to the people who put up the decorations, and so benefits them. The royal yacht is permanently manned and maintained, so that fuel and food are the only extras for the honeymoon. As you see, I grow more militantly Royalist daily.

Leonard Russell's piece in the *Sunday Times* has so far called forth *eleven* new Oscar letters—none of prime interest, but several quite good—and more may still be reported.

I never knew Audrey Van Oss, but like to think that you brightened her last days with the story of Winston's fly-buttons.

So far Vyvyan is playing up splendidly, but the bits he most dislikes are still to come. I have suggested dedicating the book to him, his wife and their son—not wholly as a sop, but because it seems to me fitting. Mrs V. told me the other day that they look on me as almost one of the family, so there is hope.

There is no need to take *How Green* to the cottage: that great work awaits me there, if the mice have spared it.

Oh yes—I hate contrōversy worse than cold boiled veal—make no mistake about it. Last Thursday I went to one of the world's longest operas, Berlioz's *The Trojans*. One is in the theatre from *6* till *11*—too long for me—but since my host Garrett Drogheda (our new Lit. Soc. member) is Chairman of Covent Garden, we were most comfortably accommodated in the Royal Box. Behind it is a private dining-room, where we ate and drank copiously during the three intervals. Two of my companions were Sir Solly Zuckerman, head of the Zoo and Government scientific adviser on defence (whatever that means) and his very agreeable wife, a grand-daughter of Rufus Isaacs. I was glad that I hadn't yet published the forthcoming book about the Marconi scandal. The opera itself has some excellent moments, but to a non-musical person the convention and idiom are hard to take, and it transpired that the name Aeneas is a difficult word to sing.

[1] Of Princess Margaret and Anthony Armstrong-Jones.

One evening Ruth and I had drinks with Alistair Cooke and his wife, there meeting the film-star James Mason, who seemed modest and agreeable. He had just finished playing the part of Carson in one of these frightful Oscar films. Incidentally, a musical version of *The Importance of B.E.* has just been successfully produced on Broadway. The old boy's definitely in the news.

Peter has at last handed in his Younghusband manuscript, and I can see that we're going to have a helluva job to get it out this year.

11 May 1960 *Grundisburgh*

You are now there—browning, probably already, happy as a sandboy, whatever a sandboy may be, and Ruth somewhere in the immediate offing, looking quite lovely against the background of heather and hill—that endless sky which the children evacuated from London to the country in 1939 found so horrible and terrifying. Not that she depends on background. She would give grace to the goodsyard-wall of St Pancras Station. Fancy your imagining that I might have forgotten your holiday address! You remind me of an imbecile aunt who told my sister all about her (the aunt's) brother, who, in cold fact, was my sister's father. Otiose (or supererogatory) is the adjective isn't it, or hasn't anyone used either for years (except Max, of course)?

Adam has started well. As the foolish golf-reporter said of a player who was one up, he has only to stick to his lead to be sure of victory.

My excellent nephew from N.Z. was here on Sunday and confessed how little interest *he* takes in 1960 cricket—nothing like the same game as he remembers played by Hammond and co (and he never even saw Trumper!). Am I to be interested in an art practised by such men as Halfyard and Titmus? You may say what about Gaukrodger, but there is a certain magnificence about the ugliness of that, as in a Notre Dame gargoyle. And if you object to my saying there is so much sheer *bogus* in county cricket, look at the Sussex v Yorkshire match today, when in reply to Sussex's 280 Yorkshire made 281 for *none*, but lost the match. In match after match declarations are *de rigeur*, because three days without them produce nothing but draws.

In old days Yorkshire would have won easily with that start—and deserved to.

Poor old Murray. To deal at one time with Byron and later with Carlyle would have taxed any man's wits and patience. Publishing must be a very difficult vocation. For one thing the difference between silliness and genius must often be very hard to discriminate. One post brings Della Crusca or Dada and the next *Tristram Shandy* or Ezra Pound (a good seller, I imagine, though to me unreadable). And would any sane man spot *Lucky Jim* as the book which everyone *must* read?

I saw nothing of the royal wedding, though everyone says it was lovely. I don't feel strongly about the £25,000, and in any case always hate to find myself approving of anything done by Gaitskell and co. Everyone hereabouts has commented on the black depression on the Queen's face, and the rustic mind likes to invent the causes of it as jealousy, snobbery etc. But how can you rely on a photograph? Probably she was wondering whether she had left the bath-tap running; and anyhow, like her grandma, when she isn't smiling, she *does* look over-serious. You don't say anything of what they tell me are the countless rumours about and against the poor young photographer. Probably you will say, as Johnson did when surprise was expressed at his ignorance of some town scandal, 'By those who look close to the ground dirt will be seen'.

Two most intriguing books (isn't 'intriguing' a necessary word somehow, though an upstart? It seems to me to express something which 'interesting' doesn't) have just arrived from you with great appreciation. The one about a house[1] Pamela has bagged and is enjoying, and I have read *The Answer to Life is No*[2] with the greatest interest, though he is often too subtle for me. He is right down among the roots of human nature. I wonder what the reviewers will make of it. The blurb hints that the author could be spotted—but not by G.W.L. Anyway—though you hate being thanked as much as Jan Crace did—gratitude is, as ever, your portion.

I shall miss his memorial service, and my lecture at the Leys School, for a rather humiliating reason. I had a heavy fall on the top of a bus yesterday and have cracked a back rib. The leech prescribes rest for at

[1] *The Living House* by George Ordish (1960).

[2] By Wrey Gardiner, published anonymously (1960).

least a week and says at my age etc a cracked rib is not to be sneezed at. Not that I would dream of trying. Every movement is infernally painful. Dressing is purgatory; changing position in bed is hell; merely to clear the throat *very* gingerly would start Himmler or even Heydrich chuckling. And I always thought a cracked rib about equalled a mildly sprained ankle. The only *soulagement* to my feelings is that it was not my fault but that of the damned bus, which stopped with a hideous jerk as I was making my way to the steps, and hurled me to the ground, where I must have caught the edge of a step. Apparently a lorry suddenly got in the way. Pamela wants to sue the bus, the lorry and whoever made rather a blind corner on the road. Bless her.

I have a letter from Wilfrid Blunt with whom you have recently corresponded. A good man. He says he can't imagine how you get through what you do. Nor can I or anyone else. I suspect Ruth must sometimes have urged you to leave me out *this* week when you are clearly overdone. 'After all the old stuffy has had any amount of good stuff from you, not to mention forty or so excellent books.' She has every possible reason for saying that, and, to use that slightly stupid expression, I couldn't agree with her more. But not one of your letters shows any sign of strain (I have read and re-read each one pretty carefully) so I want nothing at all to change.

The opera! It is an immensely ridiculous art-form surely; 'an exotic and irrational entertainment' the old man called it,[1] but it survives with apparent ease for all its absurdity. When King Mark found Tristan making love with Isolde, instead of laying T. out with one swashing blow, he merely lamented the situation for twenty-two minutes in notes of indescribable fatness (he was a superb basso-profondo). What is the Oscar film in which J. Mason appears as Carson? It hasn't come Ipswich way, but then lots of things don't. I have just read Roger's book. A very pleasant bit of bookmaking indeed. The royal family circle must always have been fascinating—in one way. Not one single solitary remark ever made indicating the slightest understanding or appreciation of anything at all three inches below life's surface or two inches off the beaten track. What did George V and VI *read* in their spare time? Our little Queen I believe is fond of

[1] Dr Johnson, *Life of John Hughes*.

Jane Austen. John Raymond in his new book of criticisms has one of those articles on J.A. which always irk me—practically putting her above all other novelists that ever wrote.

Well, the thought of you two at Kisdon is a very happy one. Tell me *all* about it and send any spare snapshots you can. I shall forget when I get them that picking a letter up and opening it is a definitely painful movement—but not mentally.

15 May 1960 *Kisdon Lodge, Keld*

Even as you unerringly remembered this address, so you will doubtless recollect that the postal arrangements, especially the outward ones, are erratic. Our good farmer, Mr Hutchinson, duly brought up your excellent letter, and will always post things for us, but we never know exactly when he's coming, and sometimes miss him. In fact I hope this will reach you by Tuesday, but while I am here you must be patient with delays.

I don't know what a sandboy is either, but we are certainly as happy as any two of them. Our journey went smoothly according to plan, and we arrived to find the cottage swept, scrubbed and polished, with a good fire burning (all done by the Hutchinsons). Within a few hours it seemed we had never been away. The first night we slept exactly twelve hours (10.30 to 10.30), since when we have averaged ten hours a night. The first morning, when we were fetching water from the spring in the next field (six gallons, carried in two buckets and two plastic water-carriers given us by Elisabeth Beerbohm) in hot sunshine, Ruth spotted a ring-ousel's nest in the stone wall. On Friday we almost stumbled on a meadow-pipit's, and now the only regular birds of Kisdon whose nests we haven't found are the snipe and the golden plover. (We have found curlew, grouse, plover, lark, redstart and yellow wagtail. Also sandpiper.) The fields are thick with wildflowers, which Ruth arranges in the most enchanting way all over the cottage. Just now there are kingcups, primroses, cowslips, oxlips, forget-me-nots, anemones, heartsease and masses of deep purple orchids. We have been to one village sale, where in an afternoon of pure enjoyment we spent 21/6 on a looking-glass for the bedroom, two pillow-cases, three curtains and a quantity of plates and dishes. The weather has been Aprilish—hot sunshine between hailstorms—but we are just as happy inside as out. Oscar proofs arrive most days and we are busy checking the letters against photostats of the originals. *How Green* is still on the shelf, and so are Roger's book and the second volume of T.C.'s *Reminiscences*, which I brought with me. So far I have read a good Buchan (*The Dancing Floor*), part of an idiotic woman's memoirs (in search of Oscariana) and a chunk of the first volume of the big new edition of Swinburne's letters. Unfortunately the two vols so far published (out of six) go only to 1875, which is exactly where Oscar's letters begin, but I find them most interesting all the same.

I'm glad you got some enjoyment out of *The Answer to Life is No.* The author's name would certainly *not* be known to you. He has published a number of books, but, as you can imagine, they were all failures, and I told him I would publish this one only if it were anonymous. He reluctantly agreed. I still hope the very fact of anonymity may arouse some interest. Since he wrote the book I gather that his financial position has improved as a result of his letting his basement to a call-girl who pays a substantial rent.

We are both most distressed by the account of your accident. Must you travel on the *top* of buses? I've often almost come to grief myself in the same way. Your doctor is surely right to prescribe rest: do please obey him: we don't want to lose you.

Ruth is outraged at the suggestion that she might ever, in any circumstances, try to prevent my writing to you. So you had better make your peace in your next letter.

Up here—and nowhere else—I always keep a brief daily diary, and Ruth is even now reading the entries for 1955–58, reminding me of many incidents we had both forgotten. The grandfather clock is ticking placidly; the Aladdin lamp sheds its splendid light; the fire burns brightly, and another is already lit in the bedroom. There is no sound outside, save now and then the mournful cry of a curlew. If one stands outside the cottage door one can see four lights strung out along the bottom of the valley: three are in farmhouses and the fourth in the telephone-box in Keld. It is on all night, and doubtless we all pay for it. The lady who keeps the only shop in Keld is stone-deaf and has been courting for thirty-five years. This year we hear she has acquired a deaf-aid (*verb. sap.*) and has so far regained touch with life that she insists on shutting the shop at the regular hour of 6 p.m. (and then removes the deaf-aid to avoid hearing the knocks and shouts of the outraged villagers) instead of obligingly staying open till all hours, as she has done for many years. The couple who run the Keld post-office are giving it up on July 31. They are sick of being tied all day and everyday for £4. 10. 0 a week, which is apparently all they get. No one else is keen to take the job on, so perhaps there will be no post-office next time we come. The old-age pensioners are already pitifully asking how they will get their money. Our village, you see, is full of its own problems, although the population is something like thirty-eight.

Much love from us both.

18 May 1960 *Grundisburgh*

The plot thickens. The doctor—like all of his trade a simple psychologist—told me I had a cracked rib, by which he really meant not cracked but broken, confident that the milder word would soothe me. But after two days it seemed to me that the pain was altogether on too majestic a scale for a mere crack, so I had it X-rayed, and that revealed *three* ribs temporarily but effectively bust. They are now sullenly mending. I can now clear my throat without feeling sick, and can walk much as usual, though, to adapt Flurry Knox on Miss Bobbie Bennett,[1] you would still look a long time at Deerfoot or Jesse Owens before you thought of me. The body is very odd. I asked the doctor if anything I did in reason could have a bad effect, and he answered 'only staying in bed'—rather as if, say, an ingrowing toenail *could* result in gastritis. Apparently passivity when wounded invites pneumonia.

But how bored you will be with all this. Pain makes one a fearful egoist. Your letter arrived second post yesterday, which is only one post late (but what about your p.o. disappearing?). Your letter breathes happiness, which is wonderfully refreshing in 1960. All

[1] In *Some Experiences of an Irish R.M* by E.Œ. Somerville and Martin Ross (1899).

Lytteltons are hopeless ignoramuses about birds and flowers, but I like their names, and though the shape and size and colour of practically all remain mysteries, somehow the thought of you both surrounded by ring-ousels, meadow-pipits, redstarts, oxlips and heartsease gives me a lovely holiday feeling, vicarious though it is. We are not very rich in birds here, though I have a suspicion my ears may be partly to blame. But alas the nightingale has been banished from his old group of trees by building, and his note is distant and sounds discouraged. No longer 'singing with fear for none, true on the note, sharp at the edge, loud, fat with tone, with a trill and a tremolo to make you frozen with wonderment to hear' (from *How Green!*).

I am still puzzling over *The Answer to Life is No.* He seems to have such a lot to say which often does not emerge into intelligibility. Even short apparently simple statements; e.g. what the heck does 'I have brought my humming-bird to the glass of time' mean? I doubt if you will make a penny out of it, but what do I know? I have seen no review yet. Pamela is entranced with the other book; she hasn't finished yet. I raced through the new life of Charles Kingsley. A tedious old hearty in many ways, but a goodish chap I expect. Not up to Newman's class with the foils, but wasn't he mainly right? And wasn't there something faintly repellent about Newman, described by Scott Holland as looking 'as delicate as an old lady washed in milk'. Remembering many boring pictures of saints in the galleries and churches of Rome I like K's calling them 'prayer-mongering eunuchs'. And after all he did write the finest English hexameter, *n'est ce pas*? 'As when an osprey aloft, dark-eyebrowed, royally crested.'[1] Do you know about N. saying of Manning: 'Ah yes, Cardinal Manning, ambition, ambition, ambition.' Some kind friend told M. who flushed and riposted: 'And shall I tell you what was wrong with Cardinal Newman? Temper, temper, temper.' Both bullseyes, no doubt.

Ruth! The finest defence ever made of what at first sight looked harsh was of course Johnson's to a lady who said when they had met previously, he had called her a dunce. 'Madam if I had thought so, I certainly should not have said so'. That shall be mine adapted. And I will add that anyone who had been in her company for ten minutes, and thought she could ever do or say anything mean or ungracious or

[1] From 'Andromeda.'

jealous or stupid would be instantly certifiable. Any further reparation you think I should make shall be instantly made—and all with my very best love.

Boswell was a great standby last week, when each day was a long ache punctuated by stabs apparently of a dagger both sharp and serrated. I was pleased to be reminded of the mathematics lecturer, who, when he bored his audience, was made to yawn by their deliberately yawning, and invariably dislocated his jaw when he did, and could utter no word till his man was sent for to set it.

I say how *savage* reviewers are on a man who is out of fashion. Poor old Barrie kept on getting it in the neck last week, and a day or two ago one young man said *Margaret Ogilvy* was *nauseating*, an idiotic exaggeration. You can say that to modern taste it is sometimes sentimental, but no more. Much of it (e.g. the chapter 'RLS') is very charming, and I love the old mother's reply to J.M.B., after she had said how proud Jane was and she would have been to look through the door at Thomas Carlyle and think how famous he (her mon) was. J.M.B. said 'Yes but what when he roared at her (Jane) to shut the door?' 'Pooh! a man's roar is neither here nor there'. That surely is part of what every woman knows. Of course he *could* be tiresome. How cross old Agate was at his commenting on 'the courage of flowers' in wartime, going on and looking so bright and happy.

No, let us use words rightly. What *is* nauseating is the cant, very current just now, that one of the first essentials of civilisation and culture is that *Lady Chatterley* should be published unexpurgated, not in the least because pornography is popular, but because every teenager is passionately anxious not to miss a word D.H.L. wrote. One man ten days ago actually wrote that D.H.L.'s physiological details, interspersed with words commonly met with only on the walls of public lavatories, really made the book cleaner than when they were left out!

My nephew was here recently. He says there is not much hope for Hagley.[1] It is too near the Black Country and, there being only one park-keeper, toughs and teddies swarm at will in the park. When they want to come into it, they kick out three or four palings and come. There is a good deal of fern and bracken in the park, and the sardonic

[1] George Lyttelton's ancestral home in Worcestershire.

keeper told Charles that much of the recent rise in Birmingham's population was the result of what happens in the Hagley bracken every summer evening. Old George finished building the house *exactly* two hundred years ago. *Tout passe, tout casse, tout lasse.*

22 May 1960 *Kisdon Lodge, Keld*

To say the least, your doctor sounds to me an ass—but they are all the same, seldom knowing what is the matter, and failing to treat their patients as responsible grown-ups. Thank goodness you had the X-ray: *three* ribs *broken* is surely something to boast of. I do hope they're mending, however sullenly.

Your soft and affectionate answer has turned aside Ruth's wrath, and she sends you more loving messages than I think it good for you to read.

I visited our shopkeeper the other day for an ounce of tobacco. Certainly her deaf-aid has brought her to life. I also discovered that her only means of getting bread these twenty years has been an itinerant vendor who drives up the dale once a week with a travelling shop. But she has never been on speaking terms with him, so every week a neighbour, some way off, buys and pays for the bread and then carries it down to her.

This week we had three sunless days of bitter east wind, which kept us at the fireside and greatly benefitted the galley-proofs of O. Wilde. We have now checked 448 galleys against the photostats of the originals (finding just enough errors to make it worthwhile and amusing) and await more by tomorrow's post. The dear fellow has still two and a half years and a hundred or two letters to go. I should be doing lots of other work on the proofs, but our days seem all too short and full, and we still sleep our solid ten hours each night. I have almost finished the first volume of the Swinburne letters, and mostly find the matter more interesting than the manner. To his Etonian friends A.C.S. went on using Eton slang ('in the bill', 'after twelve' etc) for many years. Naturally enough the American editor has failed to notice or remark on this, but otherwise he has done quite well.

Although I have never seen Hagley, I hate to think that it is finished: will it become a loony-bin or what? Ruth is now enjoying Roger's book, and I shall read it next. *How Green* still looks reproachfully from its shelf. No more birds' nests, but plenty of birds and flowers: I'm glad to think that their very names gave you some pleasure. The wheatears (the word, they say, is a mangled form of 'white arse') have just come back: they lay delicious little blue eggs in walls and under big stones: we have only once found a nest.

They sent me a proof of the London Library sale catalogue, which I think will look quite impressive: you shall have a copy when I get back. It all seems delightfully far away, and I spend *no* time anticipating the ghastly pile of letters which must be accumulating in Soho Square. I gave E. Blunden this address, and his letter got here in *three days* from Hong Kong! He writes cheerfully, but clearly longs to see some cricket and get among the secondhand bookstalls.

We are in the middle of prolonged and delicate negotiations which we hope will lead to our getting (at a cost of £30) water piped to a (so-far non-existent) tap in our kitchen from a spring in the next field. The owner of the field seems very friendly, but the blacksmith from the fairly neighbouring village of Gunnerside is dilatory: we opened negotiations almost a year ago. We're very happy climbing over the wall each day and spooning water out of the animals' (spring-fed) drinking-trough with an enamel mug, but we can foresee days when we might prefer an indoor tap.

We have been for one long walk—a circumambulation of Kisdon. It took six hours, including two hours for picnic lunch and reading on the river-bank. It was hot and sunny, and we saw *no one* except a very distant farmer on a horse. Tomorrow, if it's fine, we plan another such walk, to visit a ruined farmhouse called Crackpot Hall, which is set in an astonishingly wild and beautiful place. There are spectacular waterfalls (here called 'forces') at Keld, which is where the Swale proper begins.

You must forgive the disjointedness of this letter: we are so relaxed that concentration is difficult, and I just scribble down whatever comes into my head. Write here again this week. We shall sadly return at or soon after the end of the month. I must be home for the Fourth of June. Only one more, which will be my tenth as a parent. Nurse your broken ribs.

There is a delightful holiday air about your last letter, slightly reminiscent of Tennyson's lotus-eaters reclining by their nectar, far away from everyday affairs. Just as it should be. And I fear you must find my half-baked observations on literary topics sounding very like the bloodless twittering of ghosts that Aeneas heard in Hades. Never mind; I have your assurance of loving messages from Ruth (though how right you are in realising how easily septuagenarian heads are turned).

You are pretty right too about my doctor—a good man, but like his tribe a childish psychologist. My ribs have abandoned their attempts to emulate the rack and the thumb-screw, and now merely ache, and that apparently they will do for another three or four weeks. However, at seventy-seven an ache is neither here nor there—or more accurately, if it isn't here it will be there—and I am back in circulation, if that is not too big a word for my mild activities. I am coming to the Lit. Soc. on June 14, though probably my doctor would purse his lips over the possibly dangerous effect of meeting Lockhart or Sir Cuthbert. I am told Lockhart's book has a reference to me—rather an inaccurate one it sounds—in connection with K.G. Macleod. But is anything ever *entirely* true?

Any news about your shopkeeper is welcome. I hope her non-speaks with the travelling baker is/are not only because of deafness. Those village animosities can be Olympian. Here Mr Dunnett has not spoken to Mr Willy Cook for seventeen years; Mrs Patemorrer, though living next door to her, will deny to her last breath any knowledge of the existence of Mrs Pizzey.

The Victorians had something we haven't. I have just got from the library Sir Charles Petrie's *The Victorians* and am a little disheartened to see in the index that Tennyson is mentioned twice, Carlyle and Ruskin not at all. Surely that is to describe a country's military activities and omit the artillery? The Ipswich library is in rare form nowadays; the last four new volumes it has acquired are *Pawn-power in Chess*, *British Monetary Experiments*, *Public Enterprise in Sweden*, and *Theoretical Elasticity*. I believe *you* would read the last long before *How Green*.

Hagley won't be got rid of till my nephew comes back from N.Z.—over two years, but I see no hope after that. The cussedness of things! My brother sold ten years ago a lot of land near Birmingham and got £110,000 for it. Very nice? Well, today it would easily fetch £1,000,000, and as my nephew says, you can do a lot with a million, and even get parlour-maids and gardeners.

What do our top-chaps care about old tradition, family seats etc., venerable and obviously valuable institutions like your L.L.? The Inland Revenue clearly contemplates bankrupting Shrewsbury, and takes the infantile point of view that as parents have so far faced the increase of fees, they will go on doing so. But in several schools I know the limit of parents' patience and indeed capacity is pretty near. Beaks' pay will continue to rise, and, let me tell you, few are worth more than they are getting now, though nobody dares say this in public. But enough of that. Fancy talking about education when you are listening to the white arse carolling away! I wish you could buy Crackpot Hall. What an address to have, and what fun counting—on the fingers of one hand—the people who did *not* make a joke about it.

We have a new neighbour here, one Patrick Barrington who used to write excellent light verse in *Punch* and elsewhere. (Do you remember his pet hippopotamus which he nursed through hippopotameasles and hippopotamumps?) Last week he came to tea at 4.30 and left at 7.45 without once drawing breath. Pamela says it was my fault and I encouraged him in capping quotations etc.

Meanwhile special thanks for *The Living House* which I greatly enjoyed, and Pamela adored. Fascinating and original. Is there *any*thing the man doesn't know about lepidoptera and coleoptera etc? I have seen only one review of it so far.

Love to Ruth—it must have been someone very like her the poet had in mind when he wrote No 70 in the Oxford Book, original edition.[1]
P.S. I very seldom cob you in a mis-spelling, but shouldn't 'benefitted' be 'benefited?' Beak! Pedant! Prig!

[1] 'There is a lady sweet and kind' (Anon).

I am writing this out of doors, in a sheltered dip behind the cottage in hot sunshine. Ruth is beside me, repairing some gay curtains (destined for the bedroom) which we bought at that (one and only) sale. A cuckoo is calling across the valley. There is no other sound. I meant to write to you last night, but by ten o' clock I was too sleepy. The final batch of Oscar galley-proofs (ending up with No 542) reached us on Saturday, and we spent most of yesterday (a still and warm but largely sunless day) checking them against the originals, finishing after tea. We breakfasted this morning at 10.15, and after seeing to the fire, washing up, making the bed and fetching the water, *nous voici*. The post leaves the village below at 3.15, and when we post this we shall also fetch the milk and the day before yesterday's papers.

In the same bundle as the last Oscar proofs there arrived *all* the galley-proofs of Diana Cooper's third volume. (What, you may ask, is holiday, and what work?) But there are only 160 of them, and I should be able to read and correct them all during to-day and tomorrow. I may conceivably have to go to Chantilly next week, to go through them with Diana, but that depends on her movements. We shall leave here in great sorrow on Wednesday, stopping the grandfather clock and locking the door soon after 11 a.m., and reaching the noise, dirt and stuffiness of Soho Square about 9 p.m. Two days in the office, and then to Bromsden for Whitsun, the Fourth etc—looking forward to your letter greeting me. We're determined to get up here again for a week or two, possibly in August, by which time the spring should have been tapped for our water-supply. Did I tell you that both the farmer who owns the spring and the blacksmith who is going to do the job are called William Calvert? No relation, but luckily good friends. Ruth is also plotting to get a little calor-gas cooker to take the place of the Primus. Soon we shall be as sophisticated as the Savoy Hotel.

Ruth can't wait to look up No 70 in the *O.B. of E.V.*, which we haven't got here. So far our chief anthologies are *Nightingale Valley*, compiled by William Allingham (1862)—an excellent book: do you know it?—and a good Everyman volume called *A Galaxy of Shorter English Poems*, or words to that effect.

(The sun has momentarily gone behind a cloud, and a curlew is calling.)

Last week we made two longish walking expeditions—one to Crackpot Hall, where we would indeed like to live (jokes or no jokes), for its situation is superb, but the central part of the house collapsed some years ago—the result, they say, of centuries-old lead-workings under the hill. The other expedition was to various places, including Summer Lodge Tarn, a large and rather sinister mountain lake, miles from anywhere, in the midst of bog and heather, where thousands of black-headed gulls come every spring to nest—it must be a good sixty miles from the sea. They build their nests in reeds on the edge of the tarn, and rise in screaming multitudes at one's approach. Later they gradually settle, and apparently each bird unerringly flies straight back to its own nest. They are beastly birds, constantly dive-bombing the open nests of peewits, curlews etc and destroying their eggs. Often one sees a peewit driving the much bigger and more powerful gull away. If my last letter had a holiday air, what will you say to this one?

I don't think a great deal of Sir Charles Petrie—indeed, as Oscar would say, I never think of him at all—and so am not surprised at the deficiences of his index or his book. The Ipswich library seems to deal largely with what C. Lamb called *biblia abiblia*: you must let Patrick Barrington loose in it. He was at Eton with me, and I rather liked him. I thought 'benefitted' looked funny when I wrote it: I trust you to point out all such solecisms. I won't promise to write them all out ten times, but I shall probably remember them.

I have finished both large vols of Swinburne's letters One can't *like* him much, and his shrill tirades against 'the Galilean' and in favour of the Marquis de Sade are tedious and childish. But his devotion to poetry is fine, also his passionate championship of Shelley, Blake, Landor, Victor Hugo etc. There are four more vols to come.

Goodbye, dear George. I wish you could see the magical beauty which lies all around me.

At this moment you two must be approaching the sodden and unkind midlands, every minute or two a mile further from paradise, 'so late their happy seat'. But I am afraid you will take rather a sardonic view of the subsequent lines 'The world was all before them where to choose Their place of rest'.[1] The last word will *not* seem to be *le mot juste* to you; I suppose Milton really meant 'abode'. If not Adam too might have indignantly asked how 'rest' was in key with all that menacing stuff about the sweat of his brow. I remember how unattractive each year at Eton the resumption of the collar was every September—always glorious weather, and the realisation that there was some sour stuff to come before the feet could be again on the fender. And football in September was usually just as incongruous as cricket in May. I once inadvisedly caught a very hard hit in a trial match at Cambridge. Brilliant and all that yes, but not worth the split hand which the bitterly cold day brought about.

Comic about your Calverts (the chief factotum at Pamela's home Babraham was one William Calvert for years). It is much the same here; Pipes and Dunnetts swarm, all disclaiming any relationship with each other, though everyone knows they are connected, however different their social levels.

We went on Sunday to an exhibition of modern pictures at Framlingham (the home of P's sister, Lettice Colman). To my Victorian eye most of them looked like a painter's palette before scraping—a mess of bright confused colours. They literally said nothing to me whatever. But the afternoon's entertainment was an address by Roger on George II, which was excellent value, and very characteristic, humorous, naughty, impish, very easy to listen to. But the room was rather hot, and one or two of the weaker brethren—and sisters—got rather repellently drowsy, mouth sagging, head drooping obliquely. A famous ex-international polo-player composed himself for sleep from the start, then woke up with a jerk and strode out of the room, watch in hand, giving the impression that he had to catch a train. But he did ample justice to an excellent tea half-an-hour later. Yesterday R. was lunching with the Lord Beaverbrook, not on business, just a friendly

[1] Part of the antepenultimate lines of Milton's *Paradise Lost*.

lunch, the Beaver apparently having forgotten that in a correspondence with R., not long ago, he said what R. had said in some speech referring to the *Daily Express* was 'most offensive'. Not that he really could have cared much. Only yesterday three judges stigmatised the *Daily Express* and *Daily Mail* in unmeasured terms. I shall be interested to hear R's account of his lunch. I fear he won't be at the Lit. Soc., as he and Sibell are taking a holiday in Spain.

Summer Lodge Tarn is a good name, in spite of its sinister aspect. Lakes can look really rather terrifying. There is a small one near here, closely surrounded by trees, black, absolutely silent; no bird comes near it. And Wastwater amid all those grim screes is pretty unfriendly. Do you know Loch Ness? The mother of a boy in my house was drowned there, and her body was never found, all of course put down to the monster.

I am glad to see *John o' London's Weekly* has revived, and there has been some interesting reported talk with Gilbert Murray; *inter alia*, that Henry James meant 'The Turn of the Screw' to be terrifying to every reader, but was convinced it was a failure as he dictated it to an unemotional Scot, who, after each hair-raising episode, merely asked 'What next, please'. And I like G.M.'s telling of the great (but absurd) Cambridge philosopher McTaggart that he always wore a string round one of his waistcoat buttons. 'Why?' 'I keep it handy in case I should meet a kitten'. The White Knight in person. But so were a good many Cambridge dons half a century ago.

How right you are about Sir Charles Petrie. *The Victorians* is poor stuff—superficial, chatty, quite inadequate. Reviews are misleading; only one that I saw observed that a survey of the Victorian age was an odd one which mentioned S.W. Gore as a tennis-champion but said nothing of his brother the great bishop. No, it won't do.

Love to Ruth. I don't *think* she will mind what poem No 70 *O.E.V.* says, but one never can be sure.

P.S. I have lost nine pounds avoirdupois.

Once again I write out of doors, but this time *in the shade*! The house is covered with huge red roses, and the laburnum-blossom is drifting down over me as I write. (I wish you didn't always have to come here at midwinter.) Outside the library window, in the morello cherry tree, a flycatcher has a nest with five eggs. Over the porch in the clematis a pied wagtail has built, and under the eaves the house-martins have returned in their dozens. A cuckoo with laryngitis is calling in the wood. Altogether a pastoral scene of high summer, but my heart is aching for the windy uplands, green green valleys and surrounding majesty of peaks. We drove south sadly in hot sunshine on Wednesday, and have both felt pretty miserable and *désorientés* ever since. What Henry James called 'the real right thing' takes a lot of snapping out of. At Soho Square the accumulation is appalling. Every-one I have ever heard of or dimly known seems to have written me a long complicated letter. Vyvyan Holland wants me to expurgate the later letters, and altogether my heart sinks. Kisdon is the place for me.

Ruth has gone to her son's cottage in Essex for the week-end. She was enchanted to discover the identity of No 70 in *O.B.E.V.* and is much looking forward to seeing you at 6 p.m. on the 14th. When do you leave for London? It mercifully looks as though I shan't have to go to Chantilly, since Diana is coming to London, but I may well spend next Saturday in Oxford, getting Sparrow's remarks on the Oscar letters and checking the ones in Magdalen. I'll hope to write to you on Saturday night and post it on Sunday.

I thoroughly enjoyed Roger's book: if this is book-making it's most agreeably done. Am now reading Cecil Day Lewis's autobio-graphy *The Buried Day*. I appear once with my name misspelled. I shall warn Cecil that when *my* autobiography appears it will contain many flattering references to C. Day *Leavis*. That should draw him!

Adam came over yesterday for the Fourth and spent a quiet day in the garden. Comfort took him and a girl-friend back for the fireworks. He seemed in good form, enjoying everything. He is supposed to be in Lower Club, but they haven't yet had one club game: instead they masquerade as the Third Eleven (XXXIII) and Fourth Eleven (XLIV), for which A. played against some school or other and took three for one.

Duff's Schools began at Oxford on Thursday. He telephoned yesterday to say the first three papers weren't quite as bad as he'd expected—which may or may not be a good sign. Adam's G.C.E. (Advanced and Science) begins on the 22nd (the day of the London Library sale). Yesterday Comfort looked at one of last year's Maths papers and couldn't begin to understand a single one of the *questions*!

Experts are predicting high prices for some of the manuscripts at the L.L. sale: I only hope they're right. Christie's say that a little preliminary champagne always has a tonic effect on the bidding, so I'm trying to raise some more money for that. T.S.E. is all for it, and I'm sure will receive the guests most graciously. Did I tell you that I asked Birley to contribute to the sale, and he sent a copy of the Nonesuch Press Herodotus? It's a lovely book, which I wouldn't mind having myself. E. Blunden reports that a Hong Kong schoolboy wrote 'In Hong Kong there is a queer at every bus-stop'. I have told him that in London the answer would be 'So what?'

Ruth and I went to the Robert Morley Wilde film on Thursday and thought it rotten, except for the Trial dialogue, which is *verbatim* from life. We shall try to see the other film too. Next Friday is R's birthday and I am hoping to take her (on Thursday) to the new Rattigan play about T.E. Lawrence, which sounds pretty good. Sometime soon we are going to check that immensely long Oscar letter (*De Profundis*) in the British Museum. There is too much to do, and I don't much want to do any of it. Have your ribs quite recovered? It will be a sad day when you can no longer scramble up to the eyrie in Soho Square.

9 June 1960 *Grundisburgh*

As I hope you know, the widespread conviction that, without my counsel, the finances of the Abbey School Malvern would be entirely precarious compels my annual visit to Oxford, where the Finance Committee meets under Sir Douglas Veale. I am staying with Roger and Lavinia Mynors. Last night I was taken to dine in Corpus and had a pleasant talk with the Vice-President, and the printing pundit whose name, I suspect, has half-escaped me when I say it was Regler.

It was an oddish dinner for a guest-night, all cold, slabs of unidentified but not wholly untoothsome made-up meats. A good white wine, and of course I followed (was it?) Saintsbury's advice in preferring Madeira to port or sherry. I spoke with several others; more than one claimed to know R.H-D. (who doesn't?). One literally called him 'a great man' and clearly meant what he said, so you will see I was in the right atmosphere.

Pamela and I spent last week-end in a curious *omnium gatherum* at her brother's near Cambridge. A picturesque French lady was there, who, Robert Adeane told us, has had three children by Picasso, whose pictures R.A. does much to boost at the Tate. The house is full of ultra-modern paintings which to my ignorant and philistine eye look like the uncleaned palettes of painters—just a confused mass of colours. The one question one must *not* ask is 'What is the subject'? That puts one at a stroke back among the fans of Alma Tadema and Watts.

I hope the shades of the prison-house are gradually becoming less black? You suspected that Vyvyan Holland might be tiresome. There can surely be no point in expurgating O.W. I do hope you will be able to overrule him. Does he think that at this date O.W.'s moral opinions can be glossed over or whitewashed?

I leave for home to-morrow and go to London on Tuesday—the day your letter usually arrives. But, my dear R., you have far too much round your neck. We meet on Tuesday 6 p.m. Why not give yourself a brief rest from writing to G.W.L.? You really should. I shall be climbing your stairs at 6 and shall always do so, moving with the slow and rhythmical steps advocated by mountaineers.

I haven't yet read *The Buried Day*. Your suggested revenge for (I imagine) 'Dav*ies*' is excellent, though Roger Mynors tells me that Leavis's *pupils* are devoted to him, even after ceasing to accept all he says as gospel. I suspect he may be one of those apropos of whom G.K.C. (was it?) wrote 'If you want to keep your dislike of someone alive be careful not to meet him'. Macnaghten (H) at Eton constantly got letters from the Rev. H. Daman, spelling his name McNaghten. At last M. riposted 'If you go on leaving out the first 'A' in my name I shall address you leaving out the second 'A' in yours'. These witty old pedants!

Oxford is looking lovely—or would do if the traffic was not impossible, and the populace far too numerous. The streets are full of examinees fresh from a paper—though 'fresh' is not the word. Most are a bit pallid and strained. I hope Duff is not one of these—in fact I am sure he isn't. Adam, I think, has gone well beyond Eng. Lit. (O level) and will pass his tests with colours flying.

I like 'a queer at every bus-stop'. I think it may be true here, but what do I know?

I missed the Oscar Wilde film in Ipswich and am glad at your saying it is rotten. Anyway I know the trial almost by heart.

I was mildly interested by John Lehmann's second autobiographical volume[1] and quite a lot by *Waterloo*.[2] It seems that both Napoleon and Wellington made any number of what would appear to be almost fatuous blunders and misapprehensions. As for Ney, he never once did anything right. One constantly has the feeling of hideous carnage, but the sum total of English casualties is very small beer besides *one* day of the Somme or Passchendaele. Is there an expert in the Lit. Soc.? B. Fergusson? Tim? Probably Peter F. knows as much as anyone. My old brother, who never wrote a line, knew all there was to be known about Waterloo, and I was interested to find that this new book says just what he did about the undeserved load of blame which historians, following Napoleon, have put on Grouchy. Does one know the full truth about anyone or anything? And yet the air is thick with the dogmatisms of 'spokesmen' every day. The latest BBC change from facts at 9 to facts and comments at 10 will diminish my listening still further. It is grim evidence that people have got to the point of wanting their minds made up for them. 'Tell us what we *ought* to think'. And yet individuals I meet still seem to have some independent notions.

11 June 1960 *Bromsden Farm*

Your account of the conversation at Corpus is clearly apocryphal, but none the less welcome. Ridler is the name of the Printer to the University—a very nice and able man.

[1] *I am my Brother* (1960).
[2] By John Naylor (1960).

Duff has finished his Schools, for better for worse, and next Friday retires from Oxford, though he may conceivably be recalled for a viva in July. Yesterday he came over, and, in a fit of post-examination euphoria, cut *all* the grass in the garden between lunch and tea. This made the brick-path look so weedy and unkempt that I have spent most of today putting it in order, housemaid's knee or no.

Last week in London, though a short one, was well-nigh intolerable. Apart from the noise, heat and stink, my office was seldom free of callers and the telephone rang incessantly. Everything had stood still during my absence, so all books are behindhand. Vyvyan Holland is trying to make me bowdlerise Oscar's letters. Of course I won't (still less will I falsify some of them, as V.H. suggests) but the copyright belongs to him and I see a deadlock looming. I can't tell you how fed up I am with it all—and how I long to retire to Kisdon's happy hill.

Needless to say, Ruth has sustained, sympathised and comforted in her inimitable way, though she finds the London scene as unattractive as I do. Next week her daughter is arriving from Italy with a four-year-old child and an Italian girl, to await the birth of a second child somewhere about the end of July. This will clearly be a great nuisance. You mustn't mind my unburdening myself to you: it will be a joy to see you on Tuesday.

I met Leavis once and thought him quite revolting—dirty, messy, rude—but perhaps he grows on one. I shall certainly give him no opportunity of so doing.

The new *John o' London's* seems to me pretty poor: they refused to take Swinnerton back.

You must ask Gerry Wellington about Waterloo: I fancy he knows a good deal.

16 June 1960 *Grundisburgh*

An excellent evening, as always, only needing the presence of Ruth to make it perfect. I was glad to have a crack—for the first time—with James Laver, who was most pleasant and interesting. So too was Gerry Wellington. I asked him a good deal about Waterloo, and you may (or may not) be surprised to hear that the Duke did not make all that many mistakes. But, as the D. himself said, there are so many different versions of what happened that he really became quite doubtful whether he had been there himself. Jonah and Ivor and I sat for another hour afterwards. J. does seem much better, but is still breathless and the doctors are now really on their mettle and making test after test. Pamela's diagnosis is that it is some form of hysteria, as they all say his heart and lungs are as sound as bells. Maybe. We have a neighbour who now and then cannot walk across the room—in fact can do little else but tremble, and it is nothing at all but nervous imagination. It seems to me half-way to the firm belief that you are either God or a poached egg, which are apparently the commonest hallucinations, but somehow I don't think Jonah will end by thinking either. I like old Ivor very much, but doubt if he is a happy man. Yet as his old thrawn fellow-countryman said, nobody conscious of what is below the surface, i.e. the fundamental tragedy of man's life, can possibly be really happy—not even Leigh Hunt, 'idly melodious, as bird on bough'.

Your frank derision at my delicacy emboldens me to tell you that in your last list *The Laughing Fish*[1] sounds exactly the kind of book I love reading in bed. Sleep always comes to me late and goes early. On Tuesday night I had very little and put it down to your admirable vintages. But as I again had a hot head last night after a teetotal day, the cause must be elsewhere—hysteria perhaps. But how could an evening when Cuthbert and Lockhart were both absent induce hysteria? I suspect that after seventy-seven something goes a bit wonky every few days; all the bearings are getting a bit loose.

Lockhart's book[2] is mildly interesting in places, but doesn't amount to much—and why do I savour and rejoice in all *your* vignettes of heath and birdery at Kisdon, but never want to accompany him fishing in obviously lovely places? I am all for hearing about the playing of a salmon, but the description must be as skilful as the playing. Lockhart's writing is colourless, and after a time one gradually ceases to share his deep interest in Lockhart.

How good it was to see D. Somervell again—and looking so well—surely one of the very nicest of men.

[1] By Selwyn Jepson (1960).

[2] *Giants Cast Long Shadows* by R. Bruce Lockhart (1960).

Next week from Tuesday to Friday I shall be at North Foreland Lodge—Mr Chips to the life. Dreadful. Last year I brightened their young lives through my chair collapsing at girls' dinner. But I cannot expect such a stroke of luck again.

17 June 1960 *Grundisburgh*

I wrote and sent off my short-measure letter yesterday, and to-day arrives really the noblest non-birthday present that ever was—*five* books if you please, of magnificent variety and obvious readableness. I am equipped with occupation for my abundant leisure for weeks, not that next week isn't a bit depressing with *three* speech-days and a committee meeting. This goes to Soho Square, as I doubt if, posted to Bromsden F. to-day, it would reach you to-morrow. Well, what can I say but 'bless you' again. They say that prayers reiterated gain in force (how do they know?) so perhaps blessings do too. And how the devil can I ever hope to repay you in any way at all?

We dined yesterday in a small company, in which was a god-daughter of Malcolm Sargent's, and a lifelong friend of Vyvyan Holland's, so I walked warily. The lady told me that M.S. is fundamentally an unhappy man and very lonely—marriage broken, daughter dead. *Pauvre humanité*—another Eugene O'Neill in fact. Our eupeptic Victorians despised Euripides, especially in his view that the best thing of all was not to be born, the second to die as soon as possible. And Omar K. had no vogue of much account until Victorianism was on its way out.

18 June 1960 *Bromsden Farm*

I shall just scribble a page tonight, and continue in the morning. I spent most of to-day in Oxford, which was boiling hot and stuffed with mostly very unattractive people—bearded youths naked to the waist, negresses and other exotics, all sweating and jostling. I lunched at All Souls with Sparrow and John Bryson of Balliol. They have both read the Oscar galleys and are most enthusiastic. Bryson gave me material for three splendid new footnotes. Afterwards Sparrow and I walked down to Magdalen library, where we spent two hours checking their Oscar letters, Sparrow reading them aloud while I followed on the proofs. The road going and coming was packed with vehicles bumper-to-bumper—hideous! It is becoming increasingly clear that this part of the proof-correcting is going to take weeks, if not months, and I must just face the fact and get through it all as fast as I conveniently can. Now for bed and more of T.C.'s *Reminiscences.*

Sunday morning

The second volume of T.C. is excellent: I'm still on Jeffrey, with Jane to come.

Comfort is much disheartened because the squirrels have taken to lifting up the strawberry net, popping underneath and eating all the fruit. It has taken them twenty years to learn this trick, the little pets. A farm cat has destroyed the flycatchers' nest—tooth and claw everywhere.

Even as Cuthbert at the dinner-table sheds around him a baleful aura of *ennui* and *malaise*, so do you, my dear George, surround yourself with an infectious gaiety and pleasure. Whenever my eye falls on you, your noble brow, towering above its brachycephalic neighbours, is always the centre of laughter and anecdote, wit and repartee. Truly your presence always raises the Lit. Soc. level to what it's supposed to be. You mustn't mind my slipping away after dinner: I have almost always had enough by then, and Ivor is delighted to have you to himself. No, I don't think he is a happy man—a disappointed one perhaps.

As I left, James Laver said to me: 'What a delightful person G.L. is'. Needless to say I put him right.

Ruth was much pleased by the edited selection of your messages that I passed on to her. The advent of her daughter, grand-daughter etc has temporarily submerged her in a welter of cooking and tiresome domesticity, poor lamb. I sent you a parcel of books last week: *The Laughing Fish* shall follow.

Air travel is surely the most tedious and time-wasting invention ever—for meeters and see-ers-off, that is, and often for travellers too. Ruth and I went to meet her daughter at London Airport on Wednesday. Her plane from Milan was scheduled to arrive at 10.35 p.m. (a tiresome enough time in itself) but a telegram from Milan announced a postponement till 11.55 p.m. (This L.A. first denied and then corroborated.) We got there at 11.50, and, after some anxious minutes, the plane landed at 12.15. Customs etc took so long that it was almost 1 a.m. before we were able to drive away.

Next evening (Thursday) I dined with the Huntingdons at Roehampton: he a Labour peer, she a beautiful woman and good writer (Margaret Lane)—both charming. I was driven there by Lord Montagu of Beaulieu—and his wife. The other guests were Dorothy Dickson (marvellously preserved at sixty-four), Paul Dehn (Agate's godson) and a glamorous American woman. She drove D.D., P.D. and me back to London, and I set fire to a whole box of matches in the back of her car. Paul Dehn deftly put it out, but the car was full of fumes, and it transpired that none of the windows would open. The American lady explained this by saying that the car was borrowed.

22 June 1960 *Grundisburgh*

What a very nice letter to get! I remember my old tutor (or 'tootor' as my aunts always pronounced it; and it was a dear old Victorian snob great-aunt who, when a relative married a Headmaster of great distinction, said gloomily, and frequently: 'No, I must say I do think it is rather—as in 'gather'—dowdy to marry a tootor') Arthur Benson saying (not that no one else ever said it) '*Everybody* likes praise, deserved or undeserved, though many will pretend they don't'. But if you *will* produce such easy and charming people as James Laver to sit next to, how can I help bubbling away? And the excellent fare you provide does what it should to blunt their critical faculties. I am not so sure about your reference to my noble (*sic*) brow '*towering*' above those of my neighbours. The Creator has a frequently malicious sense of humour. He sent me into the world with an outsize head, and fifty years later gave me Paget's Disease, of which one of the results is a slow but steady increase in the size of the head. I don't yet—like Jeeves—take no. 9 in hats, but am not so very far off. So I adopt the feeble but very human device of practically never wearing a hat. Don't sympathise about Paget: it honestly doesn't bother me at all; there are many varieties, some hideously crippling, some quite harmless, and it was worth the exorbitant (I thought) £5. 5. 0 that I paid to the great Rowley Bristowe twelve years ago to be told a) it would trouble me very little and b) don't waste any money going to Droitwich. I was glad especially to hear b), as, with the possible exception of Stourbridge and Dudley, Droitwich is the most unattractive of places. Wigan—like Hell—has something majestic about it. Not Droitwich. Hester Alington was nearly drowned there, as the water is so salt that if you go upside down in it you can't right yourself. Didn't that happen to Kinglake in the Dead Sea?[1]

I have just finished the life of Eugene O'Neill you sent me. *Very* absorbing. As with so many geniuses the commonplaces of moral judgment are best left unexpressed. That picture of him in the frontispiece is really appalling in its tragic misery. Tell me about his plays. I have just got three or four of them from the library but not yet embarked on them. I remember somewhere in the book it says that they are—like so many of Shakespeare's—much better when acted than when read. I don't take much to Carlotta somehow. Am I wrong? Agnes sounds much nicer. And what is Shane doing now? And is Oona's marriage a success? Why did E.O'N. object to Charlie Chaplin —a greater genius than himself?

You told me the Bennett-Wells letters weren't up to much. After about p. 67 the editor had rather to scrape the barrel, and they don't talk enough about other people and things. But they say many shrewd and perceptive things. How right B. is about W. as an artist. But he was wrong surely in putting—who was it? *someone*, in one of W's lesser books—above Mr Polly as a comic character.

I shall tackle Druon when I get back. What a noble present you sent me. You always assert that gratitude is not your due, but again I remember Arthur Benson. 'Never take a kindness for granted, however regular or repeated it may be'. And if that isn't wise and just advice I'll eat my hat.

Your squirrels are, I hope, those grey criminals, not the little red fellows. Show them no mercy. Tree-rats they should be called.

Dorothy Dickson's looks thirty or forty years ago were entrancing.

[1] A.W. Kinglake (1809–1891) found it difficult to swim in the Dead Sea (*Eothen*, 1844, chapter xiii), but made no mention of capsizing.

I know of one young man who really did put an end to himself for love of her. Wasn't her daughter also a smasher? What has happened to her? Paul Dehn I surmise is making a name. What was that strikingly good play, revue, fantasy, pageant? of his somehow connected with Shrewsbury? James Agate thought a lot of him.

I am at the present moment at North Foreland Lodge surrounded by 'a knot of little misses', feeling, *à la* J.M. Barrie, how much nicer girls of fifteen are than boys of that age—so unshy and intelligent and friendly. Too strong perhaps. Boys can be very nice too.

What shocks one has. Harry Altham, President of M.C.C., *approves* of modern cricket—even of matches in which every innings till the last is declared and the result is awfully sporting and exciting—and bogus. A game which you lose after using only half your resources, in order to please the crowd, is to my mind rather a silly game. So I was always taught by C.M. Wells, who had the greatest contempt for cricket that wasn't serious. He didn't mean 'solemn'.

26 June 1960 — *The Swan Hotel*
Newby Bridge, Lancs
(My bedroom is called Coleridge)

It's biro to-day, on a bench on the bank of the River Leven—in hot morning sunshine. It was charming of you to write an *extra* letter last week, and your regular one reached Soho Square just as I was setting off for Euston. Full of questions it was and lively comment. Droitwich, which you roundly condemn, has been the salvation of Comfort's stepmother, who goes there twice a year for her rheumatism or arthritis and always with benefit. I daresay she doesn't worry about the scenery or other horrors.

Eugene O'Neill's plays are mostly excellent to *see*, but I imagine less so to read. Shane is still a drug-addict, Oona's marriage is a tremendous success. She has six or so children and is reported placid and beautiful. All three of E.O'N.'s wives are still alive. Clearly Carlotta is intolerable, and E. could never forgive Agnes for having behaved so well. *What* a story!

Dorothy Dickson's daughter—Dot Hyson—is indeed a smasher.

She married the actor Anthony Quayle and renounced the boards, sensible girl.

The London Library sale exceeded all conceivable expectations—realising a grand total of £25,600!!!! Added to the £17,000 we have already collected in cash, this more than doubles the sum we originally appealed for, and should keep the Library solvent for some years. The high spot was the manuscript of Forster's *A Passage to India*, which, you remember, I travelled to Cambridge to fetch, and brought back higgledy-piggledy in my brief-case. Believe it or not, this fetched £6500—from America. Next highest was £3800 for two address-books belonging to T.E. Lawrence, and £2800 for the manuscript of *The Waste Land* which I persuaded T.S.E. to copy out last winter. The manuscript of Strachey's *Queen Victoria* fetched £1800, that of Maugham's *Up at the Villa* £1100, and so on. It was a very exciting, if hot, evening. Ruth and I dined first with the Eliots at their flat and went along with them. At dinner we spoke of Shaw, and T.S.E. said he thought S's best plays were *The Chocolate Soldier* and *My Fair Lady*—which I think better criticism than it sounds: there's nothing like a few good tunes for bolstering up a rather outmoded play.

When the T.S.E. manuscript was knocked down for £2800, the audience clapped and cheered and the old boy beamed modestly. We are devoted to him, but worried by his breathlessness and general frailty. His marriage is a tremendous happiness to him.

I arrived here on Friday evening in perfect weather, and yesterday (when the radio told of rain at Wimbledon and darkness at Lord's) the sun burned down all day from a clear blue sky (as it does to-day). There is mercifully no spare-room in the Ransomes' very uncomfortable cottage, so I am quartered in this excellent hotel, a few miles away, and they have hired a large Austin for the week-end. It has a wicked gear-change, but is otherwise okay. Ransome is pretty immobile—shuffling with a stick—so yesterday I drove him all day through the lakes—Esthwaite, Rydal, Grasmere, Thirlmere, Ambleside, Derwentwater, Keswick (where I visited Hugh Walpole's grave), Bassenthwaite (we picnicked on the road above the lake) and on to Cockermouth (birthplace of Wordsworth), where we sat in the sun by the Derwent, from which Ransome has pulled innumerable sea-trout and salmon. He is much grieved by the (scarcely acceptable) realisation that he will never be able to fish again. To-day I shall drive him about some more, and tomorrow morning take train for London, where another over-crowded week awaits me. I am reading Peter Quennell's new book *The Sign of the Fish*, which you must order from your library: it's autobiographical, and its theme is an enquiry into the ever-fascinating question of why writers write. P.Q. himself writes beautifully. I hope you can read this scrawl.

29 June 1960 *Grundisburgh*

I really should have sent you a wire about that magnificent auction for the L.L. which gave *me* immense pleasure, knowing something of your ceaseless efforts for it. Now who will paint your portrait to hang near that of Thomas Carlyle (and isn't my grandfather somewhere there too?). How does Comfort like the prospect of being Lady H-D. in the next honours list or two? It is inevitable—unless you refuse like John Christie and get a C.H. instead, even more distinguished they tell me. I do hope you are indulging in an orgy of self-satisfaction. I feel fairly confident that Ruth will see that you do. It is a very splendid achievement.

My letter. Yes I know. 'Questioning is not the mode of conversation among gentlemen'. And you may make the same retort as J. made to B. who feebly said he was encouraged to do it because J. was 'so good': 'Sir, my being so good is no reason for your being so ill'. But your knowledge of men and things in the world of drama, literature and indeed the world generally is so much greater than mine that I just have to pick your brains. And so you will continue to be good and I to be ill. It is one of your crosses.

Eugene O'Neill. I have read four of his plays, which seem to me fully to explain the appalling despair in his face. In *Desire under the Elms*, *Strange Interlude* and *Mourning Becomes Electra*, human nature is portrayed as of almost unrelieved blackness, 'no cakes or ale nor nothing pleasant'. I found them quite absorbing to read, and they must be terrific on the stage. *The Iceman* I am finding rather boring; all the conversations go on too long, in fact the whole play is too long. In bed I am enjoying the Jepson story you kindly sent. But how did your reader overlook 'corpus delict*us*' on p. 70?

To revert to O'N. and your grim dictum 'He couldn t forgive Agnes for behaving so well'. Isn't that first cousin to D.H.L.'s insufferable trait of writing with the most venomous malice about those who had most helped him? Katherine Mansfield said there were three Lawrences—the black devil whom she hated, the prophet in whom she did not believe, and the man and artist whom she revered and loved. But I did not know him as a man, and am not clever enough to appreciate him as an artist, so all that is left is Nos 1 and 2, alas! But couldn't his executors have offered you something for the L.L. sale? Perhaps he thought it should be razed to the ground and the site sowed with salt, as that old ass G.B.S. suggested for Oxford.

The names of the places you passed through with Ransome—Rydal, Thirlmere, Bassenthwaite sound like vintages (though W.W.'s home *would* be called Cockermouth) but you ought to keep away from Westmorland. Nostalgia can be very debilitating. '*Tendebantque manus ripae ulterioris amore*'.[1] Virgil knew all about it. It would be worse if you weren't fairly soon getting another spell there.

Do coalmine disasters always hit you in the wind? They do me. Is there a grimmer death than being cut off by a fall of coal and being slowly suffocated or starved? I agree with the man who wrote that no man should be doomed to such a life. But then where would our fires and factories be? Other bad news in to-day's paper is that in a few years' time the larger apes will be no more throughout Africa. What will life be without gorillas? Apparently they are the mildest of animals, even if they have faces like enlarged H.K. Marsdens.[2] But you mustn't anger them; if it comes to a showdown you won't win. An irate gorilla once gripped a gun-butt so tightly that his fingers sank into the wood, and in a tug-of-war he can pull over seventeen men with one hand. He has a very sensitive spirit and can suffer acutely from disappointment—like (also improbably but truly) the pike. If Ruth is not chez No 36 on July 12, I shall show how strong my kinship is with both. I shall be there, though I oughtn't to be, as there will be a mort of exam-scripts here. The next three months are my busy ones. My real holiday-month is February, and a plucky lot

[1] 'Their hands outstretched in longing for the farther shore' (*Aeneid* vi, l. 314).

[2] Eton master.

of use that is. Love to R, and gently point out that to cast no eye upon her from April, no—March, till October is an infliction the Inquisition might have thought up.
P.S. And there are a lot of questions in this letter too; but practically all of them are rhetorical.

2 July 1960 *Bromsden Farm*

First—before I forget it—will you be an angel and propose Adam for the M.C.C.? He will be seventeen on Monday, and so eligible under the latest rules. I think—don't you?—that you know enough, at second hand, of his cricket interests and prowess to avoid perjury. Last week the *Chronicle* congratulated him on receiving his Middle Club, when he had not in fact done so, and the paper now has to retract and apologise. Many boys would be upset by this clumsy mistake, but Adam seems unmoved. Apparently the Lower Club side is now considered the Eton Third Eleven, and the Middle Club side the Fourth Eleven (and they play matches as such), while dear old Strawberry is left in the cold. As you will see, proposal entails both your signature on this form and a brief letter. If you can send me both in your next, I'll ask Fred Coleridge to second him. Adam is home for Long Leave, very cheerful despite his G.C.E. (A & S) which is in progress. To-day we all drove to Aldwick, near Bognor, and had our first swim of the year. There wasn't much sun, but no rain fell, and the sea was *warm*—very refreshing and enjoyable.

I have had three or four charming letters about the London Library sale, including one from Harold Nicolson, but have been too bedevilled with other things to spend much time in self-satisfaction. Your harping on an imaginary knighthood is a delightful fantasy. In the extremely unlikely event of one being offered, my instinct would be to accept. I have no worldly ambition (only peace at Kisdon) but while one is engaged in the merry-go-round, it seems churlish to refuse any rewards from the sideshows. There is surely a great deal of snobbery—straight and inverted—in these matters. My old friend Edward Garnett refused a C.H., saying that it was 'given only to dentists'. He was a lifelong 'agin-the-Government' radical, but I have heard many people sneer at honours of all kinds because they are mostly given to nonentities. True, but one might well refuse to do *anything* on the same grounds.

There my pen gave out and I went to bed. Now it is eleven o' clock on grey Sunday morning. So glad the O'Neill plays interested you: they are indeed terrific on the stage: even *The Iceman* held Ruth and me gripped for all its length.

I shudder at corpus delict*us*: I suppose I must have missed it in the typescript, but can't imagine how. Can I have been skipping?

My last day in the Lakes was hot and sunny: I drove A.R. all over the place. We lunched at Gosforth, in the shadow of the Atomic Pile, and then sat by the sea at Ravenglass, an enchanting little dead-end, consisting of one straggling street leading to nowhere, a huge natural (high-tide) harbour, said to have been used by the Vikings and not since, and beyond it a large island or isthmus which is a bird-sanctuary where several kinds of terns nest. I should have liked to join a boat-load of people who were being taken over to see it, but Ransome is too crippled to get into a boat. Altogether his situation is pitiable, for he needs a strong male nurse constantly in attendance, but has only his wife, who at the moment seems headed for a nervous breakdown, and is mildly irritated by the poor old boy. I left them feeling utterly exhausted, despite the wonderful weather and lovely scenery. Last week was black with engagements, none interesting enough to chronicle.

July 5 or 6, anyway Wednesday *Grundisburgh*

Form filled in and enclosed for Adam—with great pleasure. I always resent 'block capitals', but as they might easily say the form was not properly filled in, I do so, not in block capitals, but in the script of Cardinal Bembo's secretary[1]—and I doubt if any candidate has been so sponsored before. I hope it won't stand in his way. Is there a possibility of his getting his eleven next year? That *would* be fun. I should

[1] In 1513 a papal brief of Pope Leo X was written in exquisite italic by an anonymous chancery scribe and signed by the Pope's secretary Pietro Bembo (1470–1547), who was later a Cardinal.

like to see you behaving exactly like a cat on hot bricks, and I can think of no other circumstance that would bring that about. A cricketer of such imperturbable nerves as A. has great potential value.

The Ladies Plate gave me immense pleasure. Bobby Bourne told me at Xmas the VIII would be nothing much; but on Saturday he said that quite suddenly, a week before Henley, they '*clicked*', like some machinery being adjusted and lubricated, and he went to Henley full of hope. Peter Haig Thomas five or six years ago told me he considered Bobby was in the 'Havvy' (de Havilland) class as a coach, and whatever rot he might (and did) talk about much else, he never did about rowing (like Flash Harry and music).

Of course you must accept the knighthood when (n.b. not 'if') it is offered you. You are right about the snobbery of those who sneer at it (or mere conceit, like Housman refusing the O.M. because Galsworthy had it). I have in my day done a little wire-pulling when Anthony Bevir[1] was in charge. But he is so no longer, and in fact is fairly deep in liquor nowadays. I regret the elevation of Hobbs and Gordon Richards but that was a sop to our *soi-disant* democrats. Surely old E. Garnett was quite wrong about the C.H. being given to dentists. Wasn't he mixing it up with the M.V.O., fifth class, which, the legend was, Edward VII gave to his bridge-partner who left the declaration to Tum, who had four aces.

Very interesting to hear that you and R. were thrilled by *The Iceman* on the stage. It just shows you can't judge by merely reading. I think the debased Yankee diction and slang rather got on my nerves (or 'noives'). The complaint that nothing happens except talk is of course as irrelevant as it was in Shaw's prime. Do any of the characters emerge as 'likeable' on the stage? Perhaps that is irrelevant too.

I was a little disappointed in the new Druon.[2] Didn't quite get the point of it, which of course may not be his fault; but his other books I recall as having plenty of subtlety as well as vivid colour, and in this one I get only some of the colour. What do *you* think of it?

You know, Rupert, the fundamental—and slightly depressing—

[1] Anthony Bevir (1895–1977). Private Secretary to Prime Ministers Chamberlain, Churchill, Attlee and Eden. Knighted 1952.

[2] *Alexander the God* by Maurice Druon (1960).

difference between my letters and yours is that yours are full of interesting things you have done, and ditto people you have seen. I, having done neither, am reduced, largely, to not very inspiring chatter about what I have been reading—with an occasional diversion onto, say, gorillas or other large animals for which you do not share my taste. What can be done about it? Nothing that I myself can see. Shall I tell you what Miss Smith (nicknamed 'the Drip') said about teaching Eng. Lit. to girls who confuse Ben Jonson with Dr Johnson and are not in the least abashed by her horror? Shall I tell you how I scored off the Inspector of Taxes last week, or that the reason why George Dunnett the local carpenter won't now go up a ladder, is not because, at seventy-five, his balance (like mine) is untrustworthy, but because, his weight being eighteen stone, he is sure that sooner or later a rung will wilt beneath his foot and bring him 'with hideous ruin and combustion down'?[1] No, the beer is very small and not comparable for a moment with your rich and varied vintages. I can't (honestly) think why you like my letters, but I believe you do. One, I suppose, of the anfractuosities of the human mind. Well there it is.

Now a small problem. Henry James wrote to R.L.S. that *Tess* was '*vile* . . . pretence of sexuality . . . abomination of the language' etc. But in *The Legend of the Master*[2] I read that in a later letter to R.L.S. he said that in spite of its faults it had 'a singular beauty and charm'. Well, where *is* that letter? It isn't in Percy Lubbock's two huge volumes; it isn't in your selection of his letters. But he oughtn't to be left with that slightly obtuse judgment. I am delighted to re-find that he regarded Carlyle as 'perhaps the very greatest of letter-writers'. But I suppose H.J. was not far wrong when he wrote 'your demolitions of the unspeakable Froude don't persuade me that C. was amiable . . . perhaps the most disagreeable in character of men of genius of equal magnificence'.

[1] Milton, *Paradise Lost*, book I.

[2] A compilation, by Simon Nowell-Smith, of anecdotes about Henry James (1947).

Considering that your last excellent letter began 'My dear Peter', and that you forgot to include in it the letter of recommendation for Adam to the M.C.C. (bring it with you on Tuesday if you can remember) you're jolly lucky that this letter doesn't begin 'My dear Cuthbert'. Anyhow you made up for it by your splendid substitute for 'block capitals'. Alas and alack, Ruth will not be with us on Tuesday, as she is being taken that evening to *Der Rosenkavalier* at Glyndebourne, which, as you know, means leaving London in full evening dress soon after lunch. She is most distressed at missing you once again. Her second grand-daughter was born safely on Monday morning, and will soon be back in Ruth's house, together with its mother, father, sister, nanny and Italian girl—a regular menagerie with which R. simply hasn't time to cope.

Last week, for most of three days, we escaped to the comparative peace of the Manuscript Room of the British Museum, where we checked the manuscript of Oscar's *De Profundis* (his longest, best and most important letter) against our proofs. The manuscript was given to the B.M. by Robbie Ross in 1909 (to ensure its not falling into the hands of Lord Alfred Douglas) with a fifty-year embargo on anyone's seeing it: R. and I are therefore almost certainly the first people who have scrutinised it properly, and to our surprise and great excitement we discovered that the so-called 'complete' version (first published in 1949) is a travesty of the original (it was printed from a wildly inaccurate typescript of Ross's). At least 1000 words were omitted, many hundreds misread, paragraphs transposed and goodness knows what. You can imagine what fun the checking was. I fear my proof-correction-bill will be appalling (I would never have set up from the printed version if I'd had the faintest inkling how corrupt it was) but the *Letters* will benefit enormously from containing the first complete and accurate version ever to appear.

You are quite right about Druon's *Alexander*. It was intended as the first volume in a series of *biographies* of Famous Bastards: Druon is one, and is therefore interested in the subject: he prefaced the book with a long introduction proving that all the greatest men in history were illegitimate (this seems to me idiotic: who knows who's legitimate for certain?). Anyhow the series never materialised, and we were left with this isolated volume. I decided I couldn't possibly publish it as a biography in English, so I changed its title, removed the introduction, and put it out as a novel—to all which Druon most helpfully agreed. *The Times* gave it a good review on Thursday, Raymond Mortimer is doing it in the *Sunday Times*, and the Critics are to discuss it tomorrow, so it should be well on its way. But it's nowhere near so good as his French history novels: I've just corrected the proofs of the new one, *The She-Wolf of France*, which will appear in the autumn. It includes an appallingly graphic description of the murder of Edward II in Berkeley Castle.

I think I have (at Soho Square) a typed copy of the James letter to Stevenson about which you ask: if I can find it I'll send it along. Remind me of it on Tuesday. Meanwhile here is a splendid piece of Oscar, rescued by us from the B.M. last week. It describes the recipient's father, Lord Queensberry:

> And I used to feel bitterly the irony and ignominy of my position when in the course of my three trials, beginning at the Police Court, I used to see your father bustling in and out in the hopes of attracting public attention, as if anyone could fail to note or remember the stableman's gait and dress, the bowed legs, the twitching hands, the hanging lower lip, the bestial and half-witted grin. Even when he was not there, or was out of sight, I used to feel conscious of his presence, and the blank dreary walls of the great Court-room, the very air itself, seemed to me at times to be hung with multitudinous masks of that apelike face.

Good strong stuff, eh?, and you are almost its first reader. I'm longing to get the book into page-proof, so that you can have a go at it. But when will that be? How long, oh Lord, how long? I have no time to work on it properly, and I keep on letting myself in for tedious, time-wasting and quite unnecessary chores. Tomorrow (Sunday), for example, at 3 p.m. I am opening an exhibition of Victorian first editions at Stratford-upon-Avon. Why, in God's name? you ask, and I can only say that I felt sorry for the organiser, who means well. I shall speak for ten minutes (goodness knows about what), and I shall waste *eight hours* doing it. This includes all the driving, and luncheon with the Priestleys at their new home, Kissing-Tree House, Alveston, just outside Stratford. Angus Wilson is staying with them for the week-end, I believe.

I have just read the new Michael Innes, which is great fun, and am now embarking on Tony Powell's latest. Mind you get the Peter Quennell book: it is reviewed in the current *Spectator* by Evelyn Waugh with a feline savagery which can only come from an old friend with a grudge.

We have a glut of raspberries, now rotting in the rain. The worst of growing fruit is that one either gets *none* or *much too much*. One hates to see it going to waste, but everyone else always has too much at the same moment. Anyhow thank God we're not in Cuba or the Belgian Congo! I can't wait to get back to Kisdon. London life has lost its spell for me. The noise in Soho Square seems to increase daily. Please come and add to it at six on Tuesday.

14 July 1960 *Grundisburgh*

Short measure this week, which should come as welcome relief. I arrived back yesterday to tackle a mountain of scripts on *Julius Caesar*. All the last twenty-four hours the morons of Liverpool College have made hideous with their half-baked ineptitudes. I am always mystified by the beaks of these third-rate schools. They go through the play repeatedly, and you would have thought that one time or another, on meeting the line 'Ate by his side come hot from Hell', someone might have asked and someone might have said who *Ate* was;[1] but so far of forty candidates *not one* has got nearer than saying Ate was Satan. And a good many spell Caesar Ceasar, and that I put to you is even worse than addressing someone called Rupert as Peter. The mystery of that still baffles me.

Tuesday again was an excellent evening—though Ivor, poor man, can't eat kidneys, and old Cuthbert practically can't eat anything. But I have never seen him (C.) in better form. Tim thought Peter F. was too heavy-handed in his ragging of the old chap, but from what

[1] In Greek mythology the goddess of vengeance and mischief.

I saw he thoroughly enjoyed it—and he certainly stayed longer than he normally does.

I say, did you see that dreadful grief that poor dear Pam Spanoghe has had—only daughter, aged eighteen, killed in a motor-accident? It simply doesn't bear thinking of. Elisabeth was the apple of her eye, and, I am pretty sure, her one real happiness in life. She is fond of the son, Benjie, but I think he was always second to E. What *can* one say on these hideous occasions that is of the smallest use? And yet one must say something. Fate is always quite indiscriminating in bestowing rough deals—no sign of ever thinking A. has had enough of them, let's send some to B. who has had few or none. I can't quote it, but Allan Monkhouse made a good remark once to the effect that he wasn't going to be satisfied with any but the best defence that the First Cause put up about the injustices etc of what Henry James called 'this horrible world'. I like the deliberate way in which the old agnostic avoided the name God.

I hope Ruth enjoyed Glyndebourne. I wonder if she met John Christie. He is a very Pickwickian figure now, physically as well as mentally, which he always was. He took enormous trouble over everything at Glyndebourne down to the smallest details. There is something engaging about what one could call the Prussian thoroughness, but for the sly fun in it, that in the cast's lavatories the ladies' seats are of different sizes, because, as J.C. simply explains, the rumps of prima donnas vary greatly in size. He once gravely admitted that the shapes as well as the sizes varied, but regretfully decided that it was too delicate a problem to tackle.

I very much want in October to sit next to D. Somervell, which I haven't done for a very long time. I had quite a lot of talk with Sir C. much of which, on his part, I didn't hear—to his obvious pleasure. I don't think we shall have him with us much longer; he looked incredibly thin and weightless on Tuesday, and I suspect, to use Carlyle's expression, is 'twinkling away' pretty quick.

I hope you are settling down to Oscar in every moment of spare time. No more Stratford jaunts. But you are hopeless.

I thought those kidneys were particularly good, didn't you? But Cuthbert and Ivor between them can eat practically nothing. Cuthbert's presiding kept him well away from me. When I rang up Tim to congratulate him on his barony, he reiterated his belief that Peter was too brutal with C., but I daresay he prefers rough attention to none. I had a good evening with Donald S., Leslie Hartley, Jonah and Tony Powell. In October we must certainly arrange for you to sit next to Donald. If you do, you must encourage him to let me see the anthology of wit which he has been compiling all his life. As I told him again on Tuesday, his retirement is just the time to polish it up and off, so that I can publish it, but he is shy about it.

Yes, I did read the Spanoghe tragedy, and wrote Pam a hopelessly inadequate little letter: it simply doesn't bear thinking of, as you say.

Ruth loved Glyndebourne and reported all the arrangements first-rate, working like clockwork and well thought out. She always sends messages of love and devotion, but I don't always pass them on, fearing to turn your head.

On Wednesday we went to *Ross*, an excellent play about T.E. Lawrence,[1] miraculously well acted by Alec Guinness, which held us both spellbound.

I only wish I could follow your instructions and concentrate on Oscar, but yesterday the proofs of *four* of my most important autumn books arrived simultaneously—bad planning you will say, but one simply has to push books through with different printers as quickly as possible. So goodness knows when I shall get back to Oscar.

Yesterday on my way to Paddington I looked in for half an hour at the nursing home where T.S.E. has taken refuge. What with asthma, breathlessness and determined admirers, peace is hard for him to find. He was in excellent spirits, reading a detective story, with a Penguin book of crossword-puzzles beside him. He is determined to preside at next Tuesday's Annual General Meeting of the London Library, returning immediately to the nursing home. He is unwilling to order a car for the afternoon, mistrusting the discretion of firm or driver (so far are our great men persecuted by the press!) and I have promised

[1] By Terence Rattigan.

to fetch and return him in a taxi. 'You're a great comfort to me', he said, and my heart melted. I truly love him, and so does Ruth—so you see you have a rival!

19 July 1960 *Grundisburgh*

I did nothing about Tim's barony, thinking he would prefer *not* to write a letter. I cannot quite make out—is he now Lord Nugent? Pamela says not but I am not sure. I shall certainly do what I can about Donald Somervell's anthology of wit. He mustn't be shy about it. The late Rev. P.A. Donaldson, Master of Magdalene, used to maintain shyness was a form of conceit. Once at dinner someone couldn't quite remember a certain song, so Donaldson sang it through. He had an unattractive voice.

I am sure old Cuthbert *enjoyed* Peter's badinage. I think he took Peter's list of his pessimistic views as in some obscure way a compliment. But I shall be surprised if he lasts until October; there is *nothing* of him inside those clothes.

I am sorry to hear T.S.E. is so frail. He has been only once to the Lit. Soc. since I have been a member. I had his company and greatly enjoyed it. He is clearly one of the best and nicest of men. I wonder why (or if) he likes Ezra Pound, whose utterances, many of them, reveal him as a really prize ass, but I suppose he isn't really, though I suspect Graham Hough thinks he is. Do you think G.H. is right in his view that whereas Wordsworth's and Coleridge's revolt inaugurated a century of new poetry, T.S.E.'s and Ezra P's 1920's revolt is so far sterile? Do you and can you read Auden? He says nothing to me, but that means nothing. Oh no, I see you share my view of him. What does T.S.E. think of Auden? I read a pleasantly sour review of A's recent volume,[1] though Connolly still seems to think he is very fine—and no doubt he too thinks so.

I wrote this yesterday at the club, and resume now having finished with the young women. They weren't so bad as I expected, their chief defect—as always—being to 'sow with the whole sack'. When asked to describe 'a day at the village school' most of them described

[1] *Homage To Clio* (1960).

the walk to school, the building and furniture, the schoolmistress's appearance and clothes, the two mistresses who succeeded her and the Inspector's visit, which took place once a year. They write like Herodotus in fact, though less entertainingly. Do you remember his tale of how some drug was discovered? It was like the house that Jack built. He began by describing the home of the explorer, then the boat in which he set out to sea, and how he rowed it, then his fishing-tackle, then the fish he caught, and how he extracted its liver from which he extracted the drug. In fact there is every reason for supposing it was nothing less than cod liver oil.

I thought Waugh on the Quennell book poor stuff. Mildly sour without any 'tang' to it. Meanwhile tell me about T.E. Hulme, who, they all say, is very important, and I recall nothing that he ever wrote. I looked at his life in the library and did not find him attractive. But it was fairly petty of the John's people not to admit him to their list of war-dead after 1918, because of some row they had had. I find some claim that T.S.E. owed him a great deal. Is that true?

It is very wrong of you not to hand on anything nice that Ruth says. You don't perhaps realise that my generation of the family is profoundly diffident—quite the opposite of my uncles ('all cheek and charm' as Inge said), who, as a result, all got jobs which they weren't quite up to—except my father who had no ambition at all. But you evidently think my head is easily turned, or perhaps, with the Doctor, that 'there are few things that we so unwillingly give up, even in advanced age, as the supposition that we still have the power of ingratiating ourselves with the fair sex'. Well, I don't care, and continue to send her my very best love, knowing full well though I do, what a peck of dry dust at seventy-seven she must think it (and quite rightly). What *would* life be without illusions?

24 July 1960 *Bromsden Farm*

It is Sunday morning—grey and overcast—and I have more work to do before to-morrow than I can possibly accomplish, even without sleeping to-night. This is partly my fault for having spent most of Friday and Saturday on a jaunt to Stratford. I was driven down by

Diana Campbell-Gray (née Cavendish), a charming widow whom I have known for thirty years. We stayed with my ex-wife, Dame Peggy, in a very comfortable cottage in the country nearby and in the evening saw P. act in *The Taming of the Shrew*—a negligible play which in this production they have made enchanting. I last saw it in 1927, when it was the first play in which I appeared (playing a non-speaking servant) as a student at the Old Vic. This fact, combined with Peggy's astonishing youthfulness and beauty in the part, took me back forcefully, and with exquisite melancholy, to the time when we and the century were in our twenties. This in its turn made me long to write down some impression of those days. My love for Peggy, which will be with me always, was (I now see) chiefly an intellectual and spiritual passion, tied up with poetry and music, drama, youth and spring. Basically it wasn't a physical passion at all—which is why the marriage foundered—but all the rest is still there, although we seldom meet, and a brief visit like this can be an inspiration. Forgive me for pouring it all out to you: it is still very much in my mind, and you are my conscience.

You're quite right about Cuthbert's frailty: when I helped him up from the sofa before dinner it was like lifting a parcel of bones wrapped up in tweed.

T.S.E. wasn't well enough to preside at the Annual General Meeting of the London Library, so I had to ask Harold Nicolson, as Vice-President, to deputise. He agreed with his usual quick kindness, but made a fearful hash of the proceedings, getting things wrong and leaving out some of the agenda, which I managed to force in later. E.M. Forster turned up (as an ordinary member) and I particularly asked Harold to say something nice about him. But H. muttered that he (E.M.F.) was a grossly over-rated writer (which is to some extent true, I think) and scarcely mentioned him. I managed to remedy this, when it came to my turn to present the Report, by saying a few words about the sale, and pointing out that, except for the chap who gave us £10,000 anonymously some years ago, E.M.F. (by giving that manuscript which fetched £6500) was the greatest single benefactor in the Library's history. This got him a round of applause—which he certainly deserved—and made him beam with pleasure.

Next day I visited T.S.E. in the nursing home to report. He was in excellent spirits, but his breathing is very bad. He is hoping to go home to-morrow, and to his wife's family in Leeds on Thursday. Later they're going to Scarborough for a fortnight, but I fear they will have left before R. and I get to Kisdon, whence we could easily have driven over to see them.

As for Ezra Pound, he is (or rather was) one of those people whose *influence* is infinitely greater and more important than their writings. He undoubtedly had a great and beneficial influence on both Yeats and Eliot, and yet his own works seem to me largely wind and rubbish. T.E. Hulme wrote practically nothing, and I think you can safely pass him by.

Your description of Herodotus and your female examinees reminds me of the Warburg Institute, for they feel obliged to trace every irrelevance back to its origin, so that forward movement becomes almost impossible. I hope you will read Quennell: as a book it lacks shape and cohesion, but there are fine things in it, and it is beautifully written.

If you don't hear from me again you will know that I have been suffocated by the proofs of other people's books.

27 July 1960 *Grundisdurgh*

Plebeian paper I grant you, but I can no other. Next week I should have my head above water, and see about a visit to the Ipswich stationer. But even that is not certain, as in a rash moment I said I would look over and mark essays by juveniles at Oxford schools—the whole thing organised by the Oxford Preservation Trust. Well last year about seven schools sent altogether thirty–forty essays. This year one school kicks off by sending 101; their manuscripts are of all shapes and sizes, elaborately bound and illustrated by themselves—a really ghastly job, and I am plucking up courage to send them all back with a few well-chosen words of hatred and contempt. And I' rather think my eyes may be temporarily giving out. Little bouts of double vision—one eye at cross-purposes with the other. The doctor plays his comfortable trump card by saying it 'will probably pass off. It is not the thing to say then 'But supposing it doesn't'.

I love your 'pouring out' as you call it. What else are great friends there for? Your story is a wonderfully interesting one—and oddly enough has a strong resemblance to H.G. Wells's first marriage, which I was reading about yesterday.

They still refuse to cough up P. Quennell's book in the library, though I know it has been accepted. In *John o' London* last week there was an article about English words, and *inter alia* the wrongness of 'from whence'. I remember Cardus was on the mat for using it, and when he feebly said x. and y. well-known writers used it, the formidable C.P. Scott said: 'They wouldn't have in my paper'. C. ought to have taken leave of C.P.S. with the words 'Then I will lift up mine eyes unto the hills from whence cometh my help'. But I suppose he would have been instantly sacked.

Harold Nicolson ought to have remembered that, on an occasion like the L.L. general meeting, mentioning benefactors is in the same category as obituaries; 'In lapidary inscriptions a man is not upon oath.'[1] I rather agree with you both about E.M.F. It is odd that no one has ever set about debunking him—or have they? I was much bored not long ago by *The Longest Journey*, but then, as you know, I am poor at novels.

Shall we ever see T.S.E. at the Lit. Soc. again? He sounds in rather poor case, I fear. All the examinees in the G.C.E. (Alternative Ordinary) paper wrote of him with great respect—obviously dictated—though they based it on qualities which I rather doubt his claiming. What would he think of 'child-like', 'old-fashioned', 'bitter' and 'very reminiscent of Pope'? The cumulative effect of reading second-hand pretentious rubbish is in the end depressing. One lot of candidates referred with airy omniscience to Baudelaire, Dante, and Nietzsche; one young puppy was condescending about Nietzsche's 'phrose' (*sic*).

30 July 1960 *Bromsden Farm*

This last week has been a nightmare of proof-reading and index-making, from which I am still reeling. Oscar has now lain untouched for five weeks. Although there are two long manuscripts to be read

[1] Doctor Johnson.

and corrected, I brought down also the Oscar galleys, together with an armful of letters and notes which have collected, and this afternoon stole half an hour for the old labour. The delay doesn't matter much, except that for proper annotation and cross-reference one should have *everything* in one's head, and mine is now stuffed with irrelevant and boring details of the R.H-D. autumn publications.

Did you see that Duff got a second in Greats? I think it very creditable, since he was up for only three years (instead of the usual Greats four) and did a lot of other things as well. Now he is in search of a journalistic job, and the *Sunday Times* (Roy Thomson group) boys are proving most helpful.

I hate to hear of your eyes playing you tricks; couldn't you arrange to correct *fewer* rather than more exam-papers, which you seem to be doing just now?

I doubt whether we shall ever again see T.S.E. at the Lit. Soc. Apart from his physical weakness, he is so happy at home. They went off to Leeds last week to stay with her mother.

Comfort came up to London last week and went to a couple of theatres, which she enjoyed. She stayed at the flat, but I scarcely saw her, so engrossed was I in everybody's proofs. One night I dined with Veronica Wedgwood, where I met Sir Somebody Something, one of the joint heads of the Treasury, and so one of our chief rulers. He might have appeared, without make-up, as 'Self-Love' or 'Complacency' in a morality-play like *Everyman*, though his performance might have been thought a little exaggerated. As you will have gathered, I didn't take to him. When we left it was pouring with rain: he had a government car and chauffeur waiting but was too nervous to take us an inch out of his own way, so I and another chap were deposited in a streaming Oxford Street. God save us from such piddling bureaucrats!

Ruth is still overwhelmed by her grandchildren, but directly they all go back to Italy we shall hasten to our beloved Kisdon. About August 24 or so.

Have you got Lytton Strachey's *Portraits in Miniature*? I took it down this morning and read the little essay on Carlyle: some good things in it. Have a look.

Only eight grandchildren! I shall tell Ruth how lucky she is only having two. Please give my respectful greetings to the lovely Rose, and congratulate Bobby on winning the Cricket Cup after his Henley triumphs. Did I tell you that Adam *did* get his Middle Club in the end? So his scug-cap days are over. Mine never were.

3 August 1960 *Grundisburgh*

It really is heart-rending to hear that for five weeks you haven't been able to get at Oscar. You must be in a continuous state of irritation, and what is more wearing than that? Shall you get some chance at Kisdon? Winston or somebody defined the perfect holiday as 'a change of work', but there should be at least a period of *dolce far niente* at first.

I am delighted to hear of Duff's second in Greats. All the *best* men have got seconds from Newman downwards. Housman was ploughed, C.B. Fry got a fourth. People like Blue-tooth Baker[1] get firsts, do nothing very striking, and end up as Warden of Winchester. About the most brilliant scholar ever at Eton was Carr Bosanquet, of whom you have never heard—irretrievably lost as some kind of permanent official.[2] But one thing he did which should not be allowed to die. He described *The Yellow Book* as a book 'which binders would buy to bind and bounders would be bound to buy'. Which I am sure you will agree is pretty good. You have a good brainy pair of sons—but I am sorry to see Adam did not figure in the schools' chess championship. I expect he is more pleased with his cricket colours. Why *shouldn't* he get his XI next year?

My 'diplopia'[3] is nothing to do with excessive reading of exam-papers, and indeed is really very unimportant. Some years ago an oculist said I had 'splendid eyes'. As I have worn specs since 1900 I demurred, to which he said 'Oh yes, the focusing needs adjusting, but I was speaking of their sound lasting prospects; they will easily last your time'. And it is true they have never ached or given me the smallest trouble.

[1] Harold Trevor ('Bluey') Baker, Liberal politician (1877–1960).

[2] Robert Carr Bosanquet (1871–1935), archaeologist. Director of the British School of Archaeology in Athens 1900–1906.

[3] Double vision.

Quennell is still on his way, and I am first on the list. I shan't be disappointed. The *shape* of a book never enters my consciousness, but the *writing* does. Ivor gave me a month ago his *Dark Ladies* (i.e. Helen, Sappho, Cleopatra, and *the* Dark Lady) which I enjoyed, but entirely understood why, as he told me, it had no sale. There is too much historical information, and there isn't now the interest in (or knowledge of the background of) those old myth-histories that there used to be. It astonishes me all the more that Druon's book should be so popular (though delighted for the publisher's sake). I frankly found it rather hard going—so many bloodthirsty battles and necessarily all the same, and I couldn't somehow get very much interested in Alexander himself. But I *am* enjoying the Andrew Young poems[1]—so lovely and *short*, and every one with its flavour, and very soon shall be enjoying the Stanley book.[2] *Thank* you, as always. Stanley once came and lectured to the prep-school where I was. I can't imagine how they got him, as I suppose he was then (1893) at the top of his fame. For a long time he was looked on as a pushing little bounder, but I suspect he was a pretty good man, and that public opinion, led by the papers, was just as untrustworthy in the Nineties as in the subsequent Sixties.

Sir Somebody Something! Yes, you make me shudder. Those stuffed shirts are—what is the word? Shall I venture on 'rebarbative'? Rather a good mouthful, but I am not absolutely sure what it means. Couldn't you somehow have managed to hit him in the wind or even tread on his toe? Jacks-in-office are the devil.

I thought I had *Portraits in Miniature*, but it seems to have vanished. I seem to remember old Carlyle being described as 'that dry, neglected crater', as of an extinct volcano, which I suppose he is. So few appear to be conscious of (a) his enormous power of pen and (b) his glorious humour. But you and I know all right.

Next week I go to Cambridge for a week for tedious (but not badly paid) work on the G.C.E. borderline cases, and rectifying the blunders of examiners. I shall be here to get your letter, and shall answer it from the University Arms Hotel, which will be full of Yanks, affable but strident. Humphrey and family will be here just when I am not.

[1] His *Collected Poems* (1960).

[2] *Stanley's Way* by Thomas Sterling (1960).

Did you see about his loss of his trumpet and its return? It was actually in the 9 o'clock news, being apparently of equal importance with Lumumba and Castro and Cousins etc. No doubt some genial gossip-writer will hint that he had it stolen on purpose—like a film-star's jewels. I once asked who William Hickey was, and got the caustic answer that he was several people. 'No one man, or even woman, could be such a cad as W.H.'—a nice wide-flung denigration.

Luncheon is imminent and I must stop. It will be a good noisy meal, though luckily not all at one table. The children are in the kitchen, the grown-ups in the staff-hall next door. Two of my grandsons are born teddy-boys, their motto being that anything like a book, hat, tool, or utensil of any kind is merely there to be destroyed, damaged or thrown away *quam celerrime*. One of the most boring traits in *all* the young is the irresistible urge to take away my stick. But there is a Mede and Persian law on *your* stick, which so far holds good. I shall bring it to the October Lit. Soc.; but am pleased to tell you that *at least* four people have already said it is the best they ever saw. But perhaps it will bore you stiff. You must pretend it doesn't. Apropos of boring I picked up the Shaw-Mrs Patrick Campbell correspondence after many years and found it *quite intolerable*. His voluble amorousness in letter after letter very quickly turned my stomach. What do *you* think? Give my love to Ruth. The idea of her as a grandmother is wholly incongruous. But then Nature *is* incongruous. My aunt Georgina married Lord Leicester and found *two* step-daughters several years older than herself.

6 August 1960 *Bromsden Farm*

This heavy sunless weather induces, I find, an immense lassitude, not to say sleepiness, which goes ill with work of any kind. Today I drove over to Wiltshire to lunch with the Devlins, and it was all I could do to keep awake, even on the way *there*!

On Monday Comfort and Adam are journeying to Scotland, to spend a fortnight with my sister, so write to Soho Square this week. On Friday Ruth and I are nipping over to Dieppe for the week-end. We plan to bathe and eat and laze, and visit Oscar's post-prison retreats. We both need freshening up—the grandchildren are overpowering Ruth—and we can't get away to Kisdon till the 24th. I shall try and scribble you a line from a café-table.

Duff looks like starting his journalistic career on the *Western Mail* at Cardiff in a week or two. Meanwhile he is toiling nobly in the garden.

Carr Bosanquet's quip about *The Yellow Book* is brilliantly good. I warned you (or meant to warn you) that *Alexander the God* wasn't up to Druon's usual standard. I knew you'd like Andrew Young, and you'll certainly enjoy the Stanley book. Incidentally, after I had passed Diana Cooper's proofs for press, what should I find but the hideous LYTTLETON (referring to Oliver)! An S.O.S. to the printer just caught it. Phew! What would you have said to me?

I'm much looking forward to meeting my stick in October: I daresay it will be a case of love at first sight.

To-day, when I might at last be spending an hour with Oscar, I am (for love of Max) correcting the proofs of Sam Behrman's forthcoming book on him (not published by me).[1] In it he records Max as saying that he was so disgusted by the Shaw-Campbell letters that he couldn't finish the book: so you are in good company. Now I am going to bed: more in the morning.

Sunday morning

After nine hours' sleep I feel a little brisker, and it's as well, for there is plenty to be done. Yesterday when I reached the Devlins, I found the judge in a secluded corner of the garden on a *chaise-longue*, reading a book on birth-control. 'Too late to be any use , he said, ruefully indicating his delightful family of four sons and two daughters. I think he might be an excellent member of the Lit. Soc.

On Tuesday I am making a lightning dash to Edinburgh to see the Estate Duty people about Dorothy Walpole's estate. Admirable though my co-executor is (he's a Writer to the Signet) his knowledge of copyright and publishing procedure is minimal. I am travelling each way by day—first class at the Estate's expense, 4 p.m.–10.40 p.m. This will give me more than twelve hours in which to read and correct a typescript about the Marconi Scandal. I am to spend the intervening

[1] *Conversation with Max* by S.N. Behrman (1960).

night with Robin Walpole, the surviving brother. I feel sure those two days will be the hottest and sunniest of the summer.

Adam is now learning to drive—on our car—and I tremble for the clutch and brakes. No news of his A levels yet: I think the end of August is the time. I shall think of you in Cambridge, discussing pass-marks with your fellow-examiners and going to strip-tease movies in the evenings.

10 August 1960 *Grundisburgh*

I have greatly enjoyed the Stanley book, and am glad to be corroborated in my belief that, for all his bounding and pomposity, he was a fine and immensely tough chap. How he survived really passes one's comprehension. And I rejoice to have my opinion of Shaw's letters corroborated by M.B. What other support on a question of literary taste is needed?

I say, Rupert, your autumn list! If I wasn't quite sure I had quoted Mr Squeers before I would now. Druon back again on his own ground, Peter Fleming, and old Shaw on music—about which he is always first-rate reading. Also his dramatic criticism. I was delighted to find Max, when I met him at Butterwick's, put it at the top of his writings. Why does one never hear of Janet Achurch except from him? And he put her right among the Terrys and Bernhardts. *Trumpets from the Steep* is a fine challenging title[1]—if one precisely knew its relevance. I am taking Middleton Murry and Ivor's *Shakespeare in his Time* to Cambridge—and a new Carter Dickson for bedtime. Mind you tell me if and when you ever come across a first-rate detective story. The last Allingham I read was very poor.

I have got used to Lyttleton (though always annoyed by it). Half the pedagogues who send me exam-papers get it wrong. I feel inclined to fire Housman at them: 'Accuracy is not a virtue; it is a duty'. Yet another book about the chippy old Cassandra by a Yank lady called Hawkins. She claims to have talked repeatedly with Gow—who denies ever having heard of her. She says *inter alia* that the Oxford exam called 'Moderates' (*sic*) has as its Cambridge equivalent the 'Littlego',

[1] Of the third volume of Diana Cooper's autobiography.

in which Housman examined. It surely is not easy to be much wronger than that.

Odd that you should mention Behrman, because I have just returned to Wilfrid Blunt a lot of stuff by him on Max B. Talks, not yet gathered into a book—which surely must be the one you are proof-reading? Is M.B.'s remark about the Shaw letters in it? Because I didn't notice it. Anyway my memory nowadays is hopeless.

Why not Mr Justice Devlin in the Lit. Soc.? Judges are almost always the ripest company (I was omitting the 'almost' when I suddenly remembered old Avory, whose talk I believe was as dry as his skin, and one can't say more than that).

That was a sour leader in *The Times* about the Oxford by-pass. They *must*, as David Cecil says, take it at *any* cost well clear of Oxford. (But they won't.) We are all engaged in plans and policies which were profoundly stigmatised by Juvenal, '*propter vitam vivendi perdere causas*',[1] or in our own less dignified idiom 'not putting first things first'. Did you see that remark by a woman in a traffic-block in Oxford 'They never ought to have put a university here'.

Love to Ruth. Why has the poor dear to take her grandchildren so seriously? Probably because she is a much more conscientious grandmother than I am a grandfather.

P.S. I have just discovered that there was a saint Bugga (*D.N.B.*). It almost reconciles me to the approaching collapse of civilisation.

P.S. *In Quest of a Mermaid*[2] is *good* reading. What a real fairy godmother you are!

13 August 1960 *Bromsden Farm*

As you see, I am not in a waterside café in Dieppe, awash with brandy and local wine, but at my old post in my library, with the rain falling steadily outside. We had to cancel our trip because Ruth felt she couldn't leave all her family, and maybe it was just as well, for the seamen's strike seems to have disorganised all yesterday's Channel services.

[1] 'For the sake of life to lose life's aim.' (Juvenal, *Satires* 8, 83).

[2] By J.H. ('Elephant Bill') Williams (1960).

Duff and I are here alone, but tomorrow if it's fine enough, Ruth is going to bring down a carful of her family for a picnic lunch.

Duff is expecting a call to begin his life's work at Cardiff, and meanwhile he is feverishly repainting the kitchen as a surprise birthday-present for Comfort. This evening he went to a cocktail-party nearby and on the way home shot three rabbits from the car with a .22 rifle. Nothing like being an all-rounder!

How are the giddy examiners at Cambridge? Plenty of night-life for them I hope. Tell them to read the strip-tease article in this week's *Spectator*, and they'll surely arrange the next examiners' meeting in Soho.

My trip to Edinburgh went according to plan. Very comfortable all-Pullman first-class carriage, in which, each way, I consumed a whacking tea and an immense dinner. The tea was especially good, and since it is a meal I usually miss, I particularly enjoyed it. I stayed comfortably with Hugh Walpole's brother, and woke on Wednesday morning to hot sunshine and a sky of unclouded blue. Edinburgh was looking its loveliest, and I rejoiced to see so many of its noble squares and crescents unharmed. The Estate Duty people proved very amenable, and the interview was over so quickly that I managed to fit in three-quarters of an hour in the best of secondhand bookshops. Altogether a most agreeable interlude. I have always liked Edinburgh, though I daresay one would tire of it eventually. Only ten days now—and then Kisdon, *laus Deo*!

Sunday morning

The sun is shining, but Ruth has just telephoned to say they can't come after all, as her daughter isn't well. So Duff will carry on with his painting, and I, inspired by his example, shall do some needed tidying and gardening. Peter and all his family are shooting grouse in Scotland. Oscar is with me, but untouched: at Kisdon I simply must read him straight through, but I should like to get rid of all the attendant letters and notes (a thick pile) before we leave.

Last Thursday I went to Sotheby's (now closed for the recess, after doing a year's business of almost *seven million pounds*) to see about the approaching sale of Max's books etc from Rapallo—a very touching but intensely amusing and interesting collection, for Max used to annotate and illustrate everything. Merton are to have enough to make a permanent exhibition in the Max Room, and the rest are to be sold. Mrs Reichmann, the owner, is threatening to give me one of the most valuable books, but I don't think she should be so generous. Across the room (at Sotheby's) was the splendid library of C.H. Wilkinson of Worcester College, waiting to be catalogued. It isn't so much the worms who get everything in the end, as the auctioneers. Except for insurance, auctioneering is surely the safest racket imaginable—no risk, a sure percentage, and endless material (including often the same objects sold again and again). And they're all immensely pleased with themselves, as though they were creating the masterpieces they sell. But I suppose an annual turnover of £7,000,000 is enough to turn the solidest head.

Now I must stop chattering to you and do some useful work. The trouble is I much prefer the chattering. How many million words have we by now exchanged? Enough anyhow till next Saturday. Write *here* this week.

18 August 1960 *Cambridge*

This will be rather a scrappy affair, I fear, as we are a good deal behindhand—owing to a posse of imbecile examiners who give three for a set of answers that deserve thirteen and vice versa, and then write reports which we spend half a day re-writing in English. Well you see what we are up against. Two of our examiners, moreover, have almost totally illegible hands, and one has the impudence to pick holes in the scripts of the candidates. There have been one or two good things, e.g. in the essay on 'Jazz' in which several candidates mention Humphrey and one writes 'Humphrey Littleton (always so spelt) is the leading English trumpeter, and—like many others—plays best when he is drunk'. What can one do about that? We have been once or twice to the pictures—nothing much until last night when we saw Edith Evans in *The Importance of Being Earnest*. Excellent fun, though some of the wisecracks date very emphatically. I was interested to see Dorothy Tutin, who is whole-heartedly adored, believe it or not, by Granny Gow. I don't blame him. Her Cicely was entirely charming. I haven't read the play for years, and please tell me if: Lady

B. 'My nephew tell lies?? Impossible! He was at Oxford' is a gag or not. I have a strong suspicion that it is—but it got the loudest laugh of the evening.[1] Margaret Rutherford was somehow wrongly cast for Miss Prism—too bulky and amiable, but the rest were all right. What a magnificent absurdity it is—and how O.W. must have enjoyed writing it.

You must tell me all about the sale of M.B.'s books—and of *course* you must keep whatever is given you. Sotheby's *would* make £7m p.a. now that Cyril Butterwick is one of them. He always falls on his feet and must put by a tidy annual packet. Whenever he bought a share it at once rocketed—and fell like a stone the day after he sold it. Mine always do the opposite.

I am reading Middleton Murry in bed. A good critic surely, but I find it very easy to get out of my depth with his aesthetics. I am delighted to see that *Lady Chatterley* is again postponed. One of my colleagues says that, unexpurgated, it is D.H.L.'s best novel. He is a northern professor of philosophy and ought to know better. But the inner circle of D.H.L. fans are deranged in their wits. Leavis is only about 450 yards away from this hotel. I shall not call upon him.

Apologies for this vapid (and rapid) scrap, but you won't mind with Kisdon so near. Keep Ruth's family away with broom and bayonet—and give her my love.

20 August 1960 *Bromsden Farm*

The blessed day approaches. If you should suffer from insomnia on Tuesday night, think of us at 4 a.m. on Wednesday, when we shall set out from Soho Square in Ruth's tiny car, lights on, streets empty. Out through St Albans and Dunstable to Northampton. At 6 a.m. we stop by the roadside for coffee (from a thermos) and biscuits. Mounting excitement as the morning lightens. On through Market Harborough and Leicester to a road which bypasses everything till at 8 a.m. we reach Bawtry, just south of Doncaster and *inside Yorkshire*. There we breakfast at the Crown Hotel. Sundry shopping at Bedale,

[1] 'Untruthful! My nephew Algernon? Impossible! He is an Oxonian'! (*The Importance of Being Earnest,* act iii).

Leyburn and Hawes; a picnic luncheon high on the pass between Wensleydale and Swaledale—first taste of that incomparable air and silence—then drop down into Swaledale and report at 2 p.m. to our farmer, who will be ready to drive us up Kisdon in his tractor, with all our luggage, books and provisions. Thereafter perfection.

Meanwhile the best news is that Adam has been awarded a State Scholarship, which seems to me excellent at seventeen. So far as I can gather from the mass of bumf they've sent, you get £50 a year even if you're a millionaire, and the rest (if any) depends on your income. He and Comfort come back from Scotland on Monday night, and I shall give them breakfast in London on Tuesday.

Duff starts his reporting at Cardiff on Monday. He has blued his savings (£200) on a 1955 Ford Popular, which looks sensible and roadworthy.

I am desperately trying to tidy everything up before Wednesday, so as to keep Kisdon for Oscar and idleness, but no sooner have I cleared everything off than some other horror crops up.

Your Cambridge outing didn't sound very gay. I certainly don't remember that line in *The Importance*, but will look it up. Fancy Granny Gow falling for Dorothy Tutin: he should journey to Stratford to see her Cressida, which is said to be excellent.

The question of my present from Max's sister-in-law is now happily resolved. She wanted to give me the plum of the whole collection (a biography of Bernard Shaw heavily annotated and extra-illustrated by Max), which Sotheby's have valued at £500+. I managed to persuade her to give me instead (1) a first edition of Oscar's *An Ideal Husband*, with a caricature of Oscar by Max on the flyleaf; (2) Max's copy of the first edition of *The Importance*, inscribed to him by Oscar, and with four most interesting notes by Max. These Sotheby's had valued at £150 and £200, so I have done pretty well, and am quite delighted. Both books have suffered forty years of Rapallo sun, but inside they're fine.

I have been asked if I am willing to be called as a witness for the defence of *Lady Chatterley*, and shall reluctantly agree. I'm all against the prosecution, though in fact I think it a sentimental, contrived and occasionally ridiculous work. Anyhow they must surely have plenty of more important witnesses.

Some of Ruth's family have gone back to Italy, but she won't escape from the others till we drive north. She is exhausted, poor lamb, and I daresay we shall break even our own high record for hours of sleep. We usually have a coal fire in the bedroom, and dropping off to sleep there in the flickering light, in the certain knowledge that one won't wake for ten hours, is so unspeakably agreeable that I sometimes try to keep awake a little longer to prolong the enjoyment. Very different from the incessant car-park noises in Soho. As you can see, my thoughts are there already, and I have to keep pulling myself back to the proofs and manuscripts which must be coped with before I leave.

I had a most touching letter from Geoffrey Faber, resigning from the Lit. Soc. because he now realises he will probably never see London again. This makes a vacancy, and the whole cumbersome business of an election (which I was hoping to avoid this year) will begin again in November.

Next week's letter will be pastoral-rhapsodical, and I may call in Ruth as collaborator.

24 August 1960 *Grundisburgh*

I get a vicarious glow from all you say about Kisdon—before, during, and after. My mind's eye reproduces it very convincingly as resembling that enchanting country along the Roman wall, or that surrounding the hamlet—it may be no more than a farm—which has the appealing name of Pity Me, which is somewhere up in the Walter Scott country, or at any rate Melrose. As to the mind's ear, I conceive the cough of a sheep or an occasional curlew as pretty well all you hear when the wind is low. What of the mind's *nose*? The sense of smell is the most vivid remembrancer of all five. Now and then I am recalled instantaneously to the prep-school I went to in 1892. What are the 'murmurs and scents of the infinite'—'weald' shall we say instead of 'sea'[1] or is it a little too literary and garden-of-Englandy? Four a.m. is a noble hour to start at. Please tell me exactly what you have for breakfast at Bawtry. It should surely be one of those great breakfasts

[1] Matthew Arnold, 'The Future'.

of fifty years ago. The North used to be good at them. I still remember the one I had at Scotch Corner thirty years ago. Wensleydale and Swaledale!—you must by then be feeling as full of music as Milton was when he wrote of 'Horonaim, Seon's realm, beyond The flowry dale of Sibma, clad with vines'.[1] Let me share your happiness in that lovely land you will reach at the otherwise prosaic hour of 2 p.m. Every and any daily detail will be a delight.

What a very distinguished pair of sons you have. That State Scholarship is a fine achievement. Will Adam go for a scholarship at Oxford in December? He sounds of the right calibre, and Etonians nowadays do sometimes get science scholarships, which they never did in my day, though one or two, like Alfred Egerton,[2] went to the top eventually, plus an ornithologist or two. Does Duff start by sending 'stories' about a man found dead at Bognor, which are ignored or cut down to four lines? Don't even the Montagues and Nevinsons start like that?[3]

Cambridge *wasn't* very gay—the whole day practically taken up with reading the work of the victims of very inept teaching. A name here and there pleased me. Among Browns and Joneses of some very English school there suddenly appeared *Parapolidikok* which I assure you is real, though it oughtn't to be. One good story I heard, which I hope you haven't. Old Maugham, talking to a girls' school about the art of writing short stories, told them that the essential ingredients were religion, sex, mystery, high rank, non-literary language and brevity. The schoolmistress next day told her young charges to try their hand at writing one according to this recipe. After a minute one raised her hand and said she had finished. The incredulous mistress told her to read it out, and she did: 'My God!', said the duchess, 'I'm pregnant. I wonder who done it'. That girl should surely go far.

Lady Chatterley. It is absolutely essential that you should not for a moment think that I am in *full* disagreement with you. I wholly agree that this police-court attempt at censorship is ridiculous. The fatuity

[1] *Paradise Lost*, book I.

[2] Alfred Egerton (1886–1959), Professor of Chemical Technology in the University of London. Knighted 1943.

[3] C.E. Montague (1867–1928) and H.W. Nevinson (1856–1941), leading journalists.

of a lot of men in the jurybox, every one of them straight out of a drawing by the late George Morrow[1], listening to E.M. Forster testifying to the deathless beauty of *Lady C.* cannot be described in words. But what nauseates me is the flood of *cant* which so very many of those who support the publication pour out. I read that there are 250,000 copies ready, and what the defenders say (or imply) is that this mass of readers wants to read it because it is a (or *the*) masterpiece of the great genius D.H.L. And everybody knows that the great sale will be to all the adolescents in the country who, like George Forsyte, have a liking for the 'nubbly bits'. I have actually heard a man maintain that the book, expurgated, may be dreary, but the addition of D.H.L.'s fourth-form physiological crudities makes it a work of genius. If my view is Victorian, well I can't help it—but I would maintain that the inhibitions, the dislike of seeing all these crude words for the sexual functions flung onto the page, are every bit as 'natural' as the impulse to fling them. It was wrong to write the book, and it is wrong to print it. Them's my views. 1883 was a great year for 'squares'.

Comic, your saying Gow should go to see D. Tutin at Stratford. He has already been, I think twice! He has seen every part she has played in, and is just as critical over the way she plays as over a colleger's elegiacs. What pleases him is her acceptance of and agreement with his strictures. Old Edith Evans, of course, was splendid as Lady Bracknell, but I was rather horrified by her striking ugliness. She is plainer now than Dame Edith Sitwell, and one can't say more than that. Have you heard any of these poetry recitals by the authors? Someone told me that the records of Dylan Thomas reading are magnificent. I remember thinking him the only one worth listening to when he was alive. The Dame, I gather, is inaudible.

Best love to Ruth. Don't go and say that I have sent '*regards*'. I like to think of her enjoying peace perfect peace, with loved ones far away. Mind you both come back completely rested, ready to face even the world of 1960 with equanimity.

[1] *Punch* artist (1870–1955).

I went outside just now to write to you, but the fickle sun withdrew, so I am back in our sitting-room at the big table. On the other side of it Ruth is working away at Oscar, checking the formidable lists of recipients and manuscript-locations. This letter won't go down the hill until our farmer comes up to milk in the late evening, so won't be collected till to-morrow, and should with luck reach you on Wednesday. Your letter was faithfully brought up by the farmer on Thursday. Our drive north went according to plan, except that it rained the whole way, and three different minor things went wrong with the car, so that we reached Bawtry three quarters of an hour late. We did indeed have a fine breakfast there—porridge and what they call 'a full house', i.e. egg, bacon, sausage and tomato, with masses of toast, butter, marmalade and tea. Since we got here we haven't left our hilltop except for a brief shopping expedition to Hawes on Saturday. Yesterday was my fifty-third birthday, and we celebrated it cosily in blissful isolation. Apart from its magical view, the first thing that strikes one with wonder here is the complete *silence*—a blessing almost unknown in most places today. At this moment for instance, with the door open, I can hear *nothing* except the tick of the grandfather clock and the faint bubbling of a milk pudding which R. is cooking on the range. The mildest cheep of a bird, let alone the mournful cry of the curlew, is a noticeable event, and when there is no wind (as now) we can occasionally hear the distant barking of a dog far down the valley. The weather has been mixed, with rain most days and intermittent sun, but we are equally contented indoors and out. We have never been to the Roman Wall, but I feel sure your comparison is pretty exact. We have often planned that and other such expeditions, but once we get here we never want to move, and our days seem so few and so fleeting. One day perhaps we shall have world enough and time. You ask about smells, and I don't quite know how to answer, for one's first impression is of the astonishing *absence* of smells, and of the purity and freshness of the moorland air. Just now, when the sun shines there is also the lovely smell of cut grass, for the wretched hill-farmers, who began their haymaking in June, are still not through with it. The field in front of us is cut but not gathered, and field behind not even cut. Three fine sunny days and we shall be helping with large wooden rakes, as we did last year.

So far we have slept ten or eleven hours each night, with an occasional after-lunch nap as well. Our promised tap and pipe are not yet fixed, so we still climb a stone wall each morning and fetch six gallons of lovely spring-water from the next field. Our two Aladdin lamps still warm our evenings, and for my birthday Ruth gave me a little lamp for my side of the bed: she already has one on hers. (Suddenly I hear the bleating of sheep far away: probably being driven somewhere by dogs.)

Adam's A-Level results read:

CHEMISTRY:	DISTINCTION
PHYSICS:	DISTINCTION
MATHS:	DISTINCTION
GENERAL PAPER:	PASS

which shows how good he must be at his own subjects, and also the dangers of starting to specialise at fifteen. We are thinking of putting him in for an Oxford scholarship in December, with a preference for Merton, where there is a closed science scholarship for Etonians as well as open ones. If he got one he could then spend nine months doing some non-scientific subject (probably languages) before going up. He should be in Sixth Form his last two halves.

We have just been out to look at the flock of sheep which are being driven up on to the fell on the other side of the valley. I've had one cheerful letter from Duff, saying that accommodation in Cardiff seems to be plentiful and cheap (he has already been offered a double bed-sitter for 30/- a week) but not describing his work, which I have now asked him to do.

Most poets are shocking readers: Dame Edith is indeed largely inaudible, but Yeats was grand and Dylan Thomas superb. Cecil Day Lewis is also very good, but most of the rest are agony to hear.

How Green gets more and more reproachful on the shelf. Since we got here I have read a new Simenon, John Fothergill's *Innkeeper's Diary* (I find J.F. was a friend of Oscar's and so worth searching) and part of the proofs of an immense (and immensely too long) biography of the Nineties poet Richard Le Gallienne (another friend of O's), kindly lent me by Martin Secker. I am also studying (with the aid of a tiny dictionary) the egregiously full notes to a German edition of *De Profundis: 'Clapham Junction ist eine der belebtesten Londoner Vorortstationen'* and things like that. If I don't break the back of the Oscar work here, I simply don't know how or when it will be done: here only is peace. Ruth sends much love and says she is already looking forward to seeing you in October.

30 and 31 August 1960 *Grundisburgh*

A blank Tuesday morning post—as of course is apt to happen when you are at Kisdon, so I am writing this at the club in Ipswich where I have finished the papers and am storm-bound by the punctual daily downpour. I do hope you are not getting all this monstrous hysterics of Nature, though it might be all to the benefit of Oscar. I still await some 300 papers from British Guiana, and have a faint hope that they may have been sunk on the journey. *Wednesday*. Still no letter. You are probably cut off from any postal facilities. I shall post this after the second delivery today. The possibility must always be considered that one of the chores which you are delighted to get away from is your weekly letter to G.W.L.

Well now, what is there from Suffolk? Little of interest I fear—and it becomes daily clearer that quite soon there will be as big a gulf between me and what is going on as there was between Abraham and Dives. My attitude to the daily paper is almost Balfourian. It is no good reading about Cuba, the Congo, Ceylon, Algeria etc unless one has followed all the news from the start—and even then! I am *not* excited by a young English girl getting a bronze medal for swimming. And, apropos of the Games, will you kindly tell me what *repêchage* means? French presumably, but it rings no bell, though it is now compulsory in any article about the games. Yesterday I browsed for an hour in the library on *Shakespeare and Company* by Sylvia Beach. Is it very fine? I was handicapped by ignorance of most of her dramatis personae; but to you I suppose Bryher, Djuna Barnes, Adrienne Monnier, Harriet Weaver, Eugene Jolas, George Antheil, Robert

McAlmon, Archibald McLeish, Valery Larbaud and Stuart Gilbert are household names? I have never heard of a single one, and so the lavish praise each gets from Miss Beach leaves me rather cold. There is a tremendously grim and formidable photograph of T.S.E. Am I right in surmising that it was taken just after he read or had been asked his opinion of *Ulysses?* The meeting between Joyce and C.K. Ogden must have been interesting—one wanting enormously to develop and enlarge English vocabulary, the other to reduce it to 500 words. I haven't the smallest interest in either, so write me down an ass and a philistine.

I say, the *Lit. Sup.*!! The two main articles last week were on the Soviet Cinema and the poet John Oldham. Is this remotely sane? It looks as if Pryce-Jones's feelings as he contemplates his successor may be much the same as those of Sin when she first saw her offspring Death.

I was a good deal bored by Swinburne's letters—all that interminable stuff about Hotten and Chatto should surely have been cut down. And I found the informative notes on the origin of such expressions as 'tender mercies' and 'apple of his eye' very irritating. I suppose Yankee editors are like that. S's deep interest in flagellation is very odd to my Victorian mind, and his eulogies of Count de Sade, but I know little about such anfractuosities of the human mind. What I *should* like to know about is his friendship with Jowett, who cannot really have had much in common with de Sade. Where does the story come from of S., staying with J., sitting in a neighbouring room to one where J. was taking a tutorial, and from time to time a high triumphant screech from S. (who was reading some classical researches of J's) 'Another howler, Master, another howler!' and a demure 'Thank you, Algernon' from next door? It is an engaging tale—not, I think, told in these letters.[1]

I like Andrew Young very much, though I don't always follow him. But the proof of how little I know about modern poetry is that the comments and dicta of modern critics on these poems are *completely* mystifying.

[1] But in *The Life of Algernon Charles Swinburne* by Edmund Gosse (1917), p. 213.

Wednesday, second post.

All well; letter on hall-table. Thank you for breakfast menu at Bawtry. I was with you in spirit. Smells. Yes, cut grass is among the best. Almost my favourite is sacks in a coal-cart, especially after rain. Surely with the sheep in the offing you can't be smell-less? Hay-smell of course is superb. My old and very great friend C.D. Fisher (killed in the *Invincible* at Jutland. His brother the Admiral in the *St Vincent* swept into the battle past the wreck) maintained that his favourite smell was the top of a very small baby's head. And—*verb. sap.*—he wasn't far wrong. Gosh how you would have liked C.D.F.

You should surely send Adam in for a scholarship. His father will see to it that he doesn't develop into a Lancelot Hogben.

I have given up all hope about *How Green*. Couldn't you get Ruth to read it while you are at some special proof-reading? Only a few pages are necessary; I would rely on her judgment with entire confidence—so would you. It really is a shame not to read it at Kisdon. It cries to Heaven, as the butler said about what was in Dr Jekyll's room. But I suppose, in fact I am sure, that being a publisher, you are very stubborn.

P.S. No, T.S.E. was sickened not by *Ulysses* but by *Leaves of Grass*.

5 September 1960 — *Kisdon Lodge*

I was both touched and conscience-stricken to read of your so eagerly awaiting my dull letter and being so often disappointed. I only hope that this week you will have learnt to expect nothing from Kisdon until (with luck) the second post on Wednesday. Your letter flew back and was in my hands by Thursday evening. Why have I not answered before? Because, as I've always found, the less one *has* to do, the less one *does* do, and how enjoyable that is! It has rained every single day since I last wrote, but so far not to-day, and this morning we helped the farmer, his son and daughter-in-law to turn their sodden hay in the field up here, which has lain cut and awash for sixteen days. Saturday too was fine till the evening, and we descended the hill after a solid week up here (our longest unbroken sojourn so far) and drove to a sale in a little village near Thirsk. It proved a total washout—nothing one would have gladly taken as a gift—so we ate our picnic and drove home, doing various shopping at Hawes, Bedale, Thirsk and Ripon—all of which we like.

Oscar is limping on: another three weeks up here and the job would be almost done: as it is, with the piles of proofs, manuscripts and letters which will certainly be waiting, I simply don't know how or when I shall be able to finish. Incidentally I have recently, and quite by chance, acquired a new helper—an O.E. called Henry Maas (aged thirty-one) now schoolmastering in Surrey. His fresh, and extremely perceptive, mind is pointing out many errors and anomalies, asking pertinent questions, and generally improving the book. But it all means more work. Have the British Guiana contingent rolled up yet?

I once had Einstein's theory of Relativity explained to me so lucidly that for an hour or so I completely understood it: now nothing remains. In the same way have I several times been instructed in the meaning—and indeed the *working*—of *repêchage*, but alas! The French word must mean 'fishing up again', and I *think* here refers to some kind of proportional representation in timings—but who cares?

I've no doubt you're right about Sylvia Beach's book, though I must confess that all those names you list are comparatively well known to me—but then I am a literary bloke, immersed in all such nonsense, so take heart. When Richard Le Gallienne, the long-haired poetaster of the Nineties, published a book called *If I were God by Richard Le Gallienne*, some wag commented: 'If I were Richard Le Gallienne by God I'd get my hair cut'.

What you say (rightly) about the note-excesses of Swinburne's American editor makes me ever so slightly shiver in my shoes, for it's much harder than perhaps you think to decide where to draw the line. Young people today seem to know almost nothing. When Oscar wrote to Reggie Turner in 1899 'I hear you joined the Fleet Street Kopje at the Cecil', I feel obliged to explain Kopje *and* Cecil, both of which would be obvious to you.

You have twice referred to Andrew Young as 'modern poetry', but Andrew is 75, and surely his verse is timeless. Or do you see modernity lurking in his landscapes? Ruth is revelling in *Middlemarch* and wants to know whether you have read it lately, so that she can talk to you about it in October.

Duff writes very happily from Cardiff, where he has taken the 30/-

a week bed-sitter and finds the work most congenial. I am going to send him a thriller I've just read called *The Progress of a Crime* by Julian Symons, which is all about a young provincial reporter. I think you might find it enjoyable—or at any rate readable.

We are, alas, driving south on Thursday (leave here 11, picnics on the way, reach Soho 9 p.m.) so write to Bromsden, which I shall reach on Friday evening. The perfect relaxation, deep peace and easy slow rhythm of our life up here make the immediately subsequent days and weeks almost intolerable, and next May or June (when we can hope to return) seems a long way off. *Perhaps* I shall then be able to come without any proofs, with plenty of time for *How Green*—but in fact I daresay poor old Oscar will still be on the stocks. The index alone will take months.

7 September 1960 — *Grundisburgh*

Wednesday second post. I was prepared for it this week, and the starting tear called for no drying. You were quite right not to attempt answering my letter before. An answer must be allowed to come to the boil, not forced with a blow-lamp. And how right you are about the ease of doing things when time is ample.

I must tell you that I feel sad this evening—not because of the weather, Lumumba, the end of 1960 cricket or growing consciousness of senility, but with a vicarious sadness about you two leaving Kisdon. Such is the happiness that breathes through your letters from there, and then the return to the great ant-heap. I know how I should loathe it. I was afraid you must be getting a lot of rain. This is a notoriously dry corner of England, but we have had enough to hold up the harvest most days, and—as to-day—though dry, the sky is all over the colour of the belly of a dead fish. No doubt it is no more than we deserve, as an evangelical aunt of mine used to say—and how mealy-mouthed and soft was that generation which did *not* murder her. How right Thomas Hardy was in his remark 'It has been obvious for centuries that the Supreme Mover or Movers, the Prime Force or Forces, must be either limited in power, unknowing or cruel'. Can you see any way out of that?

Maas K.S. must have left about when I did, but I never came across him. I wasn't taking English Extra Studies at the end of my time. He sounds a competent chap.

You make me feel very ignorant, being totally unaware of all those authors mentioned by Miss Beach, whom you know all about. I shall throw up the sponge, and abandon the vain struggle to keep up. Next time we meet I shall babble of Besant and Rice, and Miss Braddon, and Mary Cholmondeley. But one thing makes me strike the stars with uplifted head, and that is that *Middlemarch* has always been my favourite novel. I read it first in 1904 and have read it at least three times since then. I am delighted to hear that Ruth likes it. It is simply crammed full of good stuff of all kinds. I often think of it when they babble (in speech or print) of the 'incomparable' Jane Austen, who just tinkles along in comparison. I could talk about it for hours, so dear Ruth had better look out. And if the British Guiana exam-papers still delay their coming, I may very well read it again. Didn't V. Woolf call it one of the very few really grown-up English novels? Even so one thing is missing, *viz* Dorothea's physical reactions towards her dreadful old husband. I don't want any *Room at the Top* stuff, still less the probing obsessions of Lawrence, but dash it all she must have had the matter much in her mind. I wonder why G.E. called him Casaubon. Could one bring a great sailor into one's novel and call him Nelson? Because the real Casaubon was actually a great scholar.

Richard Le Gallienne. Thank you. A lovely story. How immensely dead many of those chaps are—Stephen Phillips etc. And Vernon Lee —who the devil was she? I know absolutely nix about her.

You needn't surely be nervous about notes to Oscar; you never put a foot wrong with *Hugh Walpole*. But what a lot of incompetence there is about. *Old Mortality*, set for next year's G.C.E., is as you know full of full-blooded Scotticisms. Well, believe it or not, Everyman's edition has a glossary in which words like 'blithe', 'bracken', 'cannily', and 'feckless' are explained, but about 'grane', 'cess', 'tow', 'marts', and many others, no solitary word. I doubt if the Board, which chooses the books, are wise to choose Scott. He is so tremendously long-winded, and half the speeches of his ladies and gentlemen have the air of pieces set to be put into Ciceronian prose. And his young women!

Yes, the young are very ignorant (as I expect they always were) about the generation or two just before their own. Practically no undergraduates remember the declaration of war in 1939. An Oxford don told me recently that not one of the class to which he was lecturing had any idea what *Lebensraum* meant. A good many, of course, just don't read the papers. No one except me in the Ipswich Club ever reads the *Spectator* or *New Statesman.* I expect they regard them as just as devitalising as I find the *Express* and *Mail. Punch* seems to me positively abysmal nowadays, but my daughters tell me it is immensely funny, and they don't resent one or two of the pictures being (i) incomprehensible and (ii) not at all funny when explained. Well, Caran d'Ache[1] dispensed with captions or stories, but was surely very much funnier than our modern Johnnies (who, incidentally, don't draw a quarter as well).

I read *The Progress of a Crime* and greatly enjoyed it. Are his others good? Tell me. My bedside book is the new Ngaio Marsh. A prime theatre bitch has just passed out, and no doubt to-night Roderick Alleyn will blow in. She writes well. My nephew Charles says she is charming, and that counts quite a lot. Probably you have known her for years. The library is extraordinarily slow in producing P. Quennell's book, but I fancy nothing at all happens in August when all are on holiday. (Thursday) you are at this moment starting from K.—a horrible moment.

10 September 1960 *Bromsden Farm*

Your letter was waiting faithfully for me yesterday (Friday) evening when I arrived, heavily homesick for Kisdon, missing Ruth, loathing London and all its inhabitants, publishing and all its ways. The rain, which fell pitilessly through our blessed fortnight, cleared off only as we left the cottage, and we got more sun on the drive south than we had had during our whole stay. Yesterday the hot sunshine in London was almost unbearable, but to-day I have relaxed again in the garden here, reading first the weeklies since I left, and then a once-famous play called *Frou-Frou* by Meilhac and Halévy, which Oscar mentions and I couldn't annotate in ignorance. Now, on the same

[1] French caricaturist (1858–1909).

errand, I am reading Part III of Balzac's *Splendeurs et Misères des Courtisanes*—good full-blooded stuff.

I think it wonderful that, without having been there, you can so truly sympathise with, and enter into, our passionate love of Kisdon, our happiness there, and our ever-increasing sorrow at leaving. Everything you have ever written about it shows that you perfectly understand, whereas most people are perturbed by the thought of its primitiveness and isolation.

On our last evening at dusk we watched *five* hawks hovering over the hilltop. Suddenly a huge owl got up, was attacked by the hawks, and gradually drove them away, one by one. We watched, spellbound, in the fading light. Stopping the grandfather clock wrings our heart—but I need say no more—you know it all. London yesterday was unspeakably awful—jostling crowds of hideous people everywhere, stinking cars bumper to bumper, all my dear colleagues full of their own problems, my office piled high with waiting paper (I counted forty-two letters that need answering), and at mid-day my beloved friend Leon Edel, American professor and expert on Henry James, arrived to stay in the flat for a fortnight. Both Ruth and I love him dearly, but yesterday it was all we could do to be decently hospitable. I managed to arrange for him to spend the week-end with a friend in Sussex, thus gaining a brief respite.

Ruth will be delighted to hear of your love of *Middlemarch*, which she brought back with her to finish. Her daughter-in-law is now pregnant, so she will soon have three grandchildren, though I doubt if she will ever challenge your impressive brood.

I could write you pages about Vernon Lee, the great unread, if not unreadable, but I will spare you. Stephen Phillips's story was tragic: from incredible success ('the elder Dumas speaking with the voice of Milton' was how one of his plays was described) he faded into total failure, and so far as I know not one of his plays has ever been revived.

The sort of thing that holds up Oscar interminably is this: a few months ago I managed to get from Paris photostats of two letters from Oscar to Mallarmé, the French poet. One is undated, the other clearly postmarked February 1891. I put them both together, only to be reminded by one of my invaluable helpers that in the Stetson Sale

Catalogue (1920) there is a quotation from a Mallarmé letter to Oscar which is dated 10 Nov 91 and is clearly an answer to my undated letter. This entails moving my letter from February to November and shifting the main Mallarmé footnote to the other letter, which is now the first to him. Multiply this by several hundred and you will see the problem. Many things which I have laboriously read during the last five years (including this catalogue) couldn't then disgorge their full relevance, and there's a limit to what one can keep ready in one's head. I enjoyed the new Ngaio Marsh, and all Julian Symons's thrillers are good or goodish.

Duff writes enthusiastically of Cardiff, and his life and work there. I find I did Adam an injustice, since the only results in the General Paper are Pass or Fail, so in fact he couldn't have done better. At present he is pining for love of the fifteen-year-old daughter of a neighbour, who isn't very nice to him. His appetite, usually immense, has quite disappeared.

Peter can't find a subject for his next book: all I need is time to finish mine, but when shall I get it?

14 September 1960 *Grundisburgh*

How often the Ancient of Days indulges in sardonic humour. That you had ceaseless rain your whole fortnight at Kisdon and golden September days the moment you got back to Soho Square is a fine instance of it. Sheer cussedness! Did you see in to-day's *Times* the definition of a Combination Room—'a strange mixture of vestry and pantry'? My fourth-form mind liked it. Did you know, by the way, that, according to Macaulay, Soho Square in the 1700's was the most fashionable spot in all London? Your front-door bell in fact was the very latest thing in 1670, and people watched those who rang it (as they do me now). I shall be more careful on October 11 (is it?) not to deracinate it.

Fancy your ending up with five hawks and an owl! The sardonic gods again—they wanted to put the last edge on your regrets at leaving. And it is clear that what mainly oppresses you in London is my exact *bête noire* too—that horde of hideous people—mud-coloured, devoid of any sign of interest or intelligence or fun, noticing nothing, that is how they appear, and they are the people on whom democracy stands or falls. It is not hard to see which of the two it is in process of doing at the moment.

Everything is very costive here. My British Guiana papers have not *yet* arrived (is there some hope they can get no transport?) and that infernal library will not produce Quennell's book, though I am sure I am the first applicant for it. (The latest book on the new bookstand is the *History of High Wycombe* in two volumes—also an exciting-looking volume called *Solutions*, which deals however not with mystery-problems but with liquids.) Whenever I ask for the librarian or deputy, or secretary, they are all on holiday.

You must get rid somehow of the good Edel. Very odd people are. Gow used to come and sit in one's room and expect to be talked to between schools in the afternoon. And yet no man ever was quicker to get rid of a visitor when *he* had work on hand. And he was good value when one was not busy—a dry wine, but very palatable, though never quite the 'chatty and confident claret' once advertised in a catalogue, or even from the same place a 'champagne of great wit and repartee', which would no doubt produce the 'sober incalescence and regulated aestuation' approved of by Sir Thomas Browne, followed, you may remember, by his deprecation of any indulgence which leads to 'dementation or sopition of reason'.[1] If you don't know these quotations you will like to meet them; if you do know them, you won't mind being reminded of them (the prize bore's apologia).

I glanced yesterday at *Middlemarch*, and put it to you confidently that the very first three pages have more satisfying food for thought than fifty pages of—but I won't specify! I hope Ruth agrees in loving that charming prig Dorothea. In the story of Mr Casaubon's arid, indeed bloodless, courtship there is one quite delightful sentence: 'D. said to herself that Mr C. was the most interesting man she had ever seen, not excepting even M. Liret the Vaudois clergyman *who had given conferences on the history of the Waldenses*'. What a lot of the Victorian age, as well as of D., is in that sentence.

Tell me who or what to read about Vernon Lee. I dislike being so wholly ignorant as I am about her; I have never seen anything to do

[1] *Pseudodoxia Epidemica* (1646), book 5, chapter xxxi.

with her, or any kind of picture of her. Does she come into *no-one's* biography? Because I must have read most of them.

Do you know Leonard Woolf, whose reminiscences are interestingly reviewed? It isn't quite easy to take Bloomsbury very seriously in 1960—or the great G.E. Moore, whom I tried many years ago and stuck in irretrievably. Did they, in spite of the good things they wrote, amount to much *collectively*? And isn't the last word on them in Max B's devastating 'From Bloomsbury to Bayswater'?[1] Is anything less attractive than faded arrogance—or more ridiculous? One gets the impression of rather pinchbeck Ozymandiases. I find that much the really best things in Lytton Strachey's writings are those in which he is *not* mocking, however subtly—though these can still amuse when, like e.g. Monsignor Talbot,[2] the victims really were absurd.

I have to write a paper on Gilbert for the Ipswich G. and S. society of which I am President. Yesterday I got Hesketh Pearson's Penguin on G. and S. which is excellent reading. What a good face H.P. has, at least on the back of this volume. I think you once said he was a capital chap—even though he dislikes Mr Gladstone. So did Gilbert, whose dislikes were largely fortuitous. He must on the whole have been a detestable man. His dialogue in the plays (not his lyrics) is dreadful reading now. You will be pleased to know that dear Queen Victoria thought the plot of *The Mikado* 'rather silly'.

18 September 1960 *Bromsden Farm*

I fear you won't get this before Tuesday. My whole week-end was disjointed by yesterday, when we were obliged to drive over to the Victor Gollanczes' new cottage near Marlow and play bridge with them for *six hours*. I am very fond of them both, but as you know I seldom play bridge (or anything else) and have a great deal to do. However, I think Comfort enjoyed it, and we eventually staggered

[1] Published in Max Beerbohm's *Mainly on the Air* (1946).

[2] George Talbot (1816–1886), fifth son of the third Lord Talbot de Malahide. Private Secretary to Pope Pius IX, who helped Manning to become Archbishop of Westminster. He ended in a lunatic asylum. See Strachey's *Eminent Victorians* (1918).

home the richer by 7/6. Now I am trying to cram two days' business into one, and the sun has been seducing me out of doors.

Adam was much pleased and flattered by an extremely nice letter from Birley, congratulating him on his scholarship etc. An excellent gesture, I thought. Apparently a Distinction in A-Level counts as one in Trials, so Adam now has *seven* to his credit.

Last week in London was most exhausting. No one could be a less demanding guest than my dear friend Leon Edel, but Ruth and I have come to depend on the flat for moments of escape and peace—coffee and the crossword at 10.30, often lunch, a quiet whisky-and-soda after the office, and so on—and to find even the nicest of guests always there, having to talk when one longs for quiet, is persistently frustrating. However, the dear fellow flies home next Saturday, and somehow we'll stumble through till then.

My spies tell me (*this is frightfully private*) that the big City investment firm which owns Heinemann (and me along with it) is negotiating to sell the whole caboodle to an American tycoon. Nobody can guess what this would mean, but I don't much like the sound of it. I'll let you know as soon as I know any more.

Where exactly does that splendid bit of Sir Thomas Browne come from? I don't immediately know where you can read about Vernon Lee, though there's certainly a bit about her in Maurice Baring's autobiography, *The Puppet Show of Memory*. I shouldn't bother about Le Gallienne. When he emigrated to America, Max sent him on a postcard:

> Bewitched by American bars,
> Pan whistles you home on his pipes.
> We love you for loving the stars,
> But what can you see in the stripes?

I do indeed know, and like, Leonard Woolf. I have bought his book but haven't yet begun it. Your wise strictures on Bloomsbury sum it all up beautifully, but I'm sure you needn't worry; time winnows away the chaff of arrogance etc, and the grain (of which there surely was some) will remain.

Many Oscar notes still elude me, and the galley-proofs are little nearer completion than they were this time last week. My wild Irish boy, a child-prodigy of research, is with me for another fortnight, adding to the confusion in Soho Square with a powerful gift of the gab. But he is biddable, and I have prepared a long programme for him in Somerset House, British Museum, London Library, Record Office etc.

How dull the papers are without any cricket—and soon the clocks will be altered, and darkness will close in.

Peter is meditating a book on Siberia 1918–1919, Admiral Kolchak, and the Russian civil war—but this too is secret for the moment. His present (Younghusband) book we have postponed till January. Diana's third volume begins in next week's *Sunday Times*, but please don't read it there: I'll soon send you a proper copy. I dined last week with her and her son, and although it was all very nice I didn't enjoy myself much. Maybe I have reached some kind of climacteric or change of life, but I certainly feel ever less social, gregarious and tolerant, and long to do what I want to do in a place of my own choosing. Perhaps one day it will work out that way, and meanwhile I must grit my teeth and carry on. Seeing you on 11 October will be most cheering.

22 September 1960 *Grundisburgh*

Your Duff's article is *excellent* reading; he makes it all very vivid. And what substantial support he brings to that dictum of Oxenstierna's[1] which Dr J. was fond of, saying to a young man: 'You will be surprised to find when you go out into the world, with what little wisdom human affairs are managed'. Not that to my limited and impatient mind the Creator has all that much to boast about. I wish I shared the belief of many that some day we shall know all about it. Meanwhile there is Clough:

> But play no tricks upon thy soul, O man;
> Let fact be fact and life the thing it can.[2]

You really are an amazing man. *Six* hours of bridge with all that mountain of work waiting to be tackled. Do you *always* do what

[1] Count Axel Oxenstierna, Swedish statesman (1583–1654).
[2] 'Dipsychus', part 2, scene ii.

friends want you to do? And then you go and fill another hour with a lovely letter to me. You will get to Abraham's bosom very much sooner than I shall--which I *suppose* is a highly delectable region??

I have at last finished my exam-papers—about three hundred of them from overseas. And am I sick of vague and vapid jaw about Brutus and Cassius, or am I? But they are well up-to-date in British Guiana. One candidate stated that Caesar was a homosexual, the proof being his saying 'Let me have men about me that are fat'—which recalls a scabrous limerick which I found in my psalter in Eton chapel in 1896—which I shall *not* tell you.

Yes, there is a glut of apples here too, which doesn't seem to be doing much good to anybody—too many to gather, and no profit in selling. And this is just the moment when our half-gardener takes his ten days' holiday. But following the old advice to 'count one's blessings', well, of course my chief one is having you as a fairy god-mother—for I go nearly as far as Southey in finding my cheeks 'often bedewed with tears of thoughtful gratitude', whenever I contemplate my revolving bookshelf, *entirely* filled with gifts from R.H-D. And now the beloved Tim has sent me Alan Ross's cricket anthology,[1] which I was on the brink of buying last week at The Ancient House, and was stopped by a spasm of economy. There are splendid things in it, and a good deal I have *not* read, plus old favourites. I wish R. had found room for C.P. Foley's superb account of Alletson's innings in 1911, when he ended his vast innings by getting 139 in half-an-hour, *89 of it in fifteen minutes*. He clearly went quite mad—and remained so, for he never made another run practically, nor even tried to hit, though A.O. Jones told him that if only he would hit he should play in every match, however few runs he made. But of course, half the fun of an anthology is picking holes. This looks a very good one—even though Lyttelton is spelt Lyttleton. I hope *you* foam at the mouth when called Davies? It is almost incredible what a vast percentage of G.C.E. candidates agree that '*Philippi*' is the only incorrect way of spelling the name. By and large 'Philpi' was furthest from the truth, from, I think the same chap who said that Brutus followed the 'sotic' philosophy.

Adam, I hope, had (till last week) his feet on the fender reading

[1] *The Cricketer's Companion* (1960).

non-scientific literature. Warn him that Darwin, when he ultimately found himself at leisure, realised that he had completely lost any taste for literature, especially fiction (not that that matters) and Shakespeare. I wonder why Gilbert disliked S. so much. I have to read a paper some soon day to the Ipswich G.S. Society, and am lazily collecting stuff for it (it is on Gilbert alone) slightly daunted by a feeling of increasing dislike of the man—practically always in a temper when not getting his own way, and with such an obvious relish for bloodshed, torture etc. His famed witticisms (like many of Oscar's?) are pretty flavourless now, less witty than Housman's, and with the same edge of snub and rudeness (though I *do* like—having a vulgar mind—'Where is Miss X'? 'She's round behind'. 'Yes, I know, but where is she'?). The librettos and dialogue in plays one never saw or heard, and therefore can't call up any tunes, are rather heavy-going, though Hesketh Pearson says that G. never was more brilliant than in *Ruddigore* and *The Mountebanks*. I can't quite see it.

I shall be interested to hear what you make of Leonard Woolf's book. It is on my list, but the library has been very dilatory of late. The reviews stimulate one's curiosity. I rather wish he had avoided the modern fashion of proclaiming his virginity up to such and such an age. Is *anything* of less general interest?

25 September 1960 *Bromsden Farm*

The sun calls me outside, so you will get poor measure to-day, I fear.

After last Saturday's bridge-marathon, I had another long day of frustration yesterday. I brought Leon Edel down here on Friday night, and we set off for London Airport (25 miles) at 11 a.m. yesterday. L.E. is a nervous traveller with ever-mounting gangplank-fever. We got to the airport at 12 and I took him to the huge central section, where 10,000 cars were parked. With some difficulty I found room for ours, lugged his heavy suitcase a long way to the first floor, only to be told that we were in quite the wrong part of the airport. Lugged the suitcase back, de-parked the car, was roundly ticked off by motorised police for going the wrong way (it's very confusing) and drove off to the *right* place. Here we were told that the flight had been postponed from 1 p.m. to 5.30 p.m. It was by now 12.30, the sun was shining hot and strong, and I felt I simply *couldn't* leave the wretched fellow to hang about for five hours. So I put him firmly back into the car and drove off.

Meanwhile, as they say in clumsy old novels, Duff had come over from Cardiff to pick the apples, found there were *far* more than we could use or store, so rang up Julia Coleridge and sold her 200 lbs at threepence a pound.

Meanwhile, again, Adam had telephoned delightedly to announce his election to the Library[1] and to ask for his tape recorder, portable wireless, box of electrical equipment, two spare recording-tapes, some eggs and other food, and (once again) his braces.

So, laden with all this clobber, and the undeparted guest, I drove to Eton. As we reached Fred's Boys' Entrance a boy, twitching and groaning with pain, was carried out on a stretcher and driven off in an ambulance. (It turned out that his name was Romer-Lee and his trouble a slipped disc.) We found Adam, and with some difficulty persuaded the dame to cough up £2. 10. 0. for the apples. Adam and the odd-job-man almost ruptured themselves getting the fruit out of the car. We admired the Chess Cup in the dining-room; Adam said he was playing football at 2.15, so didn't want to come out to lunch. Leon acquiesced in all the hurly-burly—and then I drove him to Monkey Island, which was looking very beautiful, and had a good lunch. I could see that L.E.'s anxiety-neurosis was growing rapidly, but managed to divert his attention by asking him to tell me about the time when he was psycho-analysed. This kept him going happily through a protracted lunch, and at 3 p.m. I suggested that we might examine the secondhand bookshops of Windsor and Eton and then return to the airport at 4.30 as instructed. He said he'd be happier if we rang up the airport for confirmation, so I sat in the sun by the river while he got the necessary pennies. Soon he came disconsolately back to say he'd pressed the wrong button and lost all his pennies, so I got some more, rang up the airport, and was told the flight had again been postponed—till 8.30 p.m.! This news completely shattered him, and I simply didn't know what to do. I could have brought him back here, but he would have hated that as much as anything else. Instead

[1] The boys' governing body of an Eton house.

I drove him to Windsor and we pottered in the bookshops, buying a few odd books. Then he said he must telephone again, so we sweated to the Post Office at the very top of Windsor Hill, and got some more pennies, and the flight was still 8.30.

L.E. was really very touching, saying he realised I was being very kind, and he knew he ought to be enjoying the sunshine and the adventure and the bookshops, but that he simply couldn't control his exasperation, so after giving him a cup of tea I drove him back to the airport and left him there at 5.30, with three hours still to go. I got back here at 6.30 utterly exhausted, having driven eighty miles and spent all the apple-money.

I have got Alan Ross's cricket anthology, but needless to say haven't had time to examine it. I am enjoying Leonard Woolf very much, and I think you will too.

Tomorrow is T.S.E.'s seventy-second birthday, and Ruth and I have been bidden to drinks at 6.15. On Thursday I am to take part in a hideous evening party given by the Society of Authors in (goodness knows why) a room in the House of Commons. An 'informal discussion' is to take place between Compton Mackenzie, Rebecca West, A.P. Herbert and *me*! How on earth did I let myself in for such folly? 'It was an insensate step', as Henry James once said. The full horror shall be reported to you next week. Now I must finish correcting the proofs of the Gissing-Wells letters, and read the Sunday papers and spend a little time with Oscar's dog-eared proofs. I see no daylight at the end of the tunnel: your diagnosis of a surfeit of people is a jolly good one, but what is the cure? My London life is all or nothing: one either participates or withdraws: half-measures simply aren't possible.

Now you've got six pages of complaints and I shall try the sun.

28 September 1960 *Grundisburgh*

'Poor measure indeed' followed by *six* pages of the best! Irony, or litotes (or if you prefer it, meiosis)—of which my favourite example is Swift's reference to the woman who had been flayed alive, 'and you cannot think how much it changed her appearance for the worse'. A blood-freezing man with, as Taine says, 'his terrible wan eyes'. There are some deeply grim stories about him, as you know.

This is the perfect summer-house day—coldish east wind and bright sun, and I as warm as a toast, whatever that may mean. We are beating up for a fine October, which is very common in these regions, though it is rather like the brief heartiness and eupepsia of a septuagenarian, with November in the offing, when 'Not till the spring recapture Joy as it flits along, Shall we regain the rapture Either of scent or song!'.[1]

What a nightmare of a time you and Leon Edel had over that flying. The only faint silver lining was that you sold 200 lbs of apples, which surely no one else has done this year. There seems to be a glut everywhere—and I suppose we are importing millions, or is that potatoes? I met John Hare, recently released from the Board of Agriculture and clearly happy about it, as he said bluntly that three out of four of the problems that come before the Minister are insoluble. I reassured him by saying that *all* government problems are the same in 1960—except of course such perfectly useless ones as hitting the moon. The last word (as so often) was said by Johnson—in *Rasselas*, no doubt—that the scientists had much better busy themselves in discovering a cure for asthma rather than in learning how to fly. You must have been entirely exhausted by the end of the day, but I suspect you very often are (like everybody—not that there are all that many —who does exactly what any friend asks him to do).

I love the refrain of Adam's braces—invariably sent after him with much else. The young are like that. We never have any part of the family here without sending half their wardrobe after them. I have simplified packing by having a list inside my suitcase of everything I could possibly want. It saves a lot of time. Not that I didn't, last winter, carefully pack a hot-water bottle minus its stopper. As Swift might have said, you would be surprised to find how little use it was when I arrived.

I wonder what bookshops you found in Windsor. There used in my day to be—literally—none. Only W.H. Smith, and he didn't go much beyond Penguins etc. Mrs Brown at Eton set up her shop twenty years ago and makes a good thing of it, or used to. I sold her a lot of

[1] Galsworthy, 'November'.

books when I left (*all* of which I have wanted since) and saw some of them in her window priced a good deal higher than what she had paid me, but as she once explained, when you buy a library, you find three-quarters of it practically unsaleable and only a few make the buy worth while.

Alan Ross's anthology has lots of good stuff in it, and—as one might expect—plenty that one could spare. Are you *very* good at the MCC match in *Tom Brown's Schooldays*? I am not, and still less so at Vachell's Eton v. Harrow. In fact, to come out into the open with trailing coat, I am not permanently a-giggle over Macdonell's famous match in *England, their England.* But the explanation of that may be that, as my daughters say when I condemn *Punch*, my sense of humour is going the same way as my hearing, sight, memory etc.

At last the library has coughed up Quennell's book, and I start it this evening. After sampling an odd page or two, I know I shall enjoy it. He seems to think T.S.E.'s appearance is or was, very incongruous after *The Waste Land.* E. Pound looks much more 'agin' everything and everybody. What does T.S.E. really think of E.P.? I think you ought to garner a good deal of interesting stuff from T.S.E.—not necessarily with a view to publication, but, say, to conversation with G.W.L. Does he write any reminiscences? They should be very good. Perhaps, like General Alexander, he is too much of a gentleman.

I get some definite pleasure from the *T.L.S.* reviewer who begins a paragraph about Kingsley Amis's last novel: 'This is a very nasty book'. He is, as you know, one of my steadily lengthening list of *bêtes noires.* A sure sign of old age. I become steadily deafer, the arch of my right foot steadily descends, my shins steadily itch, one deltoid muscle creaks and stiffens. Otherwise, thank you, I am perfectly well, though, as Lord Clive who is no longer alive said, there is a great deal to be said for being dead.

I should like to hear you at the H. of C. with your sparkling party. Rebecca West always strikes me as the cleverest woman in England (as J. Agate maintained) though I haven't read her last one or two. A.P.H.? Well some don't like him, but *What a Word*, *Topsy* and *Misleading Cases* are frequently at my bedside, and I should like to meet him and tell him how one of his poems 'The farmer will never be happy again, He carries his heart in his boots', etc was regarded as sheer gold by my father-in-law when he was President of the Royal Agricultural Society and recited the poem at at least twenty dinners through the winter instead of a speech and had his audience in fits of delighted laughter. Over and over again they told him that 'For either the rain is destroying his grain, Or the drought is destroying his roots' is not only very funny, but contains in a couplet the *whole* problem of farming. Do hand this on if you get a chance with him.

What line shall I take in my paper on Gilbert to the Ipswich society? It is not easy, I find, to like him. Q.[1] dallies with the problem of the popularity of the tremendously Victorian operettas long after people were turning up their noses at Tennyson and Browning. Fundamentally he has only about three–four plots, and practically all his young women are identical, and all his old ones fat and wrinkled and repellent. I wonder why Q. thought *The Bab Ballads* were better than his lyrics in the plays—'much' better, I think he says. I found the *B.B.* definitely hard to read at all continuously, a few days ago. As to his plays, away from Sullivan, well, in that nice French expression, they do not permit themselves to be read, and the poor man thought so highly of them. And as to Sullivan, have you ever heard his 'Golden Legend' which a critic, after its first performance, said combined the merits of Haydn and Beethoven? It is a very odd story.

Well, my dear R., here are six pages. Too long I know, but you began it. *Vous l'avez voulu, George Dandin*[2] (not that yours were too long for me).

1 October 1960 *Bromsden Farm*

Last week's six-sider was a *lusus naturae*, unlikely to recur for ages, but since it drew from you an equally long answer, I may one day be tempted to send you a twelve-sider, just to see how you react.

The coming of winter is depressing enough without this wilful encouragement of darkness by putting back the clock. We still have masses of *strawberries* in the garden, though to-day they are soggy with rain. Squirrels and rooks squabble for the walnuts, though in

[1] Sir Arthur Quiller-Couch in his *Studies in Literature, Third Series* (1929).

[2] Molière, *George Dandin, ou Le Mari Confondu* (1668), act I, scene ix.

fact there are plenty for all, and I gathered a large basketful this afternoon. No children here this week-end, and all is peace. I have just read three hundred pages of a draft of my old friend Wyndham Ketton-Cremer's history of Felbrigg, his house in Norfolk. It's not exactly sparkling, but I know the house well, and any competent and documented family history of three hundred years is interesting as a sort of microcosm of history. Before Monday I must also read *six hundred* pages (typescript) of the first volume of Guy Chapman's history of the French Third Republic (1871–1940). Also a French book on the Algerian war, which I fear would be out of date before it could be translated. Also I must cut, edit and partly re-write Jock Dent's sloppy introduction to the Agate anthology I am to bring out next year. And, in case I have time to spare, I have brought along a 300-page (typed) 'extravaganza' by Arnot Robertson. So you will not be surprised to hear that the Oscar galleys are locked in the safe at Soho Square for the week-end: if they were here I couldn't resist fiddling with them.

Mrs Brown now belongs to the ages, but her bookshop goes marching on, and it was one of those we visited last Saturday. Now (long since my day—and yours, I fancy) there are two good secondhand shops just over the bridge, both on the right: one opposite the cinema and the other exactly on the first rounded turning of the road up the hill (used it to be a furniture shop?). Both are well worth a visit, though the first (like so many of its fellows) is gradually surrendering its front room to paperbacks and gramophone-records.

T.S.E.'s birthday party was most touching and enjoyable: just the two of them; her mother (very nice, from Leeds); a dear old friend of T.S.E.'s and mine, called Mary Hutchinson; Ruth and me. A tiny one-candled cake and champagne (which this time I opened without drenching the Epstein bust, as I did two years ago). Tom still looks terribly grey, but better than he did two months ago. We talked of Leonard Woolf, and *Lady Chatterley*, and the theatre, and this and that. I wish I remembered more, or knew shorthand, or didn't always have each episode pushed aside by an immediate successor. I doubt whether he (T.S.E.) is writing anything much now, though I fancy he's continually brooding over a new play—and I wish he wasn't, for his plays aren't getting any better, and he has probably written enough.

Reminiscences—I fear not, though I will try and raise the subject one of these days.

The Society of Authors rout in the H. of C. turned out (as so often happens with something one has long been dreading) to be rather fun. Some two hundred authors were crammed together, each with his (or more often her) name pinned to the lapel. (Most of them seemed to be called Margaret Bulge or some such.) The main attraction was the Brains Trust, which lasted well over an hour, and seemed to give general satisfaction. A.P.H. was on the right wing, then Compton Mackenzie, then the chairman Denzil Batchelor, then Rebecca, then me. I had previously given dinner at the Garrick to Robert Holland, a nice young Lecturer in English from Liverpool, and the drink I had had (two whiskies-and-sodas and one glass of claret) must have been just right, for I suddenly felt on top of the Brains Trust and more than able to cope. The questions were quite sensible, and enabled everyone to speak a little about themselves. A.P.H. actually quoted 'The farmer will never be happy again', to the delight of the massed authors. Rebecca was most amiable, and afterwards her husband (deaf, friendly, hospitable) begged me to drive over and see them.

I am much too ignorant of Gilbert to advise you about your speech, but it seems clear that neither he nor Sullivan was any use without the other, whereas in partnership their complementary second-rateness became in its way first-class. And I *still* haven't seen a single G. and S. opera!

Tommy has great hopes of getting Siegfried Sassoon into the Lit. Soc. and indeed you would find him most congenial—cricket and all. I've told Tommy I'll happily second him, and I fancy T. is planning to bring him as a guest to the November dinner.

I greatly enjoyed Leonard Woolf. He says most things three times, like the Bellman, but one soon forgives that, because most of what he says is interesting. A batch of R.H-D. books should reach you soon, if they haven't already arrived. The list for next year looks pretty thin so far: it's a fearful effort trying to keep up output *and* standard, and I increasingly feel that I've been at it long enough.

I can hear the rain hurtling down outside, the Third Republic is waiting, and it's another six-sider. No precedent, I promise. No need to reciprocate.

P.S. I had a huge plate of fresh ripe strawberries and cream for supper!!

5 October 1960 *Grundisburgh*

'October *rediit, rediit pars tristior anni*'.[1] Do you remember your Clivus? O. is very often the best of months in Suffolk, but it has made —meteorologically—a poor start, though nothing like what it has in Cornwall, the English Riviera. But all horizons are lightened by a parcel with a lovely quintette of books from R.H-D., whose generosity beggars gratitude of any adequate words, for they have all been used. Talk about fairy godmothers! What a rich feast of reading awaits me! And I have just finished Quennell's book, a great deal of it with great pleasure. I found the Prologue and Epilogue a bit dry and difficult, like—to me—all writing about the principles of art, but whenever he gets on to people he is fine. 'Camp-followers' is an absorbing chapter. 'Stylists' too, with its visit to old George Moore—and much else. Is P.Q. bilingual? There is a great deal of quotation from French writers.

I am all for Siegfried Sassoon. I wonder what Sir Cuthbert would say about him. You will have to let me off Sir C. on Tuesday week; the plain truth must be faced, *viz* that I grow steadily deafer. The National Health hearing-aid is really unwearable—so clumsy and undiscriminating—you hear your own heart beating, and, much louder than anything else, your own voice. My cynical Scotch specialist said in answer to such complaints: 'Yes; I suspect half the hearing-aids in England are put away in cupboards'. But they do improve as time goes on. Not that at seventy-seven plus there is much of it to spend waiting.

Have you noticed how putting back the clocks seems to shorten the day by much more than one hour—or rather bring darkness over an hour sooner? Partly no doubt because at five the sky is heavily clouded. But it isn't a conspicuously pleasant time of year, anyway, after youth. Your strawberries are rather offensive—a second crop! We rarely have any at all. Pamela discovered (as with fowls too) that to grow them costs more time—and money as well—than buying

[1] October has returned, a sadder part of the year.

them. And of course mushrooms too. What humbug the advertisements are—pretending that anyone can grow crop after lavish crop with a minimum of trouble. I expect those lessons on how to earn several hundreds a year with short stories are much the same. How, by the way, are Jonah's coming along? You are suspiciously silent about them.

Heavens, the jobs you take on! Six hundred pages on the Third Republic! I thought Brogan had written the last word on that in 1939. I remember being impressed with his certainty that France was about to collapse months before she did. I am surprised at Jock Dent's writing being 'sloppy', because it used not to be. I have a persistent but quite irrational feeling that he has gone downhill these last years. You will probably know for certain. I am glad you were well-primed for that Brains Trust. Did you tell A.P.H. about my father-in-law? Perhaps you didn't get as far as that in my letter. His satisfaction must in his seventies be that he has certainly added to the gaiety of nations.

By the way, Cyril Foley in his excellent account of Fowler's match makes a very grave error of fact in saying that T.O. Jameson was laid out for a bit through being hit 'on the head'. It was really a much more vulnerable place—and a commoner, especially *on a wet wicket with none but slow to medium bowlers*. I met T.O.J. three years ago when he told us in a very husky voice that he had cancer of the throat and would die in six months. He seemed entirely cheerful about it. And in fact he is still alive. I read that old Maugham too contemplates death with perfect calm—what would appal him would be the prospect of eternal life, and how right he is, especially if, as Arthur Benson said, there are many people who appear to think that in the next world they will have a prescriptive right to one's company. The old S.M. is very corrugated now, but after all at eighty-six one has a right to be.

The Quashiboo Rangers. Author totally forgotten. There was an arrogant regiment in India that regarded itself as invincible. Some man with some kind of grudge against them trained an eleven of black men who batted and bowled very sketchily, but could catch literally anything however close to the bat. They made practically no runs, going in first, but the regiment made *none*—all caught *the moment* they hit the ball. The black eleven were named after the twelve apostles. I will try and find out about it. Unluckily Rockley Wilson[1] is dead. He knew everything about cricket history.

I should have liked to hear you and T.S.E. on *Lady Chatterley*. I suspect that the book is one of the very few things we disagree about —I mean its publication unexpurgated. I wonder what the gutter press will make of the trial. A lot will depend on the judge. I am sure my cousin the late Sir George Talbot[2] would have been very fierce about it; so would old Avory[3] but then of course they *were* Victorians. So are most judges. Have you read, shall you read, Kingsley Amis's last? Some man in the *Spectator* says it is his best, in total opposition to the *T.L.S.*

Shall you, by the way, attend the Johnson Club dinner on the 25th? I think I must go, as I have not attended one for a year. But I shall tell the good secretary that I will *not* propose the guests' health. Why should anyone? It is an otiose proceeding.

9 October 1960 *Bromsden Farm*

Is this the second Flood? Have you an arkwright handy? Goodness knows what our rainfall has been to-day alone. Except for stacking a few logs in the woodshed I have stuck to proofs and manuscripts in the library. I am struggling through the birth-pangs of the Third Republic, of which I assure you the good Brogan has scarcely scratched the surface. So glad you have enjoyed Quennell at last: he is not, to my knowledge, bilingual, but is clearly well-read in French lit.

Jonah's short stories are in the printer's hands: the book is to be called *The Bishop's Aunt*, after what I think the best story in it. Last Tuesday I dined alone with Jonah and Evy in their St John's Wood eyrie. They gave me a superb dinner (they have a daily Viennese cook) of smoked salmon, a huge melting *vol-au-vent*, a fine bottle of Mouton Rothschild, and a wonderful *soufflé surprise*, topped up with

[1] E.R. Wilson (1879–1957) played cricket for Rugby, Cambridge and Yorkshire. Assistant Master at Winchester 1903–1946.

[2] Barrister, and judge of the King's Bench Division (1861–1938).

[3] Sir Horace Avory (1851–1935), barrister, and judge of the King's Bench Division.

coffee, liqueur and an excellent Partagas cigar. Afterwards we sat and gossiped most agreeably. Jonah is definitely much better: his breathlessness greatly reduced and his colour better. Jock Dent has indeed deteriorated lately, and his writing has gone soft. I didn't tell A.P.H. about your father-in-law, because I didn't get your letter about it till *after* the Brains Trust.

I *can't* go to the Johnson Club on the 25th, being already bespoke for that evening. It's much more than a year since I attended, so I shouldn't let that worry you. Ruth and I will be waiting for you at six on Tuesday, expecting you to be deaf, breathless and drenched; we will stay you with flagons.

13 October 1960 *Grundisburgh*

On Sunday we go up to Westmorland; Pamela, I really think, enjoys the journey; I rather hate it. Senility of course. I am always convinced the car will cease to function in the middle of some northern moor.

I have just finished Diana Cooper's book. I do hope it will be decently reviewed because it is really a lovely book—all beautifully done and the end *very* moving. Pamela thinks so too (and is a very good judge). My dislike of the *New Statesman* in general and R.H.S. Crossman in particular was strongly reinforced by C's review of Pug Ismay's and Horrocks's books—so sneery and omniscient and entirely blind to the obvious fact that both men are outstandingly good chaps. And then of course he praises the man—name forgotten—who runs down Monty in favour of the Auk. To call, as he does, Churchill 'the little white politician' is schoolboy stuff—and not very high in the school either.

I shall take Druon to the north and send you a report. Is the Wells-Gissing correspondence any good—or was G. too gloomy—admittedly with pretty good reason for most of his life? I address the Leys School sixth form on Saturday. The gist of my address will be that they will get very little education from beaks but a lot by themselves, if they read properly. Half the staff, I believe, are to be there. I also intend to abuse Leavis. Half the staff worship him.

I forget how long you're staying with Roger, but hope this will catch you there. Both Ruth and I thought that on Tuesday, far from being deafer as you announced yourself, you were definitely *less* deaf—so there! Perhaps the contraption in your ear is more use than you think.

So glad you liked Diana's book: she is apprehensive about its reception and refuses to be reassured, even by Evelyn Waugh, who has sent me this for use in advertisements:

> '*Trumpets from the Steep* is as brilliant, diverse and poignant as its two memorable predecessors and triumphantly crowns one of the great autobiographies of the century.'

What more could one ask?

The Wells-Gissing correspondence is pretty small beer, but you shall have it as soon as it's ready, sometime early next year. And I must chase the man who is supposed to be editing the Shaw–Wells volume: it should be the best of the four, but I haven't seen any of it yet.

This week-end I have only a 200-page monograph on Christopher Smart (by Christopher Devlin) to keep me from Oscar.

Everything in the garden is so sodden that we can get the bonfire going only by 'borrowing' some waste-oil from Peter's huge grain-drying machine. P. himself has gone for ten days to Roscommon on what I told him was certainly in every sense a wild-goose chase. He answered an advertisement in *The Times*—'guns wanted' or some such.

Next week *may* see me in the witness-box at the Old Bailey. I've never set foot in the place, have you? Anyhow I'll describe it all for you, despite your disapproval of *Lady Chatterley*.

I long to know whether your drive took you anywhere near Keld or Kisdon. Have a look at a map, and let me know. How I wish I was there now! I have just heard on the telephone that I have to be at a meeting in London at 11.30 tomorrow (Sunday) morning—the usual intrigue and skulduggery of Heinemann's. Twenty-five years ago one of the typists in my office said to another: 'Mr Hart-Davis is very nice as long as his own personal comfort isn't interfered with', and the older I get the truer does that home truth become. All my complicated arrangements depend on my having Sunday clear for reading and writing. Damn them all!

Please give my love to the charming Sibell and to the impish demure and beloved Roger. Is he safe among those schoolgirls, or should you go along to protect him—I mean *them*?

Having made all my arrangements to travel to Rapallo on All Saints Day for the unveiling of the plaque, I now hear from the Consul in Genoa that the ceremony may be postponed for some days. Damn *them* all too! Kisdon Lodge is the place for me.

Forgive all these outbursts and send me cheerful tidings from the north.

19 October 1960 *Barbon Manor*
Kirkby Lonsdale

Your letter duly arrived, though I had a sudden compunction that I had not given you Roger's address; only second thoughts reassured me that of course you have known it for years. We had an excellent journey from Cambridge on Sunday, and go back next Sunday, having firmly decided that that is the best day for travel—especially if—as we did—one starts at 7.15 a.m. Roger and Sibell are both in excellent form and clearly much pleased by your mention of them. How right was the man—name forgotten—who said that anyone who said he did not like being praised by his fellow-men was either a fool or a liar.

What you and Ruth say about my deafness is really very interesting—because one or two others have said the same, but I myself am conscious of nothing at all except that my worse ear *is* worse, and the other much the same, except that the little contraption makes it continuously tickle; which is tiresome but I suppose I shall ignore it in time. The gadget isn't *supposed* to produce any improvement for at least a fortnight. I shouldn't wonder if faith has a good deal to do with it. We shall see.

It is very pleasant up here and Pamela is having a grand rest from her numberless chores in Grundisburgh, where half the inhabitants' first idea is 'When in doubt about *anything*, send for Mrs L.'. The last before we left was from a woman whose husband had to go to hospital, and *would* dear Pamela just nip over and help to pack his clothes. I imagine this country is very like Kisdon—rolling moorland and vast horizons (usually obscured by cloud) and 'solitude of shepherds, High in the folded hill'.[1] When they come in I will look at a map and see how near we have ever been to Kisdon. The name has never passed my lips to anyone but Pamela. I believe even Ruth's lovely lips would be pursed in censure if it ever did.

You will, I hope, be pleased to hear that both Pamela and Roger greatly like Diana C's book, and both were quite expecting *not* to. I can't believe that any honest and competent reviewer could do anything but praise it—but perhaps those two adjectives are too extravagant? I agree with every word Evelyn Waugh says about it.

R. has many of the latest books and I batten on them. Lloyd George by his son: my Victorian view is that it *may* be interesting, amusing, and important to reveal that a big man's chief relaxation was promiscuous fornication, but that the revelation ought not to be made by his son. R. is a bit cagey about it, but I rather gather that to his cynical, 1960, man-of-the-world eye the bulk of readers may well praise the father's contempt for old-fashioned conventions and the son's courageous frankness. If they do, my conviction of the Gadarene course of all standards will be still further strengthened.

L. Woolf's *Sowing* did not wholly please me, though full of interest. Doesn't he jeer too much at all other views and convictions than those held by the Stracheys and Stephens and Keyneses etc? Do you know all about G.E. Moore and his philosophy? He is, as always, extravagantly lauded in this book—though represented by two curiously dull letters. When I went up (October 1902) I was urged to read his *Principia Ethica*, but I made no more of it than Dr Johnson did of playing the flageolet. But he does appear to have impressed a great many very intelligent people, though for many years his name has very rarely been mentioned, so far as my observation goes. I wish there was a picture of L.W. at twenty-four instead of that very unattractive one of him as a boy. And, Rupert, *surely* nothing flatter than those two imitations or parodies of Henry James on pp. 110–116 has ever been written? They seem to me to bear no relation whatever to

[1] A.E. Housman, 'The Merry Guide'.

H.J. It may, of course, be the same with me as with Hume when he said he had no fear of death. 'Sir, his intellect is disordered'.

I look forward to seeing you reported as an enthusiast for *Lady C's Lover*. Please tell me all about it. It is all a fine piece of fantasy—jurymen all looking like figures drawn by George Morrow, quite clearly mystified, almost certainly shocked, very probably flattered by being told they are men of the world into denying what they *really* think. I wonder who will be the judge. Will passages be read *aloud* in court? Will there be women on the jury? Gosh, how I feel like Housman's Terence: 'I, a stranger and afraid In a world I never made'.[1]

That typist who spoke of your personal comfort. Dash it all, do you *ever* stop putting yourself out for other people? To want your Sunday clear, while bustling about through all the other six days. Well that is very much what the fourth commandment enjoins.

I have been looking at maps. After Doncaster the road here is north-west through places like Skipton and Settle. But I asked about Swaledale and Sibell says we will go there to-morrow, as it is superb. So far the little village of Dent is about the closest to Kisdon, though on a previous visit we went one day to Hawes which I have heard you mention.

Roger to-day is at some function at Giggleswick of which he is a governor. Yesterday S. took me to Sedbergh where Brendan Bracken fitted out for them the nicest library I have ever seen—quite perfect. We talked to a nice prefect. When I told him I was Humphrey's father his jaw fell.

23 October 1960 *Bromsden Farm*

This has been a most tiresome week, beginning with my having to spend five and a quarter hours of last Sunday arguing in London with two Americans called Benjamin and Mannheim. In the middle was a heavy lunch in a private room at the Dorchester—so is big business done—and the best one can say is that our side won a complete victory.

On Wednesday afternoon my old father (eighty-two) fell down in his service-flat in Knightsbridge and broke his femur (hip). Had it not

[1] *Last Poems*, xii.

been for the janitor bringing round the evening papers, the old boy would have lain on the floor in agony till morning. (The whole problem of old people who will insist on living alone is insoluble.) When I went to see him next morning he was not in pain, but grumbling as usual. His doctor told me on the telephone that if they put him to bed for three months and let it mend naturally he thought the old boy would never get up again, so on Friday they operated and inserted a 'pin'—all very successful, but my sister, who visited him yesterday in the London Clinic, reports him as a shocking patient, refusing to try and get up, as they want him to do, and being generally tiresome. I shall have to go and see him once or twice this week.

On Friday about 6 p.m., when Comfort was driving to Henley to meet me at the station, an idiotic little man, coming the other way, suddenly swung across C's bows and she hit him at about 55 m.p.h. That the fault was entirely his is little consolation, and it's a miracle that Comfort wasn't killed or badly hurt. In fact she is only very bruised and shocked. By the time I had been to the hospital, seen the police and collected Bridget from the station it was almost 9 p.m. We put Comfort straight to bed, where she has been ever since. She has a fever each evening, aches all over, and her teeth chatter if she gets out of bed. The doctor says these are all normal shock-reactions, and he thinks she will be all right in a few days. I didn't like the idea of her being alone here at night during the week, so this afternoon I bundled her up and took her over to a friend's where she is now in bed. All yesterday she wanted me to sit by her (very unlike her usual isolation), so one way and another Oscar has once again suffered. The car is a ghastly mess and will take weeks to mend, so I have had to hire a Hillman at huge cost—oh dear!

I couldn't help being a little cheered by this morning's *Sunday Times*, where Leonard Russell (the Literary Editor) writes: 'There are three men on my beat in London whom everyone loves—Sir Compton Mackenzie, Rupert Hart-Davis, and John Betjeman'. Even when such words are spoken in error (as here) they cannot fail to be encouraging.

Lady Chatterley has been adjourned till Thursday. I am apparently still on the short list of thirty defence-witnesses (selected, I am told, from four hundred volunteers), but can hardly think I shall be called. I hope however to see a bit of the fun. The defence were very keen to get some women on the jury, believing them to be more tolerant: please tell Pamela this.

I long to hear of your Swaledale drive. We love Hawes, and shop there, but it's in *Wensleydale*, which we like less than our beloved Swaledale.

27 October 1960 *Grundisburgh*

What a wretched week for you! I *am* sorry. All old men living by themselves have a fall sooner or later—and all men of character are shocking patients, chiefly because they don't really believe in doctors—and indeed there is a dreadful lot that doctors don't know, and the honest ones will admit it. And then Comfort's accident. I am always being horrified to read of accidents where *all* the blame is on one side, and how disturbing that thought is to one like me who always in any case expects the worst. Bed, they tell me, is the only thing for shock, so keep C. there till all symptoms are gone.

Pamela drove me over five hundred miles in all to and from Barbon, and we met no imbecile on the road, and also, which was odd for 1960, only an hour or so of rain altogether. There was quite a lot at Barbon and unluckily the worst day was that on which we meant to go to Swaledale. At Hawes we found ourselves in the middle of a wet dark cloud and could only come home. I wanted to get a picture of S. in my mind. But I suppose it is not very different from the majestic Barbondale or even Wensleydale, where we saw several little establishments advertising the famous cheese—but they tell me it isn't so good as it used to be. (But what is?)

I duly noted L. Russell's sentence in the *S.T.* and see no reason at all to doubt its truth. I don't think there will be an angry contradiction next Sunday. I never felt more sure of anything than that *Lady C.* should *not* be published unexpurgated. I hope you won't be summoned as a witness, for, if you are, I can't imagine what answer you will give to the question which any decent counsel must ask, *viz* 'How do these dozen passages lift the book from what it has been for thirty years in its unexpurgated form (which many think dullish) into a work of genius which mankind simply cannot do without?' Surely practically all the *real* reasons for 250,000 copies being printed are pornographic, and the pretence that they aren't is sheer *cant*. An Ipswich lawyer told me yesterday that the jury will condemn it, but I gather his prophecies in the past have nearly always been wrong.

The last book I read at Roger's was the life of Dr Arnold. I found myself hating him. That episode of his giving *eighteen* blows to a boy for lying merely shows him up as foully cruel and dreadfully stupid and impatient and self-assured; he made no attempt to find out if the boy might be telling the truth (which he was). And when the boy stayed out for two days the egregious old ass was convinced he was malingering. He should have been sacked after that caning—and nowadays, would be. It is clear Strachey didn't know about it. I wish he had. What portentous prigs Arnold's sixth-form boys were when they went to Oxford. The uncle in Clough's 'Dipsychus' described them very well.

29 October 1960 *Bromsden Farm*

I was disappointed to hear that you had missed Swaledale, for Wensleydale isn't a patch on it. Never mind—next time you visit Roger you must insist on going to Keld.

I'm happy to say that my old father is fast recovering, and Comfort is up and about again, still a little groggy but determined to resume her teaching on Monday. The car is still a crumpled ruin.

Your insistence on the suppression of *Lady Chatterley* is the only symptom of age that you have ever shown me, and I realise that the longer a tabu has been cherished, the harder it is to eradicate. Surely if you remove words from smoking-room stories and lavatory walls, and allow them to be printed in their proper context and meaning, they cease to be obscene and become ordinary—not in a moment, but in the course of time. As far as *Lady C.* is concerned, the expurgated passages seem to me the whole point of the book—but you will have read the evidence in *The Times*, and indeed I shall be thankful when the trial is over, for (being readily accessible by telephone) I have become a sort of Perpetual Twelfth Man for the defence witnesses. They never know whether any particular person is going to be five minutes in the box (E.M. Forster) or an hour and a half (Hough and Hoggart), so they keep having too few or too many witnesses waiting. At lunchtime on Thursday they thought they were going to run out, so sent out a three-line whip, as a result of which I sat from 2 till 4 gossiping with Tony Powell and Anne Scott-James. Asked to reappear at 10 a.m. on Friday, I found *fifteen* waiting. I sent in a message to the solicitor, saying that there were more than eleven waiting to bat, and if we had a batting-order, some of us could fall out. On this I escaped, but was urgently recalled for 2.30, when I probably *should* have been called if a legal argument had not occupied an hour and three-quarters. As it was, I talked to Dilys Powell, and for a short time watched Mr Justice Maude dealing with a teddy-boy knife-slasher in the next court. Now Dilys and I are both called for 10.30 on Monday. It must end soon.

In the middle of all that I attended a two-hour meeting, outspoken and acrimonious, about the direction of the Heinemann group, which, with two dinner-parties, produced such a rushed and exhausting week that I began to lose the power of sleep. However, ten hours last night helped a lot. Did I tell you (I'm sure I repeat myself much more than you do) that I am travelling to Rapallo next Thursday to attend the unveiling of a plaque on Max Beerbohm's Villino? It will mean forty-eight hours' travelling and ten hours there, but it will be a good change, and I look forward to the meals on the trains. You shall hear of it next week. I should get back here on Saturday night. I shall take Oscar with me: the Rome Express seems just the place for his letters to be corrected.

There seems to be a chance of Andrew Young's *Collected Poems* getting the Duff Cooper Prize this year, but it's not certain, so mum's the word. I should be delighted if it happened, for A.Y. is seventy-five and pretty hard up. The prize is worth only £150, but that's tax-free, and the publicity is bound to sell some copies of the book.

The Durrell book (*Zoo in my Luggage*) has gone off with such a bang that the first edition of *25,000* copies is almost exhausted: another 10,000 will be ready on November 18. A few more winners like that, and publishing would be a lot easier. Have you looked at *Hired to Kill*[1] yet? As usual, I can foresee *no* selling books for 1961, except Oscar if

[1] By John Morris (1960).

I can get him out, but perhaps something will turn up. Oh yes—yesterday I talked to Bernard Levin in the Old Bailey. He looks about *sixteen*, and at first I thought he was someone's little boy brought along to see the fun—very Jewish, with wavy fairish hair, very intelligent and agreeable to talk to. I imagine he is 'covering' the trial for the *Spectator*. Look out for it.

2 November 1960 *Grundisburgh*

Yes—old, narrow-minded, prim, stubborn—the perfect square in fact. That is what I mainly am, as you have spotted. *Lady C*'s jury must be much the same, but I suspect the temptation to show that they are not may sway them—though the first part of the judge's summing-up looks this morning to be rather against *Lady C*. I don't think the prosecutor was very forceful, but he was no doubt handicapped by the odd legal ruling about witnesses for the prosecution *not* to be asked about the book's decency. The rock I founder on is this. No doubt all those high-minded experts were quite sincere in their views about D.H.L.'s loftiness of aim, his support of marriage, and hatred of promiscuity, the book being an allegory etc etc, but how many of the 200,000 new readers will take it like that? Some day, you say, the essential beauty of all that frankness will be seen. A devilish long time, surely, before the giggle will be taken out of sex?

You weren't called, I gather. As you say, it was odd to see how differently witnesses were treated. One thought E.M. Forster would be a star witness, and he was in the box for five minutes, while e.g. Hoggart was a good deal badgered. (By the way, might not the absence of witnesses agin the book be owing to so few common readers having read the unexpurgated book? I wonder if there is anyone on the jury who holds firmly the old advice: 'Always consult experts, and always distrust them'.)

You *very rarely* repeat yourself—and your journey to Rapallo is new to me. So you won't get this till when—Sunday? Like old Shaw, you do a lot of work in the train. Good for Oscar. And what excellent news about the Durrell book. P. is enthralled in it at the moment. That *must* surely mean a few more bobs in the R.H-D. kitty, though according to A.P.H. no money is to be made out of books now. You ask about *Hired to Kill*, but, my dear R., I have never yet seen it. An intriguing (a banned word?) looking book about Tibet awaits me, from my ever-generous fairy godmother; and I have just—shuddering—finished *The She-Wolf of France*. What an almost appalling amount Druon knows about French history. There are so many characters that they close in on one like a jungle now and then. But I have discovered that to be a *little* hazy about all the relationships doesn't really matter and the story is very gripping. I looked up the further history of Mortimer in the *D.N.B.* and find he had the same end which he had inflicted on the younger Despenser—*not* a very kindly one. No doubt Dr Arnold would have approved—as indeed Queen Isabella did, with relish, in the front row of the stalls. And it gave a gust to her reception of Mortimer that night. Another *Lady C.*?

I am rather coming round to Bernard Levin—so long as he keeps off party-politics; his comments on things are full of point and wit. I never see his dramatic criticisms. Is he good at them? His fellows in it seem to me very capricious and untrustworthy. I see Doris Lessing thinks the end-pages of D. Cooper's book are artificial and so fail. She is, I need hardly say, quite wrong. Was it in the *T.L.S.* that I read a really first-class review of the book, and do you know who wrote it? Out of sight more understanding than any other I have seen. I think you will have to read Christopher Hollis's history of Eton, just out. As he says, much of it is based on Maxwell Lyte,[1] but M.L. had nothing about the last 96 years, and, even on ground common to both, H. is much the livelier. How Eton survived rapacious and hostile kings, the ineptitude and brutality of some of her headmasters, and her own fantastic and ridiculous ways down the centuries, is a mystery just as 'spirit-searching, light-abandoned' as any mentioned by the literary ladies of America to Martin Chuzzlewit. Hollis is excellent on my uncle Edward. The book is dedicated, if you please, to *me*—odd that the only error I found in a proof he sent me has been left uncorrected, viz that E.L. captained the last Cambridge side to beat the Australians, when of course everyone knows they did so again in 1882—after which one of their genial toughs said to a Cambridge man: 'In

[1] Sir Henry Churchill Maxwell Lyte (1848–1940), deputy keeper of the public records, published in 1875 *A History of Eton College 1440–1875*.

future you'll only have to hold up a light-blue cap and we'll run'. They have never run since.

The only other Australian dictum I know is, I think, Noble's (as good a judge of the game as ever was) after playing v. the Universities, that Oxford were so superior that it really was a pity the match should be played. The match was won by Cambridge (experts again!).

Thursday.

Well, so *Lady C.* won. The judge, surely, really summed up against it, but the jury, as I thought they would be, were either intimidated by that highbrow phalanx, or resolved to show that they were as jolly broad-minded as anyone. And I remain in (I suppose) a small minority —with however the brother and nephew of D.H.L. (his sister hails the verdict with rapture, but her face in the *Daily Telegraph* rouses a strong suspicion of insanity). I see that lofty moralist Sir Allen Lane hopes to publish a further 300,000—making half-a-million. What an unsuspected love of culture the public are showing! It is all very odd. And now we shall see what we shall see. I shall be surprised if we like it much.

Love to R. of course. See you both on Wed. *Lady C.* shall not be mentioned!

6 November 1960 *Bromsden Farm*

I got here exhausted late last night, so didn't read your letter till this morning. Don't be depressed about *Lady C.* See the last words of the full-page review in the *T.L.S.*: 'Young persons of either sex are the last out of whose hands anybody should think of keeping this book. The worst it could do to them would be to make them a little over-solemn'. See also Levin in the *Spectator*, and a splendid article by Ken Tynan in today's *Observer*. Anyhow that beastly Archbishop is on your side!

As you surmised, I was told on Monday morning that I wouldn't after all be called, so Ruth and I spent the morning in court as spectators and then went back to work. Everyone seems agreed that Richard Hoggart was the star-witness. I honestly don't foresee any evil consequences to this trial: pornography can still be prosecuted, and if a wedge has been driven between it and literature, as I think, *tant mieux*.

On Monday night Ruth and I were taken to *The Playboy of the Western World*, which I last saw in Dublin thirty years ago. I enjoyed it all over again, but shan't mind if I don't see it again for some time. By the end of the evening that poetic idiom of speech begins to sound like a trick, which is only *just* strong enough to support the Irish-whimsy anecdote. On Tuesday, agog, we go to *The Importance of Being Oscar*.[1]

Adam is home for Long Leave. He reports South Meadow totally flooded and Bud Hill's (once Piggy Hill's) garden awash. I was asked to review Hollis's *Eton* for the *T.L.S.*, but simply hadn't the time. Had I known that it is dedicated to you, I should have felt obliged to squeeze it in somehow.

I can't think why you haven't had *Hired to Kill*: it shall set off to waterlogged Suffolk tomorrow. The *T.L.S.* review of Diana was written by Alan Pryce-Jones: naturally it delighted Diana, as it did you and me.

Now for my journey. Ruth saw me off at Victoria at 9.30 a.m. on Thursday. A gale was raging in the Channel, but with the aid of two Kwells pills and a large brandy-and-soda I survived unsick in an armchair in the bar, and was able to do full justice to a wildly expensive but wholly delicious lunch on the Paris train. Altogether I ate five huge meals (four on trains and one at Rapallo), each of five courses and a half-bottle of wine, and felt all the better for it. I got to Paris at 5 p.m. (6 p.m. by French time), transferred my bags to the Rome Express, and strolled round the Gare du Nord till 7. A superb dinner (soup, a trout cooked with almonds, chicken, cheese and ice-cream), an hour's work on Oscar and a pretty good night in my sleeper. Got out at Rapallo at 10 a.m. A grey day, no sun but warm and dry. The little town put on all it knew for my benefit: first a fine funeral with purple-robed priests and much ornament, then banners bridging every street in honour of forthcoming elections: VOTA COMMUNISTA, DEMOCRAZIA CRISTIANA and so on. I had scarcely had a bath and

[1] A one-man performance by Micheál MacLiammóir, Irish actor, writer, painter and linguist (1899–1978).

changed when, right outside my window on the sea (by which open horse-carriages ply for hire under the palm-trees) an Armistice Day procession (the Italian armistice with Austria was on 4 November 1918) marched up with wreaths, bands, veterans and much fancy dress. Half an hour later when I went out for a walk I saw them all returning in a huge motor-boat—where from? I had some delicious coffee in a café, made a few purchases, and then worked on Oscar in my very comfortable hotel-room until 1.30, when I descended for the luncheon-party, twenty-two strong, given for the Ambassador (Ashley Clarke) by the Consul General from Genoa. I was between the retired C.G. (a Scotswoman called Fowler) and a writer called Cecil Roberts, a tolerably agreeable old queer. The lunch was Italian—shellfish (assorted), ravioli, *fritto misto* of local fish (so good that I had a second helping), excellent cheese and a fine chestnut pudding. Local wines, white and red. At 3 p.m. we were conveyed in three cars to the Villino, where a small crowd was waiting. As the Ambassador's Rolls pulled up opposite the house, the police stopped the traffic both ways on the narrow steep crowded road. The local mayor read out a speech in Italian, which I naturally couldn't understand. Then H.E. spoke (also in Italian) about Max, and I could follow most of it. By the time he pulled the cord which released British and Italian flags from the plaque, the traffic-jam stretched for several miles in both directions, with every horn hooting. Nevertheless there was just time for a last look at the terrace and garden, all very desolate and wintry, with house and study shuttered. Ichabod! As I was driven back to my hotel, infuriated motorists were still hooting, bumper to bumper, for miles.

I then had a nap and worked on Oscar till it was time to catch the Rome Express at 7 p.m. Another good dinner (Italian—the restaurant-car changes over at the frontier), more Oscar and another goodish night. At 8.30 a.m. yesterday I had *brioche* and *café-au-lait* in the dining-car and then settled down to a couple of hours of Oscar while the train first waited in the Gare de Lyon and then trundled round the *ceinture* to the Gard du Nord. Altogether I corrected more than a hundred galley-pages of Oscar, the longest consecutive stretch I've managed since Kisdon.

After putting my things in the Calais train I had an agreeable hour strolling round in the sun, examining a bookshop and having a drink in a café. A last delicious lunch on the Calais train, a smooth crossing, tea in the London train, a blissful reunion with Ruth at Soho Square, and down here by the 9.30 p.m. train. The whole thing was rather fun, and any guilty feelings of truancy were obliterated by such splendid progress with Oscar. Another such journey or two, and the back of the work would be broken!

The Heinemann business is dragging on, but there's little more I can do, so I refuse to let it worry me. My old father has now left the London Clinic and is back in his flat with day and night nurses in attendance, but my sister and I simply don't know what to try and arrange for his future. He has no constructive idea of any kind.

13 November 1960 *Bromsden Farm*

No letter this week, as arranged, but here, instead, is a one-question exam-paper. *Who* wrote this and *when*?

> If I am right it will be a slow business for our people to reach rational views, assuming that we are allowed to work peacefully to that end. But as I grow older I grow calm. If I feel what are perhaps an old man's apprehensions, that competition from new races will cut deeper than working men's disputes and will test whether we can hang together and can fight; if I fear that we are running through the world's resources at a pace that we cannot keep; I do not lose my hopes. I do not pin my dreams for the future to my country or even to my race. I think it probable that civilization somehow will last as long as I care to look ahead—perhaps with smaller numbers, but perhaps also bred to greatness and splendour by science. I think it not improbable that man, like the grub that prepares a chamber for the winged thing it never has seen but is to be—that man may have cosmic destinies that he does not understand. And so beyond the vision of battling races and an impoverished earth I catch a dreaming glimpse of peace.
>
> The other day my dream was pictured to my mind. I was walking homeward on Pennsylvania Avenue near the Treasury, and as I looked beyond Sherman's Statue to the west the sky was

aflame with scarlet and crimson from the setting sun. But, like the note of downfall in Wagner's opera, below the skyline there came from little globes the pallid discord of the electric lights. And I thought to myself the *Götterdämmerung* will end, and from those globes clustered like evil eggs will come the new masters of the sky. It is like the time in which we live. But then I remembered the faith that I partly have expressed, faith in a universe not measured by our fears, a universe that has thought and more than thought inside of it, and as I gazed, after the sunset and above the electric lights, there shone the stars.

You shall have the answer next week.

16 November 1960 *Grundisburgh*

Thank you for that very fine passage. It might well have been written by Judge Holmes, a very great man. In his letters there is often that deep bourdon note—he often looks at things *sub specie aeternitatis*, but not, of course, usually for as long a spell as this. Tell me all about it next week. G.K.C. sometimes strikes this note, e.g. in the account of the Battle of the Marne, Shaw never except in one tiny sentence about Ellen Terry. There was of course something rather shallow about him. He saw and knew that some Shakespeare passages were tremendous, but I don't think he *felt* them.

Hired to Kill has arrived and I start it to-night. What a memory you have for kind actions—I mean for *doing* them.

I have just been to the oculist—five guineas and new bi-focals which will cost about £10. Am trying a hearing-aid which is modestly priced at £63. I hear with it everything I don't want to hear much more clearly, voices only a little. Last Sunday I wore it till the first hymn in which the organ, plus a handful of now stentorian voices, nearly blew me from my seat. On the whole I hate it, but whether I shall be brave enough to tell Mr Plume so on Saturday, I gravely doubt. But £63!

I had a good crack with Roger and then Jonah on Wednesday, and Ivor Brown joined us. Lift home with R. and Roy Jenkins, clearly an excellent chap. How bad of Betjeman to shirk and leave an empty place next to his old tutor. Old Cuthbert was merely one protracted smile; I think being next to the most distinguished guest pleased him. Very natural.

I am writing 500-word biographies of sixteenth- and seventeenth-century literary men for Dick Routh. How *devilish* difficult it is to be brief and not dull. I told every new division at Eton of Wellington's apology for the length of his despatches from Spain: 'I had not time to make them shorter', which I suspect may be as '*crambe repetita*'[1] to you as Habakkuk. But there it is. I am sure Johnson has somewhere a majestic defence of repeated stories etc, but all I remember is a rather slighting reference to it as a habit of Swift. But he hated Swift and was as unfair about him as—comparing small with great—I am about Lawrence. Levin, by the way, begged too many questions; it is a little schoolboyish to overpraise all who take one view and sneer at all who take the opposite one. How hard our journalists find it to make *balanced* comment.

I suppose you don't yet loathe the winter as much as I do—more every year. It rains every night—not very much but enough to keep everything dank. Indoors is pleasant of course and would be even more so if coal cost the pound a ton that it used to. But let us count our blessings. Books are much easier to handle, print is better, and e.g. the Pastoral Symphony, now playing on a long record, is better than my aunt Sybil's piano-playing and Jack Talbot's throaty rendering of Maude Valerie White's 'Devout Lover'—'It is not mine to sing the stately grace, The great soul beaming in my lady's face' etc. The second line rather puts the lady with Mrs Wititterley who, you remember, suffered from being 'all soul'.[2]

Have you read Hollis's *Eton* yet? It is in many ways very good but a bit uneven, and oddly careless in places. Anyone who writes of Eton should not call *Wasey* Sterry *Walter*, or write '*on* the bill' instead of '*in* the bill'. I am glad he pillories Dr Goodall simply as 'that wicked man'. He wouldn't have *anything* changed, though he knew perfectly well that the conditions in College were sheer disgrace and that the Fellows were barefaced robbers. Eton in the first half of the nineteenth century was a ridiculously bad school. I can't think how it survived. I am glad too that Hollis—not *too* strongly—shows up the snobbish

[1] 'Cabbage hashed and rehashed.' Juvenal *Satires*, vii, 154.

[2] In *Nicholas Nickleby*.

arrogance of Julian Grenfell and co at Oxford; they were as bad as the segregationists of Louisiana and Milton's 'sons of Belial flown with insolence and wine'. Eddie Marsh loved them, but also hints at this unlovable trait in his autobiography. Still there remains 'The naked earth . . .'[1] and their deaths. *Per contra* Sir Philip Sidney wrote 'With how sad steps . . .' and 'Fool said my Muse; look in thy heart and write', and was loved by *everybody*. Would Julian Grenfell have given his water-bottle to a wounded Philip Sassoon? Did you know that Sidney, going into battle with a friend, found that the friend had left off some of his armour, and Sidney, therefore, doffed his own greaves that he should be at no advantage. So he was hit in the leg and subsequently died. Pamela's comment on this ultra-Quixotic heroism was, 'I think he must have been a bit dotty'. *We*, my dear Rupert, are the romantics. Women are delightfully matter-of-fact. Will dear Ruth corroborate this?

We shall see you this day week; we go to Diana's on Friday. I believe you will meet my two favourite nieces, both very good fun. Lavinia Dennys has the most impregnable derision for the game of cricket, thereby, considering the age-long atmosphere of Hagley, showing a considerable strength of mind. She was in the W.A.A.F.'s or A.T.S. in the war, and you cannot tell *her* anything she doesn't know about words of many letters or few. And the knowledge never did her a moment's harm (one for you and *Lady C.*!). The other, Anne Riddell, helped to run the Oxford University Registry and then, I gather, completely ran the University of Khartoum. Unmarried and apparently quite content. I accused her once of misanthropy. She denied this warmly, but added that the trouble was that all the men she most liked were middle-aged and happily married. That was at Oxford. In Khartoum she says that on the whole the Egyptian young men she meets are more civilised, intelligent, courteous, and generally nicer than the British—but you can't marry an Egyptian. So what?

[1] In Julian Grenfell's poem 'Into Battle'.

Sorry this paper has turned blue: it was the only colour Ruth could find. Full marks for your test-question. Those words *were* by Judge Holmes, and the astonishing thing is that they were spoken at a Harvard Law School dinner in New York on 15 February *1913*. Look at them again, and marvel at the old boy's foresight and perspicacity. When you've got your new spectacles and a £63 hearing-aid, there'll be no more mobbing in div.[1]

I fear T.S.E. will haunt the Lit. Soc. no more, after an evening with Cuthbert on one side and vacancy on the other. Leslie Hartley sent an abject apology next day, but Betjeman has made no sign. I now think I should have bullied you or Ivor into moving over to the other side of the table, but I couldn't believe that *two* people would default without notice. Jonah was in goodish form: you should have discussed *Lady C.* with him, for he seemed to share your views. I am in the middle of correcting the proofs of his stories, which read a little better in print (most things do), but are unlikely to set the smallest stream on fire, I fear.

The Duke of Wellington's admirable remark about brevity in writing was quite new to me—so there! And I'm prepared to bet that I *do* hate the winter as much as you do. Hibernation or Jamaica seem the only tolerable cures. I haven't yet read Hollis's *Eton*, and don't know who took my place as *T.L.S.* reviewer. If you haven't already done so, *do* write Frank Swinnerton a fan-letter. He's a pet, and his address is *Old Tokefield, Cranleigh, Surrey.*

You seem to think Diana's dinner-party is on Wednesday, but I have *Thursday* down in my book. I much look forward to meeting your favourite nieces, cricketing or otherwise.

Last Tuesday I attended the sixtieth birthday celebrations of my old friend Hamish Hamilton, the publisher, who first insinuated me into the lamentable trade. The proceedings began with a gala performance of *Romeo and Juliet* at the Old Vic, which I thoroughly enjoyed. Wonderful scenery, and every word audible—and *what* words! I know the play so well that I was outraged by a number of pointless cuts, and the Mercutio ruined the Queen Mab speech by trying to

[1] i.e. ragging in school.

make it funny instead of allowing the poetry to carry it through, but on the whole it was pure pleasure.

Then back to the Hamiltons' house in St John's Wood, where at midnight we sat down eleven strong to a sumptuous dinner (bortsch, pheasant, and a superb Italian sweet—Mrs H. is Italian—good white and red wine, champagne and brandy). I was blissfully placed between Lady Drogheda (an angel and old friend) and no less a person than the Duchess of Kent, for whom I fell hook, line and sinker. Very attractive, intelligent, charming and cultivated. Her sister, Princess Paul of Yugoslavia, to whom I talked after dinner, is another charmer. She speaks countless languages, including Yugoslav and Swahili. I said 'I'm sure your sister can't speak them', and she said 'But, you see, she's much younger than me', which I thought delightful. Altogether the evening, which I had been dreading for weeks, was pure joy.

I had sent my host, as a birthday present, a fountain pen, which I knew he wanted, and in an accompanying note I described him as 'just the man to put the sex into sexagenarian', which seemed to please him.

How soon is your *Times* cast away? Duff had an article in last Thursday's (November 17) on the court page, anonymous and called 'Mysterious Altercation'. Do look at it. He is now film critic of the *Western Mail*, has had two articles on Welsh spas accepted for the leader page, and is to broadcast from Cardiff!

26 November 1960 *Bromsden Farm*

Habit dies hard, but this won't be a letter, just a tiny snack between meals. And talking of meals, that was a delightful dinner at Diana's, and I was so happy to be between her and Pamela. I thought your two nieces charming, and only wished I had had more opportunity of talking to the married one. The male American must surely be one of the stupidest men at liberty? He seemed to be suffering from concussion, I thought.

On the way to dinner I had paid a brief visit to my old father, and couldn't help being moved by the pathos and irony of two excellent women (nurse and physiotherapist) *forcing* the old boy to walk again, when he has nowhere to walk to, and no desire to move.

Adam has just rung up to say he will be home for next week-end, on his way to his scholarship-exam at Oxford, and that he will be bringing a boy called Fitzhugh with him. It could scarcely be less convenient, as Comfort will have all her own exam-papers to correct.

I am once again deep in Oscar, pausing only to read through the *Satires* of Juvenal in search of a quotation (if I ever achieve retirement I shall try to regain a little Latin through the excellent Loeb Classical Library) or to seek for French Anarchists in the *Encyclopaedia Britannica*. Jonah's proofs must be finished by Monday, but I have had enough of those stories. I am reading countless books (mostly bad) about the 1890s, and am slowly coming to know quite a lot about that maligned decade.

The oak-tree in front of this window is still clinging to some of its leaves, and there are almost always a couple of cock-pheasants eating underneath it: do they particularly like acorns? The nuthatches are back at the bird-table, but today they gave place to a spotted woodpecker. The world is so full of a number of things . . .

I should have liked to attend D. Somervell's funeral, but it was in the country and I couldn't, as they say, make it.

St Andrew's Day 1960 *Grundisburgh*

Thank God I am not playing at the Wall to-day. It is anyhow an immensely absurd game, but in mud—well, there aren't any adjectives. Glance at Hollis's *Eton*, where there is a picture of it—in mud!—which in a sane society would kill it. But then of course a sane society would kill county and test cricket too. And if it comes to that a *perfectly* sane man wouldn't have written to me last Sunday. On the whole I am glad we *don't* live in a completely sane world—partly of course because that is what E. Summerskill and others of her kidney would like (how nauseating to think of E.S.'s kidney!).

I knew you would like whichever niece you had a crack with. Alexander and Diana always like *large* parties. The American mainly talked finance with Alexander. I gave him a widish berth. We saw

Anne Riddell again on Sunday. She confided to us that R.H-D. was simply 'it'. I knew she would. Of course she ought to be married—she is thirty-five, *but* I live in hope. Diana married at thirty-seven, and nothing can be happier than *that*.

Your old father. Yes, there is something immensely pitiful about old age when, basically, the wish is to be left to pass quietly away—but they never let one do that—excepting of course such benefactors as good Dr Bodkin Adams (bad luck for him that he should have the *face* of a murderer!).

We called on the Cranworths yesterday. He has (*aetat* eighty-three) also taken to a hearing-aid—of the type that *my* good man said was *not* now regarded as satisfactory. He doesn't like it (Lord C.) any more than I do mine, but I handed on, to his comfort, the unanimous testimony to the good results of use and patience. At present if anyone drops a pen I am deafened by the din, but hear much less well the human voice. However *my* comfort is that Pamela definitely says she no longer 'has to bellow like a bull' (wives *do* exaggerate you know) at our *tête-à-tête* meals, so all is not lost. Poor old Cranworth seemed to me to hear no better than before (such was his belief too) but I fear that often his brain was not taking much in. There would surely be literally nothing to be said against euthanasia if it wasn't for nears and dears. I like the story of the old Roman who lay in a hot bath with a vein open, chatting with his friends, and plugged the vein whenever the talk was interesting, and removed it when the interest faded. The Yank's talk you met at the Hoods' would have led to no plugging of *your* veins, I opine (such a good word. I haven't used it for years).

I had an excellent evening with Jonah *tête-à-tête*—a delicious dinner which he said was *exactly* the same as the one he gave you—just as it should be. I can never see that the old boy is at all a bore, as I believe some still find him. He was full of good observations—humorous, pertinent, percipient. His deep affection for the Lit. Soc. is very pleasant.

Do you ever dine at *Prunier's*? That is where Alexander took us on his cook's night-off. Marvellous food, and gosh! the fistful of notes which A. disbursed at the end. If he was anyone else, how abashed we should feel at the fare he gets here—e.g. soup, scrambled eggs and cheese—but he takes it in his placid and amiable stride.

3 December 1960 *Bromsden Farm*

I have just been listening to Mahler's Second Symphony on the radio—did you hear it? I enjoyed it enormously, and all the more in contrast to Alban Berg's opera *Wozzeck*, which I heard last night at Covent Garden. It is based on a German Expressionist play (someone in the interval said it was like *Carmen* written by Freud) and is written in what I believe is called atonal music. To a non-musical novice this seems like a free-for-all in the orchestra-pit, with distressing results. Nevertheless I found it all interesting, and the Droghedas' box (which is really two boxes) is attached to a private dining-room in which an excellent dinner is served *seriatim* during the intervals. The French Ambassador was of the party but consumed only a glass of water.

On Thursday I was summoned to a drink at Kensington Palace, to tell Princess Alexandra the drill for the Duff Cooper Prize, which she is to bestow next Wednesday. I thought her enchanting—infinitely easy to talk to, intelligent, and very attractive, with pale chestnut hair and a lovely skin. Her photographers don't do her justice. The Duchess of Kent was there, and their nice secretary Philip Hay—all very enjoyable.

On Wednesday I went to Cambridge and spent the night with Madeline House. We both dined with Graham Storey in his rooms in Trinity Hall and talked about the Dickens Letters, which they are jointly editing.

On Monday (sorry to work backwards so relentlessly) I dined very cosily with Joyce Grenfell and her husband (very old friends) in their flat. Joyce has promised to write a book (autobiographical) for me to publish.

Yesterday, before the opera, I had a feverish two-hour session on the Oscar proofs with the excellent Henry Maas, who is helping enormously.

Adam is home, en route for Oxford, and is even now playing bridge with Comfort, his friend Fitzhugh, and a neighbour. His Second Five side was beaten in the final, but he still has a chance of getting his House Colours, since Fred's are in the final of the House Cup, and their regular Goals is a doubtful starter. A. is in the semi-final of the Chess Cup.

Duff may have the chance of a job on the new *Sunday Telegraph* in London in February. He saw the editor in London yesterday and will know the result on Monday. If he gets it, he will speedily get married, and since Bridget looks like getting her chap to the altar in August, I shall spend next year in and out of Moss Bros.

Jonah's proofs are still with me. I went through them with him on Thursday, but his writing is so illegible that I must transfer all the corrections on to a clean set of proofs before sending them back to the printer.

I wonder how your deaf-aid responded to Gilbert and Sullivan. I'm sure you ought to persevere with it, and I assure you it doesn't *show* at all.

I have only once or twice flown as high as Prunier's, when it was quite first-rate.

On Monday Ruth and I are giving the Eliots dinner at the Garrick, on Tuesday we trek to Twickenham for The Match, and afterwards dine with Max's sister-in-law. Wednesday is the Prize-giving—and so it goes on.

I read nothing but memoirs of the 80's and 90's, though I have ordered Betjeman.[1] The wind is wailing, the rain lashing. I shan't go out tomorrow if I can help it. The library is warm and cosy. Please give my love to Pamela—and to yourself.

7 December 1960 *Grundisburgh*

I like paper which turns blue—light blue of course, which reminds me that you saw a fine Cambridge victory at Twitnam. My blood-thirsty soul wishes they had topped twenty points in the second half. They seem to have been a pretty hot side. Scotland of course is a bit of a genius; the first try reads finely in both *Times* and *Telegraph*. (I see the blue paper was your November 19 letter: I am an incurable leaver-about.)

Mahler. You are, *pace* your declaration, a higher-browed music-lover than I—but I don't really know Mahler and didn't hear his symphony. Encouraged by you I will try him next time he is on. I

[1] *Summoned By Bells* (1960).

have heard a bit of *Wozzeck*, and like the stuffiest of Victorians (which I fundamentally am) I find it hard to believe anyone who says he enjoys it. I would as soon listen to the road-drillers (who I see have been afflicting Dame Edith Sitwell). 'Atonal' frankly means 'cacophonous'. I wonder what 'interested' you in it. My tastes are very mild and old-fashioned. I don't really stretch much above Beethoven's Pastoral Symphony. Summing up, I enjoy quite a lot, but I don't think I understand very much. You can probably follow the plan of a symphony and have a notion of its structure. I don't and haven't. Drogheda's box sounds all right, but really the French Ambassador and his glass of water! Like Edward VIII when Prince of Wales being lunched by the Harlech golf-club, which scoured the principality for viands and vintages—and he asked for rice-pudding and lime-juice, neither of which they had. But that was either bad manners, or bad organisation by his major-domo. However we were still eating the lunch meant for him weeks afterwards, so good came out of evil.

Did you realise that Reggie Grenfell was a cousin of mine—and also a pupil at Eton? I have never heard you mention him. I have met Joyce only once or twice, and—like everybody else—liked her immensely. Keep her up to that book. Where is their flat? I must call on them.

The news of your family sounds good. I suppose A. has the Chess Cup in his pocket—or is there some morbid K.S. who has played since he was two? Duff seems to have his foot firmly on the ladder. Are you happy about his marrying so young? There is no general rule about such things. Circumstances alter cases. But the chap who said 'A young man married is a young man marred' wasn't talking 100% rubbish. I still have wedding-garments—about thirty years out of fashion, and as a brilliant daughter put it, more Moth Bros than Moss ditto—and relish the feeling that I shall never wear them again; I would give them to Humphrey, if he ever wore anything but sacking.

We will aim at a Monday for our annual—and invariably delightful—luncheon *chez vous*. The mud round about you will not actually engulf us I, presume? My exam-papers start piling up on Saturday and I must miss the Lit. Soc. next week. Please tell me all about it. Jonah's writing is baffling, though I know worse. I have no sympathy with the really illegible, though I suppose some cannot really help it, however hard that is to believe.

We went to *The Mikado* last week, myself well furnished with hearing-aid, which, *more suo*, was fairly good at the voices but made the trombone etc deafening. But I shall, they tell me, learn to discriminate.

Talking of criticism, how bad Sir Charles Petrie is in the *Illustrated London News* on Behrman's Max book. Who *is* Sir C.P. and why should anyone suppose he is capable of appreciating Max? He says that M.B. liked the Paddington Hotel perhaps because a royalty died in it. Evidence? I hate writing like that, and so many indulge in it.

I have just written biographies of Spenser, Sidney and Marlowe for some venture of Dick Routh's. To get any of 'em into 550 words and be interesting—well how the devil is it done? I wonder if I have sufficiently concealed my opinion that *The Faery Queene* is unreadable. Columbia University in their rather disgraceful plebiscite on 'the ten most boring classics' had it second to *Pilgrim's Progress. Paradise Lost* was third or fourth and later in the list came *Silas Marner*, *Ivanhoe*, and *Boswell's Life of Johnson*!! All of which makes me very dubious about alliance with America in spite of Abe Lincoln and Stonewall Jackson—oh yes and *certainly* Judge Holmes, as great as any. I must go and hew wood, but *not*, you will be surprised to hear, draw water. Really the rain!

Love to Ruth. You didn't send me hers in your last letter. I grieve—but understand!

10 December 1960 *Bromsden Farm*

This afternoon I drove through snow and icy wind to Oxford and fetched home Adam after his week of scholarship-papers. To-morrow he returns for two interviews, and on Monday a Chemistry Practical (how many marks should *we* score in that, dear George?), so we should know the result pretty soon. He thinks he did pretty well, but we shall see. It is now certain that he is to play in the final of the House Cup on Wednesday, so his House Colours seem assured. The Chess Cup is still in the semi-final stage, but Friday is the beginning of the holidays.

Duff has apparently heard no more of his London job: at least we've heard nothing from *him*.

I certainly can't follow the plan of a symphony or any other musical work, but I can get lots of pleasure out of it. Do try Mahler: he is very lyrical and romantic, and several of his symphonies introduce singers. He is nothing like *Wozzeck*. Nor is Sibelius, that doom-laden Finn, whose Second Symphony I enjoyed this evening. Try him again too.

I certainly didn't realise that Reggie Grenfell was a cousin of yours, though from his niceness I might have guessed. Their address is Flat 8, 34 Elm Park Gardens. It's between the Fulham and King's Roads and would be handy from Chelsea Square. Reggie and Joyce have been dear friends since 1927, though I don't see them as often as I'd like.

Duff's marriage? Since I was first married at twenty-two, and again at twenty-six, I am not in a strong position to tell him he is too young at twenty-four and a half. In any case marriage is surely partly a matter of luck—whether you grow at the same pace in the same direction, and things like that—and, though wisdom of a sort comes with age, luck is impartial.

Sir Charles Petrie is a bearded DUD. On no account read anything he writes. I'm sure Max stayed at railway hotels because (1) they were comfortable (2) he was unlikely to be bothered by anybody he knew (3) the child in him responded to the romance of trains leaving for distant places.

I shall attend the Max Beerbohm sale at Sotheby's on Monday, Tuesday and Wednesday, and have agreed to be interviewed by the B.B.C. Television on Monday morning, though goodness knows what I'm supposed to say. Last week Ruth and I spent two lunch-times examining the stuff that is to be sold— and we did a lot of other things too.

On Monday we finally penetrated the fastnesses of the Home Office and were allowed to examine and check Oscar's prison-petitions and other documents—very interesting and touching. That evening we dined very agreeably with the Eliots at the Garrick. T.S.E. seemed unmoved by his exposure to Cuthbert, and was altogether more robust than he was in the summer, though his lungs and heart (his wife told me privately) are still as dicky as could be, so that he might pop off at any moment.

On Tuesday the rain miraculously held off for Twickenham, and our corner seats turned out splendidly, for all the scoring—and

Dawkins's terrific last-minute efforts for Oxford—took place right in front of us. Cambridge were infinitely superior, and the great Sharp was made to look paralytic.

That night we had a terrific German dinner with Elisabeth Beerbohm's sister and brother-in-law—a wonderful fish-dish of sole in a sort of bun, flooded with a delicious sauce of lobster and shrimps; very good pheasant with sour cream sauce, cherry jam, potatoes and sauerkraut; a superb almond cream sweet, and a heavenly Riesling (two bottles among four). We both felt stupefied afterwards but thoroughly enjoyed it all.

On Wednesday was the unveiling of the Duff Cooper plaque in the crypt of St Paul's—very well handled by the Dean and Harold Nicolson. On in a hired car to Hyde Park Gate, where Princess Alexandra very charmingly gave the Duff Cooper Prize to my poet Andrew Young.

From your silence about *Hired to Kill* I imagine you hated it.

Oh yes—in one of George Moore's books Max wrote:

ELEGY ON ANY LADY
by G.M.

That she adored me as the most
Adorable of males
I think I may securely boast . . .
Dead women tell no tales.

Max's books are full of delicious little *jeux* like that. I only wish I could afford to buy a few, but I expect they'll fetch thousands.

14 December 1960 — *Grundisburgh*

It has rained all day. The glass is rather high, the forecast said there was an anti-cyclone over England. Such are the facts. I make no comment or complaint; only an occasional question like Sam Weller's crosses my mind, 'Ain't somebody going to be whipped for this 'ere?' Incidentally this is the driest region in England.

Your letter arrived yesterday just as I was going into Ipswich—in a black tie, of course, as no doubt you were, it being the day of the month on which Dr Johnson died. Quite a good day to choose. I always thought the period between St Andrew's Day and Christmas Day the gloomiest stretch of the year. Pitch-dark, dank, thoroughly sulky, no character. But don't forget next Saturday p.m. is *one* minute longer than it was last Saturday.

I expect you may have had news of Adam's venture by now. I do hope it was successful. You are right about my knowledge of chemistry. One thing alone I retain from Tubby Porter, viz that 'a body immersed in liquid loses in weight the weight of the liquid displaced'. I have found it most useful in life. For the rest I am incurably non-scientific, and full of pro-humanity saws like Dr J's 'We are perpetually moralists, but we are geometricians only by chance'.[1]

Anyway warmest congratulations to him on his House Colours. Let us hope he won't emulate the boy spoken of by a preacher at Eton (oh yes, *Crum*). The boy's *one* ambition was to play goals for his house in the final, and so after many vicissitudes he did—the day of his life. All his family came to watch and hoped he would distinguish himself. And so he did—by putting the ball through his own goal.

Stupid of me not to have looked up the Grenfells before. I somehow thought they didn't live in London. Her father Paul Phipps was a delightful man. I remember a nice simple witticism of his. My sister on the way to church with large party said: 'I do hope the hymn books won't run out'. To which P.P. said 'If they do, I'll run after them'.

I love asking you about X. and Y. Your replies are so direct and have an air of rightness—no doubt partly because they so often corroborate a suspicion of my own. I pay no more attention to the bearded Dud. Max's sale seems to have made a mort of money. I hope you are pleased? I have a feeling that the *sneerers* are soon to have a go at him—as they will too at Betjeman.

What did you say on TV? The hour is surely nearing when we shall have to get a TV. Not *quite* yet. Sixty guineas for a hearing-aid and a cool million on the roof has temporarily put me back a bit.

I am interested in your saying Sharp was obliterated in the O. and C. match. It proves that though in the first class he is not yet at its

[1] *Life of Milton.*

top. You couldn't obliterate Stoop or Monro or Davies in old days. Like Hitler's their motto was '*So—oder so*', i.e. 'If not in this way, then in that'. But someone told me weeks ago that the Cambridge forwards were tremendous.

I have been reading *The Duke's Children*. I forget whether you are a Trollope fan. I love him—and am maddened by him. The snobbery thick—a slab of the times and circles he wrote about, and those infuriatingly virginal young women. They all need a soupçon of *Lady C.*! Apropos of which I see Sir Allen Lane, contemplating the sales of one and a half million of 'em, expressed distress that many people had bought them from the wrong motives! I suppose that the tiniest whisper of 'humbug' would have made R. West, Joan Bennett, that bishop, K. Tynan, B. Levin (and R.H-D.?) red with indignation??

Oh dear, I thought I had told you how much I liked *Hired to Kill* at least a fortnight ago—and certainly Young's poems two months ago. Forgive apparent gracelessness. But *H to K* also humiliated me—not that I didn't know it already—by proving what a rotten critic I am. I liked the book very much, but couldn't for the life of me say why. The only silver lining was that a good many of the reviewers suffered from the same disability. He is a delightfully *honest* writer. Perhaps honesty is as rare in literature as in life.

How good you are about menus. I share your gulosity at second-hand. That embunned sole and its sauce! It added a relish to Pamela's kedgeree, which, I may say, is by no means to be despised.

Thank you for M.B. on G. Moore. Delicious. I should like to see his jottings on A.C. Benson's *Beside Still Waters*, one of those sweet spinsterish books he used to pour out like Tupper.[1] I have heard M.B.'s parody of A.C.B. in *A Christmas Garland* called very cruel, but that seems to me rot. The smallest exaggeration made A.C.B.'s stuff *wholly* absurd. Was that M.B.'s fault? But he was wrong about Kipling. I suppose his nausea at K's bounce and noise and vulgarity blinded him to the tremendous merits of K's best.

[1] Martin Tupper, poet and inventor (1810–1889). His versified *Proverbial Philosophy* sold many editions.

16 December 1960 *Grundisburgh*

Ten million cheers! I haven't been so pleased for years! I have sent Adam congratulations, but doubt if they will get to him till Monday. I should have rung you up, but for believing that Friday sees you *en route* for B.F. It really is quite splendid.

17 December 1960 *Bromsden Farm*

This has been an exciting week. On Tuesday night we heard (as you have probably since read) that Adam had been awarded an Open Scholarship (or, as they call it, Postmastership) at Merton, having apparently been placed top of all the scientific candidates! Much jubilation at Eton, as you can imagine.

Next day A. played (as substitute Goals) in the final of the House Cup, the only player on either side in a white shirt. It was *bitterly* cold, with ankle-deep mud. I went down by train to Slough, thence by taxi. It was an exciting fast game, but I walked round a good bit, trying to keep warm, and talked to the Coleridges, the Headmaster, Van Oss, and one or two friends (Kenneth Wagg, Michael Astor) who had boys engaged. Two-all at full time. Ten minutes extra each way. Still two-all. Darkness falling rapidly. After a lengthy consultation in midfield they agreed to play five more minutes each way. After some three minutes a boy called Perkins got the ball through Snow's goal, and Coleridge's had won for the first time, after four previous failures in the final (including Duff's year). Adam was given his House Colours on the field, and I almost wept with pride and joy. He hadn't had much to do (having Lumley, the Field Long, in front of him), but he did it adequately. I wonder if he'll ever have two such exciting days again?

Meanwhile Duff has finally clinched the job on the new *Sunday Telegraph* in London, and is to start work there on January 9 at £18. 10. a week. This means he can get married, since his girl (Phyllida Barstow) already has a similar job in London. Easter week is being considered as a suitable time. The wedding will be at her home in Wales. When they all arrived this morning (after a dance in London last night) we cracked a bottle of champagne in general congratulation. (Adam is in the final of the Chess Cup—to be played off next half.)

The Beerbohm sale was fun, with high prices. My television interview about Max was conducted at Sotheby's at 10 a.m. in riotous confusion, and was shown in the news at 10 p.m.—not, thank goodness, to me.

Ruth had a beastly cold and cough on Monday, so I put her to bed in the spare room in the flat and nursed her whenever I could. She slept a lot and went home yesterday much rested and improved.

The Lit. Soc. was ruined for me by that ghastly Lockhart, who sat (as usual) next to me, with (as usual) an empty chair on his other side, and talked of the sales-figures of his own books. We had fillets of sole, saddle of mutton and vanilla soufflé *or* mushrooms on toast. All quite good.

I say, what about that Test Match in Australia! If only that tempo and spirit could be preserved into 1961! I think Sharp's chief trouble in the U.M. was that his scrum-half was so slow in getting the ball to him, and the Cambridge forwards were so quick, that they were always on top of him before he could pass or even kick.

Adam is to spend his last two halves doing German and French with Van Oss. Since he will be in Sixth Form and will presumably have no exams, he should have a good time. At the moment he is concerned only with his Driving Test, which takes place on Thursday. Sorry there's so much family in this letter, but it has been rather a family week. I have done *nothing* so far about Christmas presents—oh dear!—and this week I have to lunch with the editor of *The Times* and go to another opera. When do you go to Eton? And what address there? Oscar, as you can imagine, lingers in galley-proof. I fear you will be sick of hearing about those letters long before you see them. And there are moments when I despair of finality. At the Max sale I saw S.C. Roberts, who reported a good Johnson Club evening (with himself as speaker). Shall we ever go again?

Shortest Day 1960 *Holland House*
Eton College

This is rather a hectic affair after a perfect day's journeying from Grundisburgh, except for the too-dazzling sun in P's eyes (December 22!) and an occasional patch of ice or muddy grease. Whereas in Suffolk every road was as dry as a D.H. Lawrence novel.

I did send you a card and the Postmaster a word of congratulation the moment I saw the great news, but I fear it didn't reach either before Monday. It was a magnificent achievement, and already I gather the science staff here are walking about looking several inches taller, as Mr Shandy said all women look after producing a baby (and every right they have to do so). You too should be what one can only call cock-a-hoop—in fact *I think* your letter shows signs of it. After all it really *was* a week for you. Duff's weekly wage sounds very handsome. In my day it would have been £4. Wage-earners of all kinds, grave and gay, are, roughly, the new well-to-do. The poor old *rentier*'s number is up—those who live on their savings and investments. No doubt we have had our day, and anyway there is nothing we can do about it.

You are too kind about Lockhart, and ought firmly to plant him next e.g. to Jonah or Harold Nicolson; both of whom, in their different ways, would deal with him faithfully. Last Lit. Soc. sounds a good party—good fare too. I share the Forsyte view of saddle of mutton. In the pre-pre-war Simpson days no man of taste had anything else for lunch (second help—or should I say 'additional portion'?—*free*!). Total cost—with cut of Stilton—four shillings. Have you read Harold N's last book?[1] As a worker, he looks to be in the R.H-D. class. But I was sorry to read that one reviewer thinks H.N. 'doesn't much like Dr Johnson'. That would be a grave failing in an otherwise good man. I shall tackle him at the next Lit. Soc.

We have in mind and joyful hope coming to you for lunch on Sunday week. How does that strike you? Pamela pessimistically thinks the track to Bromsden Farm from the road must surely be impassable with mud. I—never having had much opinion of Nature's common

[1] *The Age Of Reason* (1960).

sense—have a notion that the track is for some reason just as stolchy (Suffolk) in dry weather as in wet.

Boxing Day 1960 *Bromsden Farm*

Adam was particularly delighted by your letter, and it was charmingly thoughtful of you to write. A letter from the Headmaster announces his award of O.S.[1]—which nicely matches Duff's. I do indeed feel very cock-a-hoop about the boys and their satisfactoriness. I'm glad to say they'll both be here next Sunday, when we shall expect you about 12.45. Does Pamela remember the way? If not, telephone and I'll remind you.

So far our Christmas has passed off peacefully. I have had a number of 'useful and acceptable' presents, including a superb case of Riesling from Max's sister-in-law, but the one which pleased me and Ruth most was two home-made cakes from our Kisdon farmer and his family. How I wish we were there now, with perhaps some of that snow on high ground of which the radio-announcer so fruitily speaks.

It isn't a question of my being *kind* to Lockhart, but rather of my failing to take adequately defensive measures by inviting two others to sit beside me. Harold N., who was responsible for introducing this giant bore to the assembly, always takes good care to sit far away from him. I don't think I shall bother with H.N.'s latest: it sounds an unnecessary book, and he is clearly past his best. Poor Geoffrey Faber, I hear, has had another stroke and is pretty well unconscious, having to be fed through the nose. One can't wish him long continuance of such horrors.

Last week, in the intervals of frantic, and largely abortive, last-minute shopping, I lunched with Sir William Haley at the Athenaeum (potted shrimps, liver and bacon, treacle tart—all of which would have been good if they hadn't been luke-warm). W.H. neither drinks nor smokes, but graciously joined me in a half-pint of rather good cider, which he apparently (and quite wrongly) considers non-alcoholic.

On Thursday Ruth and I were taken to yet another opera,

[1] Oppidan Scholar.

Donizetti's *Lucia di Lammermoor*, a splendid rip-roaring piece based on Scott's novel and wonderfully sung by Joan Sutherland: very enjoyable, but like most operas a little too long.

I have brought the tattered galley-proofs of Oscar down with me (I've been carrying them about and tinkering with them since *May*!) hoping once again that I may at last get a glimpse of finality.

By the way, have you ever read Geoffrey Faber's *Oxford Apostles*? I simply can't put it down, and I only took it up to supply a footnote for Oscar. Do try it if you don't know it. The whole matter seems at once so remote and so compelling. Ivor Brown has sent me the typescript of his new word-book, which I think I must publish. I'm also reading a new French novel and a manuscript about an eighteenth-century quack, so you see I'm not exactly as idle as I could wish.

5 January 1961 *University Arms Hotel*
Cambridge

My dear Rupert

Now this really *is* a miserable affair—the cold fact being that we are kept pretty hard at work all day, and after dinner there has been a lot of 'Come and have a glass of port' which always dribbles on till near midnight. And one night my colleagues insisted on taking me to the pictures, if you please—a film called *The Man in the Moon* which they assured me was desperately funny, and indeed they laughed like prep-school boys at what seemed to me to be comicalities of marked insipidity. So what will you, as the French say?

Our whole trip to you was, as always, a real and refreshing break. Your welcome (being *vester*, not only *tuus*) is invariably warming to the cockles (whatever they may be) of one's heart. Your Adam is the sort of boy who reassures one about the country's future—a grand eighteen-year-old, and so Pamela thought too.

Yesterday we were among bibliographers and such, who were talking of a publication of yours of immense size and complexity, full of anagrams and other word-puzzles which do sound very baffling. Someone put the point that there could be no money in such a venture, to which another replied to the effect that R.H-D. didn't worry very much about that side of publishing. And subsequent remarks would have added to the tingling of your ears, if not to the pricking of your thumbs. (Would *Sir Richard Roos* be the book's name?)[1]

I go back to-morrow or Saturday and—*more meo*—am sure that the roads will be icy. Pamela picks me up here, she is at present at the Lawrences' house at Great Milton near Oxford. I was there once with friends who had a caravan. The horse was called Aaron and strongly supported my conviction of horse stupidity. It resisted capture every morning with a sort of lumpish skittishness, and playfully bit the

[1] By Ethel Seaton (1961). A study of a fifteenth-century poet.

owner of the caravan in the elbow, not really meaning to hurt, but as the animal weighed about a ton, it *did* hurt a good deal. I was always busied with setting out the breakfast arrangements.

Yours ever
G.W.L.

7 January 1961 *Bromsden Farm*
Henley-on-Thames
Oxon

My dear George

Knowing the orgiastic nature of all Examiners' Nights at Cambridge, I think it noble of you to write at all, let alone such an admirable letter. Your visit was, as usual, a tremendous success with all ranks, and I'm only sorry you missed Duff, who is now fully recovered and preparing to start his London career on Monday. This afternoon Adam played chess for Bucks v. Surrey in the Slough Community Centre, and I'm sorry to say was beaten in the thirty-fourth move.

I haven't sent you *Sir Richard Roos* because in any ordinary sense it is unreadable. Don't tell your Cambridge friends, but it has been entirely paid for by its author, so its lack of sales leaves my withers comparatively unwrung.

Today I have wasted much time observing the six long-tailed tits on the bird-table. None has ever come there before, but these six seem to have taken to it, and their combined weight deters even the bullying nuthatch. I hate starlings, don't you? Predatory, clumsy and verminous. Here are two of Max's triolets, which he wrote in a copy of Arthur Benson's *Beside Still Waters*:

I wish I had been Papa,
That arresting Archbishop.
Crozier'd Cantuar!
I wish I had been Papa,
Whenever folk murmur 'Bah!
What sermons you dish up,'
I wish I had been Papa,
That arresting Archbishop.[1]

[1] A.C.B's father Edward White Benson was Archbishop of Canterbury.

Nevertheless, it is my bounden duty to drone on;
And, even were it not, on I should drone.
'Tis hard to keep an always Christian tone in Babylon.
Nevertheless, it is my bounden duty to drone on.
The eighteenth-century divines' tone in comparison
With mine was an inebriating tone . . .
Nevertheless, it is my bounden duty to drone on;
And, even were it not, on I should drone.

There were two others, which I stupidly omitted to copy. One day it might be fun to bring out an elegant little volume of Max's poetical works, but now they would take some rounding up.[1]

I have finished *Oxford Apostles*[2], having enjoyed and admired it enormously. But how odious Newman was! A wonderful preacher and writer, no doubt, and of great personal charm—but chock-full of egotism, self-importance, self-pity, self-concern, the most tedious aspects of femininity—a real stinker, I should say.

By way of contrast I have begun Graham Greene's new novel, which is set, suitably enough, in a West African leper-colony![3]

Did you ever get Lady Lytton[4] and Charles Tennyson Turner?[5] They were supposed to go off to you last week, but our packer disappeared with bronchitis and his relief (a Heinemann man) is almost completely blind—he walked through a glass door recently—so that parcels have been going to extraordinary places. I'm delighted to say Lady Lytton is flourishing after her send-off last Sunday, and Raymond Mortimer rang up to say he was going to review Fleming, so the year is starting well.

Somehow soon, dear George, I shall simply have to put a term to my Oscar researches and reach some sort of expedient compromise between perfectionism and practicality. Ruth says, truly, that at this rate I might go on for years (it's five and a half already) and many of

[1] This was done in *Max in Verse* (1963), edited by J.G. Riewald and published by Stephen Greene.

[2] By Geoffrey Faber (1933).

[3] *A Burnt-Out Case* (1961).

[4] *Lady Lytton's Court Diary 1895–1899*, edited by Mary Lutyens (1961).

[5] *A Hundred Sonnets by Charles Tennyson Turner*, selected by John Betjeman and Sir Charles Tennyson (1960).

the lacunae that worry me will never be noticed by anyone. I know that's right, but I hate letting anything go until it's as good as I can get it. And I so seldom get more than a consecutive hour or two. If this were an American venture (like the Boswell papers or Horace Walpole's letters) it would be limitlessly subsidised, with a team of fully-paid full-time research-assistants. English scholarship (I don't mean my nonsense) is badly handicapped, and the British Museum hasn't even got enough money to catalogue its manuscripts.

Did I tell you that E. Blunden is coming home on leave from Hong Kong this year? I'll be delighted to see him, but I'm a trifle apprehensive, since last time he stayed in the flat for six months. This time he speaks of perhaps six *weeks*, starting in June, when we may well be safely on Kisdon. My life is so full and complicated that even the dearest friend on top of one for weeks can become almost intolerable. Also I long for him to remove his 7000 books from the flat, which he originally promised to do in 1961. I could do with the shelf- and cupboard-room.

Yours ever
Rupert

12 January 1961

Finndale House
Grundisburgh
Suffolk

The really annoying thing is that your last letter is in the bag which I left in the train, and I never write to you without your last letter before me, and my memory being what it is—etc! But a genial winking official at Baker Street affirms that the bag will certainly turn up—in fact he was ready to wager five to one in shillings that I should get it back. Surely such optimists are rare. I certainly was in luck, for son-in-law Alexander Hood's pyjamas fitted me very nicely, and he is always abundantly equipped with spare brushes, razors etc, so I didn't have to sleep in the buff as in the sixteenth century nor come bearded to breakfast. Meanwhile we live in hope.

Tuesday evening was very good. I don't care tuppence whether Flash Harry is the debutante's dread, the taxi-terror etc, but I do find him quite exceptionally good company at dinner. I got some good stuff out of him about Sullivan for my Gilbert paper, and he told me a good, and unprinted, Gilbert repartee. They asked him how some play of his was doing and G.—a very conceited man—told them how good a play it was. A prim listener said 'But Mr Gilbert, you know self-praise is no recommendation'. To which Gilbert replied 'Perhaps self-abuse would be better, though it doesn't seem to have done *you* much good'. I fear that won't quite do for the G. and S. Society, even after *Lady Chatterley*. But it was a good retort in the Garrick Club in 1900.

After dinner I did what I always (rather intrusively?) do, *viz* go and talk to the members I haven't met before (or is that perhaps being the perfect clubman?). Anyway I got some excellent chat with both Sykes and Irving. With the latter, helped by Jonah and Tim, we kept going till 11, and for once Jonah didn't complain of a too early break-up. Laurence Irving seemed to me a particularly delightful chap, and was most interesting about his father, grandfather and Max. I also had a good crack with Tommy who never fails to be good value.

On the way home to-day I expended a book-token on *The Intelligent Heart* by Moore. All about the man D.H. Lawrence. I saw it recently very well reviewed and so fell, probably to your derision. But at least D.H.L. is a cut above *Lucky Jim*. I haven't got far yet, but am struck by the deterioration in D.H.L.'s face in middle-age from his fresh youth. How much was that repellent beard to blame? Diana[1] met the *Lady C.* prosecuting counsel recently and thought him about the dullest man she had met. *Lady C.* was not mentioned. I should have liked to ask him how he managed to make such a mess of it, or how he expected a British jury to decide against a side which produced thirty-five witnesses in favour of one which produced none. The man must be an ass.

Tell me exactly what you think of the new Betjeman poem.[2] The brief verdict at Cambridge was 'It stinks', which is surely a little exaggerated. Dick Routh *per contra* puts it at the very top of all the poems he has read, which again seems to lack balance. It appears to

[1] George's daughter, Diana Hood.
[2] *Summoned by Bells* (1960).

me to have every merit except the poetic. Amusing, vivid, moving, full of stuff, obviously the work of a delightful, wise and excellent man. And I suppose it *does* gain by being in blank verse rather than prose? If I say that it doesn't do to me what poetry does—or did—you will answer: 'You must remember you are old and gray and full of sleep'. Leavis has not yet pronounced; he probably thinks it beneath his notice. His disciples at Girton, it is said, send to Coventry any girl who likes it.

I hadn't a book at Diana's and re-read with great pleasure in Winston's history of the first war. With not a word of censure he shows that Joffre, Haig, Robertson and even Foch were dreadfully lacking in ideas, and that we were saved only and entirely by Falkenhayn and Ludendorff being equally lacking. The French and our losses were consistently higher than the German, whether in defence or attack. It is a grim story—but very good reading. Do you know what Winston's favourite adjective is? 'Sombre'. He uses it always relevantly but perhaps excessively. How hard it is to avoid such pitfalls and clichés generally. Maugham, in his autobiographical gallop whose name escapes me, purchases a beautiful lucidity at the cost of numberless clichés.

14 January 1961 | *Bromsden Farm*

To leave my letter in a handbag is so Oscarean that I am bound to forgive you. But will the finder now return the bag, or will he hold my letter for ransom and blackmail? I can't remember what was in it, except for the two Max triolets on Arthur Benson's essays. Here is a third, which I have rescued from a bookseller's catalogue:

> You'd think I must be a clergyman,
>   So like one do I write.
> When I break the news about Queen Anne
> You'd think I must be a clergyman.
> No dips in my ample tub of bran
>   Bring ought but bran to light—

> You'd think *I must* be a clergyman,
> So like one do I write.

All of them, you will have noticed, are aimed at A.C.B.'s essays, not at the man himself.

Tommy rang up on Wednesday morning, to say what a good evening it had been, and added: 'Of course, George is a host in himself', to which I heartily agreed. Didn't you think the food exceptionally good? The club had made a mistake in the prices, and when the waitress was ready to collect the money, she asked me whether I realised the dinner had cost 27/6 instead of the usual guinea! I said certainly not, that the demand for such a sum would cause a riot, and she must collect the usual guinea, leaving the balance (£4. 10. 0) to be paid by the club. This we can well afford, since the accounts (which will reach you soon) show a higher surplus than last year.

So glad you had a crack with Laurence Irving, the most charming of men. He is a close friend of Field Marshal Alexander, whom he quoted at dinner as saying: 'The British are warriors, but not militarists', which I thought very shrewd. Eric Linklater was stone-cold sober and very charming. He is writing what he called 'an off-beat novel', and said that if I would travel to the North of Scotland in a month or two, to read it, he might let me publish it. I shall do so.

I too have always found Flash Harry very entertaining, and welcome his attendance. Cuthbert and the loathsome Lockhart are the only flies in our delectable ointment.

I think I told you once what I thought of the Betjeman poem, but I expect you left my letter in a Gladstone bag somewhere. As B. is almost my exact contemporary, and I knew him (and most of his friends) at Oxford, I cannot pretend to be impartial. I read the poem with great interest, sympathy and pleasure, and towards the end I found I was reading it as prose. Clearly it's scarcely poetry, except occasionally and briefly. So you can put me half way between Routh and the intransigent Cambridge critics. When John Wain said that B's huge sales were the measure of the English fear and dislike of true poetry, he spoke more than a little of the truth.

I was most interested in your remarks on Winston's first-war history. If you ever get through the long and full history of the

Franco-Prussian War which I shall soon be sending you, you will see that there the ineptitude of both sides was equally appalling, and the Germans won simply because the *luck* was always on their side. When they marched the wrong way they accidentally split the French army, but when the French went wrong they marched into Switzerland and were interned. I wonder if things are any different today? Did I tell you that Donald Somervell left first choice of his books to the London Library? The Librarian has chosen splendid ones, many of them big art books, worth he thinks perhaps £1000.

My eye has been swollen and aching all the week, and on Wednesday R. and I sought out a rather *louche* Bloomsbury doctor, who operated with needle and cotton-wool, gave me some auromycin ointment and said all would be well in two days. He lied, for the damned thing isn't right yet, reading is as irksome as writing, and Oscar waits reproachfully. No one (except you and Ruth) will ever realise what this book has cost in time and trouble.

I have just read the new Graham Greene novel. In technique and sheer skill there is no one to-day to touch him. The story is gripping despite the interminable arguments on God and love. I think you should read it. Now I shall relapse upon Carlyle and sleep.

18 January 1961 *Grundisburgh*

All is well. Miss Prism has got her handbag back, letter and all. The letter should not really have been in it. They usually remain in my pocket for re-reading and answering, but it got stuffed into the bag with a handful of other papers.

How right you are about Newman. In the Holmes-Laski letters L. says 'I should have been slightly nauseated by N. had he not been too remote for anything but curiosity' and H. sums him up as 'a tender spirit, and born writer, arguing like a pettifogger'. I remember being rather repelled by him when I read that he had said his *one* thought was 'Shall I be safe if I die to-night?' It doesn't do to think too much about the next world. Old Holmes was always sound about that.

I like Max on A.C.B., especially 'You'd think I must be a clergyman'. A pity they didn't really know each other. M. would have loved him, as Housman did, and no one can suppose *he* thought anything of those *Threads of Gold*, *Beside Still Waters* etc.

I have finished Moore on D.H.L. Very interesting, and I should think well done, though he handles his (to me) uncivilised and sneery side too gently. L. seems to have hated every place he went to after a few weeks, and every friend after a few months. I find him tremendously rebarbative (if that is the right word). That letter of his to K. Mansfield, beginning 'I loathe you. You revolt me, stewing in your consumption' in 1920 surely touches a new low in sheer caddishness. Was he really sane at such times? And what of the man Leavis calling him 'the finest literary critic of our time'? Was that before or after D.H.L. had put Fenimore Cooper above Tolstoi, Tourgenieff, and Dostoevsky? And to call 'Lead kindly Light' and 'Abide with Me' 'sentimental messes' is just ordinary Philistine, not judgment or criticism at all. The picture in the book of Frieda in the Fifties, with one eye apparently closed suggests that L. occasionally scored a bull's (or should I say a cow's) eye with his plate-throwing. Anyway Medusa would have thrown up the sponge if she had seen this photo.

Betjeman—no he was not in your former letter. I agree with you. I loved the poem. The Cambridge critics can boil their swollen heads. And John Wain's comment is very pertinent. Milton, Wordsworth, Coleridge, Shelley, Keats, Browning were all derided at first, and the only popular poets roughly were Pope, Scott, Byron and Tupper—all you may say not first-class poets. Was Masefield—and is he class I? Leavis of course would say that Milton etc weren't either, but L. on poetry does not ultimately matter.

I look forward enthusiastically to the Franco-Prussian War—one of those topics I can never read enough about. Bismarck fascinates me—a terrifying man. How nice to think that the one person *he* was afraid of was Queen Victoria. What you say of 'luck' in war reminds me that the French (Clemenceau?) sacked scores of generals merely on the grounds that 'they weren't lucky', and the people understanding this brings the corollary to Alexander on the English, e.g. that the French *are* militarists—or were. They certainly understood more about war in 1914 than the English.

Your lovely book-catalogue has arrived. And as you always encourage the horse-leech side of me, let me tell you there are about *ten*—yes, *ten*—books in it which make my mouth water. And obviously that is going rather too far. I see your Oscar is announced. Will it really be ready? How wonderful if it is. Pamela has just finished Lady Lytton—much struck with the editor's cleverness in making so much of material that might often seem dull, and also disliking good Queen Victoria a little more than before. Really to put Scott at the top of all poets, at the same time regretting his occasional *coarseness*(!!). Did she approve of the draping of pianoforte-legs? They really weren't sane in those days. When Gilbert put *Great Expectations* on the stage, the censor deleted 'a lord' in Magwitch's remark 'Here you are in chambers fit for a lord' and substituted 'Heaven'. And Lewis Carroll, whose amiable hobby it was to photograph little girls naked, protested against the female chorus in *Pinafore* singing 'Why damme, it's too bad'—'Those pure innocent-looking girls, those pure young lips sporting with the horrors of hell'. And I suppose you look on my disapproval of *Lady C.* as being as frumpish as the above. I see the *Daily Mirror*, that leader of enlightened thought, hopes the dear Archbishop's successor will be more modern—which means intrinsically that he must disapprove of nothing anyone does or says and never put his foot down.

I do hope that eye is all right now. Was it some species of stye? The sort of thing doctors are usually quite good at. A *very* tiresome clog on your job's work. You must be firm about Ed. Blunden, however nice he is. Even the best can be curiously unimaginative. Did it never occur to him that you might want your own room-space? But I suspect you are hopeless at saying 'No' to any friend's demands—or even acquaintances'.

I am just off to see my doctor. I expect he will give me six months—with luck. In which case I should be writing you some such letter as John Sterling wrote to Carlyle in similar circs. It isn't a very bad letter, 'written', as T.C. says, 'in starfire and immortal tears'. Do look it up.[1] Pamela sends her love. She almost girds at me for my luck in

[1] *10 August 1844* *Hillside, Ventnor*

My dear Carlyle, For the first time for many months it seems possible to send you a few words: merely, however, for Remembrance and Farewell. On

having a fairy godmother like you. She won't hear of your disclaimer of any special generosity. 'After all what other publisher acts like that?' she says with that thudding feminine commonsense. Ruth knows too, I bet. Please give her my love.

21 January 1961 *Bromsden Farm*

So glad you got your bag back without benefit of blackmailers, and that you approve of the Spring List. Naturally you shall have any books in it that you fancy. The advance sales of Peter's book[1] (which is out tomorrow) are more than double those of *The Siege at Peking*, which I take to be a good omen.

Thank goodness your frightful Archbishop is disappearing. Ramsey looked after the Queen so tenderly at the Coronation (just like a nanny) that I'm sure he's all right, and of course he has the great advantage of never having been a headmaster!

My eye recovered after a week, but today the lid has suddenly and painfully swollen up again, curse it, and I am again very self-pitying.

Nowadays most English publishers make an annual pilgrimage to New York to acquire American books—and most do well out of it. I went in 1950 and again in 1952, but have avoided the effort ever since. Now I feel I must go again, so have taken a deep breath and booked a passage on the *Queen Mary* on February 25. I shall be there for most of March, and get back in time for Duff's wedding, which is to be at Builth Wells on Easter Monday (April 3). The all-important thing

higher matters there is nothing to say. I tread the common road into the great darkness, without any thought of fear, and with very much of hope. Certainty indeed I have none. With regard to You and Me I cannot begin to write; having nothing for it but to keep shut the lid of those secrets with all the iron weights that are in my power. Towards me it is still more true than towards England that no man has been and done like you. Heaven bless you! If I can lend a hand when *THERE*, that will not be wanting. It is all very strange, but not one hundredth part so sad as it seems to the standers-by.

Your Wife knows my mind towards her, and will believe it without asseverations. Yours to the last, JOHN STERLING

[1] *Bayonets to Lhasa* (1961).

about the trip is that Ruth is coming too. For propriety's sake we have to book separately (and so pay double), but we shall be together all the time and are hoping to stay with some very nice people called Gleaves, old friends of mine, whose daughter is married to Ruth's son. By saving all the ruinous hotel-expenses I hope to pay R.'s passage out of the firm's money. Having her there will make *all* the difference (and indeed our unwillingness to be separated for so long has played a big part in my nine years' insularity), since she will bear some of the brunt of the manuscripts and the overwhelming hospitality. I shall have to visit some six different people *every day* we're there—think of it! Except for a week-end in Boston and Harvard, I expect we shall stay in New York. Ruth has never before crossed the Atlantic and is wildly excited. It will be my fifth visit, so I shall be able to show her everything. If the sea is tolerable, the two crossings will be blessed interludes, without social obligations or interruptions. You will have to get some of those sixpenny air-letter forms, and I will write by the same means. It sometimes takes as little as two days. I shall miss only the March Lit. Soc.

Meanwhile my sailing-date has also become the deadline by which the Oscar galley-proofs must return to the printer, and there is much to be done. The book may just *possibly* be out this year—it depends on how quick the printers are, and how long the index takes me to compile. I put it in the Spring List to encourage everyone. When I finally parted with the proofs of *Hugh Walpole* I felt exactly, I'm sure, as a woman must feel after giving birth to twins—empty, proud and slightly bewildered—and now I can hardly imagine life without Oscar.

My clothes are all so old and shabby that I thought I simply *must* get a new suit for America, so Ruth and I went to Burton's in Regent Street, and found a Ready-to-Wear Sale going on. I bought two very nice suits for £8. 8. 0. and £11. 11. 0. and came away rejoicing.

Adam has gone back to Eton, Sixth Form and Van Oss. Comfort's term has begun. Duff is enjoying his work on the *Sunday Telegraph* (which starts on February 5) and has found a very nice flat in Lexham Gardens for his married start. Tim is spending the week-end with Peter, and they may come over tomorrow. Stolchy isn't the word for our surroundings, and I spend almost the whole week-end in the library.

I am reading a life of Oscar Browning (in search of material about *my* Oscar) and do not so far find O.B. very congenial. Did you know him?[1] But all the Eton stuff is interesting. How rich the beaks seemed to get, a hundred years ago!

25 January 1961 *Grundisburgh*

Just to show how shameless one can become if encouraged, merely look at the books in the enclosed list which I have marked. Clive said he was astonished at his own moderation. I am equally astonished—and indeed horrified—by my own greed. There can rarely have been anything like it.

Peter's book is immensely readable. I am delighted to hear that the orders are plentiful. And Jonah's stories?[2] I look forward to reading the reviews. What would the world of readers do without the Lit. Soc.?

Your U.S.A. trip should be fun—especially with Ruth. With her even the Antarctic would appear warm and welcoming. The really annoying thing is that I shan't see either of you 'till the almond-tree turns pink, The first flush of the spring', because I have to miss the Lit. Soc. in February, and you will in March. A sister is paying us a visit on February 15, and you will miss the March dinner when I shall be there, as I have a school meeting in the afternoon.

Are you happy about the new Archbishop? 'Too much crumb, you know', as Poll Sweedlepipe—or was it Bailey?—said about Mrs Gamp?[3] He won't be as good as dear Geoffrey Fisher.

I read my Gilbert paper two nights ago. The Society was a little sticky at first but all right in the end. I ended up my researches rather liking Gilbert, absurd though his touchiness was. He was not easy to score off. When a prima donna objected to being told exactly where to stand etc she flung out: 'Why should I? I'm not in the chorus.' All she got from G. was 'No, madam, your voice is not strong enough or you would be.'

[1] Oscar Browning (1837–1923). Eton master 1860–1875, Cambridge don 1876–1909. Author of many books, mostly historical.

[2] *The Bishop's Aunt and Other Stories* by L.E. Jones (1961).

[3] It was Mr Bailey, *Martin Chuzzlewit*, chapter xxix.

Your Burton suits make my mouth water. I always get mine there but they cost round about £20. Of course they have to be made. There are *no* advantages in being an outsize. My hats cost £4 or over.

Oscar Browning was repulsive and wholly absurd. The Eton affair was badly managed by Hornby, but O.B. was really becoming rather a menace. He was openly idle about all routine work and frankly favoured all the nicest-looking boys. Arthur Benson once told me that O.B. was talking about Oscar Wilde, and said 'I knew a good deal about all that affair' and, added A.C.B., 'his face as he said that was the face of a satyr.' Of course both Hornby and Warre (like Elliott too) were Victorianly suspicious of art and artists, and O.B. did do some good work encouraging such. Old Warre indeed was something of a Philistine, for all his knowledge of Homer.

29 January 1961 *Bromsden Farm*

Here I am, faint but pursuing, a day late but still hopeful. My eye flared up again last week, and on Friday night some sort of gastric trouble overtook me. Yesterday, in poor shape, I drove to Oxford, lunched sparingly in the Common Room at Magdalen, and spent the afternoon alone in their handsome Old Library going through the matriculation registers and other records for details of Oscar's contemporaries and friends, most of whom seem to have ended long and blameless lives as vicars or country gentlemen.

Then I got caught (without hat or umbrella) in a cloudburst on the short walk to All Souls, where I took tea with Sparrow. By the time I got home I was feeling wretched. However, by sleeping the clock round (11 to 11) I have restored myself to something like health. Did I tell you that Adam has passed his Prelims (ostensibly a test of his first year's work at Oxford) and now has no exam to do until his final Schools? He is delighted with Van Oss, he says.

Today Duff suddenly announced that his wedding-day may be postponed for a week or so: if it is, and we can switch our bookings, I think we may stay a few extra days in New York. Meanwhile we both have to be vaccinated, though not finger-printed, as I was in 1950.

You shall certainly have all the books you marked in the catalogue, and I daresay others too. Fleming is selling well: he sets off on Friday for Outer Mongolia, and I can't say I envy him. He is rather like an old charger sniffing the air of the battlefield.

I'm delighted with the new Archbishop, much preferring a nanny to an unctuous old sadist—so there!

I'm sure your Gilbert lecture had them rolling in the aisles as much as their rheumatism would allow.

I certainly *must* do the Oscar index. No one else is competent to compile the sort of one I want, least of all the electronic indexer which the Americans now extol.

When Duff was in Cardiff he made friends with a chap who has invented a new (and very cheap) method of amplifying and loud-speakering. Adam thinks that some adaptation of this invention might improve the appalling acoustics of School Hall, and this evening he and Duff are staging some sort of demonstration there.

You must forgive the disjointedness of this letter: perhaps you'll get a better one from the *Queen Mary*, where there will be fewer interruptions and more time.

Do you see the *Listener*? If so, do read Jack Priestley's excellent article on Falstaff, which appeared in two parts in the issues of January 19 and 26. It's a splendid counterblast to all that Cambridge flatulence. As I told J.B.P., I wish he would write a few more pieces like this, and publish them together in a book. He said he would whenever he had enough time and ideas.

Did I tell you that I have asked the Pilgrim Trust for a further £15,800 for the Dickens Letters (they gave me £6000 in 1954)? Their meeting is on February 9, so keep your fingers crossed. Unfortunately Tommy has retired from the Chairmanship, and I don't know his successor, Lord Evershed. The other evening I dined some three places away from him at the Garrick, and he looked charming.

1 February 1961 *Grundisburgh*

Are you going to the *very best* eye-man in London? Because it is all wrong you shouldn't be cured by now. But the gastric revolt on the top makes me wonder whether you are not suffering from overwork and fatigue. There is a lot of general debility about. I have had a nasty sore throat for five days—and I *never* get a s.t. That is what I have said for half a century and more. The winter—what a hateful thing it is! But what luck I am in. Just when I had nothing particular to do, four lovely books arrived from you—only *one*, if you please from my list, and your equally lovely promise of more. One can understand how a man who murders once and gets away with it, can't stop—people like Jack the Ripper, Christie, Tamburlaine etc. So I, having once got a book from you, am now lost to all sense of decency and just go on asking. The night before your letter—and books—came I refreshed myself with Max's *Around Theatres*. He reviewed two plays by Gilbert and put them neatly in their respective places, *viz* at the very opposite pole to *The Bab Ballads qua* wit, neatness, light touch etc. Gilbert's prose really is! M.B. says it is as bad as Pinero's, implying that nothing can be worse than that. I suppose in Victorian times your sentences were expected to be dressed up.

What a globe-trotter Peter is! Give him my love and good wishes and tell him how greatly I enjoyed his Younghusband book. What a mess the Government made of it. Brodrick of course the chief villain. I met him once and thought him curiously stupid, though he shone in comparison with his brother Arthur, who talked one entire evening at Holkham without saying anything. And what about Kitchener of Khartoum? My uncle General Neville L. who served under him in South Africa always not only disliked him but thought nothing of his brains—in that agreeing with Lloyd George who summed him up as 'a good poster'. He certainly had a tremendous presence. I have now, with your books, got from the library Shirer's Nazi history—1200 large pages[1], and one has read all of it pretty well in Bullock.[2] But somehow one—or at least I—can't resist it. The horrid truth is that Adolf was a genius, and so, in that tiresome way such men have, inexhaustible.

Very interesting about Adam and the acoustics. There must be money there for an inventor—as for the man who prevents or cures the common cold. For in both nothing is known but a few alleviations.

[1] *The Rise and Fall of the Third Reich* by William L. Shirer (1960).
[2] *Hitler—A Study in Tyranny* by Alan Bullock (1952).

He has done fine work about his exams. I wonder in what ways he will blossom at Oxford.

I have read Priestley on Falstaff with the greatest pleasure, and am with you in wanting much more stuff like that from him. Why are subtle perception and sanity so rare a combination? The fiddling little sneerers and hole-pickers turn my stomach. Why do so many always think that a change of fashion must be an advance in wisdom? It is his realisation of this—*inter alia*—that makes old Judge Holmes's comments on men and books so good. His grasp of essentials was Johnsonian. Don't you like his remark to Lady Desborough that the Boer war 'would give England a chance to pay for some of its unearned exquisiteness.'

Lord Evershed is a delightful man—he is a cousin of the headmistress of the Abbey, Malvern, where he gave away the prizes some years ago. He will eat out of your hand in any good cause—and all your causes are good.

4 February 1961 *Bromsden Farm*

It is now 8 p.m., and I have been working on the Oscar galley-proofs since 11 a.m., with briefest intervals for food. The sheer physical labour of transferring several thousand corrections accurately and legibly on to the printer's set of proofs, clipping on hundreds of new typed footnotes at the relevant places, and so on, is appalling, and I have grave doubts of my ability to complete the task before catching the *Queen Mary*. It now looks as though we may stay a little longer in America than we expected, since Duff has put his wedding off from the 3rd to the 22nd of April. This is a relief, for I couldn't see how I was to get everything into three weeks. Now our return will largely depend on what passages we can get. Ruth is always sending you messages, but as she is never (alas) at hand when I'm writing to you, she doesn't get fairly reported—and anyhow, as I've said before, I'm not sure it's good for you.

My eye, touch wood, is now quite recovered, and everything else too. I have temporarily given up bread, starch, sugar and alcohol, and have lost five pounds of weight in a fortnight. When one eats in someone else's house, all this goes by the board to some extent, as yesterday, when I lunched with the Hamish Hamiltons in St John's Wood. The party was in honour of the Duchess of Kent and her sister Princess Olga, but both of them had succumbed to influenza, so we extras gobbled up the stars' excellent fare. The Birkenheads were there, both delightful; she growing steadily larger while he shrinks. He used to drink like anything, but has now completely given it up, and sits looking thin and miserable with a glass of water and a little silver snuffbox full of saccharine tablets. Only when he accepted a big cigar did the ghost of F.E. flicker out.[1]

Desmond Shawe-Taylor, the *Sunday Times* music critic, was also there—an agreeable rattle. The food wouldn't sound much if I described it, but I was hard put to it to confine myself to one moderate helping of each course.

David Cecil looked in on Thursday to gossip about Max: he hopes to finish his book in a year, but as he hasn't yet begun the writing, I have my doubts. He says Leavis has *no* chance of being elected[2], though he may split and confuse the vote a little. Only M.A.'s have a vote, and in practice only those in Oxford exercise it.

Next week Ruth and I are going to see Peggy Ashcroft in *The Duchess of Malfi*, which I've never seen before. I suspect it will make one realise all over again the excellence of Shakespeare.

Duff's paper, the *Sunday Telegraph*, makes its bow tomorrow after weeks of stress and anxiety. Last week they set up a complete 'dummy run' for practice, and were so nervous lest the Beaverbrook press might get a glimpse of it and mock, that every proof was carefully locked up in a safe each night. Now the worst will be known. Shall you ever see it? Not at home, I imagine.

It is now 9 p.m., and the Saturday evening BBC concert is coming from School Hall, Eton! I suppose they can beat the accoustics with microphones: it sounds all right so far. I wonder if Adam is in the audience.

Do you know anything of an organisation called Voluntary Service Overseas? Fred is now strongly advising Adam to spend a year with

[1] F.E. Smith, the first Lord Birkenhead.
[2] As Professor of Poetry at Oxford.

it before Oxford, instead of going to a German university, and Adam is rather taken with the idea. He keeps pointing out that it costs nothing, which is very nice but beside the point. *Not* going to Oxford at all would equally cost nothing, and we are concerned only with what is best for him. Your advice would be most welcome. I think Adam is partially influenced by the fact that, whereas Duff has been to West Africa, Yugoslavia, Greece, Russia, Germany and Austria, he (Adam) has never been further than the Pyrenees, and I see his point.

I am reading nothing but Oscariana, and as I devote more and more time to these proofs in the next three weeks, my letters will get, if possible, scrappier and duller.

Peter must be in Moscow by now, battling for a visa to Outer Mongolia, that desolate buffer-state that surely few can visit for pleasure.

9 February 1961 *Grundisburgh (summer-house)*

Your Oscar labours make me feel like the Queen of Sheba—whom I do not otherwise resemble.[1] You are just like Boswell (not in all ways!) running, as he said, half across London to fix one date.[2] What a magnificent work it will be. Why have *you* given up all carbohydrates, and why should you insist on losing weight? If I *look at* a potato, my weight goes up. Perhaps you are preparing to let yourself go, overseas. I look forward to hearing all about it, though I know you won't really have time to tell me. Why shouldn't Ruth tell me all the news—or would *that* be bad for me, in what I can only regard as your over-cautious opinion?

I wonder what you will make of *The Duchess of Malfi*. One gets an impression of a fine grimness and resonance in the reading of it; I suspect it may be like so many Shakespeare plays, much better when

[1] 'And when the queen of Sheba had seen all Solomon's wisdom, and the house that he had built [etc, etc] there was no more spirit in her.'
I Kings, x, 5.

[2] Advertisement to the first edition of the *Life of Johnson.*

acted. 'Butcherly rant' was all Shaw saw in Marlowe, but his feeling for poetry was far from strong—he really did think blank verse was easier to write than prose. And so of course Dickens found it. And certainly Mrs Siddons in speech: 'You've brought me water, boy; I asked for beer' is richer than many lines in Tennyson's *Idylls*. Also perhaps Anna Seward's[1] 'My inmost soul abhors the bloody French.'

I have just finished Shirer's 1200 pages on the Third Reich. Quite absorbing. Do you realise on how many occasions Hitler had us *absolutely cold*, and, by (obviously) the grace of God, did exactly the wrong thing? It is almost terrifying to see every time how many and how narrow our squeaks were. And where else in human history do you find so tremendous a blend of genius and wickedness? As a human being he simply had not *one* good quality. I hope whenever you meet a German you will impress upon him that only the Germans regard 'brutal' as a eulogistic word, and that only the German language has to have a word meaning 'pleasure in others' misfortune' (*Schadenfreude*) because the trait is so common in the German nature.

So I have had time for no other reading and will talk of Jonah next week. The library lets one have a book for a *fortnight*. I wonder who but G.W.L. in Suffolk will get through these 650,000 words in that time. (A neighbour's gardener read forty pages of *Lady C.* in a week and then left it as being 'not very interesting'.)

What did you think about the 'kiss-case' (trust our penny-a-liners to vulgarise anything). Silly of the young pair to bring the case I imagine, but really! How can what a couple do in a closed car, at dead of night, in a solitary square be construed as 'indecent conduct in a public place'? But of course *all* the jury weren't going to ruin a couple of honest cops. The pair were very badly advised.[2]

I know, alas, nothing about Voluntary Service Overseas, though I

[1] Poet (1747–1809). Known as 'The Swan of Lichfield'.

[2] On 10 April 1959 a young engaged couple were enjoying a 'kiss and cuddle' in their parked car in a London cul-de-sac which they didn't know was a haunt of prostitutes. They were arrested and charged with 'an outrage to public decency' etc. In May they were tried and acquitted at London Sessions. They then claimed damages in the High Court for 'false imprisonment, malicious prosecution' etc. After one jury had disagreed, a second one awarded them damages of £5200 on 8 May 1961.

have some dim memory of it being a good show. Pick Fred's brains shrewdly and find out if he knows who can give you first-hand evidence. John Hills[1] may know all about it, and his advice on such things is worth having. It may easily be an excellent thing, started in response to a strong and sensible demand. Probably a good deal depends on who is in charge. On the other hand a German university is pretty sure to be a good and valuable experience, and at the end he will *know* German thoroughly and the Germans pretty well, both of which acquisitions are perhaps more *solid* than anything he would get from V.S.O. How difficult these balancings are!

11 February 1961 *Bromsden Farm*

Ever since I wrote last week I have spent some eight hours a day on these infernal galleys—more today, and only my devotion to you is keeping me from them at this moment. I have got (in my fair copy) to number 417 out of 559, and there are only thirteen more correcting days before embarkation. I shall scramble through somehow, so clear your decks for a pile of page-proof-reading in April or thereabouts.

At the same time my dieting has continued: another five pounds off this week, ten so far in three weeks. I feel much better so, and my trousers button with greater ease.

We didn't greatly care for *The Duchess of Malfi*: indeed we were thankful when the last two characters simultaneously stabbed each other and we could escape. Peggy Ashcroft was lovely, and the staging superb (some of the best I've ever seen), but the other performers were moderate, and the play! The idiocy of Shakespeare's plots is masked and redeemed by the poetry, but except for three or four lines, there is nothing here but rhetoric and wind. Bloodshed and horrors get steadily funnier and more absurd as they multiply. I'm quite glad to have seen it once, but please never again.

I think that kiss-in-the-car couple were most ill-advised to bring their case: attacking the police, however justifiably, is always risky.

[1] Eton master. Later Headmaster of Bradfield.

They're bound to close ranks and swear black's white, and it only needs one stubborn juryman to wash everything out. I expect the young couple started by taking counsel's opinion, which is almost always *wrong*.

You have to be vaccinated before you can enter the Land of the Free, so today I drove down to Henley and was 'done' by our doctor. I asked him for the necessary certificate, but he said I should have to get a special one from the Cunard Line, and after he has signed it I shall have to get the Town Clerk to vouch for his (the doctor's) signature. But who vouches for the Town Clerk's? How much red tape can people think up?

Ruth is busy collecting a trousseau for the trip, but I tell her to save up for the New York shops. I am collecting together a few books to read on the ship. Those five days will be a blessing.

Adam is thoroughly enjoying his German and other work with Van Oss, but is wildly excited about his V.S.O. scheme. I tried to pick Fred's brains on the telephone this evening, without much result.

Duff is getting possession of his new flat in Kensington next week-end, and is planning to camp out there and do most of the decoration before the wedding. The first issue of the *Sunday Telegraph* sold out all its *one million* copies, but they can't tell how much of that is due to curiosity. Most of the other papers' remarks have been fairly acid, as one would expect.

Q. What are Chitterlings?

A. Lady Chatterley's children.

16 February 1961 *Grundisburgh*

You must be getting positively sylph-like, but no doubt you know what you are doing. Lime-juice and a biscuit at the Lit. Soc. puts you with poor old Headlam, who scowls at the first helping he is given—and of course at his neighbour's. I am not sure that poor old Ivor Brown too doesn't reject a good deal. I hope his teeth are all right. Pamela has had tooth-trouble too and had a very tender mouth for ten days. Nature is conspicuously incompetent about teeth, which start decaying practically with birth, or fits the mouth with more teeth than it wants or can comfortably house.

I suspected you wouldn't think much of the blood-boltered Webster. Only Shakespeare can gild those ridiculous plots.

Jonah's stories are subtle and well-written, with plenty of wit and irony, but whether their *interest* is strong enough seems to me a little doubtful. Did you get the impression that one or two of the stories somehow seem too long? The title-story seems to me much the best. But I may be quite wrong about all this. I shall be interested to see the reviews. Peter F. has had some good ones lately—I hope reflected in the book's sale?

How right you are about counsel's opinion. I remember once, when a housemaster asked the Governing Body some question about responsibility in case of fire. They got counsel's opinion (price five guineas) and sent it to me. I rejoined that it was an exact parallel with the old problem and its answer about how to find the sex of a canary. 'Give the bird a lump of sugar; if it is a he, he will eat it, and if it is a she, she will.' This went to the Bursar who read it out to the G.B. and a loud cackle of laughter from Provost Quickswood prevented my being hauled over the coals for impudence.

Good luck to Ruth with her transatlantic trousseau. I bet she will look lovely in it and knock 'em all on board. No doubt you will be taking *How Green* on the trip? Odd that you should so persistently avoid a book I know would delight you!

'Chitterlings' is lovely. Thank you.

I have just written to nephew Charles about a New Zealand village called 'Taumatawakatangihangakoanstameataturipunakapikimaungahoronukupohaiwhenuakitanatahn'. It means 'The brow of the hill where Tamatea, the man with the big knee who slid, climbed and swallowed mountains, the discoverer of land, played his flute to his loved one'.

18 February 1961 *Bromsden Farm*

Last Sunday evening, just over a day after my smallpox vaccination, I suddenly developed a nasty sore throat, which during a miserable Monday in the office turned into a cold so whoreson-wild that I had to spend two and a half days in bed, missing the Lit. Soc., incapable of Oscarising, allowing my correspondence to pile up as I coughed and sneezed and groaned and cursed. Ruth cherished me superbly, and had scarcely got me on my feet again when her daughter-in-law's labour-pains began. The child (their first, and Ruth's third grandchild) should have appeared today. How we shall ever get off on Friday goodness knows, but somehow we'll manage it, so imagine us boarding the *Queen Mary* at about 6.30 p.m. on Friday, prepared to sail at dawn. Our address from March 2 to 29 will be c/o Mrs Gleaves, 220 East 61 Street, New York City. My first letter will be slow, because of the boat, but if you use an air-letter-form there should be one waiting for me when I arrive. If the weather is tolerable, the five-day crossing will be bliss, without telephones or letters or (I hope) chattering acquaintances. You shall hear all about it.

So glad you enjoyed some of Jonah's stories: so did Eric Linklater, as you will see from the enclosed. I thought the title-story so much the best that I persuaded Jonah to put it first and call the book after it. I also managed to remove three or four stories of what seemed to me excessive sentimentality, and tried to remove the one about the bulldog, but Jonah insisted on its retention. I do hope the reviewers don't spoil his fun. The book appears on February 27, when I shall be happily on the high seas.

(Ruth has just telephoned to say there is no baby yet: the labour-pains were a false alarm, and the expectant mother has been sent home —a tiresome anticlimax, poor things.)

As you can imagine, my chief concern, far more compelling than American dollars or visas or office affairs, is to get Oscar ready for the printer before we leave. It's touch and go, with many desperate decisions and wily plans for leaving, here and there, sufficient space for small insertions in the page-proofs. For instance, where I know that a three-line footnote is needed and can't be done in the time, I either write 'Leave space for three-line footnote,' or write three idiotic lines, for which the right ones can be exchanged later without too much worry and expense. Most of them will pass unnoticed anyhow.

To add to the confusion, my beloved sister is arriving from Scotland first thing on Tuesday morning, to stay in the flat. That night

Ruth and I are by way of going to Britten's *Midsummer Night's Dream* at Covent Garden, and on Thursday I have to make a speech to 150 people at a luncheon in honour of a retiring publisher's sales manager —oh dear!

Duff has gone to lecture the Marlborough boys on Greece, with the excellent coloured slides he took there. Have you seen the *Sunday Telegraph* yet? It's more like the *Daily T.* than anything else: masses of material but messily arranged, with too many too narrow columns. I daresay that's what people want.

You do realise, don't you, that the letters you will get from America will be nasty, short, brutish etc. We are to spend the week-end of March 10–13 at Boston—or rather Cambridge, Mass, just across the river. Ruth will stay with a charming Harvard professor friend of ours (they have room only for one), and I perhaps with Henry James's nephew, son of the philosopher and a darling old man —a painter. From New York I have already received invitations to lunch, dinner, theatres, operas, Sundays in the country, and God knows what. Their deep feeling of inferiority leads to a crazy excess of hospitality, and if one persists in praising the country and all its ways they are momently reassured. But oh how exhausting it all is! Almost all the food has been refrigerated into tastelessness—only coffee, orange-juice, ice-cream and oysters are always good. And most of the flowing drink is straight whisky or gin with a lot of ice. All my lost weight will, I fear, return 'with advantages'. I'm already looking forward to boarding the *Queen Elizabeth* for home.

Take care of yourself, dear George, and give my love to Pamela. *Ora pro nobis.*

Do write to Jonah about his stories if you feel you can.

22 February 1961 *Grundisburgh*

I am of course in the summer-house (only just, if you see what I mean) and all books are in the house. Being swathed in a rug, I am unwilling to move. I am only pretending that it is warm enough. What is the point of thick white cloud on a perfectly dry day? I frequently find myself in agreement with Mrs Besant in her fierce days. Genius on your part to send her life.[1] I am greatly enjoying it. Clearly one of those tremendous, admirable, intolerable women like F. Nightingale and B. Webb. Wonderful character and courage and achievement and all that. But uncomfortable for us humdrum folk whom they clearly despise. But Annie B. must have been less one-track than F.N. and B.W., who saw *no* point in talking or thinking of anything but nursing and gas-and-water respectively. I suppose there must be some of this sort; otherwise Mrs Gamp and Mr Bumble would be still with us. Mrs B's biographer is a bit stuffy and longwinded, but I have plenty of time. I look forward to the India part. At present I am at the Bradlaugh period—I remember Mr Gladstone fulminating about him at the dinner-table. But I suppose if you are sure about the Trinity you are fierce about its enemies—or still more perhaps if you are not *quite* sure.

Tell me what you thought of Britten's *Midsummer Night's Dream* (and Shakespeare's too of course). What can B's music do for S's which is often incomparable there? Old Agate always maintained that first-class poetry and ditto music spoilt each other, and that the insipid libretti of the Wagner operas were all right. He hated, too, grand opera in English—as I do—pointing out that '*Voglio la mia colazione*' did not offend one, whereas 'I want my breakfast' does. Tell me also what *you* think of Shakespeare in modern dress. I always feel I couldn't bear it, but some tell me I am wrong. Hamlet in a tail-coat, Rosalind in a skirt and jumper? But as you are beginning to suspect, I am full of Victorian prejudice. *But*, I must tell you, the man Leavis's article in the *Spectator* on *Lady C.* seemed to me excellent—both very intelligent and quite intelligible. And he ties the English language up in fewer knots than usual. Have you seen my old pupil John Bayley's new book—very respectfully reviewed by Pritchett and others?[2] I shan't understand it, but I must read it.

I haven't yet seen the *Sunday Telegraph*, on which, as you say, the other papers are rather sniffy; but it is a brave venture. I imagine Duff's writings in it are not signed; no doubt that will come later. And has Adam polished off that Chess Cup? Perhaps he will get a

[1] *The First Five Lives of Annie Besant* by Arthur H. Nethercot (1961).
[2] *The Characters of Love* (1961).

chess blue, though I believe the standard is very high. The old Ram[1] was one. He lost his match against Oxford, and was still annoyed about the mistake he made with his knight half a century ago. At Eton he sometimes played with Jelly Churchill[2] who was a stubborn but poor player, though unmoved by disaster. Once Ram took his queen and expected him to show some regret, but so unmoved was Jelly that A.B.R. at last pointed out the loss. All he got was 'Yes, I'm glad she's gone; she was rather in the way,' the fact being I imagine that no player dreams of going on after his queen has perished.

25 February 1961 *R.M.S. Queen Mary*

I somehow missed your letter yesterday: I only hope you're not ill. Anyhow this is just a brief interim report, which can be posted at Cherbourg. Despite persistent catarrh and a hacking cough, I managed to get Oscar back to the printer, and everything else more or less straightened out. We are now blissfully ensconced in two comfortable and almost adjacent cabins. Any amount of excellent food, no letters, telephones or papers, and a free cinema show every day. I am reading a proof of the new Ian Fleming—so far well up to standard.[3] During the rest of the voyage I will endeavour to compile a longer letter, in which Ruth promises to join. Apparently President Kennedy is a great one for the girls, and during the election his opponents said that if he got to the White House they only hoped he would do for fornication what Eisenhower did for golf.

1 March 1961 *R.M.S. Queen Mary*

Heavy seas, mountainous meals, a movie each afternoon, ten hours of sleep each night (including the one caused by putting back the clock), an ever-open bar—all these have proved very beneficial. It

[1] A.B. Ramsay, Eton master, later Master of Magdalene College, Cambridge.
[2] My Eton housemaster.
[3] *Thunderball* (1961).

took me three days to shake off cough and catarrh, but Ruth proves a stalwart sailor, and we are both thoroughly relishing these unreal days of suspended animation. Little walks on the icy deck, bowls of broth at 11 a.m., tea and light music after the movie, visits to the library (where this is being written) punctuate the steady rhythm of creaking timbers, throbbing floors and rushing waters. Two days were rough: now all is calm and speedy. I have so far read three thrillers, the proofs of Margaret Lane's new book about Africa,[1] Vita Sackville-West's new novel[2], and *The Bachelors* by Muriel Spark. The new Ian Fleming is disappointingly like a feeble parody of the earlier ones.

The food is excellent, and one can order almost anything one fancies. I have kept a typical menu to send you. Last night, for instance, became a Gala Night, by the general issue of gaily coloured miniature hats, and we consumed oysters (melon for R), turtle soup, skipped the fish, excellent tender fillet steaks, and a deliciously light American pudding called Nesselrode Pie. For breakfast one can have bloaters or minced chicken or onion soup, but we generally stick to the excellent bacon-and-eggs. We have a little table to ourselves, where we are waited on by a charming man who escaped from the 'Free City' of Danzig in 1936 and fought with the Royal Engineers in Italy. Now he is married to a Scottish girl and lives at Eastbourne.

Mercifully there is no one on board who knows us, so we rejoice in this trancelike existence, anonymous, overfed and half-asleep. They tell us we shall dock at 11 a.m. tomorrow—and then the rush and racket will begin. I'll try to send you a brief air-letter on Sunday.

My first written word to you, dearest George, and very little space for any outpouring of soul. The best thing so far is that R. seems so definitely rested and better and has thrown away ideas of diet and eats and drinks like his old self. Very, very satisfactory. I shall try and send you a separate word in the next days or weeks. My love to you.

Ruth.

[1] *A Calabash of Diamonds* (1961).
[2] *No Signposts in the Sea* (1961).

2 March 1961 *Grundisburgh*

I am at the moment in London, for two meetings. It will be sad no longer to find my dear Geoffrey Fisher chairmaning the G.B.A. Committee, which he always did extremely well. We shall now be dragooned by Sir Griffith Williams, one of those men who looks far more important than anyone can possibly be—knighted for some incredibly dull services in secondary school education, which have for some reason convinced him that he need not cultivate the graces. He has no manners at all, which I find invariably displeasing.

I am staying with my brother and in my bedroom are no books except a novel by Angela Thirkell and two Agatha Christies which I have read.

How I hate London—especially at the rush hour, which mistakenly I thought yesterday was finished by 6.15. My brother's station is Archway where the train completely empties. I suppose everyone lives at Highgate or Hampstead. Lady Summerskill is close by; I shall not call. They tell me the House of Lords doesn't like her manner which is dictatorial. She thinks that if you are a lord you must be lordly.

I am slowly absorbing Mrs Besant, just getting to the theosophy. She is in process of breaking with most of her previous friends, Bradlaugh etc. Conversely I am reading in bed a life of William Cory, whom I don't much like.[1] Too much sentiment, and though very learned, almost always wrong in his judgments, e.g. that Tennyson was far greater than Milton. His leaving Eton and changing his name was very mysterious and no one has ever really spoken out about it—any more than they have about Oscar Browning. Wortham in his life of O.B. merely abused Hornby—quite wrongly.

[1] Presumably *William Cory, a Biography* by Faith Compton Mackenzie (1950). William Johnson (1823–1892), poet, Eton master from 1845 till 1872, when he changed his name to Cory.

7 March 1961 *Grundisburgh*

Nice letter redolent of ozone arrived this morning (with a builder's bill which I had expected to be about £75 and was £184. But I suppose that happens to everybody—though one item on it was more than surprising, *viz* 'holidays etc').

You sound in good case (as Swithin Forsyte used to say) and it is nice to hear from Ruth that you are rested and no longer dieting. I felt in my bones that this last was somehow all wrong for you. But I also feel that you won't find U.S.A. all that restful, so you will soon be again in your natural element.

I am just finishing Annie Besant—almost equally interested by her and infuriated by the over-wordy author. The book is costive with unnecessary details. I congratulated Jonah on his stories, and got a charming letter back. No reviews out yet. The *T.L.S.* continues to parody itself with long articles of steadily increasing dulness, mostly on foreign writers I at least have never heard of. The present editor is naughtier in this way than even Pryce-Jones. I have sent you a card saying I shall attend the Lit. Soc. but presume it won't be forwarded. Jonah is going to be there.

Sorry about Ian Fleming. James Bond has been a caricature for several books now. No one else surely (except Mellors[1] perhaps?) can sleep happily with a woman a day or so after being tortured practically to death.

Please give my very best love to Ruth, with warm thanks for her little P.S. to yours. It is a pleasant thought—you and she happily enjoying sea and sun and wind, wearing gay hatlets, and tucking into Nesselrode Pie. P. and I supped yesterday on boiled eggs, which Percy Lubbock once called 'stuffy little things' but we both enjoy them. I hope my last week's letter awaited you at Mrs Gleaves's.

[1] In *Lady Chatterley's Lover*.

14 March 1961 *Grundisburgh*

I am in London and—probably—your weekly letter is awaiting my return home to-morrow, so I have momentarily nothing from you to stimulate me—except of course the mere thought of you and R., which is in no way narcotic.

The Lit. Soc. last night produced a fine crowd. The uproar was terrific and prevented my hearing anything my neighbour said to me—that is the defect of hearing-aids *pro tem.* They promise to cure it in a year or two. I sat next to Tommy, and Ivor B. was on my other side. Flash Harry was opposite—in cracking form, clearly enjoying himself madly. Alan Moorehead was very friendly and apologetic at coming so rarely. In fact he said he really ought to resign, but I took it upon myself to say that *you* would not at all approve of that. I had five minutes of Lockhart; we spoke of K.G. Macleod. I suppose he *has* some other topic, but I have still to find it.

Best love to Ruth; it must be lovely having her with you. I gathered she has been firm and salutary about your dieting. I once recommended fruit and salad diet to a cousin and only just in time did her doctor snatch her from the jaws of death.

19 March 1961 *220 E 61 Street*
New York City

Do not fancy, my dear George, that an intermission of writing is a decay of kindness. No man is always in a disposition to write, nor has any man at all times something to say. I send you this mangled quotation for the same reason that Alice Meynell on her deathbed murmured 'my bluest veins to kiss'[1]—to show that I am still sentient and at least a fragment of my usual self. This is the first letter I have sent you from America, and it may well be the last, such is the pace here, without cease. Your lovely weekly letters are happy glimpses of reality in what otherwise might be the moon. Mostly freezing days with clear blue sky and all these topless towers glittering in the

[1] *Antony and Cleopatra*, act two, scene 5.

brightest sunlight. Two appointments in the morning, an enormous lunch at someone's expense, with much liquor. Two or three more appointments, drinks somewhere before a dinner-party or theatre, or both. Home by 12 or 1 to deepest sleep, and then another similar day. We have been to three plays, two revues, one movie and one opera. Last week-end in Boston and Cambridge (Mass) was enjoyable, but without even enough time to write to you.

Baghdad on the Hudson was a pretty good name for this city of fantasy. We have a lovely little flat on the top floor of the Gleaves's house, and only wish we could spend more time in it. My reason is saved by my beloved Ruth's presence, and she so enjoying it all in the savage way one must, though we shall both be *thankful* to embark on the *Queen Elizabeth* on March 29 (arriving home April 5). I shall try to write you an Easter letter on board. We have between us read, perused or sampled several dozen manuscripts and sets of proofs—most of them quite unsuitable for English publication. Have picked up one or two little things, but so far nothing major or important. We learn that the proof-corrections in the Oscar galleys will cost £500!! and that page-proofs should be ready in April—so clear your decks. The compulsive friendliness and hospitality of Americans is both pleasing and exhausting, and seeing so many people in quick succession makes for endless repetitions. Needless to say, all dieting has gone by the board, all my clothes are tight, and Ruth says it's a very good thing. All helpings of food are enough for three, and enough food must be thrown away in this city to feed half the Congo.

There is little I can add to this wonderfully descriptive letter, though I wholeheartedly endorse it all. And darling Rupert is a total success (Americanism) and adored by all these open-armed people. Which is, after all, much like being at home. A great deal of it is rewarding and stimulating, but they have no cubby-holes in their nature where one can curl up and rest. It's all outward striving and constant movement, and my heart yearns for the curlews of Kisdon. Keep yourself warm for our return. Love Ruth.

What a beautiful Johnsonian opening. You call it 'a mangled quotation' and no doubt the old man demolished Boswell's importunity with some such swashing blow.

I wasn't in the least surprised at a fortnight going by with no letter from you, as I have a vague but strong suspicion of how full they are filling your day with business and hospitality. I do hope it will all be reflected in the balance-sheet. I note in your letter a point that I have always had firmly fixed in my mind, *viz* that it is very hard to take Americans *quite* seriously. As more than one of themselves has noticed, 'not so much an accent as a whiffle, a snuffle, a twang' was the contribution of Howells.[1] Many exceptions of course—there are no two human beings I admire more than Lincoln and old Judge Holmes. I wonder if you will come across any traces of him (H). Of course you might easily go off your rocker with all this, but for the presence of Ruth. I don't know what the statistics are, but surely there are far fewer idiot women than men?

Last night dinner with Wells (C.M.)[2] at the United University Club—his ninetieth birthday, and he was one of the least decayed men in the room. John Christie[3] has had jaundice and has gout. No excuse for the former as he drinks *cream* by the pint (literally). Old Gow[4] is vanishing—really frighteningly thin. He told me he now weighed eight stone odd (At Eton he was *twelve*!). I urged him to eat more food and he said that is the trouble—he hates the stuff. Well they know all about that; it is 'anorexia' and unless cured it kills you, because you become vulnerable to any germ that is about. His state partly comes, as he admits, from having lost *all* interest in life. I had a good crack with G.O. Allen who was at his best—and that is very nice. He knows *all* about modern cricket. He corroborated what nephew Charles told me, *viz* that since Hutton's command of 'no

[1] W.D. Howells, American novelist and critic (1837–1920).

[2] Former Eton master.

[3] Eccentric millionaire (1882–1962). For some years an Eton master. Founded the Glyndebourne Music Festival on his own estate 1934.

[4] A.S.F. Gow, former Eton master, then Fellow of Trinity College, Cambridge.

fraternisation' the MCC sides in Australia have been very unpopular —and no wonder. And do you know, and can you believe, that D. Sheppard forbade his Cambridge side to fraternise with Oxford in the match? Unbelievable but true—and quite insufferable, as G.O.A. firmly said.

I stayed with my brother-in-law Leconfield yesterday. A niece of his came in, and we chatted away. Afterwards he told me that I had talked him down—was, to put it shortly, intolerable. He is 83½ and I think had a rush of blood to the head—or is what he said true?

P.S. for Ruth

Delightful little note from you—every line of it full of *your* flavour (and if that has a horrible air of *Amplex* about it, well I can only trust you to see that it really hasn't—and I do). It is *good* to hear of R. going down so well, as of course he was bound to. Now I want to hear what they think of the other R. and I bet you won't tell me (but *he* may!). Anyway I don't really need to be told, 'they have no cubby-holes in their nature' I like that—and your longing for 'the curlews of Kisdon'.

27 March 1961 *220 E 61*
N.Y.C.

Your letter arrived faithfully, but once again the week-end, when I planned to answer it, was entirely occupied with social activities, and on Saturday we didn't get to bed till 3 a.m. on Sunday. Now our last two days are chock-a-block with last-minute shopping, telephoning, appointments, parties and goodness knows what. I need not tell you that Ruth is a *succès fou* with the American gentlemen and finds this very stimulating. We are astonishingly well, considering the life we're leading.

That was Monday morning, and now it's Tuesday evening, and we sail after lunch tomorrow. I shall airmail this before we leave, write again on the *Queen Elizabeth* and post that when we land next Tuesday, so you should get it on Wednesday or Thursday. Write next to Bromsden, which I should reach on the evening of Friday, April 7.

Here the pace quickens, and fatigue is catching up with us. After a midwinter day last week, the temperature today is in the 70s and many of the buildings still have their heating on. We find we need more and more liquor—mostly Bourbon whisky, which we love—to keep us going. The best building since I was last here is the Seagram (whisky) building on Park Avenue. It is some sixty storeys high and made of *bronze*. Very beautiful in sunlight and even more so at night when one of its thousands of windows is permanently lit up. On the ground floor is the world's most *chi-chi* restaurant, called The Four Seasons. It has a Picasso mural forty foot square in the entrance hall, and a pool the size of a swimming bath in the middle of the restaurant, with four *trees* at its corners etc etc. Everything is wildly expensive, except cigarettes, but the firm is paying, so to hell with that. Last week we found two new Oscar letters, which a kindly bookseller allowed us to copy and airmail home for last-minute inclusion.

Everything is brash and loud and brutal, but at night very beautiful. Most of the people are very ugly, but friendly and longing for praise. The subway is indescribably awful. There is no climate in New York, but rather a succession of violent extremes. The city is a vast melting-pot of races and colours and creeds which presumably will one day solidify.

29 March 1961 *Grundisburgh*

No *arrière-pensées*, no suspicions, no dark thoughts. If you miss a week I know it is for impregnable reasons; and you really are a wonderful correspondent and spoil me for anybody else. I am gradually getting used to the fact that nowadays to answer any letter—even one about money—by return is somehow considered what—? non-U, plebeian, rough manners? I simply don't know. But last week I sent two cheques and got acknowledgement of them exactly eight days later. And neither of the people concerned is one tenth as busy as you are. I am at present owed five letters—four at least from charming nieces who *adore* (their word) getting letters but abhor (not their word) writing them. My nephew does well from N.Z. for the rather sad reason that he has got nobody to talk to out there.

I grow old—physically—rather rapidly. Young ladies offer me

their seat in buses—not wholly from kindness, partly in self-defence, for they see how a lurch of the bus shoots me into the lap of some unoffending matron slow in escaping. I expect to find myself sued, like the Rev. Thomas, for embracing. His plea that arthritis and copulation in a taxi were an impossible combination was rejected by the Consistory Court. Have you been reading the case? I met the sublime and the ridiculous in juxtaposition last week—*viz* the whitest magnolia in Suffolk and under it a poster announcing 'Mrs Brandy in the Box'.[1]

The Ancient of Days, who has a fine sense of humour, as we know, must be indulging in Olympian chuckles over the circulation of the New English Bible running neck and neck with that of *Lady Chatterley*. Have you seen it? They seem to me to have altered some things quite needlessly, and surely to fiddle about with the Lord's Prayer is hardly forgiveable. So many people do not appear to realise that language *just a bit* above people's heads is right. Wasn't it Mrs Carlyle who, when an old peasant-woman praised a sermon, asked her if she had understood it and got the answer 'Wad I hae the presoomption?' But she continued to praise the sermon. 'Truly and *indifferently*,' 'true and *lively* word' would the change to 'impartially' and 'living' attract those who are now repelled? But I expect introducing lucidity into the crabbed exhortations of St Paul is a wholly good thing, and after all for centuries St Paul's Christianity has really held the field for discussion. Our rector will have none of the *N.E.B.* Indeed if it was still in print I think he would have Wycliffe's on the lectern.

Good Friday, 31 March 1961 *R.M.S. Queen Elizabeth*

First class on this ship is indeed something, and I have decided that luxury is all right, provided you experience it only occasionally and for short periods: otherwise you simply begin to complain about the quality of the caviare.

[1] It was not in a taxi but in his own car, outside Wandsworth Common railway station, and in other places, that the Vicar of Balham was accused of persistent adultery with Mrs Brandy, a forty-year-old school-teacher. He was found guilty on 28 March 1961 and subsequently defrocked.

We have two *huge* cabins with an open door between. Each contains two beds, two armchairs, two dressing-tables, a mass of drawers and hanging-cupboards, and its own bathroom and W.C. When we embarked we found three enormous bouquets for Ruth, three bottles of champagne, a bottle of Bourbon whisky, a vast box of chocolates, sundry books and a cable or two. We managed to restrict the seeing-off party to three faithfuls. So far the sea has been glassy, and all yesterday we sat out on the Sun Deck in comfortable chairs, swaddled in rugs, enjoying bright warm sunshine. Today is wet and grey, so we are catching up on our letters. Putting on the clocks an hour each day is a trifle disconcerting—in contrast to the delicious extra hour a day on the outward journey—so that everything tends to be slightly telescoped. We have a delicious breakfast brought to our cabins between 10 and 11—fresh orange-juice, coffee, rolls, butter and marmalade—then get up slowly and sit outside, or walk on the covered deck if it's wet. We try to eat only a small luncheon, though one can have *anything* one wants, and work our way through afternoon tea, a rest with books, a bath and change, cocktails in the bar, and a superb dinner. Last night we had oysters (smoked salmon for Ruth), delicious poached turbot cooked with mussels and shrimps, the breasts of ducklings done with cherries, and a marrons-glacées ice, washed down by some excellent Montrachet. Each evening at 9.30 there is a free movie in the huge theatre. We saw five on the outward journey, and so far two on this—*Tunes of Glory* with Alec Guinness, and a goodish New York one called *The Rat-Race*. Then bed, and it's an hour later than you think.

The passenger-list includes Sir Bernard and Lady Docker, who last night, so our waiter told us, kept the restaurant staff hanging about till past midnight as they argued loudly, her Ladyship getting steadily drunker and more abusive. A.E.R. Gilligan's[1] name also graces the list, but none of these celebrities has yet been glimpsed by us. The only people we know are Mark Longman, the publisher, and his wife, and I think their desire for quiet is as great as ours, for they haven't bothered us, and we are rejoicing in being alone together, after the ceaseless chatter and small-talk of New York. I am reading that new

[1] Former English cricket captain.

life of Lady Gregory[1] with much enjoyment: it's the first book I've really *read* since we left the *Queen Mary* a month ago: all the books, proofs and manuscripts we dashed through in America were read against time—and mostly against the grain too. These five days of luxurious limbo are a fine bridge between the inferno of Manhattan and the paradise of England. There is an extensive ship's library, but we have enough reading-matter in our cabins to last for weeks. We are due to dock at dawn on Tuesday, and the boat-train is supposed to reach Waterloo at 10.15 a.m.

Ruth and I are now so blissfully accustomed to being together that even our brief partings at home loom depressingly. I shall stop this now and write another page or so before the voyage ends. Despite the rigours of New York, we both feel much better in health than we did a month ago: violent change has perhaps its own therapeutic quality.

Easter Sunday

Little sun since Friday, but no waves either, so our Lucullan life drifts on. Last night we drank our first bottle of champagne with caviare, *filet mignon*, asparagus, *crêpes suzettes* and an excellent savoury. The last two movies (*The Magnificent Seven* and *The World of Suzie Wong*) weren't up to much, and we left before the end of *S.W.*

Ruth, alas, has caught a cold in the head: no wonder with all the violent changes of temperature we have experienced: otherwise we are fine. The Dockers, we hear, are behaving better. Tonight there is a concert given by the Vienna Boys Choir. What next? We are prepared for anything.

Easter Monday. Cherbourg.

We made landfall here at noon in steady rain, and don't leave again till six. We are tied up to a fine modern quay, built since the war, and could have spent three hours exploring the town if we had wanted to. But the weather is still grey and wet, and we preferred to stay cosily on board. Ruth's cold is much better, and she has been very good about it. We shall be sad to leave our luxurious cabins and endless meals, but maybe five days of over-eating are enough. I shall hope to

[1] By Elizabeth Coxhead (1961).

find at least one letter from you at Bromsden and will write from there on Saturday.

It's nearly over now—isn't it sad. I can't easily imagine life shorn of its leisured elegance after such a week of luxurious ease. But how the second week would pall and longing set in for one's kitchen sink. My hands have not been so lily-white for *years*. And with so much time to do things nothing at all gets done. What an oddity of nature that is.

We have bought a copy of *The Times* so that we can do our first crossword for five weeks. Perhaps we shan't be able to. And a rather tragic little concourse of elderly gentlemen are playing us to our tea with tunes from *The Merry Widow*—so we must go. My love. Ruth.

7 April 1961 *Grundisburgh*

I am not going to let my thanks for this *delightful* Cardus book[1] wait over until Tuesday. I am immensely pleased to have it. Your kindness is unceasing—because I remember (with blood to the face) that this book was not on that shameless list I sent you when your spring list came out. And then that unfortunate letter which went to U.S.A. and probably passed you on the way. Will the good Mrs Gleaves send it back, or is it already behind the fire, as the Victorians put it? Cardus will take the place of Behrman and Max,[2] at present by my bedside. Is it a sign of old and/or mental decay that I find Behrman's beer *a little* small—after sixty pages? Is Miss Jungmann the lady Max married? She sounds a good sort. I like Max's suggestion that a volume could and should be made out of the rot that G.B.S. uttered during his ninety-four years, and his implication that the resulting volume would not be at all a small one.

I look forward to finding you stout, rosy, with a slight accent,

[1] *The Essential Neville Cardus* (1949). Reissued as *Cardus on Cricket* (1977).
[2] S.N. Behrman, dramatist and author of *Conversation with Max* (1960).

bristling with new ideas—and Ruth too, but as regards her it would perhaps be better if she has not changed in the smallest degree. This house is pleasantly a-crawl with children at the moment—and more to come on Tuesday next. Once, about, every two days I sympathise with Herod, but not for long, and on the whole there is very little grizzling and quarrelling.

8 April 1961 *Bromsden Farm*

Your sad mistake in sending your last letter to America was balanced by your earlier error of sending the first one here, so I came back to enjoy your words of February 22—and then this morning arrived your note of yesterday. What a feast!

That Cardus book has been out of print for years, and I searching the hedges for a copy for you. On Thursday after lunch Ruth and I strolled round in bright spring sunshine to Moss Bros to hire me a suit for the three weddings I have to attend (the Devlins' daughter's on Monday, my niece's on Saturday, and Duff's on Saturday week), and on the way I spied that rather battered copy in the Charing Cross Road. Those pages I mentioned have not appeared in any other book.

We landed at 7.15 a.m. on Tuesday in dark grey rain. A most officious Customs man disarranged all our luggage and made us pay £3. 12. 0 for sundry nonsenses. Finding an English translation of *Madame Bovary* in my bag, he made sure he was on the trail of dirty books, but a couple of pages of the learned translator's preface calmed his ardour. The office was piled high with this and that, and we longed for the peace of the *Queen Elizabeth*.

Here I found six weeks' worth of bills, letters and periodicals, and have spent all today coping with them. Adam *lost* the Chess Cup—I suspect through idleness and other distractions. I have put back seven and a half of the ten pounds I had previously lost, but am quickly dropping my American accent.

We shall be eagerly awaiting you at 6 on Tuesday. Siegfried has expressed his intention of attending the dinner, but I'll believe it when I see him.

One's first impression of England in the train from Southampton is of incredible *greenness*. All grass in New York, Boston and between is at this time of year a dark brownish-grey.

15 April 1961 *Grundisburgh*

How very nice it was to see you again—and looking so well after all the obviously unhygienic ways of New York. And Ruth too—lovely! But I suppose to visit a new continent, and have everyone falling in love with you as they obviously did, *is* invigorating. I hope her dinner-party went as well as ours did. Siegfried S. clearly enjoyed himself—as indeed anyone would between Tommy and John Sparrow. To me there are no evenings in the year of quite the same quality. The hors d'oeuvres so to speak—that hour with you and R.—are an essential part of it, as you must know. And but for you this brightening of my old age would never have happened. Can't you hear Cuthbert 'Why should *he* be a member—a dull pedagogue?' Tim had some good acid-drops from the old asp. Would it not be a good notion if *he* were sent up in *our* first space-rocket?

Two families have just left here and two more just come—the larger ones. But happily only two grandchildren are spoilt and therefore unpleasing and they have gone.

Two thousand more members for the MCC! And the only match I ever go up for is the Australian Test Match when the pavilion is cram-full one and a half hours before play begins—and I only got a seat in 1956 because a man (in the best seat of all) died ten minutes before I arrived, and in Housmanly fashion I took it. I say, how tremendously good Cardus at his best is! The account of McDonald in this book you sent really is superb. What a lot of people don't know the difference between fine writing and 'fine' writing!

I am going to spare you the two full quarto sheets this week—after your nasty gibes about four letters in a week. And am now off to saw wood. Bobby Bourne has to do the splitting, and indeed all the really heavy work. My doctor is rather anile about my using an axe or 'beetle'. Last week I lugged a waggon, full of timber, a good deal impeded by several grandchildren, though when Henry (*aetat* three) was asked by his mother where I was, his answer was 'He's just been helping me bring in the wood.'

So goodbye, my dear Rupert—and love (more than ever if poss!) to Ruth. That was a delicious look on her face when she said you were *not* going to do any more banting. It had the finality (but no other similarity) of a decision of Queen Victoria.

16 April 1961 *Bromsden Farm*

I'm so sorry this is a day late. Most of yesterday was taken up with my niece's wedding in London—at that beautiful church opposite Lord's, reception at the Savile Club. Duff and Adam were ushers and all went well, including my proposing the health of the young couple. Many old family friends, unseen for twenty years, turned up and had to be identified. Luckily only two challenged me by saying 'I'm sure you don't know who I am,' and I guessed right both times. Duff's wedding next Saturday is at Builth Wells in Wales, and the distance will keep down the size of the congregation. Comfort and I are driving there and back in the day (135 miles each way), so next week's letter will be a day late too, if it ever gets written at all.

I think Siegfried thoroughly enjoyed his first Lit. Soc., and not least your anecdotes of Ranji and co. On Wednesday I dined at Tommy's: just the two of them, Siegfried and me. The poet was in excellent form and talked to me about poetry in the liveliest way while Tommy slumbered by the fire. I must confess that I was somewhat disarmed by Cuthbert's asking whether he should resign, adding that the Lit. Soc. was the only thing that kept him alive. An exaggeration no doubt, but an engaging one.

I entirely agree with your remarks on the New English Bible. A few fragments of mystery are surely an *asset* to religion, and to slaughter one of the greatest glories of our language and literature to make a Sunday-school holiday is monstrous.

The Eichmann trial seems to me all wrong, because one simply can't help feeling a trace of sympathy for the victim in the glass cage, and clearly one *shouldn't*. I should be happier if they had shot him like a mad dog when they found him. But I suppose the Jews don't want the world to forget what they have been through.

Birley has sent me his Clark Lectures, which I shall certainly publish. They are called *Sunk Without Trace* and deal with six works of Eng. Lit. which were tremendously popular in their day and are now unread and almost forgotten. They are Warner's *Albion's England* (Elizabethan), Nathaniel Lee's *The Rival Queens* (Restoration), Young's *Night Thoughts*, Robertson's *History of the Reign of Charles V*, Moore's *Lalla Rookh*, and Bailey's *Festus*. The manuscript is in longhand: the writing is legible, but it takes much longer to read than a typescript. I am finding it very interesting, and it certainly tells one all one could want to know about those forgotten favourites.

Did I tell you that the page-proofs of Oscar are due to begin arriving tomorrow? And are you still game to read a set in search of misprints and editorial solecisms? A few sets are coming in piecemeal between tomorrow and May 5, and about May 7 a larger number of paper-bound complete ones. Which would you prefer? I quail at the thought of compiling the enormous index, which must be ready by the end of May—then heigh-ho for Kisdon! Blessed thought!

I love this greening time of year, with its birdsong and promise of summer, but it makes London seem even more unattractive than usual, and I long for the great hills of the north country.

Ruth has gone to Essex to spend the week-end with her son and grandson. The simple truth is that I miss her every moment she isn't there, and that after fifteen years! It must be the real thing—and how rarely is that found!

20 April 1961 *Grundisburgh*

A perfectly noble quartette of books arrived this morning to the unconcealed envy of my daughters and son-in-law. They seemed to think it was grossly unfair that I should have a fairy godmother all to myself (and so it is!). They ask indignantly 'Do all publishers do things like this?' and my answer is easy 'No, no more than all motor-manufacturers do the same as Lord Nuffield.' I shall have great fun with them. *Pro tem* I am reading Daphne du Maurier on Branwell

Brontë, whose appearance was seemingly like the mildest of spectacled curates. No wonder he could not stand up against his terrifying sisters, but I wonder who could have. Some blend of Heathcliff and Rochester, I suppose. Could the Lit. Soc. provide such do you think?

I got yesterday a perfectly charming letter from Ivor B. asking if I would mind(!) his dedicating his forthcoming word-book to me. It was a wonderfully friendly letter. How much I owe you for the Lit. Soc.—as I have said before and shall say again whatever you may say about the stories I tell you which originally came from you (that was humiliating if you like—but it was a great success in the Ipswich County Club, so there). Was it you, perhaps, who told me of the advertisement which delighted Max B. (not in Behrman, I think) 'Medical man in Cheltenham can accommodate one female resident patient—epileptic Churchwoman preferred'?

I am glad you recognised your old friends at that wedding. I am always being non-plussed, and lack the thick-skinned ungraciousness of old Broadbent[1] whose answer to an old pupil's 'I bet you don't know who I am, Mr Broadbent' was 'You've won yer bet' and moved off. You won't be writing this Saturday—you can't, in view of Duff's wedding. Give him my warmest regards; in spite of his hair being quite a different colour from what I seemed to remember.

Do you get any kick out of the Budget? I hope the surtax cut benefits you. It doesn't me. I find it annoying that after saving what I could through a working life of thirty-seven years, and investing it in gilt-edged (which have steadily depreciated) and living in my old age modestly and mainly on my dividends, I am regarded (and called) a parasite by half the Socialists, my income is called 'unearned', and I continue to be taxed up to the hilt. And hundreds of thousands of retired professional men—doctors, dentists, lawyers, schoolmasters, dons, deans etc—are in the same boat.

Birley's lectures should be good, but I am not 100 per cent certain that they will be. When an assistant beak at Eton, his reports were curiously and conspicuously dull, for all his ability. I once knew a little about Nat Lee, and Moore, and thought Bailey's *Festus* full of good lines. All I (or anybody else) can ever remember of Young's

[1] Former Eton master.

Night Thoughts is 'Procrastination is the thief of time'. Milton has better lines but few more widely known.

All decks here are stripped for Oscar. I will go through anything you send with a small tooth-comb (whatever a tooth-comb may be). But you remember what James Agate said about proof-reading, *viz* that real efficiency is impossible. He advocated reading upside down, but even so found that as soon as you recognise a word by its first half you take the second half for granted. Anyway I will do the best I can.

I say, Rupert, the blossom! Surely all the last few days have burst all records. Here it is positively heart-breaking in its loveliness. Never have I seen it so thick and rich. The atmosphere of the summer-house is Housmanly as I survey a prunus, a cherry and an almond.

23 April 1961 *Bromsden Farm*

Yesterday Duff's wedding entailed a marathon drive for us. We left here at 8.30 a.m. and got back soon after midnight, having covered 305 miles, mostly in heavy rain. Most of the lovely hills and valleys of the Wye were obscured by rainclouds, but all went off gaily and well. The tiny church of St Bridget at Llansantffraed-in-Elfael is as remote as can be imagined, at the dead-end of a tiny valley, so that all the cars had to be left in wet grass four hundred yards away and the ladies' wedding hats and shoes were sorely tried by two muddy walks in steady rain. Every seat in the church was occupied, and we were so packed in the pews that we had to get up one at a time. The young couple looked exceedingly handsome, and it was all most touching and suitable. The registry was a leaking tent adjoining the east end of the church, but by then we were prepared for anything. Afterwards champagne flowed, with Adam as chief pourer, and we shook innumerable hands and complimented everyone. They have gone by air today to Athens, *en route* for Corfu.

On Friday Comfort and I attended the luncheon in Merton Hall for the opening of the Max Room. Considering that Merton is probably the richest of all the Oxford colleges, the food wasn't all that good, but it served. I was happily placed beside Rachel Cecil (wife of

David C. and daughter of Desmond MacCarthy), an old friend. On my other side was a breezy tutor of English called Hugo Dyson, and opposite me the extremely pretty daughter of John Rothenstein (he and his wife were there too). S.C. Roberts made an admirable speech. Jonah and his wife were there, Jock Dent and many other Maximilians. Before lunch we had a drink with Sir William Hayter, the Warden of New College and former Ambassador to Moscow—a very agreeable chap.

So you can see we've been around a bit these last two days!

I get no kick—or good—out of the Budget, since I have only once paid any surtax, and that was years ago. All my tiny income is 'earned', but there isn't enough of it to qualify.

I very much enjoyed Birley's lectures, and think you will too. Eric Linklater has sent me his new novel to publish: it's called *Roll of Honour* and is all about a *retired schoolmaster* in Aberdeen! Some of it is in an irregular sort of verse, unusual but effective. I shall try to bring it out this year.

The first thirty-two pages of Oscar arrived on Tuesday, but next day the second thirty-two disclosed a hideous blunder (not of mine, but of my colleague or the printer), which has necessitated a hold-up for revision. I hope the flow will be resumed next week, and I will send it to you section by section. Get out your finest tooth-comb and your strongest spectacles, and do your damndest.

Adam has been accepted for Voluntary Service Overseas, though he doesn't yet know where he will be sent, or exactly when. In any case we shan't see him for a solid twelve months (that's part of the contract), which is rather sad.

The garden here is lush and green and badly needs mowing. If only we could find even a part-time gardener, but they all say this is too far to come. We've just heard of a firm that goes round mowing people's grass at fifteen shillings an hour (they say they—two men—could do ours in one hour, and a weekly visit from them would be a blessing). Every drainpipe and gutter is blocked with birds' nests, and the lilac is in bloom. The wallflowers are wonderful, but it's always too wet even to look at them. This morning I burned dozens of old newspapers and clipped a few edges before I was driven in by bouncing hailstones. Oh to be in England . . . !

27 April 1961 *Grundisburgh*

Gosh, your day! It makes me feel tired even to read about. And on a day when Suffolk, bless its heart, had *one* shower lasting for twelve minutes. Last autumn we overflowed with the best, but normally there is no doubt we are outstandingly dry compared with midlands, west, and especially Wales. But I grant we cannot compete with names like Llansantffraed-in-Elfael. Perfectly superb, a poem in itself. I should like to hear you pronounce it. The champagne, poured by Adam, sounds all right, inferior and vulgar wine though it is, though its effects are good, convincing one without much difficulty that the world is in a better state than in fact it is.

Please tell me whether, in the effort to keep up to date, I ought to read the plays of Wesker and Miss Delaney. They cannot surely be as bad as *Lucky Jim* or *Look Back in Anger*. How refreshing it is when the brilliant young make asses of themselves, e.g. that letter from K. Tynan and others about Cuba, which subsequent writers have shown to be entirely wrong both as to facts and inferences drawn from them.

The Australians. Who is to get wickets when Benaud and Davidson are mastered? Who is to get wickets for us? Statham and Trueman cannot go on for ever. I hope they will find someone who takes fewer steps in his run. They both walked from crease to start in *thirty-five* steps. Mold and Brearley took seven, Larwood ten. *Verb sap.* I shall be watching with Gerald Kelly on the middle gallery, where seats are kept for us by a man who, I think, sleeps there all night. I wish my nephew was at Hagley. I saw the Australians at Worcester in 1948. Charles Fry was there. Bradman of course got 200 and C.B.F. watched every ball through a pair of vast field-glasses. In the evening he said he had never expected to see another batsman who saw the ball as quick as Ranji, but Bradman certainly did—and was R's superior in concentration, which C.B.F. said he had never seen remotely equalled. Interesting.

29 April 1961 *Bromsden Farm*

I don't really much *like* champagne either—Belloc once described it as 'wine, yellow and acid, with bubbles in it'—but it's a great morale-booster, don't you agree?

I'm afraid that Jock Dent probably *is* going downhill: he looks awful now—very fat, red and blotchy. His life of Mrs Pat[1] is a shocking mess, full of coy whimsicalities and messily arranged. All the same, it does contain most of the known facts about that unusual woman, and I can't say I was bored. Most of the reviewers, liking Jock, have concentrated on the subject and disregarded the treatment. I certainly should *not* read the plays of Wesker and Miss Delaney. They may some of them be just tolerable in the theatre (*A Taste of Honey* was more than that), but to *read*—no, my dear George!

This morning was so grey and chilly that I fairly easily conquered my desire to drive to Worcester and sit on the wet grass all day. But how nice it will be to have something interesting in the papers again. I agree about bowlers' idiotic runs—Lindwall's seemed endless, but the worst of all was that of Alf Gover of Surrey: the dreariest bowler I remember, though Nigel Haig is a hot candidate.

On Wednesday Marjorie Linklater (Eric's wife and a friend of more than thirty years) paid one of her rare visits to London, and I (in all good faith) took her to the longest and dullest film either of us had ever seen—the Italian *La Dolce Vita*. It lasts for *three hours*, and there is no plot, only a sequence of incidents. The famous 'orgy scene' is pretty tame, and the whole thing seemed to me pretentious and wearisome.

Last week, when Paris was threatened with invasion, with tanks ready at every corner,[2] my Uncle Duff's old secretary wrote to say that they refused to disconnect the telephone in the Paris flat, because it had been installed in Duff's name and they insisted on documentary proof of his death.[3] I wonder the tanks didn't get tangled in red tape.

I think I heard the cuckoo a couple of days before you did, and now I hear nothing else. The wallflowers and lilac are lovely, and the grass seems to grow faster than we can cut it—particularly with both the boys away. We have mice in the larder, and rats in the compost-heap.

[1] *Mrs Patrick Campbell* by Alan Dent (1961).

[2] On 22 April 1961 two French generals brought off an anti-Government *coup d'état* in Algiers. In fear of an airborne invasion and an attempt to assassinate De Gaulle, Paris was put on full alert. The revolt collapsed on 26 April.

[3] He died on 1 January 1954.

The walnut tree is only just showing its buds. Some rabbits have reappeared, and none of the kitchen garden is wired.

On Monday I go to *Rigoletto* at Covent Garden with the Droghedas, on Wednesday Ruth and I dine with the Eliots, and on Thursday there is a dinner at the Reform Club for Ivor B's seventieth birthday. I'm not sure whether his birthday is that day, but it's pretty close, so do send him a note of encouragement.

My old father is eighty-three on Monday, and it's difficult to wish 'many happy returns' to someone who never stops saying he wishes he was dead. Perhaps he means what he says, but I doubt it. Tommy reports that Malcolm Sargent's speech at the R.A. dinner was too long, in poor taste, and spoken too fast. 'What were the other speeches like?' says I. 'Ball-aching', says Tommy, 'including the P.M.'s.' Perhaps you listened on the radio?

I am reading an excellent life of Maupassant by a charming American called Francis Steegmuller, whose future books I am going to publish. He writes with style and learning: it's an excellent book, which you would enjoy. My bedtime reading has for so many years been largely conditioned by Oscar and the search for quotations used by him, that I suddenly feel liberated, and able for a few minutes most days to follow my fancy in an agreeable way. I see, to my horror, an announcement of a *sequel* to *How Green*. Unless you pronounce against it, I shall soon have two unread books on my conscience.

29 April 1961 *Grundisburgh*

Assuming that you want them *quam celerrime* I send the mild little results of my tooth-comb now instead of waiting till my Thursday letter. I find no solecisms by R.H-D. and let me say at once, surely no book since Birkbeck Hill's Boswell has been so comprehensively and beautifully annotated. You will laugh at my one suggestion for the alteration of your English. What the split infinitive is to some (on the whole silly) people the double pluperfect has always been to me.

2 May 1961 *36 Soho Square*

Very many thanks for your note of April 29 and for your extremely valuable comments on the first thirty-two pages. They are just the sort of thing I was hoping for.

I've hastily removed the double pluperfect and will deal with all the other matters. I checked yesterday and the Tripos is now definitely called Moral Sciences in the plural, though perhaps it wasn't in those days. Here is a note from the *Oxford Companion to Music* which will answer your query about the Skye Boat Song:

> 'One half of the tune is a sea-shanty heard in 1879 by Miss Annie MacLeod (later Lady Wilson) when going by boat from Toran to Loch Coruisk; the other half is by Miss MacLeod herself. The words, by Sir Harold Boulton, Bart, (*Speed bonnie boat, like a bird on the wing*) date from 1884. Later some other words were written to the tune by Robert Louis Stevenson, who apparently believed the tune to be a pure folk-tune and in the public domain.'

I sent you another thirty-two pages yesterday and more should follow tomorrow. Keep up the good work.

3/4 May 1961 *Grundisburgh*

I was much relieved to find that my observations were not too fiddling and pernickety, and greatly amused at your being right—as I might have expected—about Moral Sciences and the Skye Boat Song. I hope, and think, that my boats were not utterly burnt by my merely querying both and not bluntly altering them. I shall be increasingly wary, and if I find Sydney Smith referred to as 'Smoth' I shall merely append a dubious query. Today I shall tackle the instalment that arrived yesterday. It is exactly the right time of year for such work—the blank period between two G.C.E. exams. Just before the first proofs arrived I was reduced (wrong word) to re-reading *Mansfield Park*. At first my anti-Austen feelings were reinforced by the immensely insipid and trivial conversations in Chapters 6 and 9 (please have a glimpse and tell me if I am really as wrong as all that).

But I frankly confess (who is humble and I am not humble?, as St Paul obscurely put it) I enjoyed it—so much so that I must shortly have another go at my *bête noire*, *Emma*. I fear I dislike *her* too much.

I fear you may be right about the nightingale. Pamela is with you and ascribes all the *Schwärmerei* about him to the poets. And what about this?

'Fat and sweet is the song of the nightingale. A good full singer he is. A good big chest full of breath, him, and a chest to hold it, too, and up with his head and open with his mouth, thinking it no shame to sing with the voice that God gave to him, and singing with fear for none, true on the note, sharp at the edge, loud, fat with tone, with a trill and a tremolo to make you frozen with wonderment to hear. A little bird he is, with no colour to his feathers, and no airs with him, either, but with a voice that a king might envy, and yet he asks for nothing, only room to sing. No bowing, no scrapes, no bending of the knee, or fat fees for Mr Nightingale. A little bough, a couple of leaves, and nightfall, and you shall have your song with no payment other than the moments of your life while you listen. Such voices have the cherubim.' From *How Green* of course. I am delighted to hear there is to be a sequel, though the fate of sequels is grim—apart from *Alice*, *The Jungle Book*, *The Prisoner of Zenda*, *The Newcomes* and no doubt several others which I have forgotten.

My nephew Charles would corroborate all you say of Gover, and more. By the way I am conscious of decided lumpishness about your lovely Cardus volume. I suppose I wrote before I had read your *quite excellent* introduction. All said that should be said with the utmost concinnity (as Max would say). How cleverly you tell us that N.C.'s mother and aunt were both harlots!

I have sent a line to Ivor B., though in actual fact his birthday is on April 25 (*Who's Who*). I recently read a first-rate review by him of *Mrs P.C.* My aunt Edith Lyttelton was very fond of Mrs P.C. and used to have her to meals—rather to the dislike of General Uncle Neville who was *echt*-Victorian. On one occasion Mrs P.C. turned to Oliver when he was about eighteen and demanded an epigram about life, which O. gave without hesitation. I don't know what it was. The story reflects credit on neither.

Sorry about your father's gloom. I shall be saying the same as he does in five years—but not to you or Ruth! When I grouse about aches and pains to my doctor, he unsympathetically says that such are *en règle* at my age, and that he knows no man of seventy-eight fitter than I am. And my only way of scoring off him would be to die suddenly to-morrow, and then I should miss Oscar. So he has me, damn him, in a cleft stick. Do you remember in that admirable second act of *The Truth about Blayds*[1] the old man's answer to the family's wishes of 'many happy returns' on his ninetieth birthday 'Happy I hope; many, I neither expect nor want.' A good answer, and in fact he died that very night.

Oscar. Tooth-comb, magnifying-glass, hearing-aid, etc. all failed to find anything and produced nothing but a grumpy query about 'moly', so that it was really a relief when your printer gave Forbes-Robertson a life of a hundred and two years (p. 87). Archibald Forbes[2] cuts a morose figure. Surely O.W's letter of Friday March 20 cannot justly be called 'obviously offensive' and to call kindly expressions 'irrelevant expressions of cordiality' is the mark of a curmudgeon.

6 May 1961 *Bromsden Farm*

Many thanks for your excellent letter, and for the proofs of pp. 63–94. I fear your patience, eyesight and sealing-wax (very impressive) will be exhausted before we're through. The printers have been so dilatory that the other day I made a great row, and they have promised to work overtime with extra men, all through the week-end, so I'm hoping for better things next week. Yes, moly is just what you think, and I'm most grateful to you for spotting Forbes-Robertson's undeserved longevity. 1835 should indeed be 1853, and it's just those simple misprints that are most apt to escape the jaded eye. I've gone so stale on the whole thing that it will be a miracle if I spot anything. I'm now beginning to veer towards Moral Science, but will take further expert advice.

Fancy your succumbing to Jane Austen: perhaps you will soon love Emma as much as the heroine of *How Green*! I know you will be

[1] By A.A. Milne (1921).

[2] Preposterous war-correspondent and lecturer (1838–1900).

disgusted and horrified, but the passage you so kindly copied about the nightingale only increases my trepidation about the whole book—and its sequel.

This week has been hellish. Let me detail it for you. Monday wasn't too bad: a peaceful lunch with Ruth, and in the evening *Rigoletto* in the Droghedas' box at Covent Garden—very enjoyable, and a good serial dinner in a private dining-room in the intervals. Also there Sir Patrick and Lady Reilly (former Ambassador in Moscow, Lady Aberconway (remarkably sober), L.P. Hartley, Loelia Duchess of Westminster and the Droghedas' son. Afterwards in pouring rain to a party at the Redfern Gallery in Cork Street, where my cousin John Julius Norwich's wife is having her first exhibition of abstract paintings. The crush totally obscured the pictures, and I got home by midnight.

On Tuesday Ruth and I lunched with the old poet Andrew Young, and I rushed off to a long meeting of my television company, with Slim in the chair. 6–8 drinks with an American publisher, and manuscript-reading-cum-proof-correcting till 11.30. On Wednesday Adam arrived from Scotland at 8 a.m. with his friend Dunglass (Alington's grandson). I took them both to the neighbouring Lyons Corner House, where the breakfast is quick, plentiful and good. Large lunch with a literary agent. 6 p.m. drinks with an American publisher at Claridge's (with Ruth) and on to an excellent dinner with the Eliots.

On Thursday, lunch with James Pope-Hennessy and much literary discussion. Evening Ivor's birthday party at Reform Club. Indifferent food and drink but agreeable company: some thirty men, including the editors of the *Daily Telegraph*, *Economist*, *Daily Mirror* and *Daily Herald*, Jock Dent, Ralph Richardson, Compton Mackenzie, Robert Morley, Gerald Barry, P. Fleming etc. Many speeches, the best by Priestley in the chair. He said he realised his own plays were out of date, and he was meditating a play in the modern manner, for the Royal Court Theatre. 'There's only one character, a tramp. The whole action takes place in a telephone-kiosk. The tramp spends the first act making up his mind to ring up his cousin in Hackney Marshes; the second act is taken up with his search for the necessary fourpence, and in the third act he *slowly* remembers that he never had a cousin.' All beautifully told with his rich Yorkshire accent. I got drenched in a thunderstorm cloudburst on my way to the dinner, but it had cleared afterwards.

Yesterday (Friday) I attended, on behalf of the London Library, a huge and delicious lunch at the East India Club in St James's Square, and in the evening a banquet for three hundred in Stationers' Hall, to celebrate the jubilee of a publisher called Walter Harrap. Cocktails, madeira, white and red wine, port, brandy, cigar, more speeches. Can you wonder that I feel dim-witted and listless today? Nor is next week going to be much better. It's worse than New York, where the air is more stimulating. Also I've made a hideous blunder and arranged to attend Francis Meynell's seventieth birthday dinner on Wednesday, which this month is the Lit. Soc. day—oh dear!

Ruth has gone to Essex to help christen her grandson. We can neither of us believe that blessed Kisdon is only four weeks away. Shall we ever get there? Somehow we *must*. Then you will get brief notes about curlews and baby grouse.

11 May 1961 *Grundisburgh*

The truth is simply that there has never been any suggestion made to you to which you could say 'no' except one—and that is that you should read *How Green*. I was not greatly surprised by your demurrer to the nightingale sentence, for I have long sensed your allergy to the book. We agree in and on so much, but in any two people with minds of their own, sooner or later some huge gap appears as big as that between Abraham and Lazarus. I remember the shock (but I am older now) it was to find that my old friend Tom Cattley, who had plenty of humour and a feeling for words, saw nothing remotely funny in P.G. Wodehouse. Similarly you have to put up with my thinking *Lady C.* a very dull and pretentious book with all its fourth-form defiance of previous standards. The only superiority I claim is that I have read *Lady C.* and you have not read *How Green*! And there we must leave it.

I am greatly enjoying the O.W. stuff, though fully conscious how few and short (like the prayers they said for Sir John Moore) are my suggestions. I will say again how frankly astonishing the fulness, accuracy, and interest of your editing seems to me. On almost every page one detects *weeks* of hard research, and I like to see you sometimes enjoying yourself. E.g. p. 125 the 'American lobbyist, financier, talker and gastronome' and just below after O.W's ecstatic praise of *A Daughter of the Nile*[1] produced on September 6, your laconic statement 'It was withdrawn on 23 Sept.' What an extraordinarily *nice* man O.W. was, so kind and courteous, till pricked. Did his extremely beautiful wife remain loyal to the end, or was her stuffy family too much for her? It was a dreadful business really and need never have come to a head at all. O.W. didn't corrupt anybody, and everyone now knows that the clause in Labby's[2] bill making private behaviour a public offence was passed at the end of the day when all MPs wanted their dinner, and weren't attending. I hope you are as pleased as I am by the outcome of the 'Kiss in the Car' case? I followed it daily and—as so often—was puzzled by the neglect of what seemed to me a very important point, *viz* the absurdity of calling what two people do in a closed car at dead of night, in a dark corner of a dark square, an offence against *public* decency.

Why is T.S.E. not among the 'Companions of Literature,' the new order just started. He is a better man than either old Maugham or E.M. Forester (*sic* in *Daily Telegraph*). Perhaps he didn't want to be.

I have also just got Connolly's *Enemies of Promise* which I remember finding interesting years ago. Do you know him? Shall I write and tell him that he is in error saying the book was banned at Eton? Eton is particularly good at *not* being thin-skinned about hostile opinions (partly, of course because she does, or did, not, like the Duke, care one twopenny damn what hostile critics think). I remember Tuppy Headlam being much pleased by C's eulogy of him as teacher and influence, but I fear it was much too favourable. T.H. never had 'much the best house at Eton', and if as C. says he 'hated idleness' he got over it: for in his last years he was conspicuously idle in school (golf at Swinley *every* Sunday!) partly because he had formed the opinion that history was not a good subject for teaching to the great majority of boys. And he may have been right.

[1] A play by Laura Don.

[2] Henry Du Pré Labouchere (1831–1912). Radical M.P. for Northampton 1880–1905. Founded *Truth* 1876.

Slightly comic Governors' meeting of Woodbridge School yesterday. Next year we are to have tercentenary celebrations. What big noise shall we try to get? The Duke of Edinburgh? Well who do we approach to find if he could or would? The Lord Chamberlain. Who is he? Lord Nugent. Does anyone know him? G.W.L.: 'My first pupil'—but he isn't the Lord Chamberlain. Who is? Eric Penn. Does anyone know him? G.W.L:' He was in my house', but he isn't the man. Some governor 'No, the man to go for is Sir Edward Ford. Does anyone know him?' G.W.L: 'He is my cousin.' Another governor: 'I believe the right man is Sir Michael Adeane; does anyone know him?' G.W.L: 'He is my wife's cousin.' Another: 'Suppose we can't get him. What about the Queen-Mother? Does anyone know her?' G.W.L: 'She was a great friend, before marriage, of my wife's.'

So now I am in the eyes of my fellow-governors either *very* highly connected or the biggest snob in England. *Que voulez-vous*?

13 May 1961 *Bromsden Farm*

Very many thanks for your letter, and for your comments on pp. 95–222. They are most valuable, and your name will have to be added to the list of my benefactors in the Introduction. You are particularly good at spotting printers' errors in people's dates. I should never have noticed Vernon Lee's 99 years: in fact she died at 78: I must check the exact date. Of your other queries: I've no idea what a 'pen-rog' is or was, but this text is from a catalogue and is probably wrong. I like to think that you have enjoyed Lafite all your life, wrongly believing it to be Lafi*tt*e! '*Je pruse*' and '*Oxonicuris*' are the printer's versions of '*Je pense*' and *Oxoniensis*'. Doubtless my handwriting was to blame, but such obvious nonsenses are much easier to spot than those plausible but wrong dates. Do try and find the reference for Carlyle on Margaret Fuller: God (or Gad) knows where I took it from.

Your return of the misdirected pp. 223–254 was so cryptic that I'm not sure whether you got two sets, or only this one. I rang up Henry Maas, but he is away till tomorrow morning, when I will try him again. My secretary's wits are clearly going—so sorry.

Peter reports an agreeable Lit. Soc., and I wished I was there, for

Ruth and I had a pretty tedious evening at Francis Meynell's seventieth birthday dinner. There were far more men than women, and I was between Reynolds Stone (Foxy's engraver son—very nice) and a Central European typographer. The food was quite good, but there were *eight* speeches—all poor—and the final one, by F.M. himself, lasted over an hour. I twice almost dropped off.

Earlier in the day I went to Geoffrey Faber's Memorial Service, at which T.S.E. spoke well. He refused that ridiculous award, and I encouraged him to do so. The Royal Society of Literature—a miserable institution—is simply trying to bolster itself by crowning five octogenarians, who were too vain, gaga or polite to refuse. In any case, I told Tom, a stripling like him is far too young for such a questionable *galère*.

You always write as though *Lady C.* was my favourite book, whereas I feel almost exactly as you do about it.

So glad you're enjoying Oscar, though we're barely a third of the way through yet. Your praise of the notes is very comforting. After six years I have lost all sense of proportion, and simply don't know whether the notes are too long or too short, too detailed, too dull, or too frivolous—so you see I'm in need of reassurance. Yes, Constance Wilde behaved well all through, as you will see, though at the end she was quite out of her depth. Hold on—the best is yet to come.

I am reading Tyson's autobiography, which I think he certainly wrote himself. How many professional fast bowlers are capable of quoting from Keats's letters? He has some good stories too. Do you know the one of Bradman, overhearing British criticism of Australian umpires, and interjecting 'That's all nonsense. Mel McInnes played several times for South Australia before his eyes went.' Would it amuse you to read the book when I've finished it?

I had a protracted and pathetic luncheon with my old father at White's on Wednesday. He has to totter with two sticks, seldom recognises anyone, and if he does can't remember their name. He reads all day and night, but enjoys very little, finding his adored Dickens now quite unreadable. Self-pity is surely the least attractive of all faults, and it prevents one's own pity from functioning. He never stops saying he has made a mess of everything and wishes he was dead. What can one answer? He refuses to have TV and seldom switches on the radio—what a life! He has day and night nurses permanently in attendance. Sorry to be so depressing. You could easily be my father—what a difference!

18 May 1961 *Grundisburgh*

Rather a moderate harvest this week, I fear. You and your minions are wonderfully accurate on the whole. I am greatly enjoying the job and childishly pleased when I discover an error. The letters are crammed with interest.

I have searched hard but without success for the Fuller-Carlyle episode, though I have the irritating certainty that it must be somewhere in my room. I suggest you might find it in that portentous biography of T.C. by D.A. Wilson, which, though Ipswich has it not, must be in the London Library. It is a very ridiculous book in seven volumes—fattish ones too, with much triviality and irrelevance; what in the world the dear old curmudgeon would have said about it, one just dares not think. But at any rate it does tell us that his tobacco was Bird's Eye, which Froude does not. I am rather glad too that he doesn't put all the blame of Mrs C.'s unhappiness down to C.'s bearish ways. She exaggerated everything, and Froude had no more perception of exaggeration than a boy has of irony. I have a *very strong* feeling that he said 'Gad' and not 'God'. I hope you will find it. I continue my search.

I much enjoy your dislike and contempt for literary societies and—to a great extent—men. Do you remember Henry James's reply to John Bailey when asked to be chairman of the English Association?[1] Edel missed it in his volume of selected letters (published by you) just as he missed another immortal one to Walter Berry who had pre-

[1] '. . . Let me, for some poor comfort's sake, make the immediate rude jump to the one possible truth of my case: it is out of my power to meet your invitation with the least decency of grace. When one declines a beautiful honour, when one simply sits impenetrable to a generous and eloquent appeal, one had best have the horrid act over as soon as possible and not appear to beat about the bush and keep up the fond suspense . . .'
After which he delightfully beats about the bush for several pages.

sented him with a dressing-case.[1] Really a very extraordinary omission, because I have never read letters more packed with character and vivacity and humour, both incomparable in style. Do look them up in Percy Lubbock (unless of course I have said all this before!).

How right you are about the rarity of literary style among fast bowlers. Few of them have put pen to paper. I must read Tyson's book, what a pity he lasted so short a time, he was one of the very few really fast bowlers.

I am sorry about your father—knowing enough of the stresses of senescence to sympathise with him—knowing too how many people wish they were dead but manage to refrain from saying so.

20 May 1961 *Bromsden Farm*

Your comments continue to be most acute and helpful. I should *never* have noticed that the printers had changed Blackwood's birth-year from 1836 to 1886, thus depriving him of fifty years. I've *got* those portentous seven vols of Carlyle source-book, and sure enough you're right, though the phrase is given as part of a conversation between T.C. and Margaret Fuller: 'I accept the Universe'. 'Gad, you'd better!' I am most grateful. What should I do without you?

[1] '. . . You had done it with your own mailed fist—mailed in glittering gold, speciously glazed in polished, inconceivably and indescribably sublimated, leather, and I had rallied but too superficially from the stroke. It claimed its victim afresh, and I have lain the better part of a week just languidly heaving and groaning as a result *de vos œuvres*—and forced thereby quite to neglect and ignore all letters. I am a little more on my feet again, and if this continues shall presently be able to return to town (Saturday or Monday;) where, however, the monstrous object will again confront me. That is the grand fact of the situation—that is the tawny lion, portentous creature, in my path. I can't get past him, I can't get round him, and on the other hand he stands glaring at me, refusing to give way and practically blocking all my future. I can't live with him, you see; because I can't live *up* to him. His claims, his pretensions, his dimensions, his assumptions and consumptions, above all the manner in which he causes every surrounding object (on my poor premises or within my poor range) to tell a dingy or deplorable tale—all this makes him the very scourge of my life, the very blot on my scutcheon . . .'

By now you could have received up to page 446, which is about half-way through. Can you bear it? Last week I bullied some information out of the printers which makes it quite certain that the book can't appear before January. *Eighteen tons* of paper will be needed, costing almost £3000. The printing, on the biggest machine working day and night, will take fifteen weeks. And *when* am I to compile the enormous index, and fill in all those missing dates? The index I can do on Kisdon, but little else. It looks as though, for January publication, I must finish everything off by mid-July. It is a job for a team of subsidised young experts, not for an ageing publisher in his non-existent spare time.

I do indeed know the James letter to Walter Berry, and in March when I was staying in the James home in Cambridge, Mass, I made Billy James (H.J.'s nephew) read it aloud. He has a barely perceptible and rather attractive hesitation in his speech; and it might have been the Old Master himself—a delicious experience. In justice to Leon Edel, it's fair to remind you that in his introduction to the *Selected Letters* he explains that he has deliberately omitted famous letters already known or printed, in favour of others hitherto unknown.

Last week was pretty exhausting. It began with *two* cocktail parties on Monday, the earlier and more interesting one at the American Embassy in Grosvenor Square. T.S.E. was there, in excellent form, also a lot of poets and littérateurs. All that New York hospitality is coming home to roost, and last week R. and I lunched three separate lots of Americans. On Wednesday evening I went to hear Alistair Cooke give the Annual Discourse at the Royal Institute of British Architects in Portland Place. It was the first time a layman had been invited to speak, and A.C. acquitted himself nobly. Afterwards there was a dinner-party of twenty, including most of the leading architects—Basil Spence, William Holford etc, all very agreeable. And so it went on, day after day, with my Oscar proofs piling up. We plan to drive to Kisdon on June 6 and stay there three weeks. It seems too near and too good to be true.

Duff and his bride are here for Whitsun—very sunburnt and happy. Peter's annual cricket match against the village is on Monday. Duff is playing, but not I fancy Tim, who with Rosalie is staying with the Flemings.

24 May 1961 *Grundisburgh*

A *most* boring thing has happened. I read your—as always—admirable letter at breakfast yesterday, meaning, *more meo*, to read it again at least once before answering it when it is always open before me. And then in the course of yesterday (after one rapid perusal) it vanished and in my senile decay I remember only a few patches of it. Damnable. My capacity for losing things grows steadily. I know exactly where I have put something—but it isn't there half-an-hour afterwards. Well anyway—

I greatly enjoy this scrutiny of your proof-sheets, but the job grows lighter owing to your—and really your printers'—outstanding accuracy. The two lots I send herewith are practically flawless, as far as I can see. As you prophesied, the interest grows with each page. But the amount of hard labour still before *you* in the way of references is horrifying. To be done at Kisdon? But surely you need half the London Library and British Museum to give you any real help.

Have you passed the Strand Theatre recently? outside which the play is blurbed as 'Delightful, bawdy, wonderful, amoral, indecent.' A direct result, as it seems to fuddy-duddies like me, of the *Chatterley* verdict. Words are reversing their old meanings. Whereas 'bawdy' is now a word of praise, no self-respecting young modern critic will ever refer without a sneer to writing for which 'beauty' or style is claimed. I have just read a book (*Mirror for Anglo-Saxons*[1]) in which the author condemns the English wholesale for being 'gentlemanly'. U.S.A. writers are praised heartily for their 'brashness'. Have you seen the book? It says some sensible things but very many silly ones. How tiresome these young men are who complain of having been 'ruined' by being sent to Oxford or Cambridge.

Are you hot under the collar about the latest plan for the Oxford road? A.W. Whitworth[2]—*not* a Christ Church man—says a lot of rot is talked about the incomparable beauty of Ch. Ch. Meadow. I don't know it. What would be a real crime would be to spoil the Parks. But I suppose you all realise that you have literally the loveliest cricket-ground in the world. It would *not* be improved by a motor-road across

[1] By Martin Green (1961). [2] Former Eton master.

the pitch. Fenner's on the other hand would. It might also improve their cricket. Annoying your missing the Lord's Test. We could have split a ham sandwich. But I expect you regard the cry of the Swaledale curlew as superior to that of the score-card boy, and the company of Ruth as making all that you miss at St John's Wood of no account. I shall be *chez* my brother at Highgate Village—bus to Golder's Green, change, bus to Swiss Cottage, change (I think), bus to St John's W. (past the home of Jonah).

I am just off to judge a reading competition at Ipswich—the first at which I shall be using my hearing-aid. Old Rendall[1] went on judging when he could hear only treble voices, so all the prizes went to the small boys—which gave rise to the murkiest and most unreasonable theories.

28 May 1961 *Bromsden Farm*

Your question about the change in Oscar's attitude to Bosie between May 1895 and May 1896 has probably now been answered by your reading the *De Profundis* Letter. He had had a whole year to think about it all: Bosie had never once even written to him: the attempted publication by B. of O's letters and the suggested dedication of B's poems—all combined to this end.

Yesterday was joyful. Lord's only half full, and a bitter north-eastern blowing. I had failed to get a Rover for Ruth, so we paid six shillings each and sat in the front row, ground floor, in the middle of the Grand Stand, whence we had a splendid view. The sun shone on us all the morning, but in the afternoon we got colder and colder, and at the Tea Interval went back to Soho Square for a hot bath to stave off *rigor*. We sat next to an amiable young man from Hobart, Tasmania, who repeatedly lent us his superb binoculars. They were Japanese, and he told us he bought them new in Singapore for £9.

After our bath we went to a revue called *Beyond the Fringe*, which is the talk of the town. I expect you have read of it—just four young

[1] Montague John Rendall, 1862–1950. Headmaster of Winchester 1911–1926. In retirement he restored and transformed Butley Priory, near Woodbridge in Suffolk, and was chairman of many committees.

men, who wrote it all—and I must say it was vastly amusing. The best things were a skit on Macmillan speaking on TV, and a mock-sermon.

One day last week R. and I lunched with Sybil Thorndike and Lewis Casson, whom we found enchanting. She is seventy-eight and he eighty-five—a little deaf but right on the spot, and full of plans for future plays.

I hold no brief for Christ Church Meadow—a dreary flat expanse—and think the road should certainly go through it, provided they close Magdalen Bridge to most traffic. If they don't, there will soon be just as much going through the city. The Parks are indeed incomparable, though I have a great liking for Worcester county ground, with the river and cathedral alongside.

I fancy Adam may make a fool of himself at Speeches on the Fourth by not knowing the bit of *Don Juan* he has chosen to say. We never saw Duff perform, as he was playing for the XXII and excused. Pray for a warm day. Yes, write here this week—and then! I suppose I shall get everything done somehow. Taking on the whole Oscar job was, as Henry James said in another connection, 'an insensate step.'

P.S. Read this quickly before you lose it!

31 May 1961 *Grundisburgh*

Nasty little sarcasm about my losing your letter—like chaffing a man about the loss of a dear friend! I am still full of chagrin whenever I think of it. It shall never happen again.

How on earth you get through your work I can't imagine. The O.W. stuff alone is easily a full-time job for anyone. I expect most of my recent suggestions are baseless: my faint pride about 'far' for 'for' will probably be easily dispersed by you. What a perfectly loathsome man Douglas comes out as—which indeed his father's son could hardly help being. O.W's taking him up again after he left prison even odder than the Murrys' resumption of friendship with D.H.L. after the latter's unspeakable letter to K. Mansfield.

I should like to see *Beyond the Fringe*. It has had very good notices of those spirited young men. You will not, I think, have seen the Crippen trial turned into a musical comedy. There is no limit to what seems to me sheer imbecility, in which class I unhesitatingly put 'The Turn of the Screw' set to music—on the whole the most appalling story I know—making *Dracula* mere commonplace blood and bones.

I don't care much for *Mrs Patrick Campbell.* All higgledy piggledy and surely much too long. At the very start that tale of her petticoat coming down goes on and on up to p. 20. Do we want to know what *every* single critic said about it? And I agree with you about Jock Dent's interpretations. Poor stuff. He would have done better than that when in old Agate's employ, for J.A. was never arch or merely facetious. I expect Mrs P.C. was fairly intolerable. I haven't reached the Shaw part yet.

Interesting about Christ Church Meadow. Did I ever tell you Masterman's reply when I praised the lovely Worcester College cricket-ground or rather the garden in which it is. 'Which garden do you mean? We have five'. The Worcester county ground is good though surely not equal to the Parks. E. Jones the Australian fast bowler once hit a ball into the river and wistfully said to H.K. Foster at the end of the over 'I wish I had got hold of that one', to which H.K. with an unusual flash of wit said 'If you had, you would have smashed the best stained-glass window in the Midlands'. The cathedral is a third of a mile away.

4 June 1961 *Bromsden Farm*

Thank goodness we shan't have to attend the Fourth of June for many years to come. We set out yesterday at 9.30 a.m. (taking with us the sixteen-year-old girl of Adam's devotion) and got home, quite exhausted, at 12.30 a.m. It's a little too much for the middle-aged, and the constant bother of parking, deparking and reparking the car is a nightmare. Speeches lasted too long—two and a quarter hours—and varied, as usual. Only two in Greek, one in French and the rest in English. Adam did his bit well, but it wasn't a particularly good bit. The final item was an intolerably tedious chunk of the play Tennyson wrote when he was fourteen, which should have been destroyed by his executors.

Oh yes—I couldn't help thinking how delighted Oscar would be to see a tolerably handsome boy reciting a passage from *The Sphinx* in Upper School in 1961! The best thing about the day was the weather—warm and mostly sunny. Picnic lunch and tea on Agar's, and in between watched some very moderate cricket. If Harrow or Winchester have any batsmen, they should be in clover, judging by the Eton bowling and fielding of yesterday. The Captain (Wigan) rearranges the field between each ball, and his own bowling did little to improve his average, which the *Chronicle* told me was 1 for 256. I saw almost no friends except Jonah and Vyvyan Holland.

After Adam had attended Absence[1] we took drinks with the Coleridges, and then drove to Monkey Island for a tolerable dinner. Hideous parking problems again, and the poorest fireworks I remember—long intervals between, and too many behind that cypress tree. Posses of police could do little to mitigate the subsequent traffic-jam. What we go through for our children! The whole place was looking its best in the sunshine, but low-flying jets keep on blotting out all other sounds. Adam says it's only the Boeings, but there are lots of them.

Thanks so much for your two last sets of comments—all most pertinent and valuable. I will see whether that 'for' shouldn't be 'far'. I shall hope to send you some more tomorrow, and thereafter my secretary will supply you to the end. Do send them back, with your comments, to Kisdon. By the time you get this we shall be well on our blessed way. Leave Soho Square 4 a.m. Breakfast, Bawtry 8 a.m. Shopping, Bedale 10.30. More shopping, Hawes 12. Lunch on the Buttertubs Pass between Wensleydale and Swaledale about 1. Report to our farmer at 2. In the cottage before 3. I repeat all this, partly for pleasure, partly so that you can follow. Ruth's little Renault has packed up, so she is hiring a new Ford for three weeks, and we may venture onto the earlier reaches of the M.1. You shall hear all.

Last Wednesday Comfort came up for the night and we went to the Mansion House, to the first-ever Midsummer Banquet for the

[1] The Eton name for roll-call.

Arts, Sciences and Learning. There must have been four hundred or more guests received in great pomp, between lanes of trumpeters and soldiers in ancient uniforms, by the Lord Mayor, huge, hideous and charming. Fanfares, bands and mace-bearer. Huge banqueting hall with gallery. Husbands and wives all side by side. On my other side I had an agreeable woman, Lady Logan, wife of the Principal of London University. T.S.E. and wife were at the top table—perhaps you saw the list of guests in Thursday's *Times*? Goodish food—and a superb soup: cold turtle soup *en gelée*, with a nest of pink caviare in the middle and cream on top—Russian, I imagine, but certainly delicious. The chief speeches, by Sparrow and Osbert Lancaster, were far too long, and only in part audible, though I'm told heard clearly on the BBC. Eventually we were given a lift home by Hugh Greene, the head of the BBC.

7 June 1961 *North Foreland Lodge*

I am in the headmistress's study at North Foreland Lodge. We (a small sub-committee) met yesterday to tell the staff they were, in one or two respects, inefficient, and to do so without hurting their feelings—and staff's feelings are very near the surface. Well I, as chairman, poured melted butter over them and all was well—except that I think they dispersed, unanimously convinced that we had come down solely to congratulate them. I used the old trick of describing one or more of their bad practices as what other schools I knew absurdly and lamentably did. I think I deceived all except the cynical old man who teaches art and fencing who was clearly enjoying hearing his colleagues hinted at and not himself.

Do you know about girls' schools? Virginal starry-eyed, angelic, do you think? Well the headmistress showed me a letter from another school to the girls here, challenging them to a novel contest—how many girls they could get into a bath all at once. The challengers' record was nineteen. And would they kindly send a photograph of the proceedings before, during, and after. The headmistress asked me (non-committally) what I thought, and was delighted when I said what she thought, *viz* that it stank. What do you think? After all *I* am an old Victorian square and stuffy, entirely out of date.

I have long avoided June 4—an intolerable day—and decades ago I swore I never wanted to see another firework. On many ageing parents the day's effect is the same as that which results from attending an old friend's funeral in January, i.e. death. Don't *you* give way.

How lovely the names of your journey are!—Bawtry, Bedale, Hawes, Buttertubs—the diapason closing full in Wensleydale and Swaledale. Ruth and Swaledale—two lovely names and the loveliness doesn't end with the names!

There is literally nothing that I can find in this O.W. instalment, though I am a little distrustful, as I read it against a prattle of childish voices and a backfisch playing the Moonlight Sonata with the forthright vigour that one expects in 'Rule Britannia'.

11 June 1961 *Kisdon Lodge, Keld*

No need to apologise for the pencil of your excellent letter from North Foreland Lodge: it was noble of you to write at all in such surroundings. Our farmer's son has gone away to work in Kirkby Stephen, and now there is no milking on Kisdon, so we get our post only when we walk down the hill (which isn't every day) or when the farmer comes up on his motor-bike, ostensibly to look at the non-milking cows ('drybags,' he calls them) but in fact to bring us milk from below. So far, ever since we arrived on Tuesday we have been assailed by bitter cold, lashing rain and a whoreson north-west wind. We sleep anything up to twelve hours a night, hug the fire and get ourselves delicious meals. No callers, no telephones, no sound but the wind outside and the tick of the grandfather clock within. Yesterday was Ruth's birthday, for which I usually assemble half a dozen little presents, to be given at intervals through the day. This time, not through any diminution of devotion, but simply because of the crushing weight of things to do in London, I had nothing! She was very good about it, and graciously accepted a tiny fountain pen which we bought on our week-end shopping expedition to Hawes. Our drive up didn't exactly follow my traditional forecast. The hired car—a Ford Anglia—went like the wind, and by making use (for the first time) of the M.1. from its beginning to the Northampton turn we cut *forty minutes* off our total time, without covering any fewer miles! We flashed through Bawtry at 7.40, long before the hotel was open, and eventually breakfasted at Boroughbridge, after whizzing through Doncaster before its interminable traffic had assembled in the bottleneck. All we now need is a good way of avoiding the loathsome Leicester.

Your Oscar comments and corrections are most valuable. We haven't yet done anything to the index here, for I had to spend the first two days coping with arrears of mess from the office. I have been reading for the first time John Buchan's last (or perhaps penultimate) novel *Sick Heart River*, which I much enjoyed: he is surely under-rated as a story-teller. Now I am ready for Priestley's new novel, and the life of Wilfrid Blunt by his grandson. But in daytime I am mostly occupied with the Oscar proofs. Just finding and filling in those cross-reference page-numbers in the footnotes takes longer than you would think.

As for those schoolgirl pranks, you should have told them that it's most unlucky to have thirteen (or more) in a bath. What next! It sounds to me much like I imagine Rayner Wood's house to have been.

So far you have said nothing of your opinion of Oscar as letter-writer. (I find his letters make most other contemporary ones seem very dull.) Do you find yourself liking and sympathising with him more and more, as I did? Do some of his jokes make you laugh? I am thankful to say that since we found those last three letters in New York no further ones of any importance have turned up, though the book's publication will surely produce another crop.

To our sorrow there seem to be few or no sales in the neighbourhood during these weeks, but we still have faint hopes. Ruth is waiting to add a little postcript, so goodnight—and love from us both.

P.S. with my adorable new pen

To you I can confess that I carry a heavy burden locked in my heart for, quite inadvertently, when buying stamps in the post office at Hawes yesterday, I overheard the latest Test Score and may not tell it for fear of spoiling the papers for days ahead (we are always two days behind). I feel dreadfully guilty and may even give it away in my sleep.

You would have laughed to see R. wrapped up to his ears in a rug and crouched over the fire and his O.W. proofs; a tempest without and our last drop of paraffin gone. Why do people like Augustine Courtauld willingly spend a whole winter alone in an igloo? Very odd people are. But we're blissful here in spite of everything. Perhaps that is odd too.

Dear George, forgive these crooked words but I write on my knee which is nearer the fire. And they bring you my love and the nice thought that I shall one day soon again hear the tap tap of your stick on that interminable flight of stairs. My love. Ruth

14 June 1961 *Grundisburgh*

How lumpish of me not to have said what I have all the time felt, *viz* that O.W's letters are *fascinating*. But I was, before your letter arrived, intending to tell you how steadily one's liking for him grows. His bed may have been as full of boys as that bath I told you of was of girls, but what is that to me? It didn't prevent him from being far kinder and nicer and wiser and wittier than most of his precious friends. The Victorians really could be unbelievably stupid and grossly unchristian, whatever their lofty professions. His unending poverty in '97 and '98 is a heartrending tale. Why did no man with money and imagination send him £1000. But perhaps the two things never run in harness.

I am vicariously crushed by the amount of work you still have to do on Oscar, and I still remain literally astounded by the amount you have already done. How *did* you find out practically everything? E.g. how did you get on to *Giton* in Petronius's *Satyricon*, or is all literature your province? You never read Petronius up to e.g. Toddy Vaughan. I am very little good to you over the two enclosed lots. One or two tiny printing-errors and one *B*obbie into Robbie and jolly little else; but the mere reading is sheer enjoyment, though often painful. You praised Constance in one letter, but wasn't she pretty harsh and unforgiving at the end? What *did* they all expect him to live on if his allowance was cut off? Of course she loathed Bosie—and who shall blame her? Except of course D.H. Lawrence, it is hard to think of anyone who could behave more caddishly. And one finds it hard to forgive coarse second-raters like Henley running down the incomparable *Ballad*. General Wavell wrote that it was 'spoilt by insincerity'. I like to remember that when his anthology[1] came out the Lord Cranworth asked 'Is this what we pay our generals for?' Philistine comments are occasionally—even if inadvertently—bull's-eyes.

I agree about John Buchan—a first-rate story-teller—and who is there except V. Woolf and others who profess not to like a story? Did you know him? A very friendly fellow, excellent company. A pretty stout chap too; he paid practically all his Oxford fees by literary work. He died too young. I must get *Sick Heart River*.

I am enjoying Wells and Gissing, especially the former.[2] I think I have read every book he wrote, and enjoyed them all. But how furious he always was when people asked for more *Polly* and less *Clissold*.[3] But he could be unpardonable, e.g. the way he treated old Henry James.

I have lately been re-reading about two great heroes of my youth (and old age) Wellington and Lincoln. Do you realise what a vast volume of opposition, dislike and contempt both were consistently treated with *by their own side*? And neither turned a hair. That picture of Abe—a broken-hearted man—in the last year of his life is one of the most moving things I know. Also the wonderful beauty of the Duke as drawn by d'Orsay. You know it of course. And please look up Carlyle's pen-portrait of him in his journal 25 June 1850. How many biographers etc don't know their business and realise that to find a man unforgettably described you have to look in Carlyle.[4]

[1] *Other Men's Flowers* (1944).

[2] *George Gissing and H.G. Wells*, edited by Royal A. Gettmann (1961).

[3] i.e. *The History of Mr Polly* (1910) and *The World of William Clissold* (3 vols, 1926).

[4] 'By far the most interesting figure present was the old Duke of Wellington, who appeared between twelve and one, and slowly glided through the rooms—truly a beautiful old man; I had never seen till now how beautiful, and what an expression of graceful simplicity, veracity, and nobleness there is about the old hero when you see him close at hand. His very size had hitherto deceived me. He is a shortish slightish figure, about five feet eight, of good breadth however, and all muscle or bone. His legs, I think, must be the short part of him, for certainly on horseback I have always taken him to be tall. Eyes beautiful light blue, full of mild valour, with infinitely more faculty and

Wilfrid Blunt I always suspect had a good deal of the four letter man about him—but he was a good friend to some. Why not—after your gargantuan labours on O.W.—produce a biographical sketch of *Skittles*[1] and her sleeping-partners, among whom, did you know it? was the old Duke of Devonshire. I suspect she was pretty good fun.

18 June 1961 *Kisdon Lodge*

The weather is turning this holiday into an endurance test, and though we are winning, we do long for a few days of hot sun. So far in twelve days we have sat out for only two hours. A knock-me-down gale has been blowing for days, often accompanied by driving rain, but we managed one lovely long walk, almost all round Kisdon, which took us the best part of four hours. On Thursday we drove sixty miles to a sale at a farm near Thirsk, where we acquired some cups and saucers, two rugs, and a lovely patchwork quilt (this last for one shilling, the only bid). Ruth was delighted at getting a letter all to herself and will add a word to the end of this. Your kind and flattering words about the Oscar editing are most encouraging and come at a welcome moment. The final work (especially the index) cannot possibly be finished here, and God knows how or when it will be done after we get back. Here we do the index together, Ruth controlling the hundreds of cards and fishing them out as I need them. This demands table-space, concentration and no intruders. The final proofs will have reached you by now, and your labours will be done. If mine are ever concluded I shall have to turn to

geniality than I had fancied before; the face wholly gentle, wise, valiant, and venerable. The voice too, as I again heard, is "aquiline" clear, perfectly equable—uncracked, that is—and perhaps almost musical, but essentially tenor or almost treble voice—eighty-two, I understand. He glided slowly along, slightly saluting this and that other, clear, clean, fresh as this June evening itself, till the silver buckle of his stock vanished into the door of the next room, and I saw him no more.'

[1] Nickname of Catherine Walters, a famous courtesan, to whom Wilfrid Scawen Blunt wrote many of his love-poems.

SKITTLES

The Story of a *Poule de Luxe*

by R.H-D.

with an introduction on Victorian Prudery,

and special reference to the bathing

accommodation at girls' schools,

by G.W.L.

Am I right in thinking that there is no really adequate biography of the Duke of Wellington? Guedalla is too slick and sly and second-rate. Shouldn't I commission the right chap to do one? Who is he? Gerry W. is very choosy about showing people the documents, having been much harassed by journalists and Yanks, so his approval is essential. I did suggest the idea to James Pope-Hennessy, but he said military history was not his thing, and anyhow he was full up with work.

I am just enjoying Rumer Godden's latest work, *China Court*, in which she has, I think, succeeded in bringing off an almost impossible task—telling the story of a hundred years (1860–1960) of the life of a family country house in Cornwall, with all four generations interwoven, so that, although they're all quite distinct and separate, they flow into each other and build up a fine continuous unity. Do try it. You may find it too sentimental, but I think you're bound to admire the writer's skill.

I'm sure I've told you before of the tiny shop in Hawes where the eccentric owner of the Wensleydale cheese-factory deposits all the books he doesn't want, on sale for sixpence or a shilling each. In the past the shop has always been shut, and we got the key from the grocer next door, to whom we returned it with our shillings and sixpences. Now the shop is intermittently cared for by an octogenarian retired railway-signalman, who delivers the morning papers in Hawes and then potters about the shop. He knows the Bible by heart, a great deal of Shakespeare, and has a good library at home, he says, including a complete set of the English Men of Letters series. He was much delighted with a life of Beethoven which he recently bought in Kendal. He used to make a day-trip to York, so as to browse through all the secondhand bookshops. There were no books in his home when he was a boy, and none of his family or fellow-railwaymen shared his interest. Isn't it extraordinary? He is a charming old chap.

E. Blunden has arrived at Soho Square, and is to be there, on and off, till August 20, when an old lady from America moves in. What hope for the index? Write here this week: we shall sadly leave on the 27th. Now comes Ruth.

I *did* love having a letter from you all to myself and wish I had some fascinating story to fill in my tiny quota of space. One thing I can say. *How G. is my V.* has been taken from its shelf and laid on the window-seat. What this portends I cannot guess, but I will let you know any developments there may be. I read it years ago with enjoyment but shall not press it upon R., as that would be fatal at this stage.

We *long* for sun, just a pale sun would do to begin with, so long as the wind would cease battering us so mercilessly. I dare to hope to-morrow may be better but it is unwise to speak above a whisper about it.

In answer to your question. 'Does R. ever refuse to do something he is asked to do' the answer is, alas, NEVER. And this I cannot seem to change, though, in this one respect, I would dearly love such a change. What *can* we do? Please go on murmuring 'Swaledale'; it may remind someone to send us some sun. I do wish you could see it all—painlessly of course. My love. Ruth.

23 June 1961 *Lord's Cricket Ground*
London NW8

From the holy of holies—but all the writing-seats are full and this is practically on my knee. And it will only be a wretched scrap. I leave Highgate Village too early for any letter-writing; I wait a long time for a 210 bus to Golder's Green, of all dim spots, then catch No. 13 for Lord's, and the walk from the stop to the nearest entry is curiously long. Then in the evening I wait aeons for a bus home and am expected to talk all the evening between yawns and so to bed, so what would you? You must at last have had good days: surely the last three have been quite perfect. Pamela optimistically opened our garden last Sunday, in spite of my prophecies of rain and murmurs that no one would pay a shilling, even on behalf of our fourteenth-century wall-paintings, to come and sit and listen to a loud gramophone playing the Water Music, etc. And of course I was quite wrong. Ancient village crones sat about like great loaves of bread (old fashioned shape), and all said how happy they were—*especially*, and surprisingly, *because* there were no lucky dips and guessing-games etc which most people think are what get the crowd to such things.

In twelve minutes Harvey will be batting again—and then O'Neill. All depends upon what sort of a night the wicket had below its covers. Last night I dined with some nice Old Boys at an absurd restaurant in Beauchamp Place, lit—a big word—by guttering candles and cramped, but good food. I drank too many different liquors and slept uneasily. One of the Old Boys' wives whom I had never seen before insisted on kissing me goodnight. A very sinister sign surely, indicating that I am far too old for a kiss to have the smallest meaning. Never mind. The sun is shining, Harvey is in and O'Neill to come. And Gerald Kelly is said to be in Russia.

25 June 1961 *Kisdon Lodge*

Goodness knows when this will reach you. They have wantonly moved the village letter-box from outside our dear farmer's house to far down the hill, and now we can't so readily ask him to do our posting for us. Nor shall we leave our hill-top till the sad exodus of Tuesday morning. And if the publication of Oscar is unduly delayed, as seems likely, owing to the editor's failure to compile the index, the blame can be laid fairly and squarely on the shoulders of G. Lyttelton and R. Llewellyn. Almost since I last wrote I have been immersed in that infernal work,[1] enjoying it enormously, and quickly getting used to that lush-Biblical-Welsh idiom. I quite see what you mean about Bronwen. It's beautifully done, and I'm most grateful to you for forcing me to read it. I think I had been put off chiefly by its length and my lack of undisturbed leisure. I finished it yesterday in a dip of

[1] *How Green was my Valley.*

the hill—the only place where we can escape the gale, which has blown almost incessantly ever since we arrived. *You* may have been sweltering: we are swathed in jerseys. Our farmer cut his hay in the field in front of us, but yesterday when we helped him rake it together, the wind blew it to blazes, and he was thankful to get most of it heaped up under a tarpaulin.

I wish you could see Ruth's bowls of wildflowers: there are three in the sitting-room and three upstairs. The most beautiful is just pink campion, but some of the mixed ones are lovely. This year, for the first time, we have found a new kind of wild orchid which smells delicious—some kinds smell like tom-cats—and there are forget-me-nots, kingcups, wild roses, bluebells, primroses, cowslips, trollius, wild geraniums, cuckoo-pint, and so on. Tonight we are having a fry-up for supper—sausages, bacon, tomatoes and potatoes. The smell is delicious, and I shall stop to enjoy it.

Later

It was superb, followed by bread and local butter and raspberry jam. We drink nothing but tea up here—gallons of it—and are all the better.

Your last batch of corrections was most valuable. I have removed the Max appendix altogether: it's out of place there and seemed feeble. We haven't yet got to page 200 in the index: it's an appalling, endless, back-breaking job, and I simply don't know when I shall get it done.

As I write, the sun is setting over Roger and Westmorland, behind a mass of grey clouds, and the hills are shrouded: I fear our last day here will be no warmer than its predecessors. But we shan't mind, for every moment here is incomparable, and the index calls us. I shall be in the office on Wednesday, to face a pile of tiresomeness, and at Bromsden on Friday, so write there. It's nice to think we shall see you before very long. Much love from us both, and now it's Ruth's turn.

Monday. Now it is our last—but by no means our finest—hour. The sky is grey, the wind blows and I am so thankful, as a brilliantly sunny final day here would have been unendurable. We are packing everything away carefully for next time. I always hate this part and feel as if I was walking out to the tumbril at any moment.

And please understand I am *passionately* interested in cricket and have always been. My father, who captained Herefordshire in its finer days, was a great friend of H.K. Foster—that pippin-faced and delightful man, and played against W.G. himself on a few occasions.

And does this mean that I may never kiss you again without your having idiotic ideas of the kind put forward (fishing a bit I thought) in R's letter? Well—we'll see about that.

My Lyttelton collection grows—two splendid items now in mint condition. But I fear there may be no more for a whole year, which is remarkably sad. And this will be the last notelet too. My love. Ruth.

June 26 1961 *Lord's Cricket Ground*

The match just over. The last innings was fun and the Australians really had to fight for the runs. The wicket stayed a bit mischievous to the end. *All* the catches at the wicket were off bumpers. O'Neill, whatever they say, cannot be quite in the Bradman–Trumper class, for, as Cardus puts it, a champion is doubly dangerous when frustrated (W.G. first innings b. J.C. Shaw 0; second innings lbw Morley 221). George Hirst, chiselled out by a Lancs premeditated appeal which bluffed the umpire, got *9 for 32* on the next day.

The England side is giving no satisfaction—no guts, no concentration, not playing like a side etc etc, you hear all round. Cowdrey apparently melancholic at the wicket. It is odd but I have never seen him get a run, but apparently on those occasions he is superb. May in both innings looked good, but each time nibbled. Do you realise that if Lawry had let the ball drop from his thigh so as to remove a bail before he had got 10 (as happened to Dexter at 17) it would have been a very even match?

I met the great Ponsford at tea—a charming fellow. I reminded him of how he stayed in with Bradman for two days, and he replied simply 'Those days were fun.'

P.S. It is drenching and I have no hat, coat, or umbrella and there isn't a taxi and all buses are full. The *Daily Mail* man wants Trevor Bailey back and as captain. God in Heaven!

29 June 1961 *The Painted Room, Oxford*[1]

How delightful that at last you have tackled *How Green*. An immense relief to hear you are sound about Bronwen, for there is a great gulf between me and anyone who does not love her. Indeed it *is* lush-Biblical-Welsh as you put it, but also as you say, beautifully handled. It isn't of course the only way to write, but I was sure your catholic taste would not reject it once you were induced to read it. Did the gentle but irresistible hand of Ruth play any part? I make private bets to myself—and always win them.

I had a very good evening with Tim. He tells me old Cuthbert is in a sad way—not *qua* health but finance. Has he been living on capital or what? I remember an old boy in Worcestershire who decided that he could not live past ninety and lived on capital which would last till then. When he passed ninety he quietly shot himself. They brought in the silly verdict that he was insane.

1 July 1961 *Bromsden Farm*

The sad week of south-coming was cheered by unexpected letters from you—one sent on from Keld and one waiting for me here. The wind blew to the last, and I daresay all this heat-wave has passed Swaledale by. We got home in record time thanks largely to the M.1. Ruth's daughter was in her house, and E. Blunden in the flat, which, though expected, was tiresomely disconcerting. During my absence the flat had at one time or another housed *six* Blundens, *four* Chinese girls and an old Chinese nurse. To hear my daily talk, you'd think they'd all been there at once, though I think it's scarcely possible. True, the kitchen looked as though a tribe of roughish gypsies had been camping there, but now all is to rights, and only the gentle E.B. in occupation. He's the sweetest man (don't be surprised if he's there when you come) and no trouble, but the fact of his being there means that I chat to him instead of getting on with my work, and since he's on vacation he has very little positive to do. On Wednesday and Thursday evenings I escaped to Ruth's house in Hampstead (her

[1] In the Golden Cross Hotel in the Cornmarket.

daughter having left) and did some Oscar index. By means of working most of today in my library, which is blessedly cool, I have dragged the index to page 250—less than a third of the whole.

If I tried to describe our sadness at leaving Kisdon and returning to London, it would sound childish and unbecoming in a middle-aged man, but I think you realise a lot of it, and we try to cheer each other by reflecting that most people don't get even our glimpses of paradise.

I forgot to tell you, by the way, that at one of our sales several lots were knocked down to a lady aptly named Mrs Bosomworth, which delighted us.

Ruth will be overjoyed on Monday when she gets her unexpected notelet. I'm glad to say she has got out of London for the week-end—to a friend in Sussex, but oh! I do miss her. In fact she hadn't anything to do with my eventually reading *How Green*: I just felt the time was ripe, and ripeness is all.

Yesterday, with the temperature at 85, we had our half-yearly sales conference: thirteen people present for two and a half hours, and I talked almost the whole time—I hope with more conviction than I felt. Afterwards, exhausted, I fell asleep in my chair in the flat.

I haven't seen Peter yet, but probably shall tomorrow. Diana Cooper is spending the week-end with Patricia Hambleden at Ewelme, and tomorrow morning I am going to fetch her over for a drink. Bridget is here, Duff and his wife come for the day tomorrow. Adam has sold a competition to *Argosy* magazine for *twenty guineas* and is much elated. Long Leave next Friday, but no Lord's. A good batch of forthcoming books will go off to you next week: I only hope there's something readable among them. I am now reading the little book about Edith Simcox and her passion for George Eliot.[1] You have probably forgotten, but E.S. gets a passing reference in Oscar, as contributing to the *Woman's World*, and I want to improve my footnote on her.

Comfort is despairing because the rabbits have come back and eaten *all* her vegetables and most of her flowers, while squirrels have had all the strawberries, jays and bullfinches every single raspberry. Apart from all that, the garden looks brown and parched, and I dream

[1] *Edith Simcox and George Eliot* by K.A. McKenzie (1961).

of the green green fields of Swaledale. Next time you visit Roger you simply *must* engineer a drive to Keld and its waterfalls.

I have had two charming letters from Birley, who seems pleased by the care with which I scrutinised his typescript. The book won't be out till January or so. I found the usual pile on my desk, and I shan't be up-to-date for days. To cap everything, my secretary is leaving some time in July. She has been with me eighteen months and is thoroughly knowledgeable about all the people I write to. Now, if I can find a new girl, I shall have to start all over again—oh dear!

Did you see *The Times* announcement of the death of Dover Wilson's wife? It ran '. . . . bird lover and for fifty years dear wife of John Dover Wilson.' Deliberate, I wonder?

Ruth would send love if only she were here. Please give mine to Pamela.

5 July 1961 *Grundisburgh*

You are right about me and Keld. I *hate* your not having perfect weather as if it was my own holiday. And for Suffolk to beat Swaledale in the matter of sunshine is absurd. Even so I don't see you spending your next summer holiday at Saxmundham, where incidentally lives the dullest man in Europe, whose sole interest is the Jewish plot against the world, which, with heraldry, is surely the hallmark of the bore.

I still think that E.B. is lacking in perception to take up, however pleasantly, so much of your time and room, but of course you are the last person to snub anybody (I am sure Ruth agrees there). Again and again, when looking through the O.W. proofs, I thought what a hideous mass of work was still before you, dating and identifying and fixing in all sorts of ways. And the reward—unanimous acclaim by reviewers—probably doesn't excite you much, sure though you must be of it. I hope you saw Priestley's little tribute to your *Hugh Walpole* in last Sunday's *Sunday Times*. He condemns Maugham's *Cakes and Ale* but very mildly. I suppose one mayn't use perfectly accurate words like 'caddish' about a still-living writer. What is the new life of M. like?

I doubt if I shall read it, having always been rather allergic to him as a man.

I look forward to the batch from you, and hope confidently that they will lift the depression into which the perusal merely of the reviews of Iris Murdoch's new novel has plunged me.[1] I am like Douglas Jerrold after reading 'Sordello'. I haven't a notion what they mean in most of their sentences, or the quoted passages from the book. And I begin to agree with an old friend who maintains that incest and homosexuality are among the most boring of subjects. There is much to be said for being seventy-eight, at which age one *needn't* read modern novels. You will laugh when I tell you that I have been reading of an evening *The Idylls of the King*. The English is largely Wardour Street (a horse is rarely a horse; it is a steed or a charger, or, if a lady's, a palfrey) and the *dramatis personae* are china dolls. But now and then he brings off a charming little picture or a delicious chime of bells, and I don't mind if they do turn the stomach of Leavis or Amis. The latter, they tell me, has been made a Fellow of Peterhouse, where he will meet the shade of Gray who won't think much of him. Oxford is really the place for K.A. I was there on the hottest days of last week—and no place is hotter than Oxford, so I mainly stayed indoors, having found a walk from Merton Street to Carfax equivalent to any Turkish Bath. We had our meeting in 'The Painted Room' (do you know it?) where our choice was between having the windows shut and suffocating, or having them open and being deafened by the passing traffic. We chose the latter and I, for one, got a very sketchy hold of the agenda.

8 July 1961 *Bromsden Farm*

With briefest intervals for meals I put in *twelve hours* at my index today—10 a.m. to 10 p.m.—and covered *forty* pages. It's much the most I've ever done in a day, but I've still only got to p. 340, and the end is not yet. I must confess that from 11.30 to 6.30 I also had the radio turned to Headingley, and maybe I should have done more pages if the game had been less exciting. Until recently winning the

[1] *A Severed Head* (1961).

toss seemed to be half the battle: now it seems to be fatal. Did you watch or listen?

Our daily (the cowman's wife) reports that a goldfinch, nesting in a lilac bush in her garden, decorates its nest with forget-me-nots and replaces them with fresh ones when they fade. Can it be true? I must investigate.

Sunday morning, 9 July

I still haven't quite caught up on my arrears of June correspondence, piles of manuscripts await my scrutiny, and above all the index calls. I must get on with it now, and trust you will on Tuesday express your forgiveness for this half-pint letter. I reckon that with luck my six years' work on Oscar may net me £1200, which is just the minimum we shall need for Adam at Oxford, as well as his £100-a-year Postmastership. You see, I haven't £5 of capital—never have had—a great handicap. I will disconnect all bells on Tuesday.

13 July 1961 *Grundisburgh*

There is nothing new to say about yet another of those evenings which I enjoy quite extravagantly, particularly that hour before the dinner. E.B. is a charming fellow, yet anyone but you would gently but firmly point out that you haven't really a minute to spare for him. Odd that he doesn't suspect it. As for Ruth—well it would be straining the truth to say that I was aware of her new dress, but it would *not* be to say that she was more attractive than ever to eye and ear. There again I suspect she was every bit as much so in April, but time scatters its poppy, and great charm always contains some surprise. I expect you are conscious of that every time you see her.

I nearly passed out at the end of the evening. I was afraid Tim, who always lifts me home, had gone, but then found he was playing billiards with Peter upstairs. I toiled up and found no one. I came down and asked some genial Garrickians in the lounge where the billiard-room was. They told me it was *two* floors up, and added that they never played the game as they couldn't face the ascent. So once again I climbed (three hours after No. 36!) and not unnaturally found my legs very achy and twitchy in bed that night. Not that I regretted either climb. But what a loathsome place on the whole London is. Misanthropy in the street has all the look of being universal. I hate all I pass or meet in a bus, and they all hate me—and only *black* bus-conductors have good manners.

I am re-reading *A Passage to India* for exam-purposes. Is it as good as some say it is, or is it a bit over-rated? The unpleasantness of Anglo-Indians seems to me rather over-stressed, just as does Jane Austen's irony, but as you can easily see, I am no judge. I was interested to be told by Anthony Powell that he cannot judge any novel, even his own. He has found Iris Murdoch's latest novel more readable than any of the others. I was pleased to find he greatly admires John Bayley. I only had time to tell Harold Nicolson that he had written of John Wesley being at Christ Church *College*, a gaffe for which I—a poor Cantab—had been severely told off by an Oxonian fifty years back. H.N. smiled demurely but made no reply. I hope I did not offend him.

This is rather a poor scrap, but I am just back and the post is not far off. Love to Ruth (with a capital L).

15 July 1961 *Bromsden Farm*

Yesterday I fell a victim to what I first thought was gastric flu, but now incline to diagnose as a mild recurrence of jaundice. By the time I got down here the internal upset had developed into a fever and I went straight to bed. After two hours I woke in such a heavy sweat that everything had to be changed. Thereafter I slept peacefully till morning, and today am pretty well recovered, though still a trifle wobbly and listless. I shall keep off alcohol and eggs for a bit. What a bore!

So glad you found Tim in the end and got your lift home. Once again I think Siegfried thoroughly enjoyed himself, though his shyness still prevents him from talking to anyone but the person next to him. I manoeuvred Harold Nicolson on to his other side, and they got on splendidly. S.S. confirmed his willingness to house E.B.'s books in an empty room in his Wiltshire mansion, so perhaps in September I shall have some room in the flat again. E.B. is an angel, and since he has nowhere else to stay in London I should feel very bad if I didn't take him in. Nevertheless, as you say, his presence does make the index and other work difficult. On Wednesday we lunched with Tommy and Siegfried and they all went together to Lord's, where E.B. reported *no* spectators for MCC v. Cambridge University.

Adam has just learned that he is to spend his year teaching in a college at Raipur in the Central Provinces of India. In the atlas it looks a hellish long way from anywhere, but he is delighted, and at any rate there is no war going on near there yet. I shall give him *A Passage to India* to read on the way, though I agree it's over-rated. *Howards End* seems to me a much better book. Incidentally, E.M.F. wrote last week to say he'd like to give £1000 to the London Library! After all his previous benefactions, this is munificence indeed. He is indeed a good old man.

Nothing you say about London can possibly equal my own increasing distaste for its crowds and ugliness and noise. In the last ten years it has worsened incredibly.

On Tuesday I am to lunch with T.S.E. to talk about the London Library's Annual General Meeting the following week, and on Tuesday afternoon T.S.E. and I are supposed (separately) to record something for a twenty-minute radio programme on the Library *in German* for the Bosches. I said, truthfully, that I couldn't speak a word of the language; T.S.E. said he could read out a sentence or two, and then his pronunciation went haywire and sounded like bad French. So we are both to speak in English and be translated, like U.N.O. Goodness knows what to say!

Do have a look at the Agate anthology[1] and let me know what you think of it. A new batch of books should be coming in soon. My secretary leaves on Friday, and I have agreed to try a girl of nineteen, fresh from the training college. God give me patience.

Did I tell you that Ruth's daughter has taken a seaside house at a place called Forte dei Marmi, between Pisa and Spezia? R. and I are invited for a brief stay at the end of August. It would be heavenly to get some sun, but this infernal index will still be hanging over me, and

[1] *James Agate: an Anthology*, edited by Herbert Van Thal (1961).

we still don't know when Adam is leaving for India. Also I have no money, but R. says she will pay my fare.

I suppose I shan't see you till October? It seems a long way off—like Raipur. Are you visiting Roger this year? We long for a few more days of Kisdon, but I don't see how we can manage all that and Italy too. At the moment, my dear George, a private income and no responsibilities are my dream—or mirage. Perhaps it's partly the jaundice.

20 July 1961 *Grundisburgh*

A million exam-papers infest the house and, as you see, general degradation has set in—no proper paper, biro etc. I don't think I shall go on for many years more, though I admit the pin-money (about £350) is attractive, especially as stocks and shares seem to be in a downhill slither. But no good in worrying.

What *does* worry me is that you should be for any reason under the weather. Because for the life you lead 100% health is absolutely necessary. Jaundice is the devil in person; I once had weeks of it, through taking its onset lightly and *not going to bed at once*. (*Verb sap*) And I remained more or less gamboge for weeks after I had recovered. That pink-and-white complexion which you have noticed took a long time in returning. Some of the candidates clearly have at any rate mental jaundice—notably the one who writes that Macaulay's style is jerky and obscure, conspicuously weak in description and 'on the whole not worth reading.' He is at Winchester.

Adam's appointment sounds exciting. Get him to write full and detailed letters about everything and everybody—thus killing several birds with single stones, for as you know the way to learn to write is to write—there ain't any other. By the way I should have told you, A. Powell was lyrical about the goodness of your *Hugh Walpole* and wasn't old Priestley nice about it too. I enjoyed his articles in the *Sunday Times*, also Waugh on old Wodehouse. Whatever he said or didn't say in Germany in 1939 he has given intense pleasure to hordes of readers for many years. Though there *are* people who don't think him at all funny; you must know some.

I have read the Agate book with huge enjoyment. What an engaging old rascal he was. The extracts are well-chosen, though I am surprised at there being *nothing* from *Brief Chronicles*, which surely contains as good Shakespeare criticisms as there are. I mean of the plays as played. Fancy being able to write six notices of *Macbeth* all as fresh as paint. Different casts of course.

Byron is as inexhaustible as Wilde, both of them mostly second-rate as writers, but not as men. I must have told you that Housman put B. top of all for an evening's company—perhaps because both were what Swinburne in his letters calls Bulgarians. I got Vol. IV from the library—the only one in. I suppose all his 'illness' of 1878 was akin to D.T. Tell me all about this, also about the earlier volumes. He was very verbose and abusive about Zola's *L'Assommoir*. Was he right? Somehow he cuts a queer figure as a champion of propriety. What would he have said to *Lady C.* (our Lady of Pain!)? Tell me how you got on in German. I hope you were finely guttural. It *can* sound a fine sonorous language when spoken by those who manage to avoid the hawking and grunting and a too aggressive 'sch' (though *all* Winston's s's are practically indistinguishable from the German 'sch').

I have had another bout at my papers, and am ready to tell you that my interest in the character of Aumerle (*Richard II*) is every bit as small as Shakespeare's obviously was, and that I am tired of reading for the nth time half-baked dissertations on whether Malvolio was or was not 'notoriously abused'. All the beaks in England dictated what was to be said about Feste, except at Eton, where one candidate had the sense to say that the play could get along very well without him—whereas most of the rest invariably say that without Feste the play would be 'dreadfully boring'.

We shall not be going north this year—I think—though Pamela may well decide otherwise. I suspect I may never see Swaledale. My heart, lungs, liver and kidneys are apparently more or less flawless. None the less I am full of small mysterious aches and seizings-up for which there is nothing at all to be done: 'you must expect such things at seventy-eight.' It bears out old Dizzy whose reply to the young lady who hoped he was quite well. 'No one is ever quite well.'

My life just now is overshadowed by my health—as I imagine always happens to people who are not often ill. My pain persisted, so on Thursday I went in London to see a charming elderly doctor, who seemed to know his stuff. After extended tests and proddings he pronounced the major organs to be in excellent shape, and *no* jaundice present. The pain, he thought, came from the gall-bladder, and this mysterious nuisance is to be x-rayed at the Middlesex Hospital on Monday and Tuesday (two longish visits are apparently necessary). If they find huge stones in it they will presumably want to operate (I gather small ones can in some way be dissolved), and I hate operations for every reason: ordinary cowardice, pressure of work, Oscar's index etc. Yesterday I felt rotten, with a slight fever in the evening, and a constant pain, which is still with me: also complete lack of appetite. This evening, after a quiet day in garden and library, I feel a little better and more able to cope. Thank goodness dear E.B. is going to be away all next week. Ruth thinks that I have been suffering from this complaint, more or less, off and on, ever since my go of jaundice two years ago, and I daresay she's right. I have certainly felt pretty listless, depressed and lacking in energy for most of that time, and who knows but the removal of my gall-bladder might restore some of my pristine vigour. You shall be kept informed.

Forgive all this tiresomeness. I have dragged the index to p. 416, quite enjoying it in small doses, interspersed with manuscript-reading on the lawn. Once again the sunshine has been inadequate and intermittent. Two lovely bullfinches came and drank outside this window, to my great delight. There are pheasants everywhere, and the hillside opposite is purple with great expanses of rosebay willowherb. No children here and all quiet.

I saw none of the University Match, and doubt whether I shall get to Lord's to see the Australians on Monday or Tuesday—too many x-rays, and on Tuesday afternoon the AGM of the London Library, with T.S.E. presiding. I haven't yet tackled the Byron volume—it is huge and very heavy[1]—and instead am enjoying a gossipy book called

[1] *The Late Lord Byron* by Doris Langley Moore (1961).

The Pilgrim Daughters by Hesketh Pearson, all about the American heiresses who married English peers: very amusing. The first two volumes of the Swinburne letters are the best so far: the third and fourth seemed to me much duller. Watts may have had a calming effect on the poet: he certainly damped down his natural propensities and flattened his style.

My German broadcast was quite painless: it lasted for two and three-quarter minutes, during which I stopped at the end of each (impromptu) sentence, and a most intelligent German gave a rapid translation. I made him play the tape back to me and it didn't sound too bad. T.S.E. did his bit later in the day.

Sunday

I was woken this morning—not too early—by an infant house-martin which flew in my bedroom window and couldn't get out. The sun is more or less shining, and my pain is tolerable. I wish I need never see London or publishing again. But what then would you do for books? Soon the autumn rush will be on us, and I shall have some more to send you.

Adam is in his last week at Eton, much concerned over 'leaving presents'. Next week-end he flies to Norway to camp with the Corps, gets home on August 8, and leaves for India we don't know exactly when. Bridget reports that the weather on the south coast of Spain is mostly cloudy.

Someone is threatening to sue for libel if I publish a novel which is now in proof. I don't think they've got much of a case, but it will mean interviews with lawyers and much fuss. So far I have been very lucky in that respect: it's too expensive to insure against libel, so one simply has to be as careful as possible and trust to luck. My good secretary left on Friday, and the new nineteen-year-old begins to-morrow, God help me.

25 July 1961 *Grundisburgh*

This is a brief gap between ten thousand papers on Shakespeare, Macaulay and Scott, and a million on Chaucer. I am gravely disturbed to hear of your continuing malaise—and also much interested. You will be at this moment (Tuesday) full of bismuth and under examination. Well, I should like to tell you that the operation is nothing very terrific and ever since my second I have been, stomachically, as fit as a flea. The gall-bladder is one of those residual organs which we can perfectly well do without. Tell me all about it: all Lytteltons (male) have what others call a morbid interest in medical and surgical details. I used to enjoy a lot of shop with my London surgeon—the great Sir Holburt Waring. When he cut me he was plain Mr and I mischievously told him the provincial (Windsor) surgeon was a knight. When he heard the name Windsor he said coarsely 'Oh yes, those Windsor surgeons; he was probably knighted for cutting King Edward's corns', which, in fact, was not so very far from the truth; he had taken an appendix out of some royal child.

I have got the Swinburne Letters vols I and II. I quite enjoyed the 1880 or thereabouts volume, though it has its dull tracts. And through recent experience I cavil hotly at the editing. To one of *your* 'not identified' this man has ten; many points which you would have roamed half London to ascertain he leaves unexplained, while expressions used by S., such as 'Words, words words' and 'riotous living' are solemnly given their chapter and verse in Shakespeare or Bible. And how comes it that sometimes a figure referring to a note is one already in use on the same page? Old Swinburne's opinions have still a fine adolescent wildness, and I dislike all that reviling of old Carlyle over his reminiscences. He (C.) was distracted with grief and old age, and in any case clearly did not mean the reminiscences to be published. But all lovers of Charles Lamb have never forgiven C's quite accurate notes about the 'insuperable proclivity to *gin* in poor old Lamb,' and sometimes his punning must have been excruciating. And of course he would have deliberately been at his worst with a dour Scot. It is interesting to see that Watts-Dunton really did prolong S's life by about a quarter of a century. Was it you who told me some quite appalling things about W-D.'s sexual habits? Anyway no doubt you know them.

I finished marking *Old Mortality* yesterday. The difference between boys of sixteen and ditto girls is that you have to work hard to give the former 50/100 and equally hard or harder *not* to give the girls 90/100. The sheer *amount* the girls write—often four and a half pages where a good boy writes one and three-quarters. Scott's young ladies are china dolls; I suppose the conventions of his time insisted on that. As a coarse critic put it 'None of them exist below the neck, still less below the waist.'

I am enjoying Gissing and Wells of an evening. What a kindly picture H.G.W. makes in his letters. I suppose he knew that *qua* success and reputation G. couldn't hold a candle to him. I imagine he *always* resented Henry James, though below the surface before *Boon*.

Pamela has just returned from a family gathering to the memory of her great-aunts, the one who died youngest being ninety-seven and the largest under five feet. She might say that was exaggerated, but it doesn't exaggerate my impression of them. Aunt Emily's mouth at tea was well below the level of the table, food found its way to it entirely by gravity. But she was a delicious old lady—full of fun.

30 July 1961 *Woolavington Wing, Middlesex Hospital, Mortimer Street, W.1.*

Here I am incarcerated, and your letter at Bromsden—Duff will bring it up tonight or tomorrow. The X-rays of Monday and Tuesday (when I reported as an out-patient) showed the gall-bladder blameless, so my doctor suggested further tests in here. 'You probably won't get a bed for some time,' says he, but next morning they telephoned to say I was to report at 5 p.m. that same day. Unable to postpone a dinner with the Master of the Rolls (Evershed) and other Pilgrim Trustees, in a private room at the Travellers Club, I checked in here at 5, went to the dinner, and got back here at 10. On Friday morning I was subjected to tests so exhaustive, humiliating and exhausting that I have only just recovered. The worst of them—a barium enema—consists of their pouring a bucket of whitewash into one while the process is filmed and photographed. The nurses, who are all gay and pretty and twenty or twenty-one, tell me that this is far the worst, so I await tomorrow's tests with comparative equanimity.

I have a little room to myself—at £28. 7. 0 a week, of which I hope BUPA will pay most—quite comfortable but hellish noisy. Yesterday an electric drill outside operated for some six hours. I had the radio switched to the Test Match, but often drowsed off between the two noises. Today being a *non dies* and sunny, they told me I could dress and sit in an enclosed garden in the centre of the hospital block. I read the papers there, and have just come back to my room for roast chicken and a sweet made of bananas. Soho Square is only five minutes' walk, and the Matron (terrifying in dark green) has agreed to my walking gently there and back this afternoon, to change into some old clothes and fetch a few books. Ruth is staying with her sister in Somerset, so I shan't see her till tomorrow, but I have a telephone in my room, on which I have twice spoken to her. I brought Oscar and his index with me, but so far haven't felt up to tackling him. Also the indexing needs a big flat table-top. Goodness knows how long I shall be here, or what (if anything) they will find out. I still have the pain in the region of the liver.

To complete the tale of Friday's woe, I had *another* stye in my eye (I think the *sixth* this year, but have lost count). It has now entirely subsided, but must surely be a symptom of something. (A drunk has just roared down the street, singing lustily. One of the nurses tells me the neighbourhood is full of Greeks, who don't 'respect the hospital'.)

The office will have to look after itself, with Ruth's eye on it. My new nineteen-year-old secretary is a calamity and must go. She is partially deaf and blind and can't spell—oh dear!

I am toying with that new book on Byron, but find it hard to concentrate. Once one becomes a patient one loses all initiative and feels as helpless as a parcel, which may well be sent to the wrong place.

The AGM of the London Library went off well, with T.S.E. in vigorous form. The *Times* report was almost solely concerned with a minor recommendation which the members rejected—rather to my relief. I think all such meetings should be enlivened by some motion on which everyone can speak—and then if possible defeat the executive. On Tuesday all the members went away blissful.

I suppose you'd better write here this week. If I'm happily released sooner than I expect, I'll let you know at once. The whole thing is a great bore, but I suppose necessary. Think of poor Oscar! I wish I was in your summer-house, helping with the exam-papers.

1 August 1961 *Grundisburgh*

How utterly and entirely damnable! I have been thinking of you all day with a sort of enraged sympathy in your world of bismuth and barium. Please let me hear what they say after all these tests. Pamela says there is a score of causes for pain in the liver. They won't be long surely in finding out what it is. Something to do with the blood causes styes I believe. All things are linked. And of course this would be the moment when you are minus a secretary. Very odd; there are millions. Rose once, among her contemporaries when asked what she was going to be, struck an altogether alien note when she merely said 'Not a secretary'—which *all* of them were about to be. You must have someone with all five senses alert and easy on eye and ear.

This is an interim letter really but I had to write.

What a stuffy little review of old Agate in the *T.L.S.* last week, by a man without bowels. *Per contra* a *first-rate* one in *John O' London* by Moray McLaren. *All* the right pros and cons bonded with exactly the right blend of charity and justice. I shall write and tell him so. Of course you know him. How rare a perfect review is!

My papers are nearly finished and I have no more getting up at 6.15 (which in fact I rather enjoy). The last batch of papers had answers on Bailey's *Shorter Boswell.* One candidate said it was a very dull book, another that Boswell was a very solemn man and very like Johnson; he got few marks. Another of the books was *Ten Modern Poets*—highly praised by most, but from the standpoint that all poetry before 1930 was long-winded, pompous, unintelligible(!) and generally negligible. They know these modern poems very well, but their knowledge is greater than their judgment.

Hurry and get well, my beloved Rupert, I cannot bear your being ill.

5 August 1961 *Bromsden Farm*

I hope you got Ruth's message to say I had been liberated. I got out after exactly a week, to my great relief, although I enjoyed the resting part of it, and the nurses were like gay and pretty butterflies. They (the doctors) have diagnosed my trouble as a diverticulum in the duodenum! There are other diverticula elsewhere, but the one in the duodenum is causing the pain, they say. Apparently it's not an ulcer but a little sac that fills up with 'roughage', and they believe that medicine and a strict diet will put it right. No raw fruit or salad, bread, pastry etc, nothing fried. I started it only yesterday (the whole week having been devoted to diagnosis), so feel little benefit yet—am, in fact, just as I was a fortnight ago, with a pain in the region of the gall-bladder, and *no* energy at all. Nevertheless I have resumed my labours on the index in a gentle way, but it can't possibly be finished before our trip to Italy on August 21 or so. Will this infernal task ever be accomplished? My love-hate for it is overpowering.

I was delighted to get your letter in hospital (if you wrote twice the second one hasn't reached me yet) and Ruth's daily visits were lovely rays of light. All hospitals, however comfortable and considerate, are rather like prisons, and ordinary outside life seems very remote and desirable. Although I had a pile of books beside me I read little, preferring to drowse or listen to the Test Match. That last day was pretty exciting, wasn't it?

The trouble with the Byron book is that it is so big and heavy—not suitable for reading in bed, needing almost a lectern to support it. I did read a couple of thrillers, corrected the proofs of the new Druon, and toyed with some Oscariana. The good Moray McLaren also reviewed Agate excellently in the *Scotsman*, where he is all agog for Oscar. Other reviews already arranged are Sparrow in *T.L.S.*, Richard Ellmann in *Guardian*, William Plomer in *Listener*, Terence de Vere White in *Irish Times*, probably J.I.M. Stewart (Michael Innes) in *Sunday Telegraph*, and I hope Mortimer and Nicolson in *Sunday Times* and *Observer*.

One good result of all my tests is that heart, lungs, liver, blood, gall-bladder and intestines generally are pronounced A.1. except for these infernal diverticula. All very encouraging.

A postcard from Adam in camp in Norway says he is having fun but the going is hard. He is due back on Tuesday (8th) and sails for Bombay on the 17th. He goes in a cargo-boat with seven other boys bound for various jobs, and I imagine they will stop everywhere, which will be fun for him. From Bombay he is to be flown across the steaming continent to his destination in the Central Provinces.

Peter looked in today, preparing to drive to Scotland for the Twelfth. Duff is playing cricket in Wales, and Bridget is there too, so here all is quiet. If only the sun would shine! I feel completely sun-starved, and sea-starved too. Ruth is spending the week-end with an old friend in Sussex. One benefit of this diet will be that it pretty well prohibits eating out and provides a capital excuse for refusing invitations. I imagine you will soon be submerged under grandchildren, to Pamela's delight.

This afternoon, after lunch, I went right to bed and slept for two solid hours; which will show you how relaxed and listless I have become. The idea of work is disagreeable, and the grasshopper a burden fit for Atlas. No doubt the diet and some Italian sun will recharge my batteries, but I can't foresee any second Kisdon trip this year, which saddens us both. E.B., charming as ever, is still in the flat, but is to leave on August 20, when my old friend Elizabeth Drew flies in from America. She is almost your age, and a martyr to all sorts of rheumatics. When she leaves (I hope at the end of September) the flat is to be rearranged, so that no sleeping visitor is possible. A night or two one can bear, but weeks and months are quite intolerable. Did I tell you that my Lawrence portrait is to be included in the Lawrence exhibition at Burlington House in the autumn? They tell me it's worth at least £3000, perhaps more! I may have to sell it one day. Now a little more index and then more bed.

9 August 1961 *Grundisburgh*

I was immensely relieved to hear that all was fundamentally well with the Rupertian interior. And how very kind it was of Ruth to telephone. She got Pamela, and you will be no more surprised than I was to hear that merely to hear her speech over the air put Pamela at once and emphatically among the numerous pro-Ruths. Please thank her most particularly. I know just as little about diverticula as Mr Micawber did about gowans. The diet etc will put you right, but I hope it won't be too severe or prolonged. I don't want to see you at the Lit. Soc. waving crossly away all the offered dishes *à la* Cuthbert. I wonder why the 'roughage' should have behaved like that.

'Sir, you may wonder.' I let you off a second letter last week; not only was the cistern fairly dry, but exam-papers were again silting up. Pleasant little oases were provided by some re-browsing over Wilfrid Blunt's diaries. These are full of good stuff (no doubt you know his admirable page about Wilde's death, as told him by Ross). He was a wilful, and I suspect thoroughly tiresome, old man in many ways. His judgments were always emphatic, sometimes excellent (e.g. on Winston) and sometimes magnificently fatuous. *Your* blood will boil at hearing that he put Yeats *far* below Gilbert Murray as a poet. He also said that it was impossible there should ever have been a worse play than *The Tempest* and that Milton was a 'pompous windbag'.

I must tell you that Pamela a week or two ago stayed at a house where there was a copy of *David* by your uncle. She was greatly attracted, but had no time to finish it. She refused to cadge for a possible copy, but you have deliberately encouraged me countless times to do so. But I expect it is long out of print. I don't remember reading it.

Your groans over O.W. are similar to Carlyle's over Frederick, but you have about another six or seven years to go. I can't think how it didn't kill him (and hasn't yet you!).

I expect the hospital rest did you good, but aren't the days long—partly because of their insanely early start to each one. One thinks it is nearly lunch-time and it is 10.45. How doctors do hate anything *fried*! It is always the first thing they cut off whatever one's complaint. I don't know what is so poisonous about it; why for instance should it raise one's blood-pressure?

There are only half-a-dozen grandchildren here at the moment but more in the offing. P's sister-in-law (a millionairess) has given us a lovely portable hut, or rather two huts, now being erected in the garden (without a permit which they tell me is probably essential, but I am a strong believer in the effect of a *fait accompli*).

12 August 1961 *Bromsden Farm*

I'm glad to be able to report that I feel very much better than I did a week ago. For the first time in *many* weeks I begin to feel once again faintly on top of at least a few things, instead of that crushed and hopeless inertia which had for so long oppressed me, and which I now learn is a leading symptom of diverticulitis. The diet is more than tolerable, and my doctor has now agreed to alcohol in moderation—not that at the moment I feel like it, but our trip to Italy is approaching, and the local wines must surely be sampled.

Adam flew safely home from Norway just twenty-four hours before all those children crashed there, and now this infernal organisation that is sending him to India says that the cargo-boat is off (though the shipping line had just assured me to the contrary), and he will probably have to fly. Comfort is putting a good face on it, but there will be a nasty couple of days if he does.

A copy of *David* shall go to Pamela on Monday. You should by now have received Fleming[1], *The Franco-Prussian War*[2], the Whiston book[3] and *Poor Kit Smart*.[4] If any of these has failed to arrive, please send an immediate postcard to Soho Square. My lack of a secretary is an infernal nuisance: that deaf-and-blind girl lasted only a fortnight, and there's no point in trying to get a new one till we're back from Italy.

The Middlesex Hospital didn't wake one till 7.15 a.m.—very civilised. Altogether my week cost £63, part of which I am trying to recover from BUPA. Do you know it.?

I have indeed urged Adam to keep a diary, and he seems to take to the idea. I bought him the three volumes of Somerset Maugham's collected short stories to read on the boat, and *The Legacy of India*, a good Oxford symposium, to teach him something about that humid sub-continent. He is to teach English and elementary Maths and Science up to O. level, or so he gathers. In some ways he is still so childish that I rather quail at the distance etc., but I expect he'll be all right. Now for bed.

[1] *Goodbye to the Bombay Bowler* (1961).

[2] By Michael Howard (1961).

[3] *The Whiston Matter* by Ralph Arnold (1961). An account of the running battle between the Rev. Robert Whiston, Headmaster of the Rochester Cathedral Grammar School and the Dean and Chapter of the Cathedral (1848–1852), which gave Trollope ideas for *The Warden* (1855).

[4] By Christopher Devlin (1961).

Sunday morning, 13 August.

A long but disturbed night, with bad dreams and some pain. My breakfast now is not your manly oatmeal porridge, but a sieved pap of groats designed for babies. As I mumbled this down I re-read Pater's *Renaissance.* Oscar says it influenced his whole life, so I thought I had better have another look at it, in case I had missed some references. So far this is not so, but the gentle tones and modulations of the old aesthete fit well into my frail mood of convalescence.

Soon I shall have to switch over to the proofs of a strident American novel that has been offered to me. The house is swarming: all three children, plus Duff's wife and Comfort's step-mother. Last night they slept all over the place on camp-beds and mattresses, and Comfort cooks and cooks. It is the last reunion before Adam's departure—and perhaps Bridget's too. The sky is a uniform grey and there is a slight drizzle. Owing to a dearth of grass for the cows to eat, Peter's minions have strewn in the adjacent field great swathes of dun-coloured silage, whose sickly stench takes most of the pleasure out of gardening. Adam has a heavy cold and sea-lion's cough—aftermath of eight open-air nights in Norway. I enclose Oliver Van Oss's admirable report on him, which please return. It is very shrewd and perceptive. Has a fold of the mantle of G.W.L. perhaps fallen on O.V.O.?

Write here this week, and next Saturday I will send you our Italian address. I think we set off on Monday, 21st, by boat and train to Pisa, and thence by bus. Neither of us speaks any Italian, but I have a fairly up-to-date phrase-book. Luckily Ruth's daughter knows the language well. I can't wait for the hot sun and the swimming. Much love to Pamela. She and Ruth must meet.

16 August 1961 *Grundisburgh*

I have pretty well finished my G.C.E. papers now, the last batch being an incredibly feeble lot from a school in Lebanon who regarded Macaulay's English as about on a par with Henry James's last style ('The Old Pretender').[1] Several of them said that Charles II's army

[1] Philip Guedalla (1889–1944) wrote: 'The work of Henry James has always seemed divisible by a simple dynastic arrangement into three reigns: James I, James II, and The Old Pretender'.

was lacking in 'cavalcades'. I wrote a report which will probably result in Lebanon leaving the Commonwealth—which I never knew they were in. Do you ever have a mild black-out, *viz* a spell when the page or manuscript you are looking at conveys no meaning at all? I do after the numbing effect of several hundred scripts. The first one was a little alarming, but I have learnt that the bout goes off in about five minutes and I cease vaguely wondering who on earth Brutus was. I think I shall drop this examining after next year; I dislike it a little more every year of late, though a little pin-money is certainly pleasant.

Thank you for letting me see Oliver Van Oss on Adam, which I return. An *excellent* letter—as such do, throwing much light on both writer and subject. I saw lots of O.V.O. at Eton and (I hope) I to some extent explained Eton to him. Reports are one of Eton's specialities and he may have picked up something in our talks, but I claim no more than that. He is a first-rate teacher and tutor. Is he right about A's humour? I remember no puns at Xmas. Nor somehow can I see his father being very patient with puns.

Pamela is thrilled about *David*, pink with pleasure. I have received all those admirable books you sent except Peter's, which should be good fun. I had great fun all yesterday with the Whiston-Rochester imbroglio. Fascinating. As good in its scale as Bentley and the Trinity Fellows.[1] And I am particularly glad to have *The Franco-Prussian War*, which I have never really read about. I am always fascinated by Bismarck and Moltke ('*der grosse Schweiger*'). I have brought it to Oxford to fill spare hours, and my address this next week-end will be *St Edmund Hall*, where the only defect is the immense distance between one's bedroom and the lavatories. Some younger awarders than I are notably inferior to me in the matter of bladder, though I confess I am not as good as I was (I hope never to descend to the level of dear Harold Nicolson).

I am much interested by your giving Adam old Maugham to read—because I recently recommended him to a parent who was in despair about his son's English writing. For lucidity only old Shaw rivals him.

[1] The great classical scholar Richard Bentley (1662–1742) was from 1700 Master of Trinity College, Cambridge. For thirty-eight years the Fellows of the college vainly attempted to unseat him on the grounds that he had infringed some of the statutes.

If A. is interested in music give him Shaw's Corno di Bassetto volume.[1] Humphrey battens on it. Please give him my warmest good wishes (not that he will not feel quite happy without them).

Do you know Pisa? If you don't and the sun is shining you *must* go to the Campo Santo, mainly ignoring the leaning tower which is a mere freak, though a lovely tower if *not* leaning. I nearly fell off it in 1902.

20 August 1961 *Bromsden Farm*

After an exhausting week, during which my duodenum played up tiresomely, and I twice retired to bed at 5 p.m., I am now poised for Italian sun. Tomorrow (Monday) morning Ruth and I leave Victoria at 11 a.m., lunch heavily (to hell with the diet!) on the Paris train, chug round to the Gare de Lyon, change into the Rome Express, dine heavily therein, sleep in our sleepers and alight at Pisa at 11 a.m. on Tuesday. I fear the only sight-seeing we are likely to do there depends on what lies between the railway station and the bus-stop, to which we shall be carrying our luggage. Our address till 5 September will be: c/o Mrs Goodman, Via Agnelli 16, Forte Dei Marmi, (Lucca), Italy. They say the posts are terrible, and it is a help to put EXPRESS on letters, which I suppose means going to a post-office and paying more. Anyhow I'll send you my regular budget and hope for the best. I am taking *no* Oscar or other work (I can't remember when this last happened), but simply a few paperback detective stories and the World's Classics edition of *Middlemarch*. Each day I see in the papers that the temperature at both Florence and Rome is well into the eighties, so have high hopes of sun. Ruth is as excited as a schoolgirl, and as she is paying for *everything*, I tell her that at last I shall experience the full pleasures of being a 'kept man', which has always seemed to me a consummation devoutly to be wished.

Meanwhile the index, which is spread around me as I write, has reached p. 563, with another 300 to go. Darling old Katie Lewis

[1] *London Music in 1888–89 as heard by Corno di Bassetto (later known as Bernard Shaw)*, 1937.

(daughter of the first Sir George[1]) died last week, aged eighty-three, and left me, bless her, an exquisite drawing of Mrs William Morris by Rossetti—the gem of all her houseful of treasures. It hasn't arrived yet, and must wait for Probate.

E.B. evacuated the flat yesterday, after two and a half months, and apparently his daughter says she will relieve me of his 7000 books (Siegfried first said he would take them, and then thought better of it). My old friend from America, Elizabeth Drew, arrives on Wednesday for the best part of a month, but we shall miss the first fortnight of her. When she has gone I shall *never* have another visitor for more than a night or two: it's too wearing altogether.

Your exam-paper blackouts sound terrifying, and I'm glad to say that not even indexing has yet given me any such.

O.V.O. is not far wrong about Adam's humour, which remains punnish and rather third-form. He is still hanging about, quite happily I think, waiting for his marching orders.

As a bed-book I have been reading Pater's *Imaginary Portraits*, and find them just the thing—exquisitely written sketches of nothing much—four beautiful walls of tapestry with nothing in the middle.

20 August 1961 *St Edmund Hall*
Oxford

God knows when this will get to you. You say *your* posts are uncertain, and at this end an Oxford man tells me you may post a letter here for London and it takes a day and a half. Curious how *incompetent* everything is at Oxford. In the exam-room the door sticks, the carpet rucks up, the collapsed bulb took some time to replace because there were no steps long enough to reach it. In this college we are fed like fighting cocks, but there are no bath-mats or corks. I have to be very careful not to slip up on a wet stone floor. The traffic of course is beyond a joke. There are lots of genial men about; several (of course)

[1] George Henry Lewis (1833–1911). Leading solicitor. Knighted 1893, created Baronet 1902.

know you, but I gather not well. R.W. David and charming wife, Colin Eccleshare, both of the C.U. Press, and others.

I am annoyed about your duodenum. Oughtn't it to be quieting down? or is more time wanted? You don't seem to be at all fussed about it. You are at this moment browning in the sun while here the cloud persists, though it is (at Oxford) mainly dry.

I shall be surprised and disappointed if you don't like *Middlemarch* with all its (and G.E.'s) defects. V. Woolf rightly described it as one of the few really grown-up English novels. You won't like either Mr Casaubon or Ladislaw, but you will admire the way poor Lydgate's decline is pictured. I am not sure the Garths, if I have got the name right, aren't a bit boring.

Just coming to an end here, the only job remaining being to peruse all the Eng. Lit. examiners' reports and correct their English. It usually takes about two and a half hours. They mostly avoid the split infinitive but are quite prone to the hanging participle and most write 'due to' when they mean 'owing to' or 'because of'. Ignorance to-day is frightening. Hardly any candidates know who the Muses were, their answers ranging from dons, grub street authors, horses, musicians, and 'important people' to (coyly) 'people like Nell Gwyn who lived in the slums'.

27 August 1961 *Via Agnelli 16*
Forte dei Marmi

Our journey went well, despite a rough Channel, and we ate two stupendous train-meals. In the end we never got to Pisa, since we found that the train stopped at Viareggio only ten miles from here, where we got a taxi.

So far the weather has been superb—a succession of cloudless blazing days in the eighties, with three or four bathes a day, and the rest of the time spent sunning, sleeping (including after-lunch siesta), eating and reading—all done very slowly and with great enjoyment. This is a nice little bungalow with modern plumbing, and I am writing in a garden behind, which is entirely covered by vines and bunches of grapes, rather like Max's 'vining-room' at Rapallo. The sea is an easy ten minutes' walk. There are wide sands, all very clean and well organised. Under pretence of offending the Catholic Church, no one is allowed to undress in public, and this enables countless little bathing-huts to be let for the season, together with deck-chairs and large gay beach-umbrellas. No English, thank God, and the chatter of the numerous Italians is as unintelligible and harmless as birdsong or an opera libretto—'*Ce qui est trop bête pour être joué, on le chante.*'

Close behind the little town, or so it looks when one is swimming, tower the wonderfully dramatic peaks of the Carrara mountains: black and pure white, and the lower slopes pine-tree-green with tiny white villages dotted about. Florence is only an hour away, but I fear we shall stick to the sea. We are both brown and well and, as I say, relaxed to the point of inertia.

So far I have read one thriller, two American novels, and have nearly finished my American friend Francis Steegmuller's splendid book *Flaubert and Madame Bovary*: if you don't know it, do try it from the library. *Middlemarch* comes next.

Occasionally we see threatening headlines about Berlin in Italian papers, and roll over in the sun until it's time for the next swim. The ice-cream is superb, but perhaps this leaves you cold (sorry for the third-form joke)? I don't know whether Adam has yet left for India—in fact all I do know is that I feel wonderfully well—for the first time in ages—and this life suits me fine for a week or two, provided my darling Ruth is with me. Disdaining her normal postscript, she has sent you a p.c. on her own. I'll hope to write more sensibly next week.

Tomorrow is my fifty-fourth birthday, and my duodenum is behaving well.

31 August 1961 *Grundisburgh*

Your life sounds just right—*four* bathes a day, and huge meals, and seascapes, and a novel or two, and a background of Italian language, and a foreground of Ruth—well if that isn't idyllic!

I have just finished your massive book on the Franco-Prussian war. Very interesting. I admit I skipped airily through some of the battles, of which I can never follow the accounts. Now for your most welcome

P. Fleming, good bedside reading if ever there was. I have to write a tabloid biography of Ben Jonson for Dick Routh. The awful truth is that I have *never* been able to bear B.J., agreeing with Tennyson that reading him is like wading through glue. No doubt I shall find that *Volpone* is your favourite play, as it was A.W. Ward's and Saintsbury's. P. Fleming gets good reviews, which is pleasing. I thought the light 'middle' was out of fashion to-day. Coming back perhaps. Also Bernard Fergusson gets a good press for his sketch of Wavell. But why does his publisher price the book (96 pages) at 12/6? Surely 7/6 would have been right? But what do I know? Old Winston makes a slightly vindictive appearance. And he *ought* to have attended W's funeral—the only general who gave us a sniff of success for two years.

There has been some sad stuff in the recent critiques of war-books. What a pity Paul Johnson, Crossman, Alan Brien, etc were not in command. They clearly know exactly what should have been done.

Is it the Carrara mountains where the marble comes from? Your descriptions are full of sunlight and colour. *Middlemarch* may be a bit Midland English for your surroundings.

3 September 1961 *Via Agnelli 16*
Forte dei Marmi

Every day here has been lovelier than the last, it seems. Unbroken sunshine, so that instead of dashing out to catch the day's five-minutes-worth, as all this summer at home, here one arranges to avoid the three hottest hours by means of lunch and a siesta. At mid-day the soft sand of the beach is almost too hot to walk on barefoot. We spend some six hours a day on the sand or in the water—this morning I had three long swims of perhaps half an hour each—and except for the area of our bathing-kit we are a most satisfactory brown all over.

I imagine that fifty years ago this was a strip of pine-trees and sand, between the mountains and the sea, with perhaps a little village in it. Now it has been 'developed' as a summer resort, but most attractively—not at all like Peacehaven or Lytham St Anne's. In the centre of the little town—a road's width from the beach—is a large circle of shady pines, under which are a children's railway and numerous carts drawn by donkeys and small ponies. All round the wood there is held every Wednesday a most attractive market, where we have bought this and that. My birthday turns out to be the day of the local saint (St Ermete), in whose honour an extra day-long market was held, followed after dark by superb fireworks on the beach. The Provost and Fellows could get some good ideas for improving the Fourth. The English papers get here at 6 p.m. the same day, so I have kept up with the cricket and drunk to Hampshire's triumph. I am just over half way through the magnificent *Middlemarch* which I am enjoying inordinately. More of this next week, when I shall have finished. Mr Casaubon is certainly a warning ('Oh, he dreams footnotes, and they run away with all his brains'), but a fortnight here has so recharged my batteries that I positively look forward to polishing off Oscar. The book is much *wittier* than I had expected, and within its limits it is masterly—no fumbling or uncertainty in the treatment.

We are due to reach London on Wednesday evening. Write to Bromsden this week. I write in the vine-arbour at 3.45 p.m., but the beach is calling, and I do so enjoy every moment of it. When one swims out a little way the sweep of the mountains is wonderfully beautiful. I haven't left much room for Ruth.

There is little more to say in my so small space except to endorse that a 'new man' is emerging, just as good as the old. *Immense* benefit has been had by both and I am convinced it should be an annual affair. The certainty of sunshine is such a delight for a prescribed time. Not for ever.

Ruth.

10 September 1961 *Grundisburgh*

And now you are facing a mountain of toil and feeling like Sisyphus —*but* feeling in finer fettle than he ever did. Your restored vigour is *very* good to hear of. I was sure you would enjoy *Middlemarch*—to my mind her best, though what that old ass Ruskin called the 'disgusting' *Mill on the Floss* is not far behind. The Rector of Hagley (a particularly good man who hunted twice or thrice a week) wouldn't allow *Adam Bede* in his house. *Tempora mutantur.*

I am setting G.C.E. papers for next year—a curiously sweaty job, especially as one has to provide a crib, and it is hard to find twelve or fourteen consecutive lines of Shakespeare for paraphrase, because there is always a line or phrase in it about the meaning of which I feel quite hazy. I usually put something quite vague which I know Brigadier Thomas R. Henn of Cats will emend, though his version often seems as dubious as mine. Shakespeare is a very difficult author. In the *Macbeth* paper I nearly gave them that magnificent paragraph of Masefield's on how M. should be acted,[1] but Tom Henn would have it out (he is head reviser). If you have in your mind a good question about Conrad's *Nigger* and three other tales, please let me have it. A large general question about the man Josef Korzeniowski.[2] They tell me he is out of fashion now; he would be. But I like the story of a visitor to C. being kept for a bit in the garden, C. still being in the throes; suddenly a window was flung open and a pale, sweating, haggard face looked out and gasped 'I've killed her.' He had just described the death—tremendously moving—of the young woman in *Victory*.

I must go in to tea. The garden reverberates with child-song.

I enclose half-a-sheet for Ruth—very poor measure I know. I am like the saint who had endless things to say to and about the Almighty, but eventually said only 'Lord, Lord!'

10 September 1961 *Bromsden Farm*

The weather held up wonderfully until the very morning of our departure, when, as though in anger at our going, thunder crashed out over the mountains, and rain fell in torrents. First we took a local train to Pisa, where we spent three hours admiring the Leaning Tower and other antiquities. The Campo Santo was badly bombed, but has been excellently restored. The rain had stopped by this time, but the air was hot and clammy. As we entered the very stuffy Baptistery, Ruth said 'I shall get a migraine if we stay here long,' so we withdrew immediately. I don't suppose the Tower has changed much since you

[1] See vol. 4 of these letters, p. 15.

[2] Conrad's real name.

nearly fell off it in 1902—very beautiful and impressive we thought—but we did not climb up it, for fear of repeating your near-catastrophe. The bridge over the Arno, also destroyed in 1944, has been very elegantly rebuilt. We just had time for a drink outside a café before catching another local train to Florence, and as we crossed the great Plain of Tuscany, the sun, of which we had seen no glimpse all day, suddenly appeared in time to set in a blaze over the cypresses and vineyards and little stunted trees.

We reached Florence in darkness, so saw nothing but the huge, clean, modern station, where we transhipped to our sleepers in the express. An excellent dinner, quite a good night, and we reached the Gare de Lyon at 9.30 a.m. Paris too was sunless but warm. We had two little walks and some refreshment before boarding the Calais train at mid-day. A smashing lunch, a roughish crossing, and London on Wednesday evening. Both of us much sunburned, sad to be separated from each other and the sunshine. The good lady who is staying in the flat—Elizabeth Drew—will go back to America before the end of the month. E.B. is back in Hong Kong, and his married daughter has nobly said she will take the books, so directly Elizabeth leaves, I shall at last be liberated from them. All here is well. Adam flew to India last week, and we have had one good letter from Delhi, where Paul Gore-Booth (once K.S. and now High Commissioner in India) very kindly had him looked after. Adam reports the temperature as a steady 95° and very humid, and I don't envy him the 48-hour train-journey to his school at Raipur, whence he telegraphed safe arrival. Comfort misses him a lot, but is bearing up well.

Middlemarch was exactly right for that sun-drenched peaceful holiday, with only Italian voices in the offing. I finished it in the train to Florence, quite sorry to part from some of the characters. For the rest of the return journey I read *Weir of Hermiston* with sad pleasure: I think it might well have been R.L.S.'s masterpiece. This passage from it might be about Kisdon:

> All beyond and about is the great field of the hills; the plover, the curlew, and the lark cry there; the wind blows as it blows in a ship's rigging, hard and cold and pure; and the hill-tops huddle one behind another like a herd of cattle into the sunset.

The day after we got back my lovely Rossetti drawing arrived. I'm going to have the mount altered (white instead of gold) and then it will be ready for your admiration some Lit. Soc. evening. It's a massively beautiful head of Mrs William Morris, with whom D.G.R. was clearly much in love, and is to me the quintessence of Pre-Raphaelitism. I don't quite know where to hang it, but it can have pride of place in my office for three months, while my Lawrence is at Burlington House.

Duff has brilliantly contrived to make the *Sunday Telegraph* pay £1500 for the serial rights (one article) of the Oscar letters. Of this £675 will come to me, and not a moment too soon, for I haven't a penny anywhere. Adam's year in India gives me a breathing-space to collect enough for his three years at Oxford. Meanwhile the index has only reached p. 567 and must somehow be finished, though there are mountains of urgent manuscripts awaiting my attention.

Birley, with whom I am now on Christian-name terms, was delighted with *The Whiston Matter* and is giving a copy to the chairman (or whatever) of the Headmasters' Conference. I'll send you some more books next week.

14 September 1961 *Grundisburgh*

Your trip really does sound a success. There is something fitting about weeping skies at one's departure from a lovely holiday. But I fear you may not have been long enough in the Pisa Baptistery to hear its really gorgeous echo. The curator sings four or six notes and a celestial chord wanders to and fro about the roof for at least half a minute. The climate of Pisa can be awful but that 'hallowed acre' where the Tower etc are is a blissful memory. A few hours at Florence are not much good; you need a few days, because the views from round about are inimitable, 'at evening, from the top of Fesole'[1] for instance.

Adam sounds well *rangé*; it will surely be a very good experience for him. I am delighted that *Middlemarch* came up to expectation and

[1] Milton, *Paradise Lost*, book I, line 289.

hope. There are moments—I say this with bated breath—when *to me* she makes Miss Austen a little thin, but to Roger and all those platoons of women that would sound sheer blasphemy. I horrified a young woman who was here last week by saying that I thought *Mansfield Park* much better than *Emma*. And I am *quite sure* that *Northanger Abbey* is on the whole bad. *Nothing* can surely be said for General Tilney's behaviour—true neither to nature nor art. *Weir of Hermiston* I remember thinking a magnificent start. What an outstanding horror Weir's original, Lord Braxfield, must have been—like a formidable blacksmith in appearance, as Cockburn says. Illiterate, contemptuous, coarse, and often condemning a man to death with a savage joke. Didn't he send to the gallows a man with whom he played chess, with some pleasantry about its being 'mate this time'—the Jeffreys of Scotland? But Scotch judges have always been *sui generis*.

Do you admire that tiresome old ass Bertrand Russell going cheerfully to jail for his principles at eighty-nine? Because I do! And how can anyone be happy about our present bomb-policy?

16 September 1961 *Bromsden Farm*

With the arrival of two letters from you this week the rhythm is resumed. All week I have been doubled up with lumbago or some kindred complaint, and still am. At least it has served to remove, or sufficiently obscure, all symptoms in the duodenum. If it isn't one thing it's another. My guest in the flat is flying back to America next Thursday, and even the *thought* of having the flat to myself—or rather ourselves—is an immense relief. Someone has been there since the beginning of June! Last week the hot water failed, and the gas people took *four days* to put it right. Also my daily woman is on a week's holiday, so siege conditions have prevailed.

Adam writes happily from India, where he apparently lives on curry and spends every evening playing bridge in Hindi with the beaks. His train-journey from Delhi took three and a half days owing to a landslide, but he failed to describe it in detail, so my letter to him this week is largely composed of searching questions.

I don't spend much time worrying about the Bomb, having plenty of other things to occupy me. As you will long ago have recognised, I have gone stale on the Oscar job, and must somehow regain enough initiative to polish it off. At the same time I feel compelled to strive for perfection. The index is stuck at p. 600, but I have just told the printers that they will have the whole thing back finished by November 30—which should mean publication in May. At bedtime I am slowly reading through Pater's works, finding a few good things buried in layers of pretentious candy-floss, if you can imagine such a thing.

The papers announce parking-meters in Soho by November, and they should greatly lessen the noise and nuisance which now make the whole place hideous. (As I write, the Proms are coming to an end, and Flash Harry is doing his stuff.) I suppose one day I shall feel wholly well and energetic again, and it will be a nice change. One grows weary of all the extra effort caused by feeling perpetually under par. Needless to say, Ruth is forever a light and a blessing: I really don't think I could keep all this up without her. This week-end she has gone to stay with her son in Suffolk, where there is no telephone, so I can't speak to her till Sunday evening when she gets home. We have quite decided to save up for another fortnight of sun next summer, even though it means only one visit to Kisdon the blessed.

Goodnight, dear George, give best love to Pamela, please.

21 September 1961 *Grundisburgh*

Lumbago is the devil in person. I used to have a good deal of it, and my sympathy with you is accordingly profound. Old Amsler[1], who was delightfully frank and clearsighted about British medicine, used to say that *all* we know about lumbago is that it comes for no reason and goes for none either, but luckily it always *does* go. Massage they tell me is off nowadays, but heat and electricity are emphatically *on*. I do wish you could have a clear and long run in the matter of health. With health all can be faced, without it, nothing. And your normal programme demands flawless health. Is your leech a good man? Mine

[1] Eton doctor.

is the nicest man imaginable, and knows nothing at all of my recent ailments; his locum cured one on which *he* had thrown no light, a tip from the local policeman another, and Lady Cranworth a third. Anyway your flat to yourself, and not cluttered up with someone else's books, should make a difference—though stairs don't go well with lumbago. I hope for a brighter bulletin next week.

My youngest daughter with family is just off to Kenya—perhaps for three years, maybe for one, or, if Kenyatta has his way, less than that. I of course am obsessed with the morbid notion that I may have passed on before I see her again. I always hate the holidays here coming to an end; I like seeing the place swarming with children. The £50 or £60 extra catering etc is merely equivalent to the trip abroad which e.g. Roger and Sibell take every year.

Old Bertrand Russell of course suffers from that last indignity of the old; worse than bladder, heart, knees, or ears, i.e. his judgment is gone. Fancy not seeing that these sit-downs and marches merely encourage the Russians. But really our governors! The captain of a boys' house in a weak year would have spotted that the way to treat a crowd in Parliament or Trafalgar Square was to do *nothing*. Let 'em sit. If they get in the way of traffic, give abundant warning and then clear a way with a hosepipe. How long would a crowd's spirit last with such treatment? As it is, who minds a one-pound fine? But who would *not* mind looking an ass after a two or three hours' sit, and/or a suit of clothes drenched? But, as I have complained before, they never consult me.

Hammarskjöld[1] surely was murdered, though so far the press has said nothing. That explosion before the crash sounds very fishy. What a hopeless world we live in.

I have been re-reading old H.W. Nevinson's *Changes and Chances* lately—a man I have always greatly admired. I liked 'Most of us deplored and indignantly condemned the atrocious fate of Oscar Wilde, for whom many, like myself, would gladly have offered bail, if, like Stewart Headlam, we could have raised the £1000 demanded.' He became a passionate woman's suffrage supporter later and left the

[1] Dag Hammarskjöld (born 1905), Swedish Secretary-General of the United Nations from 1953, died in a mysterious air-crash in Africa on 17 September 1961.

Daily News. He wrote lyrically about Christabel Pankhurst who, I read recently, some genial chap said, was a lesbian. Did you know about this? Untrue, I expect, like most things.

Candy-floss is good for Pater. I never could really do with him 'faint, pale, embarrassing, exquisite Pater' (Henry James) though H.J. did end his paragraph with 'he is not of the little day but of the longer time.' Have you noticed that Pater's favourite adjectives were 'wistful', 'dainty', 'weary', 'strange', 'fantastic', 'exquisite', 'vague'?

Love to Ruth—a routine message and yet always fresh—like the best things in Shakespeare!

23 September 1961 *Bromsden Farm*

The Franco-Prussian War has had a tremendous send-off: leading articles promptly and everywhere, including the centre page of *The Times*, which is seldom given to any book except Winston's. I only hope we sell a few, for it's a three-guinea book.

I hope you got my mid-week note about Jonah.[1] Evy's handwriting is none too clear at best, and her ordeal in Padua had rendered it well nigh inscrutable. I wrote back at once to them both, and encouraged all the friends I could think of to do the same. Tommy responded splendidly. He *is* a good fellow indeed.

All week I have been plagued by my infernal back, seldom able to get into a painless position, except on my side in bed. At last, yesterday, after a fortnight of it I went to a charming osteopath, who said I had a clear displacement between the third and fourth vertebrae, which he was confident he could put right with a few hefty clicks—or 'adjustments,' as he called them. These he duly administered, and by Monday, he says, I should be cured. The pain may be a trifle less today, but it is still very much with me, and much the most painful position is that adopted when writing—or compiling an index—so the temptation to lie down with a good book is immense. I do apologise for harping on my tiresome maladies, but lately they have come to dominate and interfere with everything.

[1] He had fallen seriously ill in Italy and been nursed by nuns.

The best news is that my guest flew back to America on Thursday, and for the first time since *May* the flat is my own. Ruth and I had an orgy of tidying, tearing up and throwing away. Now I must get rid of E.B.'s library.

Sunday morning, 24 September

There I broke off and slept for nine delicious hours. My back feels much the same as yesterday, and I can only hope.

Now I must attack my index again. My new plan is to limit myself to an hour's work at a time, and see how many pages I can do in it. Thus childishly do I struggle to break through my staleness. As soon as Oscar is dealt with, I must speedily get to work on Max's letters to Reggie Turner, which I promised to do years ago. Everyone concerned has been very patient, but I feel rather bad about it. I had no idea Oscar would take so long. How many things would never get done at all if one knew at the beginning exactly what one was in for! Not long now before we see you. I expect Ruth will get a new dress for the occasion, but you won't know it's new.

27 September 1961 *Grundisburgh*

That disc I hope by now has yielded to treatment. My son-in-law was treated by the great Cyriax, who said he had never seen a worse disc—but perhaps they always say that. Anyway he cured it completely, so we bid you to hope, as Carlyle was always quoting from Goethe, though none the less remaining plunged in melancholy all his life. My back-aches were before the age of discs and happened at just about the time when lumbago was beginning to be called fibrositis. The conclusion of the whole matter is that in England at least nobody knows anything about it.

I wrote to old Jonah on the same day on which I got your letter—airmail, so he should have got it, though I had a feeling he might be moving off to Venice fairly soon. He will not I fear be at the Lit. Soc. (where, by the way, I *shall* be, or rather *chez vous* at 6 p.m. on the 10th).

Cardus's sketch of Beecham was not very well reviewed.[1] Who was

[1] *Sir Thomas Beecham: a Memoir* (1961).

it who said it was a brave attempt to pretend that B. was not an intolerable man? We must ask Flash Harry. Did you hear him on the Proms last evening? I wonder how cynical he—and the audience—feels when they all bellow 'Wider still and wider, shall thy bounds be set' etc. Not a convincing picture of the British Empire, or Commonwealth, in 1961 surely. Did you hear or read of the young lady who greeted Flash's quotation from Bach that music should bring honour to man and glorify God, with a shrill cry of 'Alleluia'—which reminds me to tell you Housman's exquisite poem:

' "Hallelujah!" was the only observation
That escaped Lieutenant-Colonel Mary Jane,
When she tumbled off the platform in the station,
And was cut in little pieces by the train.
  Mary Jane, the train is through yer:
  Hallelujah, Hallelujah!
We will gather up the fragments that remain.'

I do hope you don't know it, because otherwise I know you will like it. I have a letter from Roger in which he says he was disquieted by a paragraph in the cheap press about you. What would this be? He takes comfort from Macmillan's saying that 'all the graver things of our lives are inventions of the press.' I read hardly anything but headlines nowadays and not many of them.

Old Gow is here—very still-life and practically inaudible. He is annoyed with John Carter's persistence in publishing Housmaniana which for the most part A.E.H. did not wish—in fact forbade—to be published. But what attention do people ever pay to that? I cannot, myself, help being rather pleased at any score off that old curmudgeon, and all his careful defences being gradually flattened. A very ungenial spirit.

At the moment I am re-reading some Gibbon. But I am encouraged to find that Gow found exactly what I do, *viz* that one floats dreamily down the stream of that wonderful style, but remembers very few of the facts recorded. I am just approaching the chapter in which he busies himself in 'sapping a solemn creed with solemn sneer,'[1] but

[1] Byron, *Childe Harold*, canto 3, cvii.

expect to be less shocked than e.g. Boswell was. What a good man Diocletian was! He has never been more than a name to me and I was quite prepared to find his record studded with startling notes 'in the decent obscurity of a learned language.'[1] But not one.

Love to R. I look forward to the new dress.

30 September 1961 *Bromsden Farm*

Too many of the wrong people are dying. Yesterday I learned of the sudden death of Billy James, Henry James's nephew, an enchanting man with whom I stayed in March at Cambridge, Mass. He was almost eighty, but slim and active and elegant and wholly charming.

Today I drove over to the Devlins', near Marlborough, where Christopher D., who wrote the book on Smart, is fading rapidly from cancer. He looked like a ghost of himself, and one can't wish him any long continuance of this agony of pain and drugs.

To descend to the insignificant, my lumbago is still with me, and I am heartily sick of it. Sitting in the car (fifty miles each way) was a particularly painful position for it. The index is still only at p. 668. I must have a good bash at it tomorrow.

If Gow is still with you, please give him my respectful salutations. I don't suppose he remembers me, but I still cherish the prize (Rupert Brooke's poems) that he gave me in 1923. I don't think he should be too hard on Carter, whose new Housman book is simply, so far as I know, a collection of all the prose pieces that A.E.H. *did* print or publish. And if he didn't want his manuscript poems published he should have burnt them, instead of leaving the decision to his brother whom he despised. Anyhow it doesn't matter a halfpenny. Poets are judged and remembered by their *best* poems, not their worst.

Nancy Cunard once asked George Moore if he could be her father, and he said: 'Alas, my dear, no,' and then added firmly: 'You must never tell your mother you asked me that question!'

Adam writes cheerfully and at length from India. There seem to be a lot of holidays of various sorts, and next week a beak called Mr

[1] Gibbon, *Autobiography*.

Purohit is apparently going to take him tiger-shooting! He says the boys love learning English poems by heart and reciting them in class. Also they often ask for more homework! All the teaching is in English except for language-classes in three or four Indian languages. He plays cricket and football with the boys, and bridge with the beaks. He is not allowed to pay for anything, and is apparently given some pocket-money as well.

Now it is Sunday and October, and my back seems worse than ever. My bed here is much softer than the one in London: perhaps I should sleep on the floor.

I was awake for one or two of the small hours and remember saying to myself 'I must tell George that'—but what was it? The sun is shining on my books and cobwebs, and I sit uneasily with a large cushion wedged into the small of my back.

Did you see that Victor Gollancz broke his thigh watching the nonsense in Trafalgar Square? They operated and inserted a pin. I went to see him in hospital on Monday and found him in roaring form. Canon Collins was there—a much nicer man than from his antics one might imagine. Tomorrow I have promised to go back and play bridge round the bed for two hours (6–8) with V.G., his wife and some other lady. As you know, I never play bridge except perhaps twice a year with the Gollanczes, but they refuse to believe this and apparently regard me as a regular player.

Siegfried is coming to the Lit. Soc., but Ivor can't come because he is proposing the toast of Literature at the Guildhall, poor fellow. His word-book, so judiciously dedicated, won't be out till November.[1] Tommy said he had written Jonah a letter so flippant that if Evy came across it she would probably fall into the Po with horror. I've had no further word from her and don't know if they're in Venice yet or where.

[1] *Words in Season* (1961). Its dedication runs:

TO
GEORGE LYTTELTON
whose teaching of English
has done so much for
others in youth and
for me in age

5 October 1961 *Grundisburgh*

Yes, I do wish people wouldn't die the way they do. One feels a sort of indignation like James Forsyte: 'What did *he* want to die for? He was no age.' You probably never saw Reggie Spooner[1] bat. You would not have forgotten it—the purest champagne. Even bowlers enjoyed his punishment of them—the lovely grace of the stroke itself and the courtesy, so kindly without anything remotely condescending. It was Colin Blythe who after being despatched through the covers said to him 'Mr Spooner I would give all my bowling to make a shot like that.' Trueman would not have said that. Cardus is sure to have had something good about him in the *Guardian*; he was one of C's great heroes, and got compared with every kind of operatic and musical figure down the years—none of whom dear R.H.S. had ever heard of. He was one of the very *nicest* men I have ever known.

Old Gow alas had left before your letter arrived. He is of course rather proprietary about A.E.H. and it is risky for anyone to encroach on the hallowed ground. I hope John C. will recover all he can. There is something suspicious about leaving a lot of stuff intact and telling others to destroy it. I put *my* poems into the fire myself.

Duff will clearly end up another C.P. Scott[2] or Nevinson. You are silent about the latter, so may have missed his admirable reminiscences. There have been some fine reviews of your *Franco-Prussian War*. I hope *every*body is buying it—also the Agate book, despite one or two criminal reviews. See you on Tuesday if I get upstairs. I have a bad leg which I think is cancer, paralysis, ossification or lupus. P. thinks it is temporary stiffness.

7 October 1961 *Bromsden Farm*

Yesterday I paid a second visit to my osteopath, and I'm delighted to say that his clicks have greatly improved my condition. Ruth says it's almost worth being in pain for the pleasure of coming out of it, but

[1] Lancashire and England cricketer (1880–1961).

[2] 1846–1932. Editor of the *Manchester Guardian* 1872–1929.

I'm not quite sure I agree. Anyhow I'm thankful it was I who had the lumbago, and not she. Lumbago, I find, is not a word used by osteopaths: a compression of discs is my trouble, or was, and he said a fortnight in bed would have put it right after the first treatment, whereas in the rush of office life it may take four to six weeks. Two weeks have now passed, and I only hope he's right.

My dear friend Christopher Devlin died peacefully on Thursday night at his brother's house near Marlborough. I think I told you that when I drove over to see him last Saturday I realised he couldn't last long, but one always hopes against probability. As you know, I rushed out his *Poor Kit Smart* (which he wrote in his convalescence after his fearful operation), so that he should have the pleasure of seeing it out. He was an extremely good, modest and charming man—less like the general conception of a Jesuit than one could imagine, and yet I've no doubt a very able and valuable priest. I shall miss him. He was saying Mass daily up to the last, and in that sense certainly died happy. How difficult it is to imagine oneself similarly comforted!

By the way, the only person I know who has been treated by Cyriax was on his back for nine months—I won't say as a result, but afterwards.

I imagine Cardus must have written something about Spooner, but I somehow missed it. No, alas, I never saw R.H.S. at the wicket.

Victor Gollancz's accident reminds me of that verse about a race-meeting in Australia, where: 'a spectator's leg was broken from just merely looking on.' He was 'observing' the sit-downers in Trafalgar Square that night, slipped on the wet pavement, broke his femur, and couldn't be got away for two hours because of the crowds. He has had a pin inserted and was in great form on Monday, smoking a large Henry Clay (he gave me one) and using a pâté-de-foie-gras pot as an ashtray. After three hours of bridge on his bed I was the richer by 6/6, but my lumbago and my index (now at p. 706) were none the better. He is a most amusing and stimulating companion for an evening.

I did read Nevinson's memoirs long ago, and thought them excellent: I must read them again. I have just re-read Percy Lubbock's little memoir of Mary Cholmondeley and think it *first-class*. I expect you've read it. In London, before going to sleep, I'm reading M.C.'s *Red Pottage*, which is rather fun in its way. Were you bowled over by it in 1899? I had a postcard from Evy to say they're coming straight home, but she didn't say exactly when. Flash Harry *is* coming on Tuesday. If your leg won't manage the stairs, telephone and we'll make another plan. If I hear nothing I shall expect you at 6, and so will Ruth. What a pity Pamela can't come too, though perhaps she doesn't agree. My love to her.

12 October 1961 *Grundisburgh*

Very good Lit. Soc. dinner. Roger and Flash Harry and I had a good crack afterwards, while Tim and Peter F. played slosh. I must tell you that three of the four people to whom I mentioned that I was going to meet old Maugham pursed their lips and/or shook their heads. I suppose he has one way or another trodden on a good many toes. Yesterday when I lunched at White's with my beloved Tim we met Bob Boothby who said that Winston is hardly compos and fills much of the brief periods when he is with angry lamentations at still being alive. When F.E. Smith died who, according to B.B., was W's only great friend, W. said 'Well at least he went out with a bang—one thing I pray is against a protracted old age.' and not long ago he was in a little company which was talking of the Jutland battle and W. sadly said 'Once you know I knew everything about it, but now it is as remote and vague as the Battle of Salamis.' How right the Synge character was in describing old age as 'a poor untidy thing'.

Bernard Fergusson was at White's. He kept murmuring what is actually a fact but also the first line of a music-hall song. 'I'm off to-morrow morn to Singapore.'

Ruth was looking very lovely on Tuesday—what a refreshment for eye and ear—and heart and mind!

Tommy was gloomy about Jonah, and I gathered he thought the poor old thing *might* be a permanent invalid. I do hope not. I shall write to J. to-morrow. I hear he is at home.

We thought you were in excellent form on Tuesday, and at dinner I could see that Flash Harry was eating out of your hand. When you see Willie Maugham ('that old iguana', as Harold Nicolson calls him), it's possible, nay likely, that the subject of his leaving his fortune to the Society of Authors may crop up. If it does, see whether, with the utmost tact, you can suggest that one certain way of helping young authors (his avowed intent) would be to leave some money to the London Library. T.S.E. and his wife, who are sitting for their joint portrait to Gerald Kelly, are going to put this idea up to him, so they should be able to back you up. W.S.M. did give us £1000 at the time of our appeal, but that is chicken-feed to him.

I have had a letter in Jonah's own hand—the first he had written, he said. He is not yet strong enough for visitors, but soon I shall have to fight my way to St John's Wood—'the shady groves of the Evangelist', as a fanciful old baronet of my early acquaintance used to call it.

Sunday morning, 15 October

All is obscured by mist, but I can hear the hefty blows of Duff, who is reducing a thirty-foot-high hedge to eight foot or so, and thoroughly enjoying himself. Yesterday week he played for a scratch against the Field and laid himself out cold with concussion. He seems to have recovered completely, but didn't play yesterday for Fred's old Boys v. the Field. He and his wife drove over to watch, and he says the O.B.'s were a trifle lucky to win 3–0: one of those opportunist goals. They saw the Headmaster, who was clearly delighted, and rather touched, to have received a letter from Adam in India. A. himself is being taken by Mr Purohit for twelve days' holiday, which he hopes will include some shooting of all kinds.

My index has reached p. 790, and as I sniff the smell of the stable-door (p. 868), I begin to get the bit between my teeth and bolt for home. When I finish there will be a lot of re-writing, arranging and tidying-up to do, but those are trifles compared to this slogging compilation.

Forgive this half-pay scrap. You shall have more next week.

My lumbago is quite gone. Hurrah!

18 October 1961 *Grundisburgh*

I shall certainly sow what seed I can about the London Library, though I shrewdly suspect the old iguana's skin is impervious to hints. One discouraging friend tells me there are days when he is impervious to ordinary discourse, neither uttering or attending to, and clearly wishes for nothing but death. I will tell you all about it *quam primum*.

Is Adam really going for a trip with Mr *Purohit*? I suppose he just calls him *Proot*—the only word with which Stevenson could stimulate his donkey.

Thursday. Well there is nothing much to report. Old Maugham was friendly, intelligent, forthcoming, unaffected. He might have been a member of the Lit. Soc.! The London Library was mentioned, but he didn't rise much. He knew of your fine work, but censured the 'intelligentsia', whosoever he meant, for the meanness of their contributions. So I fear he may be thinking he has done enough. He looks younger than his years and less corrugated. That Graham Sutherland portrait is mere caricature, but oddly S.M. likes it! Gerald Kelly's portrait of T.S.E. looks to my unsophisticated eye extremely good. He certainly makes him look a very nice man. S.M. was very gloomy about Winston, and it is disheartening to hear that W. welcomes numberless pressmen and is grumpy if they are kept at bay. Also that he resents being asked about his period in the doldrums, before the second war.

21 October 1961 *Bromsden Farm*

Many thanks for your natural history notes on the old iguana. It's amusing that he should have mentioned Winston, since it is generally believed that, apart from diverting his huge fortune from his daughter and her children, his one ambition is to outlive Winston. If they die on the same day their obituaries will take up most of that day's papers!

My best news is that the index is finished—or rather, the first draft of it, for I now have to read it through and re-write some of the messier cards. Also tie up a hundred loose ends, fill gaps etc. The deadline of November 30 is all too near.

On Thursday at 8 a.m. six stalwarts arrived at the flat with an immense van, which they had some difficulty in parking. They unloaded eighty tea-chests and set to work. Their foreman was a stocky little ex-pugilist with a broken nose, a face the colour of raw meat, and scarcely any hearing, but he worked without stopping, and after four and a half hours every E.B. book and bookcase was loaded and off. When they arrived, more than five years ago, it took three men *eight* hours to carry them up and unpack them.

Now I am trying to find a 'little man' to paint the spare room, and when that's done I shall be able to use all those shelves for my own books. On Monday I'm going round to help Diana unpack some of Duff's, so that looks like fitting in very well.

My Duff has been down to-day, shooting with Peter. They got some partridges, pheasants and hares, and one fox (shot by Duff). They saw *five* wild deer, but did not bombard them.

I was sorry to read of Bernard Darwin's death. He was in College with my father and was always very nice to me. His death makes no difference to the Lit. Soc. election, since he had become an Honorary Member.

Siegfried has been asked to unveil the tablet to Walter de la Mare in the crypt of St Paul's at the end of November. Tommy has promised to chaperone him, but already S.S. is saying he is sure to be having bronchitis just then. I lunched with Jonah and Evy on Tuesday, and found him wonderfully better than I had expected. He has lost a good deal of weight but otherwise looks fine. He gets up and dresses for meals, and goes back to bed in between. He says he has written enough stories for a second volume and is soon to present them. He is wildly enthusiastic about the Linklater novel, *Roll of Honour*, which I had sent him, and roundly proclaims it a masterpiece. I think he's right and shall eagerly await your judgment.

T.S.E. is much delighted with the French translation of *The Owl and the Pussycat*.[1] Have you looked at it, or hasn't it reached you? I

[1] *Le Hibou et la Poussiquette*, freely translated into French from the English of Edward Lear by Francis Steegmuller (London, 1961).

think we ought to sell quite a lot of it. But everything depends on the Durrell book, which appears on Monday week.[1] I have printed 50,000 copies, and have already orders for more than 23,000. If only I had a few more authors of that selling-capacity!

Heinemann, and their big-business owners, are getting increasingly restive at the unprofitability of my business, and I foresee a fairly early crisis. If they would let me go I think I could find someone else to buy the business and leave me to run it, but Heinemann seem to think my leaving would in some way damage their prestige. Nonsense, I say, but if you really think that, you must be prepared to pay for the privilege of keeping me. What I can't tell any of them is that in general I've had quite enough of publishing and would welcome retirement—but what should I use for money? It simply isn't on.

There I went to bed, and it is now a weeping Sunday morning. The empty pond completely filled up during the night and all is drip and squelch. Comfort is making Christmas puddings, with Bridget's assistance. Yesterday I read *The Worm of Death* by Nicholas Blake (C. Day Lewis) with enjoyment. (Now comes a crisis. They have peeled almonds and made breadcrumbs and mixed a great bowl of flour—and there is no candied peel! Comfort has driven to Henley to try and knock up a friendly grocer.) When I was in New York in March I paid £50 for an option to have first look at a full-length biography of Sherlock Holmes, which one of those crazy enthusiasts has compiled from the stories, and now the typescript has arrived—more than 400 pages of it, and my spirit quails a little at the prospect.[2] I have never had much sympathy with the Baker Street Irregulars, though I love the stories. How many people would read or buy this book? What do you think? Assuming that it's decently done. I may consult S.C. Roberts.

Comfort has returned in triumph with peel and the Sunday papers.

[1] *The Drunken Forest* by Gerald Durrell (1961).

[2] *Sherlock Holmes, a Biography of the World's first Consulting Detective* by William S. Baring-Gould (1962).

I say Duff's *fox*! What will the huntin' neighbourhood say when they hear of it? Shooting a fox was the only crime the Murgatroyds in *Ruddigore* accepted as a pukka crime without cavil. Do you know the opera? We go to see and hear it this evening. I have never seen it before, and though both G. and S. respectively thought they had never done anything so good, the public has never much taken to it, and on such matters the public is usually right. Gilbert's humour seems to me to last less well than e.g. P.G. Wodehouse's, though some cannot bear *his* brand. I like to think I am in the company of Asquith, Balfour, M.R. James, Ronnie Knox etc, who at least were not trivial and foolish people. The simple truth is that we share an intense delight in seeing language *perfectly* handled, no matter what the subject. But I was amused by a recent review of him in which there was a complaint that his young men and women who fall in love are altogether *too* virginal—that the only idea the sight of a double bed puts into their minds is 'What a grand apple-pie could be made of it!' And that is true. I don't want any *Chatterley* muck, but shall we say a little more red blood in his love-affairs. I hope the new Penguin P.G.W.s will revive a few which for some reason have been out of print for years, though every bit as good as the rest. Did any popular author ever remain more constantly at his best?

I too have deeply enjoyed Eric Linklater's *Roll of Honour*. The unusual setting is entirely successful—not wholly unlike Masters's *Spoon River Anthology* but much less bitter. Hardly a week goes by without some contribution to Letters from Lit. Soc. members, and there is your O.W. just round the corner. The Linklater book is always giving one what Mark Twain called 'a spell of the dry grins.' And *The Owl and the Pussy Cat* is delicious—illustrations and all. I imagine the French to be the last word in neatness.

S.C. Roberts would be a good man to ask about that Holmes book. I am no judge, but my impression is that all that clever investigation —which as you say, was rather overdone—has had its day. 400 pages is staggering. I may be quite wrong in thinking the fashion is past; I generally am. I too am a fan of the stories (especially *Adventures* and *Memoirs*, in which I once could have passed any exam) and S.H. still cuts a brave figure. (But if there is a poorer tale than 'The Noble Bachelor' I should like to see it.)

And *The Christening Party*[1] too is extremely pleasant reading. What immense pleasure your generous gifts fill my days with. I have not yet embarked on the Walpole,[2] but I have been dipping again into *your Hugh Walpole*. These people who airily fling words like 'fake' and 'bogus' about are stuffy little folk. They forget that in the Almighty's eyes we are all to a large extent fake and bogus. (Not you or dear Ruth, to whom my love.)

28 October 1961 *Bromsden Farm*

Last week was much occupied with publishing discussions. Just when my relations with Heinemann had reached breaking-point and there seemed to be no possible satisfactory solution except the closing down of my business, or my resigning and starving, a splendid *Deus* stepped *ex machina*, or rather out of a jet air-liner, and all may now be well. My saviour is a chap called Bill Jovanovich. His father was a peasant in Montenegro (as you may know, the Montenegrins are proud mountainy men who rightly consider themselves superior to all the other Jugoslavs), who managed somehow to emigrate to the U.S.A. and worked in the Pittsburg steelworks. He married a Polish girl and produced Bill, who won every conceivable scholarship, ending with a Ph.D. in Eng. Lit. To cut a long story short, by the time he was thirty-four he was President of Harcourt Brace, one of the leading U.S. publishers for quality, though not then for size. He had worked his way up through the textbook department, and in the last six years he has turned H.B. into the second or third biggest publishing house in the world, with an annual turnover of $33,000,000.

Nine-tenths of this comes from textbooks, but the general list is still good, and Bill is the most extraordinary mixture of literary man and tycoon. He is still only forty. For some reason he seems to think

[1] By Francis Steegmuller.

[2] *Horace Walpole* by Wilmarth Sheldon Lewis (1961).

a lot of me and is prepared to buy my business from the loathly Heinemann. He would leave me to run it, as now, helped by books from his list, and would bolster it with a textbook business, which today is the only hope of survival. It's all too good to be true, and the chief hurdle is to get Tilling's (who own Heinemann) to agree. On the face of it, they would be crazy not to get rid of a losing subsidiary for cash, but they have an idiotic idea that to sell to an American buyer is in some way to sell the pass, and I am busily engaged in trying to persuade them this is not so. Their meeting is on November 10, so keep your fingers crossed. I shall never get used to the speed of modern communications. Yesterday morning I spoke to Bill on the telephone at Claridge's before he left for home, and at 9 p.m. I called him at his home in Upper State New York to report progress. Directly Tilling's agree in principle he is prepared to fly back to discuss terms.

All this makes ordinary life very difficult, and as you can imagine, everything is piling up round me. But I feel wonderfully well, with a new and very welcome upsurge of hope. The awful thing is that *everything* belongs more or less to Heinemann—my flat, my car, my office and so on.

By the way—all this is hideously secret, for obvious reasons, so mum's the word.

Despite all those preoccupations last week I managed to spend two afternoons unpacking Uncle Duff's books, dined my poetess from Lancashire, spent a long evening playing bridge with Victor Gollancz (I lost one and sixpence), visited my aged father, lunched a beautiful authoress one day, an ugly literary agent another, and had tea with a delightful octogenarian at the Goring Hotel. The combination of the Motor Show, the Dairy Show and almost incessant rain didn't help the traffic at all.

I have said I will publish the Sherlock Holmes book, if all questions of copyright can be cleared up, and in due course you may be called on to read its proofs as an expert.

Adam has got a ticket for the Calcutta Test on New Year's Eve or thereabouts. He reports a total absence of liquor in the Central Provinces, and a great shortage of razor-blades.

1 November 1961 *Grundisburgh*

And now yesterday's Johnson Club dinner. Your absence was regretted but the Secretary was very nice about it and put it down to an even busier and fuller life than you actually have—and that takes some doing. There sat with us a lively and pleasant doctor called Hubble, who has apparently been a member for twenty years. We dined reasonably well at The Cock (but regrettably there was no plump head-waiter[1]), but let me tell you the dinner was (1) less good and (2) more costly than those *you* provide at the Garrick. Old Powell[2] made a speech about his birthday. He looks far younger than he did when I first became a member. Probably the presence of old R.W. Chapman kept everybody old.

I will certainly and with pleasure help in any way I can with the Holmes book though I claim to be no expert with the stories after his return. There is a pleasant vignette of old Doyle in P.G. Wodehouse's *Performing Flea*, which I bought yesterday. But the Penguins haven't really got down to publishing five out-of-print ones. Only one of these have I not got, *viz Full Moon* of which I had never even heard.

4 November 1961 *Bromsden Farm*

Today Comfort and I drove to the Cotswolds and took C's aged stepmother to lunch at the Lygon Arms at Broadway. It was a day of miraculous autumn beauty—cold, but with clear blue sky and hot sun. The trees every colour imaginable, and comparatively few cars on the road—very enjoyable. On the way I snatched three-quarters of an hour in Blackwell's, which I always enjoy, but the crush in the Oxford streets made it a struggle just to walk along.

You will remember my mentioning my dear old friend Katie Lewis, who died this year and left me that lovely Rossetti drawing. Forty years ago she bought for £200 a derelict farmhouse and six acres at the end of the main road through Broadway. She converted it into a

[1] 'O plump head-waiter at the Cock' (Tennyson, 'Will Waterproof's Lyrical Monologue'.)

[2] L. F. Powell, Johnsonian scholar and editor (1881–1975).

thoroughly comfortable house with a lovely garden, lived there for the rest of her life, and the other day it fetched £17,000! The purchaser is reported to be an American who wanted 'a place in England'.

No more news of my *Deus ex machina*, but the vital Tilling meeting is next Wednesday. I have a strong and increasing belief that they will agree, and then there will only be the price to be settled. Another few weeks should prove decisive.

The Sherlock Holmes book is temporarily held up while I attempt to get a clearance from the Estate through John Murray. I gather that Conan Doyle's son Adrian is both dotty and litigious. He recently tried to sue someone for saying that *Holmes* was Semitic! Also he lives in Geneva, which doesn't quicken things up. I'll let you know if any light breaks.

On Thursday Jonah and Evy turned up at Soho Square in a hired car, Jonah looking astonishingly better in his overcoat and bowler hat. He even talks of coming to next week's Lit. Soc. We thought the stairs, even to my office, would be too much for him, so I got into the car and we drove round and round the square till Evy got giddy. Jonah gave me the typescript of his new collection of stories (all written before his illness). I haven't yet had time to read any of them, but I like the book's title, *Trepidation in Downing Street*.

Here is the joke I promised you. A couple, twenty years married, had a fearful row. The wife told the husband exactly what she thought of him, ending: 'And on top of all that, we've had your mother living with us for ten years.'

HUSBAND '*My* mother? I always thought she was *your* mother!'

End of story.

Can you get old novels (1946 or so) from your library? If so, and you haven't read it, ask immediately for *States of Grace* by Francis Steegmuller. He gave me a copy, which I have just finished with chuckling delight. It's light and witty and altogether a joy. Now I am reading Evelyn Waugh's latest[1], which as usual is compulsively readable, I find. Only twenty-six more proofing days before I part with Oscar.

Ivor came in and signed some copies of his book, including one for

[1] *Unconditional Surrender* (1961).

you, but you won't get it for another week or so, since he said he thought it best to keep them till just before publication day.

I simply hadn't time to read his proofs, and fear there are a lot of misprints and errors in the book. You might be an angel and let me have a list of any you notice. Ivor seems delighted with the book's appearance (and indeed it is quite elegant), so if he's satisfied, all is well. I have printed only 2500 and look like selling half of them before publication, which is rather good. He says he hopes to come to the Lit. Soc.

Try and go to the Lawrence exhibition at Burlington House when you're in London. I haven't been yet, but hear that my picture is well hung—sounds like game!

9 November 1961 — *Grundisburgh*

I was fascinated by *Horace Walpole*, and I am glad to see that many of the reviews praise its sumptuous get-up. One actually said that the firm of Hart-Davis were outstanding for the appearance of their books! Meanwhile we pray for the soul of Tilling; all must have been decided yesterday. I am excited about it. How splendid it will be if the situation is established when you have nothing to think of but the quality of your books.

I came across a fine 'gaffe' recently when a reviewer complacently referred to the hero of 'Mr Anstey's famous book'[1] as Mr Bulstrode. Surely every reader of the book in existence has *Bultitude* in his mind for ever. I met Anstey once, bicycling in France with Monty James—a very absurd little man. He told us that he saw 'Bultitude' over a shop-window from the top of a bus but couldn't remember where. If I weren't too lazy I would write to the paper in which Bulstrode appeared and point out that the error is in the same crime-catalogue as, say, *Foster* for Falstaff. Anstey was childishly pleased when we quoted *Vice Versa* to him. M.R.J. knew it by heart, and I wasn't too bad at one time. I suppose it is dead now.

I have just got from the library Mrs Langley Moore's immense

[1] *Vice Versa* (1882), which has now been continuously in print for a hundred years.

book on Byron. It looks good browsing, but how can one remember all the ramifications? Luckily she tells us many things more than once. I suppose B. shares with O.W. that extraordinary posthumous vitality. We simply cannot let them rest in peace.

I look forward to further information about Holmes—and the imbecile Conan Doyle. But I agree with him in rejecting the theory that Sherlock was a Jew. I cannot think what evidence supports it. He was a misogynist—except for Irene Adler—and I am surprised no one has yet suggested that he was a homo. What about that gang of Baker Street Irregulars? Highly suggestive surely to anyone but Watson ('You see it, Watson, you see it?' 'But I saw nothing.' Might be the motto of the whole chronicle).

That is good news about Jonah. I am drifting through his *Victorian Boyhood* at odd moments, e.g. at meals when P. is out. Excellent reading, though full of inaccuracies, most of them small. His character-sketches of beaks are good. I wish, after his two years at Lowry's he had come to Arthur Benson's. I cannot quite say of A.C.B.'s 'Sir, we were a nest of singing-birds',[1] but with people in it like Percy Lubbock, Edward Cadogan, L.H. Myers, we were, I am sure, the least Philistine house at Eton. Kindersley was a fine man and hopeless beak.

11 November 1961 *Bromsden Farm*

On Wednesday the Tilling board agreed 'very reluctantly' to sell R.H-D. Ltd, 'provided they get their price.' John McCallum, vice-president of Harcourt Brace, flies over tomorrow to negotiate, and the great Jovanovich himself follows on Thursday. So keep your fingers permanently crossed. All should be settled this coming week, but not by the time I see you on Wednesday. If and when (not a phrase I like) they come to terms, there will still be a hundred details to be settled and a great deal of work to be done. Somehow in the midst of it all Oscar must be despatched by the end of the month. Reading, correcting and rewriting the index has got as far as DOUGLAS, LORD ALFRED, who has sixteen closely written cards to himself. I am

[1] Doctor Johnson on Pembroke College, Oxford.

heartily sick of it all, but still in an awful way fascinated—and the quest for perfection in editing dies hard.

Doris Langley Moore's book on Byron is on the short list for this year's Duff Cooper Prize. I think Duff would have found it fascinating. And surely the last thing either Byron or Oscar would have asked was to be allowed to rest in peace. By the way, the German and the French translation rights of Oscar have been sold—each for £400 advance, of which I get half. I am now sure that this book will pay for the whole of Adam's Oxford career. Perhaps one day I'll produce a book whose royalties I can spend on myself?

Adam reports the sudden death of the energetic and popular Vice-Principal of his Indian college. He writes: 'I attended the funeral procession and cremation on Monday. This lasted from 9.15 a.m. until noon. The temperature was 90 in the shade, and there was no shade. The procession involved a rapid walk of about three and a half miles in fifty minutes, and by the time we returned I was dished.' Not surprisingly he went down that afternoon with some kind of dysentery, but seems to have made a rapid recovery. There is a hospital (and post-office) in the college, and they seem to be looking after him well. Comfort (who has a heavy cold) has taken it all very philosophically.

Jonah's new collection of stories seems to me much inferior to its predecessor, but I shan't tell him that, so mum's the word. They seem to me, the stories, to be getting steadily more juvenile, and somehow I must try and prevent his hoping for a third volume. The trouble is that he has nothing else to do, and loves writing them. Short stories are notorious non-sellers at best, and I have half-a-dozen books of them in my next list: not purposely: things have just worked out that way.

Last week I dined out twice, and on the second occasion at the Droghedas' in Lord North Street, I met Hugh Gaitskell for the first time, and to my surprise found him most charming, intelligent, amusing, and easy to get on with. An admirable Lit. Soc. member, I should say. I wonder if you know him. My chief impression was astonishment that anyone so seemingly sensible should want to spend his life in the filthy power-grabbing welter of politics. If I ever see him again I must ask him why.

Diana Cooper, who was also of the party, lent me her Mini (Morris) for the evening. 'It's like driving a swallow,' she said, and indeed it was: an ideal car for traffic. When I fetched the car I found stuck under the windscreen-wiper a piece of paper on which Diana had written 'HAVE MERCY. AM TAKING SAD CHILD TO CINEMA.' Apparently it had effectively prevented her being charged for parking in the wrong place.

Last night, as soon as I got here, I drove to Oxford and dined with Laurence Stone, a very nice historian, at the high table at Wadham. They still do themselves pretty well—soup, grilled sole, good veal and veg, apple tart, and some admirable little confections which can only have been 'cheese remmykins'. Plenty of sherry, claret and port, nuts, fruit etc. I drove home stupefied and fell asleep without reading a word—a rare occurrence.

17 November 1961 *Grundisburgh*

This is miserable work. Not for donkey's years have I delayed writing till Friday. I should really have written *before* the dinner. This has been a full week—a meeting—only one of pleasure—on every day of the week plus next Monday. All G.B.'s except to-morrow, when again I come to London to face the Revisers of the G.C.E. papers who usually tear over half my questions, their main reasons being apparently that a Reviser's job is to revise. It was amusing to find Harold Nicolson *cagey* about the real cause of Byron's separation from Lady B, as if it was too bad to reveal a century afterwards. (Do you, by the way, approve of the Oxford protest at a young student of St Hilda's being sent down after being found in bed with her boy-friend? It is all very strange to an old Victorian like myself.) I was in luck on Wednesday as while Tim was playing slosh with Peter I found Clive Burt in the lounge and had a good crack. I know quite a number of Garrick members.

Ivor's book is splendid. I have read only forty-five pages so far and discovered *one* misprint—'ra*nucu*lus' on p. 45. But I will look more carefully. It is first-rate reading. Now, my dear R., let yourself off writing this week. This scrap deserves no recognition.

18 November 1961 *Bromsden Farm*

It was splendid of you to write at all, in such a busy week, and so soon after our meeting, and I must certainly respond, if only with a half-charge.

You will be pleased to hear that the great deal is safely through. There was a nasty period—about three quarters of an hour—on Thursday morning, when the negotiations broke down altogether, and I had lost the business and everything. I think that perhaps the opposition had a faint hope that I might cave in, but luckily I didn't, so they capitulated instead. Now the lawyers and accountants are drawing up the documents, and an announcement will probably be made about Tuesday. I can't tell you what a relief it is to have escaped from the Heinemann Group, which I'm sure was the cause of all my recent illnesses. Incidentally I shall also be earning a bigger salary, which will be a great help. I feel a great resurgence of hope.

Meanwhile, since most of last week was taken up with all this, I am more than ever behind with my ordinary work. Only twelve more days of Oscar, and much still to be done, though the index, thank God, is checked and ready.

One day Ruth and I sneaked out to the Lawrence exhibition at Burlington House. My ancestor stood up very well, we thought, in distinguished company; there are half a dozen smashing portraits there.

Adam has recovered from his dysentery and is preparing for a tiger-shoot at Christmas.

So glad you're enjoying Ivor's book: it comes out on Monday. I'm delighted to say *Le Hibou et la Poussiquette* is selling like hot cakes: the 10,000 copies I printed won't last till Christmas, and I'm desperately trying to get some more printed in time. That's the worst of publishing—either one has far too many copies, or far too few, usually the former. Durrell too is going splendidly.

23 November 1961 *Grundisburgh*

I really am delighted about the great deal which you must have transacted in the most masterly fashion. It must be a vast relief to you to be free of Heinemann. What you say of your illnesses is interesting, because old Mat Hill[1], who was well ahead of his time, always maintained that the connection between body and mind was much closer than the faculty realised. Once when I had lumbago he asked me if I was worried about anything.

Fancy your being descended from old Lawrence. Very distinguished. He is, as they say, coming back, isn't he? These up and down fashions are very ridiculous, as I am going to tell the girls of North Foreland Lodge on Monday. The gist of my address is what a lot they can do to educate themselves by merely reading what they like—*and ruminating* about it. My line will be largely anti-G.C.E. Eng. Lit. (in which I examine them) and anti-Leavis, of whom they have probably never heard. I expect they will be quite a good audience, but one can never be entirely sure. And one of them, no doubt, will be the English mistress who will not like it when I tell them that at their age it is quite right that they should enjoy flamboyant verbiage and urge them to indulge in it sometimes in an essay. 'Probably your teacher will be sick, but that is one of the things she is there for.'

I had a glorious flop not long ago with a speech to the Old Boys of Ipswich—an entirely carnal and philistine crowd who had no interest at all in the history and traditions of the school but were wholly satisfied by such tales as what Smith mi said to the matron about the lavatory in 1944. A depressing evening, as I said to the Archdeacon of Suffolk who was also there. 'But you must remember,' he said, 'that they are all shop-keepers and sanitary inspectors, who have never heard of Cardinal Wolsey' (who is supposed to have founded the school—erroneously).

Did I tell you I had been reading about the intolerable *Prof*?[2] I cannot remember so strongly disliking anyone whom I had met only in a book. He seems to have had all the faults commonly charged against scientists, *viz* arrogance and narrowness and Philistinism. He had some very odd habits, e.g. his refusal ever to wipe his brow in public,

[1] Former Eton master.

[2] Frederick Alexander Lindemann (1886–1957). Professor of Experimental Philosophy at Oxford. Personal assistant to Winston Churchill from 1940. Created Viscount Cherwell 1956. Known as The Prof. His biography, *The Prof in Two Worlds* by the second Earl of Birkenhead was published in 1961.

however hot the day: and his diet seems to have been largely confined to olive oil and the white of egg. He would have been no good at a Lit. Soc. dinner.

Also Hankey's vast book all about the running of the 1914–18 war—one of the very few men who was really indispensable.[1] And how on earth we survived the incessant disasters of three and a half years is ungraspable. I suppose the solution is that, though we did not realise it, the Germans were really more incompetent than we were—and their top men more quarrelsome among themselves even than ours with the French—a very huffy and pigheaded lot these, conspicuously and persistently devoid of anything remotely resembling gratitude to any of their allies—and in fact I read not long ago that gratitude has never been one of the French virtues—coupled closely with conceit, for what else are you to call the settled conviction that only the French are and always have been truly civilised?

25 November 1961 *Bromsden Farm*

The news about my publishing plans broke in Tuesday's *Evening Standard*, with a piece on the front page headed by a blown-up reproduction of my fox.[2] Thereafter I had long telephone conversations with chaps from *seven* daily papers, all of which printed the news, more or less accurately, next morning. I was particularly anxious not to cast any aspersions on the efficiency of Heinemann, and mercifully all was well: no feelings hurt or umbrage taken. Now we are hard at work planning to resume power in January—the first *hopeful* planning that has been possible for years!

Did you see the leader about Henry James in this morning's *Times*? It was written by the Editor[3], as a result of my lunching with him at

[1] Maurice Pascal Alers Hankey (1877–1963). Secretary to the Cabinet and the Committee of Imperial Defence 1916–1938. Knighted 1916. Created Baron 1939. His book *The Supreme Command 1914–1918*, after being banned by three successive Prime Ministers, was published in two volumes in 1961.

[2] The emblem of my publishing firm, engraved by Reynolds Stone.

[3] Sir William Haley.

the Athenaeum on Monday, and is a splendid Puff Preliminary.[1]

On Wednesday I took most of the day off and travelled to Oxford with Raymond Mortimer, Peter Quennell and my cousin John Julius Norwich, for the choosing of this year's Duff Cooper Prize. At Oxford we were joined by Tony Powell and his wife, and given an excellent lunch in the Warden's Lodging at New College by the Warden (William Hayter, lately Ambassador in Moscow) and his lady. After some discussion the Prize was awarded to Jocelyn Baines's Life of Conrad (mum's the word till the Presentation next month), and then we were shown some of the College treasures, including the superb El Greco which Major Allnatt presented to the Chapel. He suddenly wrote out of the blue to say that he had been looking round the Colleges and thought the El Greco would look best in New College Chapel! I imagine he did just the same with the Rubens and King's.

That evening I dined with Wyndham Ketton-Cremer (whom I first met at my prep-school in 1917)—again at the Athenaeum: twice in one week puts a strain on the toughest constitution. Next day I lunched with Diana Cooper and talked some more about Duff's books. In fact, one way and another, I was out to every meal last week.

Sunday morning. I slept for the best part of ten hours, and still feel cosily drowsy. I've just finished Leonard Woolf's second volume of autobiography, *Growing*, which I found extremely interesting, and now I am reading Priestley's new Pictorial Life of Dickens, which is an excellent job with first-class pictures.

I fear my last letter misled you: I am not descended from Lawrence, but from one of his sitters. You ought to visit that exhibition on your next visit to London.

The 'Prof' I met only once, when Roy Harrod took me to lunch or dine in the Common Room at the House, and I took an immediate dislike to him, on exactly the grounds you describe.

[1] For the first two (1961) of the twelve volumes of *The Complete Tales of Henry James.*

I saw more than one respectful reference in the press to your Heinemann transaction. It is all very interesting to hear about. I like to think that you are at last really having the only thing really essential to life, *viz* peace of mind. Though of course the fates are pretty niggardly with it. *Il-y-a toujours de quoi*, as my doctor, had he known any French, would have said recently when I complained of small aches and pains which I suggested he should deal with.

I saw and liked that Henry James article with the impressive announcement that exactly the publisher one would have expected is undertaking the short stories. And I was glad to read that you will be mainly ignoring H.J.'s own corrections in later editions—almost all of which, I remember thinking, were for the worse. Did you read Connolly on *A Christmas Garland*[1] in the *Sunday Times*, in which he said that of the authors parodied only five were really familiar to-day (Conrad, Hardy, Kipling, James, Shaw) 'not because the parodies killed Baring, Benson and Co but . . . because their eclipse forms part of the *general subsidence into oblivion of the whole of English Literature*.' Is this really the truth—outside the schools who are still set books by Galsworthy and Wells and Bennett (who C says are 'under eclipse')? And if so, cannot one say that it always was true? C. implies that 'the leisured reader' is vanishing.

And I was talking about reading to the girls of North Foreland Lodge last Monday and telling them how pleasantly and profitably they could teach themselves. I read them Conrad's account of the return of the *Narcissus* 'Under white wings she skimmed low over the blue sea like a great tired bird speeding to its nest', and they were wonderful listeners. Do you think I was fantastic to tell them that that sentence alone contained the ideas of speed, sunshine, loneliness, spaciousness, welcome, happiness, earth's solidity v. sea and sky's opposite, and to sum up drew a lovely picture? Well anyway I did and they seemed to swallow it. With equal avidity they delighted in Ivor's officialese reproduction of the Lord's Prayer, though I didn't dare to quote more than 'We should be obliged for your attention in provid-

[1] By Max Beerbohm (1912).

ing for our own nutritional needs, and for so organising distribution that our daily intake of cereal filler be not in short supply.'

Pamela has ordered several copies of his new book for Christmas presents, and is still immersed in it, so that I still have not read any more. She is no etymologist but delights in Ivor's miniature essays. They *are* very well done.

Another book I have just read—with increasing dismay—is the Pelican *Modern Age* in their Guides to Eng. Lit. The language of modern criticism is to me so fearfully pretentious that again and again I cannot grasp the meaning, and am constantly merely guessing at it. Such a sentence as 'The final death of Gerald in the snow is only the symbolic expression of the inexorable consequence of his life-defeating idealism' means so little to me that I have decided to avoid modern criticism in future. There are some pretty grim sentences about dear T.S. Eliot too. I wonder what he thinks of them. One Bantock insists that my old Evelyns, Eton, and Cambridge contemporary, L.H. Myers, is really a most important figure. I knew him up to about his twenty-fourth year, and I think this judgment puts him rather high. He committed suicide in 1944 for the simple reason that he 'despaired of humanity.'

3 December 1961 *Bromsden Farm*

This may be the last of my interminable letters, for at eleven o'clock on Wednesday morning I am to take wing for New York, returning on Saturday. Were it not for my morbid fear of flying, it would be something of a spree, but as it is you can imagine me boarding the bus at the Air Terminal as though it were a tumbril taking me to the guillotine. The knowledge that hundreds of people fly safely each way every day is no comfort to me, and I doubt whether the tranquillising pills I have been given will have much effect either.

Last time I flew the Atlantic (in 1952) there were no jets, and the flight took the best part of twenty-four hours, with unscheduled landings in Iceland and Newfoundland. Now, if all goes well, we leave at 11 a.m. and arrive at 2 p.m. (U.S. time) the same day. I am to stay with the Gleaveses, as in March, and to spend almost all my time in conference with Harcourt Brace. If only Ruth could come with me! She doesn't mind flying at all—women are much braver than men—and would thoroughly enjoy it, but it costs £321, and one fare is enough for H.B. Anyhow, if I survive, I shall have something to tell you next Sunday.

Meanwhile Oscar is done! The proofs go back to the printer tomorrow, and thereafter only proofs of the index will remain to be done, and I shall probably spend a day at the printers' at Frome in Somerset, looking over all their corrections before the machining begins. Luckily Tony Powell lives at Frome, and has offered to put me up for the occasion. You can imagine what a relief it is to be shot of the whole caboodle, and if only I were travelling to New York by boat, the trip would be one long celebration.

That's a magnificent sentence about the *Narcissus*: no wonder the girls were good listeners. You simply *must* stop worrying yourself by reading rubbish like that Pelican book about modern literature. L.H. Myers is a deadly writer, and Mr Bantock should be condemned to read nothing else for a year.

Meanwhile the advent of parking-meters in the Square has proved an immense blessing. One can now drive right up to the door of the house, and the vans can load and unload in peace. No one is allowed to park for more than two hours, and that only in fixed areas on payment. This knocks out all the monsters who used to leave cars there every day for eight hours. The meters stop working at 6.30 p.m., so it fills up again for the evening as of old, but no cars are left there all night, and the tireless Jamaicans have a chance of sweeping the roadway before the office-workers start to arrive.

Last Wednesday Ruth and I took her guests to the dramatisation of C.P. Snow's novel *The Affair*, which proved an excellent evening's entertainment, somewhat in the Galsworthy manner. If all Snow's works could be served up in this painless way I might find them less rebarbative.

I also lunched one day with Diana Cooper, another with Eric Linklater and generally rattled about, with final attacks on the Oscar proofs up to midnight each night. One evening I dined agreeably at the Beefsteak, and as I hadn't been there for a couple of years my dinner must have cost me the best part of £40. Harold N. was there—it is his main eating-place—very sweet and woolly.

Yesterday morning I attended a requiem mass for Christopher Devlin at Farm Street, the Jesuit church. For non-believers who didn't know the service by heart no word could be recognised except twice *Dominus vobiscum.* I tried to think nice thoughts and take it all seriously.

6 December 1961 *Over New Brunswick*

I think your best chance of getting a letter this week is to endure a serial one, part written today and part during my return journey on Saturday. I only hope this Biro (the best I have found) is legible.

I daresay, with perhaps pardonable pride, that this is the first letter you have ever received which was written at 35,000 feet above the earth. So far on this trip I have found the preliminary dread greater than the fear in the air, though that is ever with me. Perhaps the two tranquillising pills I took have helped. When I arrived at the Victoria Air Terminal at 9.30 this morning I found that the absence of my vaccination-certificate, which I had mislaid since my American trip in March, might land me in for fourteen days' quarantine in the U.S., so, at the Terminal, for a fee of ten shillings and sixpence, in five and a half minutes, I was re-vaccinated and given the necessary certificate. All along it has been a day of clear blue sky, and though we are said to have a 50 m.p.h. wind against us, this is apparent only in occasional bumps. This plane (a Boeing 707) is so much bigger than any I have ever been in before that it's more like a train, and therefore a little re-assuring. I am sitting next to the President of the Shell Oil Company of America, who might well be most useful to Adam after he gets his degree—a most charming and civilised man. For lunch I consumed two large Bourbon whiskies as an aperitif, then caviare, lamb chops and beans, fruit tart, Stilton, *three* glasses of claret, coffee and brandy—all very good and boosting to the morale. I have also been able to smoke my pipe with impunity. When we passed over Iceland, *seven miles up*, the island looked like a mud-flat intersected by trickles of water. Since then we have had a carpet of white cloud below, clear blue sky and sun above. We are due to arrive in another hour, and the terrors of landing still lie ahead. The trouble is that I shall by then have endured a full day's trials, but it will only be mid-afternoon in New York, and many more hours of bright activity may well be expected of me. I *hate* leaving Ruth, even for a moment, let alone on so long and hazardous a journey. Never again I swear. Goodbye for now. More on Saturday at latest.

8 December 1961 *Grundisburgh*

I hope Jonah is not missing the Lit. Soc. for health reasons, though I expect Tommy L. is not fit enough yet. My exam-papers start coming in on Saturday, and, as always, there are a good many more than I bargained for. One lot I shall have to mark on a book whose contents I have almost completely forgotten. My cynical colleagues assure me that it is quite easy. I think, as Swift would have put it, that they are saying the thing that is not.

Your condemnation of that Pelican *Modern Age* pleases me; a great deal of it seems to me awfully bad. I appreciate too your derision of my pathetic attempts to keep abreast of the moderns. But habits are not easily uprooted. I must tell you that, having so repeatedly read that *Women in Love* is one of the greatest of novels, I have again started re-reading it, after about twenty years, and am about halfway through. There are fine things in it, but I remain convinced that when the D.H.L. *Schwärmerei* has died down the general opinion will be a lot of it is pretentious and unconvincing. So many of his subtle probings into man-woman relations are far outside any of *my* experience or the furthest range of my imagination that they strike literally no chord in my mind. If your answer is that this merely shows I am too stupid or at least too old-fashioned, I shall be quite ready to agree. But do have a look at the chapter headed 'Rabbit' and tell me how and why it isn't pointless not to say silly.

10 December *Bromsden Farm*

My plan to write some more yesterday was thwarted by my charmingly talkative neighbour—an attorney from Ohio with the reassuring name of Weller. The return trip (though equally well victualled and liquored) was less attractive than the outward one. A strong tail-wind caused such bumps, even at 30,000 feet, that we were several times ordered to fasten our safety-belts. Eventually (having taken off from New York at 10 a.m. their time (3 p.m. ours) we reached London air-port at 10.15 p.m. (our time), three quarters of an hour late. When the sickening, deaf-making descent was almost completed (down to a few hundred feet), the pilot decided there was too much fog, went into a steep climb, and announced our departure for *Ireland*! An hour later we landed in *pouring* rain at Shannon Airport. When I was last there (also unwillingly—I wonder if anyone ever goes there on purpose?) the building was a sort of converted shack. Now it is a huge emporium like the ground floor of Selfridge's, with dozens of counters at which one can buy *anything*, an efficient telephone service and a twenty-four-hour bar, at which all drinks were free (i.e. paid for by Pan-American Airways). I rang up Ruth in London, and Duff here, to find that Comfort was waiting with the car at London Airport.

Then followed an exceedingly tedious wait of two and a half hours. When I could take no more whisky I turned to coffee and ham sand-wiches. Eventually we took off again in the still heavy rain, and after another hour's flight came down safely at London A. It was then almost 3 a.m. and poor Comfort had been there for five hours. We got home and to bed by 4 a.m. I slept heavily, but all this morning could feel the aircraft throbbing under me.

My trip was, I think, a great success. All three days were cold, crisp, sunlit and blue-skied. I ate and drank and talked prodigiously, and drove almost three hundred miles to and from a seaside village in North Connecticut, where a novelist lives. Lunches and dinners were given for me, and I was presented with the magnificent Parker pen with which I am writing this. To fill it you simply hold the other end in a bottle of ink for a moment, without pressing any levers, and the ink flows in by capillary attraction! In a modest way I think my publishing fortune is made, and the whole thing is most exciting. *And* Oscar is finished. *Laus Deo*!

Next week you shall be brought up to date with home affairs, and your excellent letters shall be answered. Oh yes—Harcourt Brace are going to reissue my *Hugh Walpole* in a paperback edition in the U.S.A.

14 December 1961 *Grundisburgh*

Very good budget of interesting news from you, and now you are safe home in port. Those air-pockets must be supremely beastly and then the fog which sent you on to Ireland. Whenever one hears from anyone about a flight in winter one has the impression that the margin of safety was nothing to boast about. Humphrey was once ordered—with the other passengers—to throw all his luggage out, and the plane, after avoiding one foggy place after another, eventually landed with fifteen minutes' worth of petrol left. Diana in one plane accompanied two others to Yalta or somewhere—one of the other two planes crashed.

I am nearing the end of *Russia and the West* by George Kennan; it seems to me wonderfully good, though not making one exactly cheerful—except in comparison with Bertrand Russell's last book of essays, which literally hold out no hope.[1] In Boots I bought secondhand a book of L.P. Hartley's called *Facial Justice*. A failure, *qua* me. A sort of blend of Orwell and Aldous Huxley all about life after the third world war, when all life will be compulsorily underground. All very jolly and boring, as George Mathew said of some Wagner opera. My exam-papers pretty well fill my day.

What a grand writer for the young Macaulay is—so lucid and emphatic. They have been tackling his great Chapter III and I am stifled with exhaustive information about the Navy in Stuart times, the country gentleman, the new advances in science etc etc. They love such climaxes as 'In Charles II's navy there were both seamen and gentlemen, but the seamen were not gentlemen, nor the gentlemen seamen.' Simple and obvious no doubt, but a good true point.

16 December 1961 *Bromsden Farm*

Fog and Christmas between them must have prevented your letter from arriving this week. I was lucky getting down yesterday, for the fog was dense, and if I hadn't walked into the 4.18 to Reading at 4.55 (it left at 5.5) I might have had a long cold wait at Paddington.

[1] *Has Man a Future?* (1961).

Let me have your address at Eton: which day do you go there? Special preparations are being made for your luncheon on Boxing Day. Bridget will be here, and perhaps Duff and wife, though they may be out shooting.

The Lit. Soc. was shadowy without you. Only nine stalwarts turned up. We ate scampi with rice, roast duck and a pear dish or soft roes. Ivor was particularly sad at missing you again. It was just as well you hadn't got to negotiate the stairs at Soho Square last week, since the decorators are in charge, with scaffolding, planks and splashing paint. They are also in the flat, where confusion reigns, but all should be ship-shape and glistening by January. So far I have bought *no* Christmas presents, and the days are running out. I had hoped to find some little thing for Ruth in New York, but I simply hadn't a moment, and in any case the furious steam-heating of the shops there exhausts one in a few minutes. I can see that next week is going to be a busy one.

Sunday morning
Clear and frosty and sunny. We are just going to drive down to Henley to inspect a new Standard Vanguard, which the garage-proprietor is trying to persuade us to have instead of a new Morris Traveller (our present car is an M.T.).

It seems funny, after all these years, having no Oscar to do, and in a perverse way I slightly miss it, though for the most part I rejoice—and there is plenty of other work. This afternoon I must start reading the typescript of the second volume of Leon Edel's life of Henry James, which is immensely long and detailed. The new publishing arrangement is so exciting and many-sided that my office-time looks like being pretty full. I already have more work than one secretary can cope with, and may get a second one, or perhaps a dictaphone. Forgive this scrappy half-pay letter. Next week there should be two letters from you to answer, and I'll probably send a line to Eton before your visit.

Boxing Day 1961 *Bromsden Farm*

This is a poor substitute for several hours of your company, and we are all most disappointed—not least Comfort, who had prepared specially succulent dishes to tempt you. I do hope poor Pamela will soon be better—though I daresay bed's the best place in this icy weather. The little gifts you should have had at luncheon will be posted to Eton tomorrow, and I shall hope to see you at the January Lit. Soc.

On the Christmas tree I was given a magnificent new bird-table, specially made by Peter's estate-carpenter, but I shan't be able to instal it until the ground is a bit softer. Meanwhile the old one is increasingly popular and gives me much pleasure. Since I arrived on Friday evening I have scarcely set foot outside the house—it's quite cold enough inside.

Did I tell you that, in small print and double column, my Oscar index will occupy *eighty* of those large pages? No wonder it took me so long! I have now arranged to scrutinise each sheet of the book, after the final corrections have been made and before it is machined. They hope to send me one or two sheets (each of sixty-four pages) each week, so that will take several months. Also, when the first sheet is ready for press I shall go down to the printers at Frome and encourage them with well-deserved praise—a jay has just come on the bird-table, the first I've ever seen there. It dwarfed the other birds, but stayed only a moment.

Your description of the Grundisburgh Parish Council is most depressing. We are in the parish of Bix, but of its churchgoing or council I am woefully ignorant. I'm sure you're right, however, in thinking that nowadays everything depends on the personality and popularity of the incumbent. (The jay has returned—and departed.) Last time I took up Macaulay's Chapter III, I simply couldn't stop reading it. Soon I must try it again.

I'm sure you would be well-advised to put in oil-fired central heating. It requires *no* attention, except the occasional checking or alteration of a thermostat. If I ever amass enough money, I'll put it in here, and so greatly improve the value of Peter's property. Duff has gone shooting with P. this morning.

Evening

Duff shot two woodcock and two pigeons, walked *miles* in freezing cold, and seems to have enjoyed himself. During the holiday I have read the manuscript of the second volume of Leon Edel's biography of Henry James, which I greatly enjoyed, and also the second autobiographical venture of Vyvyan Holland, Oscar's son, which alas is very thin and banal. I don't know how on earth to tell him without hurting his feelings. Also I have done some work on Birley's proofs, and in bed have read or re-read *Kipps*, which on the whole stands up very well. The whole of Wells's first draft of the book, much longer than the published version, has turned up, and I felt I couldn't judge it without refreshing my memory. I'll report more of this next week.

A friend and contemporary of Adam's at Eton, James Loudon, went abroad at the same time as A., under the same scheme, but was sent to teach in a school in British Honduras. He had hardly got there when the whole school, and most of the town of Belize, was reduced to rubble by a hurricane, followed by a tidal wave. The boy wrote to ask if I could do anything about books, of which no single one survived. I sent him a parcel, and persuaded our trade paper, the *Bookseller*, to print a letter in which I appealed to all publishers and booksellers to send what they could: I've no idea whether they will respond. Birley, whom I met at a bibliographical dinner in London last week, told me the boy had written to him too, and he asked the school to help. This produced more than £500. Isn't that splendid!

Last Thursday the Duff Cooper Prize was presented most effectively by Mountbatten, who spoke easily, without notes and much to the point. He gave just the impression of unflappable *sang-froid* one would expect from the Navy. Champagne flowed and Diana was much pleased.

One evening Ruth and I went to Covent Garden to hear Tchaikovsky's opera *The Queen of Spades*, which we quite enjoyed. On the whole, opera is beyond my musical comprehension, but I want to see all the best ones at least once each, to make sure, and to see what they're about. Ruth has been spending Christmas with her son and his family in Essex. No telephone there, so we have been sadly separated, and I have been worrying about her ability to keep warm there. Tomorrow we shall be happily reunited. The stairs at Soho Square are now clean and bright, and the workmen start tomorrow on the bedrooms in the flat. Mine is to be painted dark red!

Pamela is still pretty feeble, though thanks be, it is not a severe attack. This house is fairly warm. Finndale, I expect, is frozen solid, but we haven't heard. The good plumber may have turned all the water off by now. I hope to come to the Lit. Soc. but I have been having bouts of 'aural vertigo' which make me *pro tem* entirely incapable of walking unsupported or even of standing up. So I may not be able to go to Cambridge on Tuesday. I will let you know. If it comes on in the underground I shall have to go round the whole circle before getting out. It is apparently connected with some kinds of deafness. Something happens in the inner ear which upsets the balance. Damnable!

I do practically nothing here except read. Neither my daughter nor her husband ever reads, but luckily my grandson has quite a readable library, though most of his books are at Oxford. He works every day at haberdasher Caley's in Windsor and is amassing quite a nice little pin-money. I have just re-read D.H. Lawrence's letters. There are far too many of them (880 pages). Many are very dull and not worth printing. What is the point of printing 'Frieda has just got herself a big coat because it is so cold'? What a bad critic he was—all prejudice and exaggeration. But I grant you there is something refreshing about his describing Joyce's *Ulysses* as 'a clumsy ollapodrida'. I don't like him; his way of biting most of the hands that fed him is not an amiable trait.

Do you know Ivor's *Master Sanguine*? Some fine satire in it about educational theories, party government, militarism, in fact most things; very good bedside reading—till one's hands become too cold.

What you say of Macaulay Chapter III applies to all of him. Fatal to look something up; you just go on reading. But I suppose to admire him is wholly out of date now. What bilge literary fashions are.

That is a heartening tale about the Belize hurricane and that school library. Eton did well and so will the booksellers and publishers of whom, you remember, Johnson always spoke warmly. Those hurricanes are a great strain on anyone's faith—as in fact a good many things are. I hope Adam won't come across one. Is he enjoying the work he is doing? Almost the only thing that matters.

Tell me all about the *Kipps* affair. I have not read it for many years, but remember liking it, although less than *Mr Polly*. To admire either is always said to have infuriated H.G.W., but I don't suppose it did really. Who said he sold his birthright for a pot of message?

You omitted to mention the insertion of a *lift* at No. 36, no doubt inadvertently. Not that my vertigo minds stairs; no one knows what it does or does not mind. Its usual moment for coming on is when I am sitting in a chair. The leech says it sometimes comes on in bed.

30 December 1961 *Bromsden Farm*

I hope you're pleased about Bernard's taking over from your nephew.[1] I don't see why your grip on that great Dominion should be in the slightest relaxed by the change, and I imagine it's an excellent appointment, though I'm doubtful as to B's soundness on the subject of cricket. We must educate him in that all-important branch of sovereignty.

Yesterday Birley came to the office, hot from addressing the School Librarians, and we went through his proofs. He is not a good proof-corrector, but lightning-quick in the uptake, and apparently grateful for my attempts to polish up his prose. I wonder what he'll do when he leaves Eton: write books, I hope. He tells me he has plenty of ideas for such.

Adam writes enthusiastically from his camp in South India. He has shot a spotted deer and explored the antiquities of Mysore and other neighbouring cities.

Today Duff and some farmer-friends of his shot 109 hares in a blizzard. The older I get the less do I sympathise with the systematic slaughter of birds and beasts—not that I was ever very keen on it.

The point about *Kipps* is that it was originally planned as a much longer, almost Dickens-sized, novel, and then reshaped in its known form. Wells believed that all the discarded chapters had been lost, but they have now come to light in the H.G.W. archive in the University of Illinois, and have been offered to me as a literary curiosity. I read

[1] As Governor-General of New Zealand.

almost half the new stuff this evening, and it's vintage Wells all right. The trouble is that I doubt whether, just now, many people are interested in *Kipps*—or Wells, for that matter. One day they will be again. Anyhow, if Illinois will take 1500 or so copies for America, I think I could sell a like number over here, and lose no money thereby.

One of my American colleagues (Jovanovich's No. 2) is over to conclude arrangements with Heinemann, and with any luck all should be tidied up sometime next week. Meanwhile there is plenty to be done—hiring new staff, buying machines, taking extra offices etc. All in the right direction and therefore stimulating. Now I shall go to bed. More in the morning.

Sunday morning

After more than *ten hours* of deep sleep I woke to find this new soft-fallen mask of snow over everything. Duff says it is eight inches deep on the front lawn, and I fear it may drift on the exposed part of the road between here and the main road. How and when we shall all get to London is a matter of conjecture.

Bridget has just announced that in ten minutes she is going to battle her way to the post-office, so I think I'd better send this, even if it's not full measure. Somehow I must be in London tomorrow morning, and maybe it would be wise to go up in daylight this afternoon.

Have I sent you a forthcoming book called *The Fleet that Jack Built*? I meant to send it, but probably forgot. I think it might amuse you. Jack is Jackie Fisher, and it's about the Navy and its admirals between 1868 and 1918—written by an admiral too.[1]

I am thinking of putting the price of Oscar up from three to four guineas, which I think it will stand.

Now Bridget is off—so I must stop.

3 January 1962 *Cambridge*

A good letter which caught me up at the University Arms Hotel Cambridge, where, judging by the forecasts, I may easily be marooned for many days, though my purpose is to leave on Saturday for 67

[1] Rear-Admiral Sir William Jameson.

Chelsea Square (Diana's). The prospect, climate, and general feeling here is Siberian, and how they delight in telling us that there is no sign of a change.

My vertigo *may* be improving, but I don't trust it yet. A friend here knows all about it as his brother-in-law has it. It *can* end in an operation which makes one ear stone-deaf but cures the vertigo. But somehow I don't think it will with me. I shall come to the Lit. Soc. if possible and will telephone to Soho Square on Monday if impossible. (And I never thought I should ever fill a page on my own health! How right Johnson was in regarding an ill man as a scoundrel.)

Yes, I was pleased to see Bernard's appointment—a very good one I thought it, though he won't hit any sixes against a visiting team. I wonder how handy he is with speechifying. To my nephew that is the real burden, as he always spends a lot of time in preparation, as all good men do except the born speakers like old Quickswood. Odd that he so bungled his speech in the prayer-book debate when a crowded house expected him to make the speech of his life. Somehow his heart was not in it. Birley is tremendously long-winded they say, Alington was as good as any, and my old uncle Edward too was very good. I have a strong suspicion that R.H-D. is too.

I agree with you about shooting. I was no great shakes at the art, but I gave it up deliberately after a few years because, simply, I did not enjoy killing things, though more than ready to devour the results of others' efforts. A roast pheasant in perfect maturity I always regard as a dish for the gods. Do you agree?

Kipps? H.G.W. is of course dead as a prophet and priest, but as a storyteller, I simply don't know. *K.* was a fine tale. *I* should like to see it at Dickens length. I rather hope you will have a stab at it.

Colin Eccleshare is here. He has somehow heard of your recent Heinemann transaction and wishes you luck. How right you are about Kitchener. My old uncle, the general, always disliked him intensely on much the same grounds as you do—an unscrupulous and heartless careerist. He also maintained that he was a very moderate general. He said nothing about his being a homosexual, repressed or open, you will be surprised to hear.

Your letter has been lying on the table while I write this and two of my colleagues have both commented on the elegance of your handwriting. How right they were. I am always writing on my knee and my writing has gone to pot. I hope only temporarily but it may be due to latent vertigo. Who shall say?

I don't know *The Fleet that Jack Built*, though I have a feeling I have seen it reviewed. My old friend Admiral William Fisher always had a great admiration for Jackie F., who surely was a great man, and no doubt at the end quite impossible.

6 January 1962 *Bromsden Farm*

I was afraid you might have been snowbound at Eton, and was relieved to know you had got safely to Cambridge. The snow was so deep here last Sunday morning and the roads so tricky that I went back to London that afternoon. Duff managed to get me to Henley station in his little car, but we couldn't even reach the main road until we had persuaded one of the farm-workers to go before in a tractor to flatten out a track for us. Altogether it took me *four hours* to reach the flat from here, but I was warm all the time, and able to read. Next morning, I learned later, the roads were worse still, and to cap it all my usual Monday morning train crashed into the buffers at Paddington and twenty people were taken to hospital. It's an ill wind . . . Most of my office staff failed to arrive till after lunch, and then we sent them straight home again. My American colleague John McCallum was in London all week, and we spent long hours, day after day, with lawyers and suchlike, before all was brought to a happy conclusion on Thursday evening. On Tuesday I never left my own office from 9 till 6.30, sending out for sandwiches for lunch, and on Wednesday I left the house at 9 a.m. and got back at 10.30 p.m.

My darling Ruth tactfully chose the week to get some sort of bronchial flu—tactfully because (a) I couldn't have spent any time with her if she had been well and (b) she had staying with her a devoted old retired lady-doctor, who nursed her delightedly. I'm hoping R. will be back by Tuesday, but she still sounds pretty feeble. If you can't face the rush-hour journey and the stairs, ring me up and we'll meet at the Garrick or elsewhere. If R. is well enough she will be longing to see you.

The painters finally evacuated the flat on Thursday, and I am now happily installed in my new scarlet-walled bedroom. Also a huge rearrangement of books is in progress, since now for the first time I can use the shelves which so long harboured E.B.'s library.

Yes, I must confess that I thoroughly enjoy roast pheasant, so long as someone else has shot it, out of my sight, but I shouldn't really *mind* being a vegetarian if need be, though I daresay one would soon get heartily sick of nut cutlets and all such.

I finished the Kitchener book simply *loathing* K, and almost pleased at his hopeless bungling of the War Office and the War. The knowledge that a massive attack at Gallipoli when it was first mooted would probably have taken Constantinople and perhaps ended the war is almost unbearable. Winston was right all along in that matter.

The Fisher book shall go to you on Monday. I stupidly thought I'd sent it already. It doesn't appear till the 22nd. Now I shall go to bed and finish in the morning. I am happily re-reading *The Diary of a Nobody* (rationed to one chapter a night, to spin it out) and *Edwin Drood*, which I had never read before and am much enjoying. Have you any strongly held theories as to what was going to happen? There's a vast literature on the subject, and most of the contestants are as cracked as Baconians.

Sunday morning

The snow has almost vanished, and everything is suddenly very green and soft. I expect you are safely in Chelsea Square. Bridget and Duff are making plans for a fortnight's winter sports in the Italian Alps at the beginning of February. Twelve of them are planning to take a chalet. I can't think of anything I should hate more—nonsense, I can think of plenty—but all the same—

Last Monday night, before Ruth took to her bed, she and I took the McCallums to a remarkable entertainment called *Stop the World, I Want to Get Off*. It was all written, words and music, by a chap called Anthony Newley, who is never off the stage all evening. Besides him there is one woman and perhaps a dozen pretty girls. Only one set, with very little in it. Newley is dressed as a clown, and the whole thing is a sort of satire on modern life. I thought it brilliant and enjoyed every minute. Goodness knows what the McCallums made of it, for a lot of the jokes are very English, if not Cockney.

13 January 1962 *Bromsden Farm*

Despite your prohibition, I think you must have at least a half-length letter to cheer you in your giddiness. You looked exceptionally well on Thursday, though I'm sure it only irritates you to be told so.

Yesterday morning I took my sister to the Augustus John memorial service at St Martin in the Fields. Apart from an abnormally high ratio of beards to pews, it was all immensely decorous and tasteful, and might have been in honour of any ambassador or social dignitary. A crowd of gipsies on a mountain-top, with plenty of wine and girls, would have been nearer the mark. I'm sure A.J. never set foot in a church after his childhood. David Cecil gave a well-written address, but his super-U accent, his tail-coat, and his position in the pulpit, made it all grotesquely unsuitable. Many of A.J.'s children and grandchildren were there, and I wondered how many illegitimate ones. He knew he was a genius and came to think it his duty to people the world with others. Did you know that Peter F's mother had a child of his? A pretty girl called Amaryllis, with his red hair and Mrs F's features. I remember the appearance of this baby when P. and I were at Eton, and even then in my innocence I thought Mrs F's account of how she had adopted this child, through Lord Dawson of Penn etc., rather unnecessarily protracted. Now she is a cellist of, I suppose thirty-seven, very good-looking and withdrawn. The most moving—the *only* moving—part of yesterday's service was when she suddenly appeared in the choir, looking very young and slim in black, with flaming red hair, carrying her cello, on which she played some unaccompanied Bach—rather too much I thought.

The first index-proofs of Oscar have arrived, and I am ashamed to see how often the compositors have misread my handwriting. Illiterate boors, I cry, wondering at the same time whether perhaps you and everyone else have the same difficulty.

My vertigo (I am pleased to find, in the teeth of all my Cambridge colleagues, that the i is long and not short as they said) is being held at bay *pro tem*, though I don't feel it to be very far away. It is, as you say, mildly vexatious to be told one is looking well and, *a fortiori*, when a leech, never yet suspected of being a humbug, says he has never seen a fitter man of seventy-nine.

Talking of pronunciation, several G.C.E. examiners maintained that ambiválent was the right pronunciation (some, it is true, were scientists) so after a bit I demurely asked for a word with an equiválent meaning, and also brought in preválent. Sheepish, my dear R, is the only word that sums up their demeanour.

The John funeral sounds very incongruous. How immensely absurd the English can be in such things. Victorianism has not really lost much of its grip. That is very interesting about Peter F's mother. But 'such a mistake' as old Sir G. Sitwell would have said, to play *un*-accompanied cello music, where very little goes a long way. The cello is (to me) the most splendid of all instruments, but not unaccompanied. A few bars emerging from the orchestra (as in the Mendelssohn violin concerto) always get me in the wind, as horns so often do in Beethoven.

Fancy the compositors boggling over your writing. I have never had a second's hesitation anywhere. They must be like those children who complain that they can't read the Italic hand (i.e. perfect legibility) because they are used to bad writing. Give these men the rough side of your tongue; they deserve it.

Rather a setback over *Edwin Drood*. My set of Dickens is by way of being complete, but *E.D.* is not there. Nor is it at the Ipswich Library. Is there a reasonably cheap edition of it? I have read *The Fleet that Jack Built* with great pleasure. What fine chaps good sailors always are. I particularly liked Tyrwhitt, who got into the navy at his third attempt thirtieth out of thirty-one! He has a splendid face—in fact they all have. Odd that old Fisher should have ignored the defensive equipment of the big ships. Anyone who knew the Germans must have known they would hit hard and accurately. The fact must be faced that Jutland really was a defeat. That the Germans never came out again merely shows that they never really acquired the naval spirit.

(Hitler didn't either.) But we had a lot of bad luck over those raids, when fog kept on saving them.

21 January 1962 *Bromsden Farm*

I am writing a day later than usual, since I only got back from Scotland yesterday, and it took twelve hours of solid sleep to get me back to normal. I travelled to Edinburgh on the Thursday morning train, eating a huge breakfast and lunch (neither first-rate. Oh for the food on French trains!), and jotting down a few headings for my speech. After Darlington I had the carriage to myself, so could try out a few sallies *à vive voix*. Robin Walpole (Hugh's brother) met me at 3 p.m., and we just had time for a cosy tea of scones etc at his house before catching the train for Glasgow. There was a good deal of preliminary talk and drink in a stifling bar, and then the annual dinner of the Scottish Bookmen, which was attended by seventy-four stalwarts, mostly booksellers or publishers' travellers. My speech went down tolerably well, and we just caught the last train back to Edinburgh. There was a bar on board, whisky flowed, and I was ready for bed when we got home soon after midnight.

Friday I spent peacefully in Edinburgh, visiting booksellers and looking at secondhand books, which I always adore. Robin Walpole lives in great comfort with *two* maids! and it was rather fun to find one's pyjamas cherishingly wrapped round a hot-water-bottle, etc. The city was looking very black and wintry, but as always beautiful, and the Castle dramatic. I enjoyed my day. I caught the 11 p.m. train, slept fairly well in a first-class sleeper, reached the flat at 7 a.m., had a bath and breakfast, and got down here in time for lunch. The new car has arrived and looks very smart, but I seldom enjoy change, and each new model seems less roomy and comfortable than its predecessor.

Steady rain has fallen ever since I arrived, and everything is awash. Tomorrow I am going down to Frome to see the ritual machining of the first sheet of Oscar. I have now passed 256 pages for press. The proofs of the index, which are still coming in, look as long as an ordinary book!

I am to stay tomorrow night with Tony Powell and his charming wife Violet (née Pakenham), and get back to London on Tuesday afternoon. Ruth came back to work last week, but is still a little feeble after her flu.

In his new book of memoirs, the actor Cedric Hardwicke is asked by an interviewer whether today he would recommend a young man to go on the stage, and answers: 'Certainly not: there's far too much competition. He'd do better to go into Parliament, where there's none.'

If you look at the current (February) number of a paper called *Encounter* you will find an article by Sparrow which seeks to prove that *Lady Chatterley's Lover* is in fact a handbook to buggery. What next? Some old Wardens of All Souls must be rotating in their coffins. I much prefer *The Diary of a Nobody*, which I am enjoying more than ever. When did you last read it? Have you got a copy?

Adam writes regularly and cheerfully from India. His coloured parrot has escaped: otherwise he seems to have no complaints, and is planning to visit Kashmir and the Taj Mahal in the next holidays, whenever they are.

So glad you enjoyed the Jackie Fisher book: it appears tomorrow, with three other books—my first publications of the year. We have managed to take eight more office-rooms, not in Soho Square but in Dean Street, immediately across the well outside my office-windows. Here we are assembling the accounts and invoicing departments which were disbanded when we entered the Heinemann group. We shall need all the new rooms—and more I daresay—when our educational books start to appear. Harcourt Brace's head textbook man has just arrived for a three-months stay, in which he is to investigate and report on the whole question. He is said to work sixteen hours a day and exhaust three secretaries: I haven't yet found him one. Perhaps the more sedative air of London will slow him down a little.

The Max B. plaque is now ready, and as soon as it is in place in the crypt of St Paul's I shall have to arrange a consecration and unveiling ceremony. If it isn't one thing, it's another. Now I must go to bed.

Your Scotch trip sounds good (except that surely breakfasts *used* to be good on English railways?). Pamela grinned complacently when I read out how at R. Walpole's your pyjamas had been wrapped round your hot-water-bottle because she always does that with mine. She has recovered from a nasty bout of flu at Christmas, when she did not avoid pneumonia by a large margin, but still rests for two hours in the afternoon. Tell dear Ruth she must do the same. Our good doctor says the main thing about this onset of flu is not to *hurry*. What a damnable complaint it is! My vertigo has not attacked lately, but I long to get rid of the feeling that it isn't far round the corner. P. robustly maintains that is nerves, and she may be half right—but not more.

Is Hardwicke's book good? I always liked his acting. Yes, it must be a dreadful, fluky, up-and-down life. 'Overpaid casual labour' was what Gerald du Maurier called it, and he was a star—and apparently always plunged in depression. Old Arthur Benson once told me the most dreadful thing about melancholia was, as Shakespeare put it in one line 'With what I most enjoy contented least', for of course some quack told him to carry on with all his favourite ploys—and they all turned to dust in his mouth. Is it not odd that if A.C.B. came into the room, I should respectfully get up and generally kowtow—and he died when fifteen years younger than I am now? Once your tutor always your tutor is no doubt true.

I am re-reading *Pickwick*. Do you realise what an old tippler Mr P. was? I suppose they all were in the 1830's—just as a reader in 2050 will see our age as one of fornication, not of drink. But the end is not yet; something much more portentous than 1914 or 1939 is on the way. Some demonstration by the Almighty that he is not mocked, or what?

I am also reading (don't laugh) Leavis's *D.H. Lawrence, Novelist*. I must try and find out what the man's greatness is supposed to be—particularly in that sticky *Rainbow* and *Women in Love*. So far F.R.L. is disappointingly peevish and sneery with those who don't agree with him, and anyway I know *that* is wrong. You seem to be wavering in your support of *Lady Chatterley*. I shall certainly get the February

Encounter. John Sparrow may be much lazier than he should be, but he has never written anything that was not abundantly worth reading.

I haven't read *The Diary of a Nobody* for a long time, but I remember enjoying it, though my favourite in that genre was always Burnand's *Happy Thoughts*, which I shall quote from to you when we next meet (February 13 unless I am still vertiginous). I am full of hope. I look forward to seeing your renovated flat, and speeding aloft in the lift. It is clear the R.H-D. publishing business is on the crest. Fine. Love to Ruth. Mind you *insist* on her resting daily.

27 January 1962 *Bromsden Farm*

Aren't you glad you're not dressed in a space-suit and waiting to be rocketed to blazes? That man must have nerves of steel, and I shall be in a much worse dither next Tuesday, when I am to have a decayed wisdom-tooth removed. I am insisting on a general anaesthetic, since I hate the suffocating feeling of the gas-mask, and a local anaesthetic leaves the horrors all too visible and audible. Ruth has promised to hold my hand and take me home afterwards.

Warmed pyjamas are heavenly: I might have known that Pamela would so cherish you. Ruth told me yesterday that she was *just* beginning to feel human again after her flu. I keep trying to persuade her to rest after lunch, but it is seldom easy to arrange.

Thank goodness you're reading *Pickwick* to counteract that frightful Leavis. One day you must just forget all about D.H.L. Life without him is fine, I promise you.

Last Monday I travelled down to Somerset and spent a delightful evening and extremely comfortable night with the Powells in their charming house near Frome. Next morning I drove over to the printer's to see the ritual printing of the first sixty-four pages of Oscar. Needless to say, after a few minutes the machine broke down, and to allay my disappointment they took me on a ruthlessly conducted tour of the works. Seeing round any factory soon produces a state of acquiescent coma, as the exact performance of each monstrous engine is bellowed out at one above the din. After a couple of hours I was mercifully driven to Bath, where I caught a train to London and had quite a good lunch on it.

That night Ruth and I went to a private showing of an excellent movie that has been made from a first novel we published called *The Custard Boys*: do you remember it?[1] On Thursday we dined with the Reichmanns (Mrs R. is Elisabeth Beerbohm's sister) and were given a dinner so deliciously rich and enormous that we felt peculiar for the next twenty-four hours. First a soufflé filled with salmon and asparagus, then a haunch of miraculously tender venison, with cranberry sauce and sauerkraut; then a pudding of the shape and consistency of a cake, which was in fact a rum-laced trifle, then some cheese. All washed down by quantities of Rhine wine that tasted of grapes. They had clearly laid it all on specially for us, and my word we did full justice to it! Talking of venison, I saw six or seven deer in the next field as I drove home from the station last night.

Sunday morning, 28 January

I am reading, with great enjoyment, that first volume of the life of J.A. Froude that appeared some months ago. I ordered it immediately, but the O.U.P. has only just vouchsafed a copy. The great merit of the book is that most of it is in Froude's own words (hitherto unpublished) and he wrote beautifully. His prose is a joy to read. Do get the book from the library. The author's name is Waldo Hilary Dunn, and he hails, believe it or not, from Wooster, Ohio. Here is Froude on his first school:

> The master, Mr Lowndes, was rector and patron of the living. He was assisted in the teaching department by his brother and by three ushers, as they were then universally called, though converted now into masters by the ambitious vulgarity of the age.

That was written in the 1890's. What would the old fellow think of *our* age, I wonder?

The devoted old lady who sends out all the Lit. Soc. cards absent-mindedly addressed Sparrow's to All Souls College, Cambridge. Some wag in the Cambridge P.O. wrote 'Try Oxford' on it, and

[1] By John Rae (1960).

it eventually arrived safely. The post seems to have speeded up a little this past week, but the only way to make certain of quick delivery is to express a letter or parcel. Stuff from abroad seems to arrive quicker than anything else. I think I can dodge tomorrow's chaos by getting a lift in someone's car from Paddington—if my train ever gets there. Quite a lot of my staff come from south of London and probably won't arrive at all. That happened in the freeze-up at the New Year, and we had nobody in the building who knew how to work the switchboard, so the telephone was happily silent. You are well out of London these days, but I do hope your vertigo and the traffic will let you come to the February Lit. Soc.

1 February 1962 *Grundisburgh*

Let me know about that tooth. I had one of my two surviving wisdom teeth out a fortnight ago—local anaesthetic, never felt a thing. I wonder what *visible* horrors you refer to; there is nothing to see but the determined face of the ivory-snatcher. I face now a lower plate, which all say is much more uncomfortable for some reason than the top one. At present I bite only on one side.

Pickwick of course was very refreshing. I skip a good deal—all about the boring fat boy, Mr Winkle, Mr Snodgrass, Solomon Pell, but there is plenty of compensating richness. I am now re-reading all the U.S.A. part of *Martin Chuzzlewit*. The Yanks' chief claim to greatness is that they forgave Dickens his really blistering picture of them. Jefferson Brick, Hannibal Chollop, Mrs Hominy, Elijah Pogram—they all scintillate with gems of absurd speech whose appeal never dims. But what an ass Dickens could be. Pecksniff should have been left a figure of fun, not become a plotter and a villain. Similarly Squeers in *Nicholas Nickleby* should have been left a grisly comic instead of developing into a serious swindler. And all the Gride etc part of *N.N.* I find unreadable, in fact I finish more or less when N. has met the Cheerybles. Sir Mulberry Hawk won't really do. (By the way, have you ever heard any explanation of the *twenty-five*-mile walk which Dickens sent old Wardle, Pickwick etc on on December 24? They would hardly have got home before breakfast on December 25. I believe Bernard

Darwin maintained that D. meant it as a joke—surely a very inferior one?)

I have every intention of coming to the dinner, but cannot yet be certain. Almost all the time I feel slightly sick, which takes all the *joie de vivre* out of one—which at seventy-nine is in any case rather a fragile plant. Many risks can be taken—heart, asthmatic onset, lumbago etc., but not actual sickness. But no one surely has *always* felt sick; there must be an end, though it may still be some weeks distant.

That was fine feeding you had with the Reichmanns. Venison needs very careful timing if tastelessness is to be avoided on the one hand and a dreadfully pungent over-ripeness on the other, though no doubt dear Dr Johnson would have relished the latter. I have a grim memory of a parent's gift of venison for my boys. I don't think it was really very long past its prime, but of course it smelt far worse than it tasted and very few boys faced it. No domestics of course will ever touch game of any kind however perfect. The only reason I have ever heard is the slightly mean one that they aren't going to eat anything that has not been paid for.

Froude has been on my list for weeks. He has always seemed to me a good man, but how they did pitch into him. His English is lovely—without, oddly, the smallest tinge in it of Carlyle whom he so greatly admired.

I am very glad the Prince is not going to Eton. The snob tourists would have made the place quite intolerable. From one or two parents who have had experience of it, Gordonstoun sounds an excellent school—with *apparently* less dead wood than many schools. Education is in just as much of a mess as anything else, in fact what isn't? Starting from my stomach.

4 February 1962 *36 Soho Square*

The decorators are at work on the hall, stairs, landing and bathroom at Bromsden Farm, so the house is pretty well uninhabitable and Comfort has gone to stay with a neighbour for a few days.

Yesterday Ruth and I went down to Brighton for the day, which we much enjoyed. It was a soft grey misty day, the sea calm and benign, as we walked the length of the front, breathing in the lovely seaweedy air. I was distressed to find that the secondhand bookshop in Hove that I had patronised since my earliest bookbuying boyhood had gone out of business. I can remember my mother urging me along the promenade with promises of this shop at the end of the walk, and I grieved at this snapping of another link with what Henry James called 'the visitable past'. However, we picked up a few trifles at other Brighton bookshops, ate an excellent lunch of fish-and-chips followed by treacle roll, breathed in a little more ozone and came peacefully back to Soho Square, to await the End of the World. I haven't yet had Adam's account of Indian reactions, but according to the press they are in a fine stew. When nothing happens they will doubtless attribute the miracle to the efficacy of their own prayers.

As a foretaste of judgment last Monday's traffic-chaos in London was quite enough to be going on with. I was lucky enough to get a lift from Paddington in a friend's car, and thereafter managed on foot. For miles round here the streets were solid with stationary vehicles for most of the day, and my poor Bridget, who had owned her first precious car for only a week, was run into broadside by a motor-bicycle in Eaton Square. No one was hurt, but it was clearly a beastly shock, and the car got a nasty bash.

The worst thing about the extraction of my wisdom-tooth was the apprehension beforehand. At the time I felt nothing—Pentothal works at once and leaves no aftermath beyond a slightly tipsy feeling for an hour or two. The chap who skilfully administered it turned out to be the man I sold our Highgate house to in 1946. Ruth came with me to hold my hand and waited next door. That evening I graciously (but with a trace of guilt and dishonesty) consented to be treated as an invalid and given my dinner in bed, but the whole thing was very little trouble. My objection to a local anaesthetic is first of all *hearing* it all happening, and then I imagine gouts of blood. Anyhow I much prefer Pentothal.

I must soon read *Martin Chuzzlewit* again: it used to be one of my favourites. I'm sure that the changes in so many of Dickens's characters (Pecksniff, Squeers etc) were due to the difficult and unnatural way he had to write his novels, for the monthly part-issues. He was seldom an issue ahead, and I imagine had only a rough plan of what was to happen, and how the characters were to develop. Also, he several times wrote two novels at once. In fact it's a wonder the plots hold together as well as they do.

8 February 1962 *Grundisburgh (Summer-house)*

First of all *I am* coming on Tuesday, unless there is a railway strike. I am not *quite* well yet, but at seventy-nine who is? And I was encouraged recently by a friend who said he once had six months, during which he felt sick every day, but after finding he never *was* sick, he got used to and ignored it. If I turn out to be too optimistic next Tuesday evening, well that will be jolly bad luck on the Lit. Soc. The vertigo has been in abeyance now for a month and more.

I am sending this to Soho Square as you may be still unhouseled. For all I know you are also unaneled,[1] but I am not precisely seized of its meaning.

To-morrow I start a lower-jaw plate, which everybody (except my dentist) says is always uncomfortable for weeks. My only originals left are the eight front ones in the lower jaw, which apparently are always the last to go. I may possibly be writing next week to the dentist, as the old woman pensioner did 'My top ones are all right but those in my bottom are very painful.' The worst thing about the local anaesthetic, to my mind, is the piercing of the gum. The actual extraction is completely painless. Of course for some seven or eight hours afterwards that half of one's face seems to belong to someone else.

My memory is awful. I read in some recent book that R.H-D's biography of Hugh Walpole was one of the really outstanding books of the last twenty years, and, ass that I am, cannot remember the author. Clearly a man who knew what was what. I was pleased to read a strong complaint by Connolly in the *Sunday Times* about modern criticism, which never says that a book is good reading, but talks aridly about technique. Apropos of Leavis's remark recently about Max Beerbohm in the *Spectator*, I nearly wrote a letter quoting Lamb's

[1] *Hamlet*, act I, scene 5.

very sharp-pointed question to Coleridge, 'whether the higher order of Seraphim *illuminati* ever sneer', because a great deal of Leavis's line about poets or novelists that he doesn't like and their admirers is not that they are mistaken but that they are contemptible. I do wish someone like H. Nicolson would blow him sky-high.

10 February 1962 *Bromsden Farm*

All here is still confusion and smell of paint; moreover the library stove has given out, and the experts are slow in coming. Instead I have got an oil-stove in temporary use: it gives out lots of heat, but occasionally emits a disconcerting gurgle. Snowdrops and crocuses (yellow) are out, but winter seems otherwise very much with us. No news from our winter-sporting children beyond a postcard to say their aeroplane had reached Geneva safely. The headmaster of Adam's school (a Sikh) is clearly a most enlightened and imaginative man. He recently told A. that he (A) was doing just as much work as any of the other masters, and it was ridiculous that he should only be paid £1 a week. He proposed therefore, not to pay him a larger salary, but to pay for his first-class fares and expenses in any travel he wanted to do, since he had come to India to see the country as well as to teach. Isn't that splendid! Adam took immediate advantage of this generous offer and travelled in state to Delhi, where he witnessed a gigantic Republic Day parade. He is now back at the school, but has designs on Kashmir and the Taj Mahal. I must write and thank the excellent Sikh.

In the middle of my last bout of correcting this afternoon, I took half an hour off, to clear my head, and read the opening chapters, one after the other, of *Oliver Twist, Nicholas Nickleby* and *Great Expectations*. All are good and made me want to re-read all three books immediately, but *G.E.* is infinitely the best—much the most sharp and assured. I wish I had time to read *all* Dickens in the right order, so as to observe his growing mastery of technique (the overflowing genius of creation was always there).

Last week Ruth and I went to *The Cherry Orchard*, which we enjoyed enormously. It is superbly acted, very funny and continuously moving. Also I had a final session with my Uncle Duff's books. Many they are keeping, some are to be sold, some given to the London Library, some given to me.

Bernard F. rang up yesterday to say he can't after all come to the Lit. Soc. because he and Laura have received a royal invitation for that evening. He is tremendously pleased and excited about his appointment, but has been overwhelmed by *seven hundred* letters of congratulation. After living in Scotland with two daily women, it will be fun for them having A.D.C.'s, ladies in waiting, butlers, chauffeurs and goodness knows what.

Sunday morning, February 11

The sun is shining, and Comfort is putting me to shame by digging outside the window. If I had one of those jobs that finish when one leaves the office I should probably be a busy (if fine-weather) gardener. As it is, each week-end I hopefully bring home more work than I can possibly do, and the garden suffers. Don't misunderstand me: all I do anyhow is the rough work—weeding and repairing the brick paths, tidying, clipping and so on. All the real gardening is done by Comfort, and she is very good at it. Duff loves really hard work, like cutting down trees, and the other children are prepared to work the motor-mower in moderation. I wish to goodness we could get a man to do it, but we are too far from everywhere, though nowadays even the cowmen seem to have their own cars.

My increase of salary since the H.B. take-over means that in a month or two I shall have no overdraft, and I simply can't remember when that was last the case. I have grown so used to hand-to-mouth economy, and never knowing where next half's school-fees are coming from, that this new situation is quite disconcerting.

12 February 1962 *Grundisburgh*

De profundis—not quite in the O.W. sense but from a welter of humiliation, rage, disappointment, and malaise. The fact simply is that with this beastly feeling, I know that at no gathering, however alluring, could I either get or give pleasure, and there you are. One can only back out. Please give my special regrets to Ivor and Jonah *qua* the dinner and, *a fortiori*, much stronger ones for missing you and Ruth beforehand.

I am now starting on *Dombey and Son*. I believe it is Jock Dent's favourite.

15 February 1962 *Grundisburgh*

I still remain the leech's headache. A liver-complaint hitherto confined to the entourage of the Akond of Swat is *my* diagnosis. The faculty's only suggestion is that in about a week, if no better, I should go and be investigated and x-rayed etc at the Ipswich hospital, so no doubt some day all will be as serene as it ever can be at seventy-nine.

You will of course be letting me know all about the Lit. Soc. (and the fare thereat). I don't often quote T.E. Brown—except of course 'God wot' etc in mockery, but I have recalled another poem of his in which I seem to recall the refrain 'And I not there!' And on Tuesday evening I felt every bit as sentimental as he did.

I like the idea of your taking a spell of *Dickens* to *clear* your head; but I suppose he is rather like a plunge into the sea. I have left off *Dombey*—found I must have read it too recently and remembered it too well. Also I found Miss Tox and Captain Cuttle a bit wearisome—as also is the incredible Dombey himself. Carker's teeth are mentioned *every* time he appears; so are Captain Cuttle's signature remarks. But I am embarking on *The Moonstone*, which I last read when a boy at Eton and have forgotten every word of. Tell me what you think of it—it may I suppose be called the first detective story. Shall I be disappointed? The Clough book is on my list.[1] The young reviewers have been, *me judice*, all wrong about him. He was much better than they say. Of course there is something faintly absurd about a man who loses his faith and then bemoans the fact, but I am blowed if there isn't a lot of good stuff in 'Dipsychus'. Easy enough of course to be superior and sniffy about hexameters and varsity reading-parties of a hundred years ago, but I enjoyed 'The Bothie' at Cambridge.

A joke I wanted to mention to Ivor (and you) is that the Prince o

[1] *Arthur Hugh Clough: the Uncommitted Mind* by Katherine Chorley (1962).

Wales's headmaster at Gordonstoun was once H.M. of Salem wherever that may be, and Mr Creakle (*David Copperfield*) was Headmaster of Salem House. But I have a frightful misgiving I may have told you that already. Don't tell me if I have. Only forgive.

Your picture of Bernard F. cosseted by a battalion of servants is too rosy. *All* domestics leave in troops directly they find that at any other job they get higher wages. Their whole wage-scale is even more monstrous than ours; it has been a constant worry to Charles's wife.

Well, that is all I am strong enough to write, and far more than you are strong enough to read, and that is that.

P.S. Clough. I should of course have mentioned 'Amours de Voyage'.

---

17 February 1962 *Bromsden Farm*

Your last week's letter was waiting for me in the office on Monday morning, and on Tuesday I got your pathetic signing-out note. Too bad: we were all, including Ruth, most disappointed at not seeing you. It was a week of ceaseless activity. On Monday Ruth and I attended a cocktail (or rather, thank heaven, a champagne) party on Campden Hill in pouring rain, then went on to dine at the Café Royal with Allen Lane, the originator and head of Penguin Books. It was the night of the National Sporting Club's annual do, and the whole place was swarming with outsize bruisers in dinner-jackets. Tuesday was the Lit. Soc., of which more anon. On Wednesday I went to the theatre with Flash Harry, Princess Marina and her sister Princess Olga. The play was *Becket*,[1] which I saw in New York last year but enjoyed again. After it we were conveyed in a huge Rolls to the Savoy Grill, where we had an excellent dinner. Flash H. told a number of near-dirty stories, which the royal ladies clearly knew they couldn't avoid, and then Princess Olga told a charming one: 'Once upon a time there was a king who had two daughters, one blonde and beautiful, the other dark and exceedingly plain. The son of a neighbouring monarch came in search of a wife, and the two girls were paraded for

[1] By Jean Anouilh.

him, the dark one in superb clothes and the blonde one clad only in her flowing hair. Which one do you think he chose? The answer is that he chose their father, for this is a fairy story.'

I like both the princesses very much, and was much flattered to think that they must have suggested my making a fourth, as I'm sure Flash Harry didn't, though he couldn't have been nicer. On Thursday Ruth and I went to *Don Giovanni* at Covent Garden: a superb production of a superb opera, but it went on for three and a half hours with only one interval, and the seats weren't made for anyone my size.

When I tell you that I was also out to lunch every day, and dictated more letters than my secretary had time to type, you will realise why I arrived home exhausted last night. And what did I find? The two painters, who had already reduced the house to piles of paint-pots, dustsheets and heaped furniture, both collapsed with bronchitis on Tuesday and haven't been seen since! Chaos reigns, but thank God the library stove has at last been mended, so all's well in here, and I have a mass of overdue manuscripts to occupy my week-end.

If you had to miss a Lit. Soc. this was quite a good one to choose—for two reasons: (1) the dinner wasn't as good as usual (and, as I have long feared they would, the club is putting up the charge from 21/- to 25/-) and (2) Lockhart was all too present. I had prudently insulated myself by asking Sparrow and Tony Powell to sit on either side of me, but Lockhart was on Tony's other side, with poor Ivor beyond him. I thought Lockhart (whom mercifully we hadn't seen for a year) was looking very old and ill, but it soon became apparent that his wits have gone. *Four* times in as many minutes he asked Ivor who was sitting on Tommy's right, four times Ivor said 'Alan Moorehead', and four times Lockhart countered 'He wrote a very bad book', meaning, I suppose, the one on the Russian Revolution, in which L. thinks he has a prescriptive right. At the coffee-stage Ivor asked if he could come and sit next to me, leaving Harold Caccia to cope as best he could. There is unfortunately nothing in the rules to remove members when they become gaga, so we must just hope he doesn't come often. Tommy has promised to take him on next time, but I don't think he fully appreciates what he's in for. Afterwards Roger walked back with me to Soho Square and stayed a little while, gossiping agreeably.

How is your lower-jaw plate? I feel most sympathetic about it, since I dread false teeth, and so far rely on my own, which are mostly metal.

Adam has visited the Taj Mahal, but ran out of money there and had to get through the day on a bag of peanuts. No doubt this fasting sharpened his aesthetic propensities. The other two are due back from the Alps tomorrow. When we last heard, only one member of the party had broken a leg.

21 February 1962 *Grundisburgh*

I was rather disappointed when your last letter came to find no reference at all to anything in *my* last letter, but then I realised I had been rather late in posting it and it might well not have arrived till Monday. I was wrong. It was posted all right but *was* carefully addressed to the secretary of a girls' school who returned it yesterday. She is a puffick lady and I am pretty sure did not read it, but I rather apprehensively re-read it, and was reassured to find it was not 'scored with startling blasphemies' as Dr Jekyll's holy book was by Mr Hyde, or even with the mildest Rabelaisianism. But it annoys me much that you must have thought that sour little grouch about my shirking the Lit. Soc. was regarded by me as my weekly letter. And in the end it is you who suffer, because you get two letters by one post, which is what the evangelist meant by full measure pressed down and *running over*. And you made no complaint about my apparent lapse!

Roger told me that Lockhart's mind seemed to be giving way—like my old uncle, who was however eighty-six; he used to be reminded, when he got to the end of a story, of the beginning, so it went like chain-smoking—very hard for the audience to keep its face. Otherwise it sounds a good party. *The Moonstone* is fine—no sign of it coming to an end for several more days. I feel there may be some tragedy to come, either via the Indians or the Quicksand which has already had one victim.

I have paid another visit to the leech and am now to go and be examined by the hospital consultant. There is something vaguely wrong round about the liver. You can't surely have gall-bladder adhesions thirty-seven years after the operation. Nature is a good deal of an ass but surely not such an ass as that.

Flash Harry of course *does* bound for all his amiability—the kind of man who, I am sure, is at his most bounding with women. Does Ruth know him? I trust her judgment. Sorry about your constricted seat at the most delicious of all operas. It always takes the edge off one's enjoyment. As Winston once said of oratory 'The head cannot take in more than the seat can endure.'

How right you are about regrets for books one has discarded. I am always wanting the books I got rid of when leaving Eton for here. I wonder what Adam's reactions to the Taj Mahal were. To my eye the mere pictures of it show it as of overwhelming beauty. Does it ever disappoint?

I must stop—slightly short measure, but I feel compunctious about inflicting a sort of *Mabinogion*[1] in one post. Love to Ruth. I bet she revelled in *Don Giovanni*.

P.S. My plate, thank you, is perfectly comfortable, and I can now eat anything—except caramels for obvious reasons.

24 February 1962 *Bromsden Farm*

Two excellent letters in one envelope were waiting for me here last night. My only fear last week was lest you might be feeling too groggy to write, and I am much relieved, even though your doctor's diagnosis doesn't sound very certain. Let me know what they say at the hospital. Perhaps you are suffering from that diverticulitis which I seem to have made so popular of late?

I didn't mention the fare at the last Lit. Soc. because it wasn't good. Harold N. (just back from his cruise) admits that Lockhart's wits are going and says we must just hope they go quickly. Harold was responsible for Lockhart's membership in the first place. I thoroughly enjoyed *The Moonstone* when I last read it (ages ago) and am sure I should again. Did not T.S.E. write an introduction to the World's

[1] A series of Welsh tales, mostly about Arthur and the Round Table. An edition in three volumes was published by Lady Charlotte Guest in 1838–1849.

Classics edition? I should also try *The Woman in White*, which I also thought great fun.

Adam was bowled over by the beauty of the Taj Mahal and used a whole roll of coloured film trying to capture some of his pleasure.

Last week was mercifully a little less strenuous than its predecessor, but on Tuesday I took part in a lunchtime *divertissement* in the Holborn Central Library. There were three performers, allotted fifteen minutes each. First I read some poems from books I publish; then Pamela Frankau spoke very charmingly about her books and others; then my dear friend William Plomer read some of his own poems. 150 stalwarts attended (free of charge) and seemed to enjoy it all. Afterwards we were regaled with sandwiches and whisky by the Mayor and Librarian.

I still have the final proofs of some 150 pages of Oscar to correct (or rather check) when they come in, but already I have begun, in a desultory, shuffling sort of way, to assemble the materials for two minor projects which have been held off for ages by Oscar's continuance. They are (1) the editing of Max's letters to Reggie Turner[1] and (2) the compiling of the definitive bibliography of the works of E. Blunden. This last is a labour of love and requires only time and a clear head, for in my office I have the most complete collection of his writings that exists. I am so accustomed to having some editing or kindred work on hand that I feel rather empty without any, and neither of these jobs will tax me unduly.[2]

I have at last managed to get Max's plaque erected in the crypt of St Paul's, and the Dean has promised to dedicate it in April, when S.C. Roberts will make a speech. In August Max's ninetieth birthday is to be celebrated by the publication of a large anthology of his work.[3]

28 February 1962 *Grundisburgh*

I am writing before the hospital visit, so there is nothing new for the moment. I don't know that I expect much, and I suspect I may be

[1] Published in 1964.

[2] The Blunden bibliography eventually passed from my nerveless grasp into the capable hands of Miss Brownlee Kirkpatrick, who published it triumphantly in 1979.

[3] *The Incomparable Max* (1962).

involved in a long series of 'trial and error' transactions. *Nous verrons.* I should like to feel perfectly well again. How impressive it would be if one day you announced to the Lit. Soc. that one of its members was suffering from diverticulitis.

I note your recommendation of *The Woman in White*. Is it still in print I wonder? How refreshing it is to make one's way through a long story full of human beings who behave as such, and when one really wants to know what is going to happen. I have finally decided (quite impenitently) that I am a square, a fuddy-duddy, an incurable middle brow, the sort of reader he who shall be nameless sneers at, as one who thinks Housman a good poet.

I have now read *A Question of Upbringing*[1] and much enjoyed it though I am mystified about its exact significance. I like his neat and pertinent English. Le Bas has a good deal of Goodhart, not much of McNeile I think, who was a frightful ass. He succeeded to my beloved Arthur Benson and had every boy agin him in three weeks with his persistent fussiness and suspicion, and all the staff too. How good Tony P's picture of that French *pension* is and its inmates, and I feel I know Widmerpool nauseatingly well. What is Tony P's next one?

Shall we Maximilians be notified of the Max B. ceremony? Not if it depends in any way on Jock Dent who must be the least efficient secretary that ever was.

(Later) I have just had an immense interview with the leading Ipswich doctor and am in for a spell of x-rays and blood-tests etc with God knows what results. All that is so far certain is that I have a slightly enlarged liver, but he added reassuringly that very many people have. I shall report to you what they say—obstinately ignoring the truth that you do not in the least want to hear it. But even Dr Johnson did sometimes report, e.g. 'Dropsy threatened, but seasonable physic averted the inundation.' I hope to feel less of a worm in a week or two. I couldn't feel more.

Love to dear Ruth. The idea of her being a grandmother is ridiculous.

[1] The first volume (1951) of Anthony Powell's *A Dance to the Music of Time*.

[*My letter of 3 March has vanished, amazingly the only one of the whole correspondence to do so.*]

7 March 1962 *Grundisburgh*

I become daily more like a Russian diplomatist capable of no answer to any proposal but 'No, no.' They keep postponing their exploration of my interior, and till that has happened, I am still too dicky to face a Lit. Soc. What particularly dishes me is the walking and stair-climbing etc, all the things one has to do in going from place to place in London. It is all thoroughly damnable, and at times I think it is going on for ever. But Pamela does not allow me to express that view.

You are determined that I shall remain a square, and I expect you are right. I shall never make the other grade. I await with hope C.P. Snow's riposte to all those mannerless dogmatisms of the Downing seer, but he perhaps prefers silent contempt. I shall go on with Tony Powell, but he is pretty popular and the library is usually short of his books. I look forward to reading the Irish tales you have just kindly sent. I see you are publishing two Ibsen plays. I hope they are better translated than the Archer ones. A. seemed, from what I can remember, to think that 'Hem' was a common English ejaculation. It always pulled one up.

I have had rather a failure with *The Return of the Native*. Not much interested. My fault probably. Among the countless questions the consultant asked me were several which seemed clearly to be investigating my sanity, so it may be that I am in the position of the sieve which complained of the pump for not filling it. You will be reminded of me in Jocelyn Brooke's literary article in today's *Times*. He admits to doing what you always urge me to do, i.e. abandon the struggle to keep up. J.B. finds D.H.L. unreadable. A man after my own heart.

I have just heard that the x-ray cannot be done for at least a fortnight. Depressing. I may score off them by passing out with an undiagnosed gastric ulcer. Unlikely, but these delays do one's nerves no good.

My outlook at the moment on practically everything is pessimistic. I am only cheerful when reading a letter from you or writing one to you. A worm and no man. Love to Ruth.

I am outraged at the way these doctors keep you waiting for their idiotic opinions. No wonder you're depressed, but you must try not to be. The spring is coming, and you will soon be holding the Lit. Soc. table in thrall once again. In fact I couldn't recommend the youngest and healthiest person to come to London as it has been just lately, with that cutting east wind and an insufficiency of taxis. Today has been warmer, but at the cost of incessant rain. Compton Mackenzie has got things properly organised: all the winter he hibernates in his warm Edinburgh flat, emerging only with the daffodils, or even later. I suppose that, if it wasn't for our hellish winter, we shouldn't appreciate the spring so much, and that to live in Southern California where the sun shines *every* day might grow wearisome—but there are days when I have my doubts.

I think you will enjoy the book on the Marconi Scandal.[1] The author started out without any *parti-pris*, and wrote the book for the best possible reason—that she wanted to read a book on the subject, and there wasn't one. Gradually she came to realise, as any unprejudiced reader must, that Isaacs and Lloyd George were saved by Asquith and the Liberals, who covered them up with whitewash. It's a disgraceful story, and I think Isaacs was one of the nastiest bits of work that ever schemed his way to the top in everything. Kipling's daughter, who is a friend of Reading's widow, has refused permission for the reprinting of 'Gehazi', though it has already been printed in countless other books. G.K. Chesterton's executor was similarly churlish about a relevant and amusing poem of his.

Have you read your friend Leavis's swingeing attack on C.P. Snow in the current *Spectator*? It's high time someone took this line, and I only wish it had been a less woolly and repetitive writer than Leavis. He says everything several times, wanders about, and, as always, writes without any style or distinction. I wonder whether Snow will answer. I fancy he must. Would you like to have the new Ibsen translations? So far I have published eight of the sixteen I agreed to bring out. Such reviews as there have been have been favourable, but the

[1] *The Marconi Scandal* by Frances Donaldson (1962).

public is not exactly stampeding for the precious volumes.

Don't be put off T.H. by *The Return of the Native*. Have another go at *Far from the Madding Crowd* and *Tess*. I wish I had time to try them all again.

Last Monday Ivor and Mrs B. gave a dinner-party for ten in the Lit. Soc. room at the Garrick—excellent food and agreeable company, including Edith Evans and Ralph Richardson. Another day I had a good gossipy lunch with Frank Swinnerton. He is seventy-eight and full of beans. He is an excellent mimic and gives lifelike reproductions of dialogues between his old friends H.G. Wells and Arnold Bennett. I introduced him to a visiting U.S. professor, who is writing on Wells and was thrilled to hear something from so near the horse's mouth.

17 March 1962
(St Patrick's Day) *Bromsden Farm*

All this and the flu as well! It really is too bad, and I am all sympathy. Please thank Pamela for her letter: it was most kind of her to write. I was planning to ring her up this evening to ask after you, but this morning some woodmen of Peter's who are felling trees in the valley-bottom with a circular saw neatly brought one down across our telephone-line, so we are cut off till goodness knows when. Ruth is expecting me to ring her up tonight—hell!

The Lit. Soc. on Tuesday was as good as could be without you. We ate scampi with rice, *escalope viennoise*, and angels on horseback. I had Ivor on one side, Sparrow on the other. Sparrow and I have put up Patrick Devlin the judge (now Lord D) as the first candidate for next November. As you may have seen, Balliol has just sent out an appeal for the best part of a million pounds, and as we discussed it, we gradually realised that of our eleven diners, no fewer than seven were Balliol men! There are 4000 old Balliol men living, so they'll have to give £250 apiece if the target is to be hit. Not very likely, I should say.

Earlier in the day I had been through Jonah's proofs with him, and the book should be out in June. I told Tony Powell you had enjoyed his book, and he was much pleased. He said the only characteristic of Goodhart's that he had deliberately given to his housemaster was G's habit of standing with both his feet pointing sideways in the same direction.

I have enormously enjoyed, and strongly recommend, Osbert Sitwell's *Tales My Father Taught Me*. They are most entertaining, and short enough to prevent O's getting involved in those endless sentences that made some of his autobiography such heavy going. Sir George is a superb character—and this whole book is about him.

Sunday morning, 18 March

I was happy to see your Diana had been safely delivered. Does that make twenty-one grandchildren? I wonder whether they were hoping for a girl this time. Diana is so lovely that she ought to have a beautiful daughter.

Apart from the Lit. Soc., last week was a great rush, since on Wednesday morning Bill Jovanovich, the dynamic head of Harcourt Brace, turned up for a week's stay. There are hundreds of business details to be settled, and we shall be at it non-stop till he leaves next Thursday.

I expect you noticed Dr Attlee's death. If his advice had been taken in 1921, and my mother had not intervened by taking me to London for an immediate operation, I should probably have died in a matter of weeks. I remember her saying to Jelly: 'I can't help it if the boy has to leave Eton. I'm not satisfied with the diagnosis and I'm taking him to London.' Jelly agreed meekly, but in later years chose to forget the incident, and always maintained that Attlee had been right.

You are not to dream of writing until you are really strong enough. I shall ring Pamela up from London tomorrow for the latest news. Now I must read a manuscript about Nepal, and some proofs about the Channel Tunnel, neither of which at the moment interests me enormously.

22 March 1962 *Grundisburgh*

Grand man you are! I have sent you practically nothing for a fortnight and here you are with four excellent sides. What can I do in reply? I tell the doctors I am very ill and they deny it, pointing to thoroughly well-behaved heart, lungs, and kidneys etc. I say 'What do they matter in view of the fact that I am tired all the time, sunk in apathy and lassitude, and faintly sick-feeling much of the time. The x-ray process yesterday (two and a half hours) was acutely uncomfortable. You lie face downwards for about seven minutes eight times with ten minutes' interval during which you relax (ha!) by lying on your *back*. You lie on a practically bare board.

I suspect that part of the treatment will be drastic dieting. And what sort of a guest shall I be then? Is there any precedent at the Lit. Soc. for a member dining off bread and milk and saying no to all the scampi and angels on horseback? Would it be in the records?

Your kind heart prompted you to ask about me and Ibsen. Well the truth is I *loved* Ibsen when I read him years ago, but I have been too tired to read much lately. I tried Crabbe whom I hadn't read for fifty years, but it didn't do. That thudding relentlessness got me down with which he grimly shows up every friendship and love-affair ending in disaster. His pictures of Suffolk do nothing to enamour one of the county.

I didn't know that habit of Goodhart's, but please ask T.P. if he knew that G. had in a drawer numberless advertisements of women's shoes. Mat Hill of course recognised at once one of the commonest signs of suppressed or sublimated sex. Human beings get odder and odder. Do you ever dream about snakes or keys? Because if so you must look out.

The Hoods are pleased about their third son. Diana always said—and I think truly—that she would not be good at dealing with a daughter, and Alexander for some reason passionately wanted another son. It is to be called James. Number 21 grandchild.

Leavis does reduce poor old Snow to monkey-dust, but one doesn't like or admire L. any the more. As you say, his style is what I call rebarbative, though never quite sure what it means. You will know. He writes as if his opinion was clearly the truth, and anyone who disagreed with it must be fool or knave. Surely Snow *must* reply: in old days he would have with sword or pistol. But I doubt if he carries the guns.

Attlee wasn't my doctor, who was old Amsler who suited us very well. How impressive lay interferences with medical ukases are. My father-in-law forbade them to do a mastoid operation on my delicate mother-in-law. He said quite simply that he knew nothing of medicine but was quite certain it would kill her. She got quite well, and lived for another fifteen years.

In latter days many of Jelly's memories were very unreliable, and of course he would *always* back Eton doctors (and others) against swells from London.

This letter is a striking example of the victory of mind over matter. I got up feeling like death and very nearly fell asleep in the bath. But I formed *one* resolve—to ignore all else but to write four sides to you, and though I must now go and lie down for a bit, I feel all the better for having done so.

I told the North Foreland Lodge governors last week that I was going to retire from the chairmanship this year. I was amused to find that their reaction was not one of horrified protest, but of quiet congratulation on having gone on so long (eleven years). In other words what they *really* meant was 'And high time too'. Such is life. I get deafer (certainly) and I suspect stupider as the weeks pass.

Bless you Rupert and give my best love to Ruth. Pamela is a wonderful nurse—and wife generally, but I have plenty left over for R.

24 March 1962 *Bromsden Farm*

It was heroic of you to write those four fine pages last week, but also very wrong. I told you particularly not to write till you were strong enough, and you *must* be sensible. I only hope the effort didn't bring on a relapse. But I must admit that the sight of your writing on Friday evening was most encouraging.

If you do in fact have to diet, I will guarantee to produce whatever you're allowed at the Lit. Soc. dinners. For some time Ivor was allowed only certain things, and we coped with that safely.

I'm glad to say I never, to my knowledge, dream of snakes or keys, but I'm sure Rayner-Wood dreamt of little else. You were clearly right to resign from North Foreland Lodge, and I think you ought also to give up all that correcting: you have done more than your whack, and earned a rest, surely. I can hear you answering: 'How the world is managed, and why it was created, I cannot tell; but it is no feather-bed for the repose of sluggards,' and I can only say that I often wish it was. From that quotation you will know what I have been reading, and here's some more of it, just for the fun of copying it out, and despite my fear that you may earlier have copied it out for me:

> If a man will comprehend the richness and variety of the universe, and inspire his mind with a due measure of wonder and of awe, he must contemplate the human intellect not only on its heights of genius but in its abysses of ineptitude; and it might be fruitlessly debated to the end of time whether Richard Bentley or Elias Stoeber was the more marvellous work of the Creator: Elias Stoeber, whose reprint of Bentley's text, with a commentary intended to confute it, saw the light in 1767 at Strasburg, a city still famous for its geese .... Stoeber's mind, though that is no name to call it by, was one which turned as unswervingly to the false, the meaningless, the unmetrical, and the ungrammatical, as the needle to the pole.[1]

If only Leavis could write like that! But he has no ear, no taste, no judgment. How *can* a man who writes as he does teach anyone *English*?

Sunday morning, March 25

Comfort always refuses to recognise the beginning or end of Summer Time, and this makes for some confusion to begin with. Bridget has just arrived from London, blithely unaware that she was an hour wrong. The wind has changed and they tell me it is slightly warmer.

Bill Jovanovich's week in London consisted largely of conferences lasting several hours each—stimulating but at the same time exhausting. He stayed at Claridge's, where I ate several meals with him. In my youth it was a resort of riches and distinction: now most of the *clientèle* look as though they had been swept up in a third-class international air terminal. Ichabod! The gradual but complete social revolution which we have lived through has undoubtedly improved the

[1] A.E. Housman, preface to his edition of Manilius, Book I (1903), reprinted in *A.E. Housman, Selected Prose*, edited by John Carter (1961).

lot of millions, but it has largely destroyed elegance and *la douceur de vivre*. What would Old Jolyon say to the bearded youths in jeans and open-necked shirts that one sees in stalls at the theatre and Covent Garden?

I am now reading *A Pride of Terrys*[1] with much enjoyment. Despite the author's lapses of taste she does know and love the theatre, and the early chapters, *circa* 1850, are fascinating. At the same time, in bed, I am reading Compton Mackenzie on *Moral Courage*. It is the book of a tired old man, just rambling memory, gossip and ideas, without any appreciable design, but he is a full man, and I much prefer the weary old to the angry young. I think you might well get it from the library.

Tomorrow I am promised the final pages of Oscar for approval—the index and the first thirty-two pages of the book (which they always print last). I shall return them to the printer on Tuesday, and all will be over—very nearly seven years since I took over the job in July 1955. I hope to have complete copies by Easter. So far we have orders for just over 1000 copies, but that is without the London shops, which should take as many again. They won't order at all until they see the complete article, whereas the wretched booksellers in the provinces and abroad see only a 'blurb' and sometimes a dust-jacket.

Months ago *The Times* sent me Edmund Blunden's obituary to revise and tidy up, but I find it almost impossible to do. If, which Heaven forbid, the dear fellow died tomorrow, I could do all that is needed in an hour or two, under pressure of emotion, but in cold blood it's another matter. And yet I'm always nagging them to have proper obituaries ready. I promised to write them one on Diana Cooper, but can't bring myself to do it. Have you ever written any?

28 March 1962
[*Dictated to Pamela*]

19 Burton Ward
East Suffolk & Ipswich Hospital
Ipswich

I write *de profundis*—which is the right address of the Ipswich Hospital, as I think you will admit, when you hear my life is one of

[1] By Marguerite Steen (1962).

crushing boredom, often variegated by discomfort and sometimes by pain. What more need of words? There shall be none. Pamela supports your contention that I should give up examining, but on the other side is what Stevenson called 'the still small, unanswerable voice of coins.' However I promise not to let it be a burden. That is a lovely bit of Housman you quote, all I remembered of it was the famous 'a city still famous for its geese'.

I say, Leavis! Have you ever known opinion so unanimous about a man's spite, bad manners, injustice, bad English and conceit? It will surely do him a great deal of harm. I don't know why you have your knife into old Snow, though I admit I don't know much about him. He is perhaps a bit too omniscient. I agree with you about *la douceur de vivre* and what old Jolyon would have said about many modern things and men. With a few prejudices his values were surely mainly right.

Did you ever see Irving act? And if so did you see the genius of him through all the faults? It must have been a great handicap to a young actor to be apparently unable either to walk or to enunciate like Edmund Kean too. Marie Tempest told a young actress that if she worked hard for a year, she might be able to walk across the stage properly.

Obituaries. I was for some time in charge of them for Eton Masters, and did several. I had a certain amount of grisly fun, e.g. in getting Eggar to do Mat Hill's, and Mat Hill to do Eggar's.

Well I mustn't fag poor Pamela any longer. I had an enchanting letter from Ruth which I will answer with my own hand as soon as I can. Give her my love.

31 March 1962 *Bromsden Farm*

All that and hospital too! It's really too bad, and I am delighted to learn from Pamela that you're probably going home tomorrow. My week in the Middlesex last summer is still vividly in memory and I can truly sympathise. Pamela is a splendid amanuensis, and her hand is beautifully clear. I haven't in fact got my knife into Snow, but I do dislike his literary scheming, superiority and self-election as pundit.

I find his novels third-rate, dull and humourless, and the sight of his fat face reproduced life-size in newspaper advertisements for the *Daily Herald* is enough to put anyone off their breakfast.

I never, alas, saw Irving act, being only two when he died, but his was clearly a triumph of personal magnetism over natural handicaps. The most magnetic performance I ever saw was Chaliapin's in *Boris*, which I thought terrific. It was in 1930 or 1931.

On Wednesday Ruth and I had drinks with the Eliots in their Kensington flat. They are just back from six weeks in Barbados, and T.S.E. was looking better than he has for years. Gerald Kelly is painting his portrait for this year's Academy, and regaling him during sittings with ripe anecdotes of the last fifty years. In many of them Willie Maugham figures more or less discreditably.

On Thursday I lunched with Tommy and Joan in their royal stables. Clemmie Churchill, Veronica Wedgwood and Peter Lubbock were the other guests, and we ate a delicious steak-and-kidney pudding. One simply can't believe that C.C. is seventy-seven, so young and alert and active and pretty is she, and so charming. Tommy was at his gayest and most mellow. He said that the only stinker of a letter he ever knew George VI to write was to Ambassador Kennedy, about his defeatist pronouncements. Winston and others persuaded him to water it down to the version that is printed in Jack Wheeler-Bennett's biography.[1] Later Tommy referred to Jack's Appendix B as the best, indeed the only accurate, account of the duties and difficulties of the sovereign's Private Secretary. Last night I read it with interest and pleasure, suspecting that Tommy inspired all of it that he didn't actually write. Then I realised that I hadn't time to read the book properly when it appeared, so I am at it now. It's pretty good, I should say, but Jack hasn't got Harold Nicolson's magisterial sureness of touch in English prose, and occasionally slips into careless cliché. I can't remember whether you read the book. (If our correspondence goes on long enough, we shall *both* have forgotten what we wrote ten years ago, and shall then be able happily to start the record all over again.)

On Thursday I passed the utterly last pages of Oscar for press, only

[1] *King George VI: His Life and Reign* by John W. Wheeler-Bennett (1958).

to be told next day that the printers will need a month more than they originally said! So now publication-day is shifted to June 25, and I shall hope to have finished copies by the third week of May. It's infuriating, but after seven years' work I suppose one month is neither here nor there.

Just to show you that I'm not idling, I should say that last week I also visited old Lady Lovat to discuss a possible volume of Maurice Baring's letters, attended a cocktail party at Veronica Wedgwood's where I got trapped by a stalwart hunting lady, gave lunch to an American publisher, presided at a two-and-a-half-hour meeting of the Phoenix Trust, interviewed an estate agent about the London Library freehold, sat through a long meeting to give relief to starving booksellers and their relicts, went through my firm's accounts for 1961 with *three* chartered accountants—but that's enough.

Ruth is very pleased because last week she sold at Sotheby's a dreary Henry Moore drawing which she had had for years and didn't care for. They told her it might fetch £300. She went to the sale, and it was knocked down for £550! If you saw it you'd realise how ridiculously out of proportion such a sum is, but how right she was to cash in on the prevailing fashion. In imagination she has already spent the money two or three times over.

5 April 1962 *Grundisburgh*

George has asked me to write and say that he feels too ill to write any letters, but is most grateful to you for yours. At the moment he says he feels he can't cope with either receiving them or writing them. I am afraid he does feel horribly ill and I have an awful feeling that there is nothing they can do. We have not yet had the hospital report. Your friendship and letters have meant so much to George, I really can't tell you *how* much, and by the same token I do thank you so much for your sympathy and understanding. Love from Pamela.

6 April 1962 *Grundisburgh*
[*Dictated to Pamela*]

I send a postcript to Pamela's of yesterday to tell you that they have at last found a name for the damned thing. It is Hepatitis. It is rarer but apparently much the same in foulness and duration of time as Jaundice, and you know all about that. So evidently I am out of circulation for some time. The odd thing is that when I had jaundice ten or twelve years ago, though it was unpleasant, I was nothing like so miserably depressed as I am now. But in some queer way it is a relief to know that the beastly thing has a name.

P.S. The doctor told me that the tests were inconclusive. A clear negative would have been better. The above, i.e. Hepatitis, *is* true and a good answer to kind enquirers, and one which I am adopting. He is a bit happier having a name and some treatment.[1] Love Pamela.

7 April 1962 *Bromsden Farm*

I was so glad to get your dictated letter, and dear Pamela's, but I absolutely forbid either of you to spend any more time writing to me until you once again feel up to writing yourself. Pamela assures me she doesn't mind being telephoned to, so I shall ring her up once or twice a week, to hear how you are, and I shall go on writing regularly, as long as you promise not to feel obliged to read my letters until you're better.

Hepatitis, rather than jaundice, is what I had in 1959, and I remember your once or twice commenting on the depth and extent of my inertia and depression, so I can utterly sympathise with all you are going through, and to cheer you can only say that though I was heavily under the weather for several months, I thereafter got quite all right, as you assuredly will. I can't help thinking too that if the spring ever comes, some hot sunshine may work wonders for you.

[1] He was in fact suffering from cancer of the liver, but he wasn't told so and apparently never suspected it.

I am reading a forthcoming book called *Great Cricket Matches*,[1] which I am enjoying. I have ordered a copy to be sent to you, ready for you to read lazily in your summer-house a little later on.

This week I met for the first time, and greatly liked, Dennis Silk, a master at Marlborough, who plays cricket for Somerset and captained the last MCC side in New Zealand. He is a great friend of Siegfried S. and knows Edmund B.

I can't tell you how *delighted* Ruth was with your letter. It was angelic of you to write it when you were feeling so low.

15 April 1962 *Bromsden Farm*

I am most relieved to learn from Pamela that you have got a nurse to look after you, for I was beginning to worry that Pamela would have too much to do. I wonder if you have felt well enough to look at *Great Cricket Matches.* I am about half-way through, enjoying it all, remembered matches and forgotten ones. I find it best to read one match each evening, so as to keep them separate in one's mind.

All the members of the Lit. Soc. asked most solicitously after you on Tuesday. Tommy couldn't come, so old Cuthbert presided, very thin and shrunken, with one foot in a carpet slipper. Peter sat on one side of him, and Gerry Wellington on the other. Gerry was full of his journey to Australia and New Zealand, which he adored. He said the popularity of your nephew Charles in N.Z. is unbelievable, and all declare he is *far* the best Governor General they've ever had. Bernard (who was also there) realises that to follow Charles will be hellish difficult.

Max's plaque in the crypt of St Paul's was duly dedicated by the aged Dean on Thursday, and S.C. Roberts gave a charming and extremely apt address. Jonah and Evy were there, and other friends of Max's. Afterwards we were all given a good lunch at Kettner's by the Reichmanns.

[1] Edited by Handasyde Buchanan (1962).

17 April 1962 *Grundisburgh*
[*Dictated to Pamela*]

We both love your notes and enquiries. That cricket book is full of interest and also strange omissions. Fancy leaving out Jessop's great match at the Oval in 1902, and the famous, though possibly apocryphal, 'Come on Wilfred, we'll get 'em in singles.' Uncle Edward on Fowler's Match I find a little prolix in places and I think there are better accounts, but it is all right. It calls up numberless memories, and as you may imagine I live during the day largely on reminiscence. One of the most persistent is those hours before the Lit. Soc. Bless you. I do wish I didn't feel so awfully ill, but *tout passe* no doubt.

P.S. The poor darling is very low today and I'm afraid feels very ill, but no pain and no nausea which is something to be thankful for. He doesn't feel able to do anything but he has enjoyed the cricket book.

Much love Pamela.

25 April 1962 *Grundisburgh*
[*Dictated to Pamela*]

There is nothing in anything except my gratitude and the wonderfulness of Pamela (she mustn't cross that out). So what then? I am not even a chaos—I am a vast infinity. She will write you any more, if there is anything. Love to Ruth and bless you both. Oh the boredom!

EPILOGUE

George Lyttelton died on 1 May 1962. His sister-in-law Sibell Fulford said that in his last days he looked like a splendid effigy, with a face which bore the marks of the dignity and strength of his mind.

Ruth and I travelled to Grundisburgh for his funeral. *The Letters of Oscar Wilde* appeared on June 25. Adam crowned his academic triumphs with a First in Chemistry at Oxford and a Ph.D. at the University of York.

In 1964 my dreams came true. After eighteen years of waiting Ruth and I were able to marry. I thankfully retired from publishing, we found a lovely old house in our beloved Swaledale and lived there blissfully, until on 31 January 1967 Ruth died suddenly of a heart-attack.

Sixteen years later, on 6 January 1983, forty Old Boys of George's Eton house dined together in London to celebrate his hundredth birthday. They generously invited me to be their guest, but I was unable to accept. Instead I wrote this letter, which was read out after dinner by Sir Geoffrey Agnew:

6 January 1983 — *The Old Rectory*
Marske-in-Swaledale

My dear George

Now that you have reached your century (*how* you would dislike hearing it called a 'ton') I feel I must add one last letter to the six hundred or so that we exchanged over those six crowded years long ago. For years after you died, whenever I saw, heard or read anything amusing or interesting, I found myself thinking 'I must remember to tell George that'.

Our published correspondence has been accused of 'elitism', snobbery, name-dropping and old fashioned 'squareness', but happily the praise has far outweighed the denigration. I have had many hundreds of appreciative letters from all over the world, many love-letters from delightful old ladies, countless references to reading-lists compiled from our letters, and two separate strangers have written to say that our correspondence had changed their life. The first two volumes have already been reprinted, and all six are soon to appear in America. So we can't complain.

When Jock Murray quixotically undertook to publish the first volume, neither he nor I had any idea of what was going to happen. My only sorrow is that you and dear Pamela weren't here to enjoy the fun, but I take comfort in the knowledge that your rich personality, which might otherwise have largely died with the last of those who knew you, is now safe in six volumes, hardbound for posterity.

As we often agreed, letters are almost always nuanced—or, as they now say, slanted—to suit the recipient, and I couldn't have written my letters to anyone but you. Raymond Mortimer, who loved the first volumes, thought it extraordinary that two people with a difference of twenty-four years in their ages could share so very many tastes. Extraordinary perhaps, but so it was. Your depth and breadth of reading, your excellent memory, your willingness to accept new ideas and suggestions, your splendid sense of humour, made you an ideal correspondent.

As I have pointed out to many of our fans, my share in the correspondence was comparatively easy, since I was leading such an active life that all I had to do was to recount my week's doings, using you as the diary I never kept. But your task was far harder. Sitting whenever possible in your beloved summer-house (the only time I tried it I *just* escaped *rigor mortis*) you had little straw for your magnificent bricks, since (except for reading) correcting exam-papers and attending examiners' conferences were almost your only occupations, until the Literary Society drew you to London once a month.

I am now several years older than you were when we made our compact at the dear Nugents' dinner-table, and though I am still busy with literary work, I couldn't now react as you did to a younger man's suggestion of a regular correspondence. You, dear George, were a wholly exceptional and remarkable man, and a born letter-writer. I wish I had been in your house at Eton.

You always dreaded your Old Boy Dinners, and always enjoyed

them enormously when the day came. I hope perhaps you are enjoying this one in the Elysian Fields, alongside Max Beerbohm, Thomas Carlyle and Doctor Johnson. Let us hope that Leavis is in another place! Wherever you are, I send you, as always, my unending admiration, gratitude and love.

Yours ever
Rupert

INDEX